POLICING THE AMAZON

This edited collection discusses the rule of law in the Amazon and the capabilities of the region's sovereign states to police their territory considering security matters. Comprised of nine countries, including a European Union member, the Amazon region features states facing political instability, poverty, social inequalities, high levels of corruption, and lack of trust by their populations. This context is aggravated by the presence of criminal organizations operating there and shaping transnational bonds. Notably, the world's foremost cocaine-producing countries—Colombia, Peru, and Bolivia—are located in the region, presenting related turmoil and instability. Moreover, as home to the largest rainforest on Earth and the widest biodiversity, the region is an object of concern due to environmental reasons. The protection of these natural resources as well as the traditional peoples living there is intertwined with issues of development, security, and policing.

The book delves into questions on the international agenda, such as: how is it possible to sustain the rule of law in the Amazon? What are the states' capabilities for controlling the territory and enforcing the law? How do these states deal with the growing urban violence in the region? What are the capabilities of public authorities for proposing laws and policies, and judicial systems to process, prevent, and suppress different crimes such as drug dealing, smuggling, human trafficking, terrorism, and environmental crimes?

The book fills a gap in English-language scholarship exploring the context of the rule of law in the Amazon and the impact on policing activities. It is ideal for a wide range of audiences, including policing scholars, law enforcement and community leaders, and students focusing on criminal justice and the Amazon.

Vicente Riccio holds a doctorate in Sociology from *Instituto Universitário de Pesquisas do Rio de Janeiro* and was the coordinator of the graduate program of Law and Innovation at Federal University of Juiz de Fora (2017–2023), Brazil. He also has worked as a consultant for many public institutions in Brazil, such as the Ministry of Justice, Public Security Secretary of Rio de Janeiro, and Civil Police of Amazonas. His research interests are police reform, legal systems in developing democracies, media, justice, and video evidence. He has organized *Police and Society in Brazil* (Routledge) book, coedited with Wesley Skogan (Northwestern University). He has also published articles and book chapters in international and Brazilian publications.

Guilherme Lopes da Cunha holds a Postdoctoral in International Relations at the University of Brasília (UnB), PhD, and MA in International Political Economy at the Federal University of Rio de Janeiro (UFRJ). He is a Professor at the Brazilian War College (ESG), and the Brazilian Defense College (ESD), at the Ministry of Defense of Brazil. He has organized *Brazil in the Geopolitics of Amazonia and Antarctica* (Lexington Books), coedited with Fábio Albergaria de Queiroz (Brazilian Defense College), and Ana Flávia Barros-Platiau (University of Brasilia).

Advances in Police Theory and Practice Series
Series Editor: Dilip K. Das

Police Behavior, Hiring, and Crime Fighting
An International View
Edited by John A. Eterno, Ben Stickle, Diana Peterson, & Dilip K. Das

Translational Criminology in Policing
Edited by The George Mason Police Research Group with David Weisburd

Exploring Contemporary Policing Challenges
A Global Perspective
Edited by Sanja Kutnjak Ivković, Jon Maskály, Christopher M. Donner, Irena Cajner Mraović & Dilip K. Das

International Responses to Gendered-Based Domestic Violence
Gender-Specific and Social-Cultural Approach
Edited by Dongling Zhang & Diana Sharff Peterson

Gender Inclusive Policing
Challenges and Achievements
Edited by Tim Prenzler

Challenges of Contemporary Policing
Higher Education, Technology, and Officers' Well-Being
Edited by Vicente Riccio, Di Jia & Dilip K. Das

Policing the Amazon
Why the Rule of Law is Crucial for the Future
Edited by Vicente Riccio & Guilherme Lopes da Cunha

POLICING THE AMAZON

Why the Rule of Law is Crucial for the Future

Edited by Vicente Riccio and Guilherme Lopes da Cunha

NEW YORK AND LONDON

Designed cover image: J Brarymi

First published 2025
by Routledge
605 Third Avenue, New York, NY 10158

and by Routledge
4 Park Square, Milton Park, Abingdon, Oxon, OX14 4RN

Routledge is an imprint of the Taylor & Francis Group, an informa business

© 2025 selection and editorial matter, Vicente Riccio and Guilherme Lopes da Cunha; individual chapters, the contributors

The right of Vicente Riccio and Guilherme Lopes da Cunha to be identified as the authors of the editorial material, and of the authors for their individual chapters, has been asserted in accordance with sections 77 and 78 of the Copyright, Designs and Patents Act 1988.

All rights reserved. No part of this book may be reprinted or reproduced or utilised in any form or by any electronic, mechanical, or other means, now known or hereafter invented, including photocopying and recording, or in any information storage or retrieval system, without permission in writing from the publishers.

Trademark notice: Product or corporate names may be trademarks or registered trademarks, and are used only for identification and explanation without intent to infringe.

ISBN: 978-1-032-36193-2 (hbk)
ISBN: 978-1-032-35501-6 (pbk)
ISBN: 978-1-003-33065-3 (ebk)

DOI: 10.4324/ 9781003330653

Typeset in Sabon
by Apex CoVantage, LLC

CONTENTS

Series Editor's Preface	*viii*
Appendix	*x*
List of Contributor Bios	*xx*
Introduction: Why the Rule of Law? Vicente Riccio and Guilherme Lopes da Cunha	1

PART I
Crime, Violence, and the Rule of Law in the Amazon 11

1 Rule of Law and Environmental Crimes in the Southern Amazonas 13
   Vicente Riccio, Giuseppe Giura, Deborah De Felice,
   Dorlí João Marques, and Antonio Gelson de Oliveira Nascimento

2 The State, Indigenous Communities, and Illicit Economic
   Activities in the Peruvian Amazon 31
   Oscar Espinosa

3 Devastating Devastation: Impact of Crime in the Colombian Amazon 46
   Juan Carlos Ruiz-Vásquez and Rubén Sánchez David

4 The Use of Intelligence for Mapping the Activities of Criminal
   Organizations in the Amazon 62
   Rodrigo Costa Yehia Castro, Giuseppe Giura, Fabio Licata,
   Sandro Sarkis, and Vicente Riccio

5 Ecuador's Presence in the Amazon: Security, Weak Institutions, Questioned Capabilities, and Strategic Opportunities 74
   Katalina Barreiro Santana and Diego Pérez Enríquez

6 Strategic Resources, Border Economies, Transnational Dynamics, and Threats in the Amazon: The Case of Lago Agrio in Ecuador 88
   Milton Reyes Herrera and Patricio Trujillo Montalvo

7 Policing Indigenous Lands Impacted by Hydroelectrical Dams in the Brazilian State of Rondônia 102
   Rafael Ademir Oliveira de Andrade, Artur de Souza Moret, and Jean Carlo Silva dos Santos

8 A Polycentric Governance Model Through the Amazon Cooperation Treaty Organization: Capabilities for Tackling Transnational Threats 109
   Carlos Alfredo Lazary Teixeira, Guilherme Lopes da Cunha, and Fábio Albergaria de Queiroz

PART II
Policing Challenges in the Amazon 123

9 Being a Policewoman in the Amazon: Motivations and Everyday Routines 125
   Ludmila Ribeiro and Alexandre M.A. Martins

10 Procedural Justice Perceptions and Use of Force at the Civil Police of Amazonas 142
   Eduardo Magrone, Vicente Riccio, Wagner Silveira Rezende, and Mario Aufiero

11 Pressure on the Brazilian Amazon Border and State Discretion in Granting Asylum to Venezuelans 153
   Janaína de Mendonça Fernandes

PART III
Law and the Environmental Protection in the Amazon 165

12 Intellectual Property Rights Legislation as a Source of Inequality: A Case Study Based on Natural Genetic Resources From the Amazon Region 167
   Marcos Vinício Chein Feres

13	The Environmental Protection in French Guiana: Normative Scheme and Stakes *Frédéric Bondil, Carole Hassoun, Mathilde Kamal-Girard, and Jean-Philippe Vauthier*	181
14	Logospiracy in the Legal Amazon *Raimundo Pontes Filho*	202
15	The Brazilian Amazon Between Geopolitics and Law *Guilherme Sandoval Góes and Antonio dos Santos*	212

Index 226

SERIES EDITOR'S PREFACE

While the literature on police and allied subjects is growing exponentially, its impact on dayto-day policing remains small. The two worlds of research and practice of policing remain disconnected, even though cooperation between the two is growing. A major reason is that the two groups speak in different languages. The research work is published in hard-to-access journals and presented in a manner that is difficult for a lay person to comprehend. On the other hand, police practitioners tend not to mix with researchers and remain secretive about their work. Consequently, there is little dialogue between the two and almost no attempt to learn from one another. Dialogue across the globe among researchers and practitioners situated in different continents is, of course, even more limited.

Dilip K. Das, a police practitioner-turned-academic, attempted to address this problem by starting the IPES (www.ipes.info), where a common platform has brought the two together. IPES is now in its 30th year. The annual meetings, the major annual event of the organization, have been hosted in all parts of the world. Several very impressive publications have come out of these deliberations, and a new collaborative community of scholars and police officers has been created whose membership runs into several thousands.

The International Police Executive Symposium (IPES) has annual meetings throughout the world. All the editors have attended these meetings. They involve a collaboration of practitioners, scholars, and other experts in law enforcement. Ideas are exchanged in a unique way as all at the meeting not only share their research but also collaborate during social events.

This volume innovates in policing studies with chapters discussing the Amazon region. Climate change and environmental protection are the most relevant issues in the contemporary agenda. There is considerable interest worldwide concerning the Amazon rainforest due to its vastness, natural richness, potable water reservoirs, and the most significant biodiversity in the world. The Amazon has been studied for a long time, but mainly by the natural sciences. In the field of social sciences, there is a lot of research on indigenous populations, the process of occupation, and land conflicts. However, studies in the field of criminology and policing are scarce. This book aims to fill this gap by discussing why the rule of law is crucial for Amazon's future.

It is relevant because Amazon faces enormous problems related to crime and violence. The largest producers of cocaine in the world, Colombia, Peru, and Bolivia, are located there, and these drugs are smuggled across the globe. Criminal organizations operate in the region with international connections and are not limited to drug dealing. They are involved in environmental crimes such as illegal logging, fires, biopiracy, and public land appropriation, among others. Besides, urban violence is also growing in the most significant metropolitan areas in the Amazon. These phenomena are interrelated and require new policies and strategies to bring more effectiveness to the rule of law in the region. This book tries to open a new debate in the field because sustainable development for Amazon would be a mirage without it.

Finally, this work represents the aim of IPES: a global forum that gathers researchers and practitioners with plural and democratic perspectives. It is an important perspective because policing challenges are becoming more global, and their effects can be observed in different places. Thus, there are new frontiers to be explored by researchers and practitioners.

An account of the IPES meetings and publications is included in the next few pages. The global influence and service of IPES was recognized by the United Nations and, as a result, IPES is in special consultative status with the Economic and Social Council of the United Nations (ECOSOC).

Dilip K. Das, PhD, Professor
Founding President, International Police Executive Symposium, IPES, www.ipes.info
Founding Editor-in-Chief, Police Practice and Research: An International Journal, PPR, http://www.tandfonline.com/gppr (2000–2020)
Editor-in-Chief, Advances in Police Theory and Practice, Book Series,
Founding Editor, Journal of Best Practice and Research in Policing (Forthcoming)
Human Rights Consultant to the United Nations,
Vicente Riccio, Associate Professor—Federal University of Juiz de Fora (Brazil)
IPES Book Editor

APPENDIX I

IPES Global Meetings

	Country	Theme	Host
1994	Switzerland	Police Challenges and Strategies	Canton Police, Geneva, Switzerland
1995	Spain	Challenges of Policing Democracies	International Institute of the Sociology of Law, Basque Country, Spain
1996	Japan	Organized Crime	Kanagawa University
1997	Austria	International Police Cooperation	Federal Police in Vienna, Austria
1998	The Netherlands	Crime Prevention	Dutch Police, Europol
1999	India	Policing of Public Order	Andhra Pradesh Police, Hyderabad, India
2000	Evanston, Illinois, USA	Traffic Policing	Northwestern University, Center for Public Safety
2001	Poland	Corruption: A Threat to World Order	Police of Poland
2002	Turkey	Police Education and Training	Turkish National Police
2003	Bahrain	Police and Community	Kingdom of Bahrain
2004	Canada	Criminal Exploitation of Women and Children	Abbotsford Police Department Canadian Police College Royal Canadian Mounted Police University College of the Fraser Valley Vancouver Police Department
2005	The Czech Republic	Challenges of Policing in the 21st Century: A Global Assessment	The Czech Police Academy, The Ministry of the Interior, The Czech Republic
2006	Turkey	Local Linkages to Global Security and Crime: Thinking Locally and Acting Globally	Turkish National Police
2007	Dubai	Urbanization and Security	Dubai Police

(Continued)

(Continued)

	Country	Theme	Host
2008	USA, Ohio	Police Without Borders: The Fading Distinction Between Local & Global	Cincinnati Police Department & Ohio Association of Chiefs of Police
2009	FYR Macedonia	Policing, the Private Sector, Economic Development & Social Change: Contemporary Global Trends	Ministry of Interior, Republic of Macedonia
2010	Malta	Tourism, Strategic Locations & Major Events: Policing in an Age of Mobility, Mass Movement and Migration	Commissioner John Rizzo and Malta Police
2010	India	Community Policing: Theoretical Problems and Operational Issues	Government of Kerala and the Kerala Police Department
2011	Argentina	Policing Violence, Crime, Disorder, & Discontent: International Perspectives	IPES
2011	Sweden	Contemporary Issues in Public Safety & Security	The Blekinge Technological Institute and the Swedish Police
2012	USA, New York	Economic Development, Armed Violence and Public Safety	In Cooperation with United Nations Dept of Economic & Social Affairs NGO Branch
2013	Hungary	Global Issues in Contemporary Policing	The Ministry of Interior and The Hungarian National Police
2014	India	Policing by Consent: Theoretical Challenges and Operational Issues	Kerala Police Department
2014	Bulgaria	Crime Prevention & Community Resilience: Police Role with Victims, Youth, Ethnic Minorities and Other Partners	IPES and the Bulgarian Ministry of Interior
2015	Thailand	Police Governance and Human Trafficking: Promoting Preventative and Comprehensive Strategies	The Royal Thai Police Association, The Royal Thai Police and Shinawatra University
2016	USA, Washington DC	Urban Security: Challenges for 21st Century Global Cities	The George Washington University
2017	England	Organized Crime & Terrorism: Policing Challenges for Local to International level	Liverpool John Moores University
2018	Austria	International Police Cooperation	United Nations Office on Drugs and Crime
2019	Serbia	Contemporary Police Challenges in Light of a New World and New Knowledge	IPES

(*Continued*)

(Continued)

	Country	Theme	Host
2022	Albany, New York, USA	Integrating Science, Technology, and Higher Education into Policing: Interdisciplinary & international perspectives	IPES and University of Albany (Criminal Justice School)
2023	Manaus, Brazil	Policing, Rule of law, Organized Crime, and the Environment	IPES, State University of Amazonas (UEA), and Center for Security Studies in the Amazon (CESAM)
2024	Thessaloniki, Greece	Promoting the Rule of Law, Protecting Human Rights and the Vulnerable Segments of the Society	International Police Executive Symposium (IPES)

APPENDIX II

IPES Publications

A) Advances in Police Theory and Practice—Routledge

1) Challenges of Contemporary Policing: Higher Education, Technology, and Officers' Well-Being
   - Vicente Riccio
   - Di Djia
   - Dilip K. Das

2) Gender Inclusive Policing
   - Tim Prenzler

3) International Responses to Gendered-Based Domestic: Gender-Specific and Social-Cultural Approach
   - Dongling Zhang
   - Diana Sharff Peterson

4) Exploring Contemporary Police Challenges: A Global Perspective
   - Sanja Kutnjak Ivković
   - Jon Maskály
   - Christopher M. Donner
   - Irena Cajner Mraović
   - Dilip Das

5) Translational Criminology in Policing
   - The George Mason police research
   - David Weisburd

6) Police Behavior, Hiring, and Crime Fighting: An International View
   - John A. Eterno
   - Ben Stickle

- Diana Scharff Peterson
- Dilip K. Das

7) Women in Policing Around the World: Doing Gender and Policing in a Gendered Organization

- Vanessa Garcia

8) Policing in France

- Jacques de Maillard
- Wesley G. Skogan

9) Policing and Mentally Ill: International Perspectives

- Duncan Chappell

10) Civilian Oversight of Police: Advancing Accountability in Law Enforcement

- Tim Prenzler
- Garth den Heyer

11) Cold Cases: Evaluation Models With Follow-Up Strategies for Investigators, second edition

- James M. Adcock
- Sarah L. Stein

12) Collaborative Policing: Police, Academics, Professionals, and Communities Working Together for Education, Training, and Program Implementation

- Peter C. Kratcoski
- Maximilian Edelbacher

13) Community Policing: International Patterns and Comparative Perspectives

- Dominique Wisler
- Ihekwoaba D. Onwudiwe

14) Community Policing and Peacekeeping

- Peter Grabosky

15) Crime Linkage: Theory, Research, and Practice

- Jessica Woodhams
- Craig Bennell

16) Delivering Police Services Effectively

- Garth den Heyer

17) Ethics for Police Translators and Interpreters

- Sedat Mulayim
- Miranda Lai

18) Honor-based Violence: Policing and Prevention
    - Karl Anton Roberts
    - Gerry Campbell
    - Glen Lloyd

19) Los Angeles Police Department Meltdown: The Fall of the Professional-Reform Model of Policing
    - James Lasley

20) Police Corruption: Preventing Misconduct and Maintaining Integrity
    - Tim Prenzler

21) Police Integrity Management in Australia: Global Lessons for Combating Police Misconduct
    - Louise Porter
    - Tim Prenzler

22) Police Investigative Interviews and Interpreting: Context, Challenges and Strategies
    - Sedat Mulayim
    - Miranda Lai
    - Caroline Norma

23) Police Performance Appraisals: A Comparative Perspective
    - Serdar Kenan Gul
    - Paul O'Connell

24) Police Organized Crime: Intelligence Strategy Implementation
    - Petter Gottschalk

25) Policing Terrorism: Research Studies Into Police Counterterrorism Investigations
    - David Lowe

26) Policing White-Collar Crime: Characteristics of White-Collar Criminals
    - Petter Gottschalk

27) Policing in Hong Kong: History and Reform
    - Kam C. Wong

28) Policing in Israel: Studying Crime Control, Community, and Counterterrorism
    - Tal Jonathan-Zamir
    - David Weisburd
    - Badi Hasisi

29) Security Governance, Policing, and Local Capacity
    - Jan Froestad
    - Clifford Shearing

30) The International Trafficking of Human Organs: A Multidisciplinary Perspective
    - Leonard Territo
    - Rande Matteson

31) Police and Society in Brazil
    - Vicente Riccio
    - Wesley G. Skogan

32) Police Reform in China
    - Kam C. Wong

33) Cold Cases: An Evaluation Model With Follow-Up Strategies for Investigators
    - James M. Adcock
    - Sarah L. Stein

34) The Crime Numbers Game: Management by Manipulation
    - John A. Eterno
    - Eli B. Silverman

35) Mission-Based Policing
    - John P. Crank
    - Dawn M. Irlbeck
    - Rebecca K. Murray
    - Mark Sundermeier

36) The New Khaki: The Evolving Nature of Policing in India
    - Arvind Verma

B) Co-Publications—Routledge/Taylor & Francis

37) Change and Reform in Law Enforcement: Old and New Efforts From Across the Globe
    - Scott W. Phillips
    - Dilip K. Das

38) Contemporary Issues in Law Enforcement and Policing
    - PhD Millie
    - Dilip K. Das

39) Criminal Abuse of Women and Children: An International Perspective
    - Obi N.I. Ebbe
    - Dilip K. Das

40) Economic Development, Crime, and Policing: Global Perspectives
    - Frederic Lemieux
    - Garth den Heyer
    - Dilip K. Das

41) Effective Crime Reduction Strategies: International Perspectives
   - James F. Albrecht
   - Dilip K. Das

42) Examining Political Violence: Studies of Terrorisms, Counterterrorism, and International War
   - David Lowe
   - Austin Turk
   - Dilip K. Das

43) Global Community Policing: Problems and Challenges
   - Arvind Verma
   - Dilip K. Das
   - Manoj Abraham

44) Global Environment of Policing
   - Darren Palmer
   - Michal M. Berlin
   - Dilip K. Das

45) Global Issues in Contemporary Policing
   - John Eterno
   - Arvind Verma
   - Aiedeo Mintie Das
   - Dilip K. Das

46) Global Perspectives on Crime Prevention and Community Resilience
   - Diana Scharff Peterson
   - Dilip K. Das

47) Global Trafficking in Women and Children
   - Obi N.I. Ebbe
   - Dilip K. Das

48) Police Without Borders: The Fading Distinction Between Local and Global
   - Cliff Roberson
   - Dilip K. Das
   - Jennie K. Singer

49) Policing Global Movement: Tourism, Migration, Human Trafficking and Terrorism
   - S. Caroline Taylor
   - Daniel Joseph Torpy
   - Dilip K. Das

50) The Evolution of Policing: Worldwide Innovations and Insights

- Melchor C. de Guzman
- Aiedeo Mintie Das
- Dilip K. Das

51) Urbanization, Policing and Security: Global Perspectives

- Gary Cordner
- AnnMarie Cordner
- Dilip K. Das

52) Policing Major Events: Perspectives From Around the World

- James F. Albrecht
- Martha Christine Dow
- Darryl Plecas
- Dilip K. Das

53) Strategies and Responses to Crime: Thinking Locally, Acting Globally

- Melchor de Guzman
- Aiedeo Mintie Das
- Dilip K. Das

C) Interviews With Global Leaders in Policing, Courts, and Prisons—Routledge

54) Trends in the Judiciary: Interviews With Judges Across the globe, Volume Four

- Wendell C. Wallace
- Michael M. Berlin
- Dilip K. Das

55) Trends in Policing: Interviews With Police Leaders Across the Globe, Volume Six

- Bruce F. Baker
- Dilip K. Das

56) Trends in Corrections: Interviews With Corrections Leaders Around the World, Volume Two

- Martha Henderson Hurley
- Dilip K. Das

57) Trends in Corrections: Interviews With Corrections Leaders Around the World, Volume One

- Jennie K. Singer
- Dilip K. Das
- Eileen Ahlin

58) Trends in Legal Advocacy: Interviews With Prosecutors and Criminal Defense Lawyers Across the Globe, Volume One
   - Jane Goodman-Delahunty
   - Dilip K. Das

59) Trends in Policing: Interviews With Police Leaders Across the Globe, Volume Five
   - Bruce F. Baker
   - Dilip K. Das

60) Trends in Policing: Interviews With Police Leaders Across the Globe, Volume Four
   - Bruce F. Baker
   - Dilip K. Das

61) Trends in the Judiciary: Interviews With Judges Across the Globe, Volume One
   - Dilip K. Das
   - Cliff Roberson

62) Trends in the Judiciary: Interviews With Judges Across the Globe, Volume Three
   - David Lowe
   - Dilip K. Das

63) Trends in the Judiciary: Interviews With Judges Across the Globe, Volume Two
   - David Lowe
   - Dilip K. Das

64) Trends in Corrections: Interviews With Corrections Leaders Around the World, Volume Three
   - Dilip K. Das
   - Philip Birch

65) Trends in Policing: Interviews With Police Leaders Across the Globe, Volume Two
   - Dilip K. Das
   - Otwin Marenin

66) Trends in Policing: Interviews With Police Leaders Across the Globe, Volume Three
   - Otwin Marenin
   - Dilip K. Das

CONTRIBUTOR BIOS

Rafael Ademir Oliveira de Andrade holds a PhD in Regional Development and Environment from the Federal University of Rondônia (2021) and a master's degree in Education from the Federal University of Rondônia (2014). He is a specialist in Higher Education Methodology from the Faculty of Porto Velho (2012), graduate in Social Sciences (UNIR—2011—degree and bachelor's degree), pedagogy (UNICS—2015–2nd degree), and technologist in Human Resources Management (UNIRON—2006). He is carrying out a post-doctoral internship in the Doctoral Program in Regional Development and Environment at the Federal University of Rondônia (2022). He is the leader of the Research Group Laboratory for Studies in Neglected Populations of the Amazon (LEPONA), deputy leader of the Amazon Laboratory for Studies in Latin America (LABLAT), and researcher associated with the research group "Biotechnology and Education.

Mario Aufiero is a PhD candidate in Constitutional Law at FADISP—Faculdade Autônoma de Direito—São Paulo. He holds a master's in public administration (Public Security) at Fundação Getúlio Vargas—RJ (2008) and is a graduate in Law from the Federal University of the State of Amazonas (2000). Currently, he is a Civil Police Commissar at the Civil Police of Amazonas. His main research interests are public policies, government planning, public security management, and police.

Frédéric Bondil holds a PhD in Private Law from the University of French Guiana and is a member of the MINEA research laboratory (Migration, Interculturality and Education in Amazonia, UR 7485). His reference works are mostly developed on the world of enterprises in the French Overseas Departments. He is the author of several sections based on the "French Overseas Departments" at the commercial and corporate law section at Dalloz. He has also written a study on the Amazon rainforest park, published in a legal environmental review.

Rodrigo Costa Yehia Castro holds a master's degree in law and innovation from the Federal University of Juiz de Fora and a law degree from the same institution. He practices law in Brasília, and he is a former Department of Formal Public Law and Professional Ethics professor at the Federal University of Juiz de Fora.

Rubén Sánchez David is a policy analyst. After studying in France at the Institut de Sciences Politiques de Paris, he became a professor at several prestigious universities in Bogota as Universidad Los Andes, Pontificia Universidad Javeriana, and Universidad del Rosario.

Deborah De Felice is a sociologist of law at the University of Catania (Italy), where she teaches "Sociology of law and deviant behaviour" at the Department of Political and Social Sciences. Her main field of study and research regards decision-making processes in legal contexts, especially in children's rights implementation. She published three books, many articles in peer-reviewed journals, and different chapters in edited volumes.

Diego Pérez Enríquez holds a PhD in Political Science (Universidad de Belgrano, Buenos Aires, 2016), master's degree in International Relations (Universidad Andina Simón Bolívar, Quito, 2004), and bachelor's degree in Law and Political Science (Universidad Internacional del Ecuador, Quito, 2002). He is a tenured professor in Ecuador's Instituto de Altos Estudios Nacionales (IAEN), at the School for Security and Defense, since 2010. As a part of this university, he has held the posts of General Research Coordinator (2018–2019) and Dean of the School for Security and Defense (2011–2012, 2016–2018, 2022–2023). He has also coordinated the Security and Defense master's program, as well as the master's program on Strategic Studies and International Security.

Oscar Espinosa has a PhD in Anthropology and Historical Studies from the New School for Social Research of New York. He is Full Professor at the Social Sciences Department, Pontificia Universidad Católica del Perú (PUCP), and Chair of the Research Group on Amazonian Anthropology. Espinosa is specialized in research related to the Amazon region and its indigenous peoples. This research has been done during the past 30 years, mainly with the Ashaninka, Shipibo-Konibo, Kukama, Yánesha, and Achuar peoples. He has published extensively about the relationship between the Peruvian State and the Amazonia, indigenous politics, indigenous youth and education, ethnohistory and history of the Peruvian Amazon region, environmental issues, and climate change, among other related topics.

Marcos Vinício Chein Feres has a degree in Law from Universidade Federal de Juiz de Fora (1994), an MA in Law from Universidade Federal de Minas Gerais (1999), and a PhD in Law from Universidade Federal de Minas Gerais (2003). He is currently Associate Professor at Universidade Federal de Juiz de Fora, Brazil. He served as the Director of the Faculty of Law from 2006 to 2014 and as the Vice-President of the University from 2014 to 2016. He is currently a Research Productivity Scholar funded by the Brazilian National Research Council (CNPq). He has research projects in the field of Intellectual Property Law and Legal Theory Applied funded by both public agencies, FAPEMIG and CNPq. He has experience in the field of law, with an emphasis on empirical legal research applied to Economic Law, acting on the following topics: empirical legal research; Argumentation, Law and Intellectual Property; social and economic rights; and Intellectual Property Law.

Janaína de Mendonça Fernandes holds a PhD in Administration from the Brazilian School of Public and Business Administration from Fundação Getúlio Vargas (FGV). Currently, she is Professor at the Federal University of Alfenas (Universidade Federal de Alfenas—UNIFAL) at the Institute of Applied Social Sciences, Varginha Campus. Her areas of interest are ethnic-racial and gender relations and forced immigration. In addition to working in the academic sphere, she has worked as a business consultant for ten years.

Giuseppe Giura holds a PhD in Sociology and Methods of Social sciences. He has professional knowledge of organized crime. Currently, he is a research fellow at IESE Business School—Centre for Business in Society—in Barcelona (Spain). In 2020, he got the National Scientific Qualification as an associate professor in Sociology of Law, Sociology of deviance, and Social change. His main scientific research interests are sociology of law, sociology of deviance and social change, sociology of crime, and methods of social research.

Guilherme Sandoval Góes is Coordinator of the Postgraduate Program in International Security and Defense (PPGSID) at the Superior War School of Brazil; Emeritus Professor at the School of Command and General Staff of the Army; Postdoctoral researcher in Geopolitics, Culture, and Law at the Brazilian Air Force University; Doctor of Law from the State University of Rio de Janeiro; Leader of the Geopolitics Research Group of Brazil at the Superior War School of Brazil; Constitutional Law Professor at the School of Magistracy in Rio de Janeiro and at Cândido Mendes University; Member of the Examination Board of the Getúlio Vargas Foundation for the Brazilian Bar Association (OAB) Exam; invited speaker at the William J. Perry Center for Hemispheric Defense Studies, WJPC, USA (2019–2023); and Diplomate of the United States Naval War College, Class 48, Newport, Rhode Island (1996).

Carole Hassoun is a lecturer in private law and criminal sciences at the University of French Guiana. She is a member of the MINEA research laboratory (Migration, Interculturality and Education in Amazonia, UR 7485). Hassoun specialized in civil law and her areas of research are mainly civil liability law and contract law.

Milton Reyes Herrera is Doctor of International Political Economy (Rio de Janeiro's Federal University). He has a master's degree in Latin-American Studies and a minor in International Relations (Simon Bolívar Andean University of Ecuador). Herrera has a bachelor's degree in Sociology and Political Science (Catholic Pontifical University of Ecuador). He is Professor and Researcher at Security and Defense School, Ecuadorean National Institute of Advanced Studies (IAEN), and Professor at International Relations Program, Pontifical Catholic University of Ecuador. He has publications in several languages in the Americas, Europe, and China.

Mathilde Kamal-Girard is a junior lecturer in Public Law at the University of French Guiana. With her PhD dissertation, titled *The Constitutional Council and Time*, she started research on legal time aspects in Constitutional Law. She also works on Law and Language interactions. She is a member of MINEA research laboratory (Migration, Interculturality and Education in Amazonia, UR 7485) and CERIJE (Interdisciplinary Research Center on Juritraductology).

Fabio Licata holds a Master of Science in "Digital Competencies in Data Protection, Cybersecurity and Privacy" and is a Senior Italian judge and expert in organized and economic crime cases. During his service at the Court of Palermo, he mainly dealt with the seizure and confiscation of criminal assets and currently serves as a labor judge at the Court of Patti. He was a member of the Scientific Committee of the Superior Council of the Judiciary and carried out several consultancy activities for public institutions and international organizations (EU, CoE, IDLO, UNICRI). He has also taught as a contract professor in criminal law and authored several legal publications.

Eduardo Magrone is a professor of Sociology of Education. He is currently an associate professor at the Federal University of Juiz de Fora-MG (Brazil), with experience in public educational policies. He has a PhD in Sociology from the University Research Institute of Rio de Janeiro-IUPERJ (Current Institute of Social and Political Studies-IESP). He is a participant in the research "Critical Analysis of Judicial Decisions on Environmental Crimes in the Amazon."

Dorlí João Marques holds a PhD in Biotechnology, in the area of concentration Biotechnology Innovation Management, from the Federal University of Amazonas (UFAM), and a master's in Society and Culture in the Amazon, in the area of concentration of Sociocultural Processes in the Amazon; specialist in Administration and Planning for Teachers, from the Lutheran University of Brazil (ULBRA). He graduated in Social Studies and Philosophy from the Pontifical Catholic University of Minas Gerais (PUC-Minas). He is a professor at the Higher School of Social Sciences (ESO) at the State University of Amazonas (UEA) and a permanent professor at the Interdisciplinary Postgraduate Program in Public Security, Citizenship and Human Rights (PPGSP-UEA). He is the coordinator of PPGSP-UEA.

Alexandre M.A. Martins is a professor in the Geography Department at the Pontifical Catholic University of Minas Gerais (PUC Minas). He holds a bachelor's degree in advertising from PUC Minas, a master's degree in Geography from Kansas State University, and a PhD in Geography from Arizona State University. He has also served as a visiting scholar at McGill University, Université de Lille, Curtin University, and Texas State University. With expertise in Human Geography, he has focused his research on subjects such as Geography of Crime and Violence, Urban Geography, and Regional Geography.

Patricio Trujillo Montalvo holds a Doctorate in Social Sciences (PhD) from FLACSO-Ecuador. Social Anthropologist, at Pontificia Universidad Católica del Ecuador (PUCE-Quito). He holds a master's degree in Social Anthropology obtained from Stockholm University (Sweden), as well as studies in community epidemiology and medical anthropology from the Harvard Institute for International Development. He is a full-time professor at both undergraduate and postgraduate levels and a researcher at the Public Health Institute of the Faculty of Medicine at PUCE. He is also the Scientific Director of the Andean Amazon Research Foundation (FIAAM). He has served as General Dean of Research at the Institute of Higher National Studies (IAEN), as well as Academic and Research Vice-Rector at the Higher Polytechnic School of Chimborazo. He was the Director of Scientific Research Development at the National Secretariat of Science and Technology. His current research interests are related to medical anthropology and oriental medicine, existential anthropology, ethnography of everyday life, neuroscience, and neuroanthropology.

Artur de Souza Moret holds a degree in Physics from the Fluminense Federal University, a master's degree in Science Teaching (Physical and Chemical Modality) from the University of São Paulo-USP, and a PhD in Energy Systems Planning from the State University of Campinas-UNICAMP. He is currently a full professor at the Federal University of Rondônia Foundation-UNIR and Professor of the Postgraduate Program in Regional Development and Environment at UNIR, at master's and doctorate levels. He was a Fulbright scholarship holder between 2014 and 2016 and Post-Doc in 2017 at the Institute for Research and Urban and Regional Planning-IPPUR/UFRJ. His research interests are technological innovation in energy and development, electricity generation with local renewable sources, and social impacts of large energy projects in the Amazon.

Antonio Gelson de Oliveira Nascimento holds a PhD in Demography from the Center for Development and Regional Planning (CEDEPLAR) at the Federal University of Minas Gerais (UFMG), a master's degree in Population and Regional Development from the Federal University of Amazonas (UFAM), a specialist degree in Population Studies from the Federal University of Amazonas (UFAM), a full degree in Literature (UFAM), and a Bachelor's Degree in Economic Sciences from the Federal University of Amazonas/UFAM. He has worked as a substitute professor at the Federal University of Amazonas (UFAM); Coordinator of the Professional Master's Degree in Public Security, Citizenship and Human Rights at the State University of Amazonas (UEA); and Coordinator of the Center for Studies and Research in Citizen Security (NEPAS) at Public Security of Amazonas State. He has also worked as Consultant and Manager of Statistics and Criminal Analysis of the Public Security System of the State of Amazonas with the National Public Security Secretariat (SENASP) of the Ministry of Justice—MJ.

Raimundo Pontes Filho holds a PhD in Society and Culture in the Amazon from the Federal University of Amazonas (UFAM), a master's degree in Environmental Law from the State University of Amazonas (UEA), a Bachelor of Laws from UFAM, and Bachelor and Degree in Social Sciences from UFAM. He is currently a professor at the Federal University of Amazonas, in the undergraduate and master's program in "Constitutionalism and Rights in the Amazon." He is also a professor of the master's program in Public Security at the State University of Amazonas. As a State Police Commissar, he has managed the Penitentiary Council of the State of Amazonas (2013 to 2018). His main research interest is violations of fundamental rights of biodiversity in the Amazon and the dialogue between law and Amazonian issues. He has published the following books: *O Terceiro Ciclo* (Third Cycle—1997), *História do Amazonas* (History of Amazonas—2011), *Logospirataria na Amazônia* (Logospiracy in the Amazon 2017), *Desafios da Segurança Pública no Brasil* (Challenges of Public Security in Brazil—2020), and *Formação Sociocultural da Amazônia Colonial* (Sociocultural Formation of the Colonial Amazon 2021).

Fábio Albergaria de Queiroz is an adjunct professor of International Relations and Geopolitics at the Brazilian Defense College (ESD). He holds a BA in International Relations (2000), an MA in Sustainable Development (2003), a PhD in International Relations (2011), Postdoctoral Studies in International Relations (2014–2015), and Comparative Studies on the Americas (2020–2022) from the University of Brasilia/Brazil. He is Winner of the Federal Coordination for the Improvement of Higher Education Personnel's (CAPES/Ministry of Education) Thesis Award (2012)—the most distinguished academic prize in Brazil—in

Political Science and International Relations with a thesis on "Security and Hydropolitics: The Amazon and la Plata Basins in a comparative perspective."

Wagner Silveira Rezende holds a PhD in Sociology from the Federal University of Juiz de Fora (UFJF) and a PhD in Education from UFJF. He is currently a professor at the Graduate Program in Law and Innovation at the Federal University of Juiz de Fora, and the coordinator of the Center for Evaluation of Basic Education (CAED) at the Federal University of Juiz de Fora.

Ludmila Ribeiro is an associate professor in the Department of Sociology and a researcher at the Center for Crime and Public Safety Studies (CRISP), both at the Federal University of Minas Gerais (UFMG). She holds a bachelor's degree in Law from the Federal University of Minas Gerais, as well as master's and bachelor's degrees in Public Administration from the João Pinheiro Foundation. Additionally, she earned a PhD in Sociology from the Rio de Janeiro Research Institute (IUPERJ) and was a visiting scholar at esteemed institutions such as the University of Florida, the University of Groningen, and Texas State University. Throughout her career, she has led several research projects focusing on the operations of the criminal justice system in Brazil. Presently, her research interests are centered on gender violence, first appearance hearings, homicide trials, and the management of the penitentiary system.

Juan Carlos Ruiz-Vásquez is Professor in the School of International, Politics and Urban Studies at the Universidad del Rosario in Bogotá, Colombia. He holds a PhD (DPhil) in politics from the University of Oxford, UK. He received a master's degree in public administration from the E.N.A. (École Nationale d'Administration) in France, a master's degree in business administration from Laval University in Canada, and a master's degree in political science from Los Andes University in Bogotá. Professor Ruiz's research revolves on police forces and citizen security in Latin America. Policing in transitional societies has been a pivotal topic of his academic and training assistance. He has served as an instructor on policing the regional training program funded by the Inter-American Bank of Development IDB "Leaders for Citizen Security and Justice Management." He was the coordinator of the master's in Security and Defense of the Colombian War College and has been an advisor at the Ministry of Defense of Colombia. Dr. Ruiz has been a professor at Los Andes University and head of the Department of Political Science at Javeriana University in Colombia. He has published six books and various articles in peer-reviewed journals. He has been a visiting professor at Sciences Po (CERI), Paris, France; University of Barcelona (Research group "Studies of power and privilege"—Faculty of Economics and Business), Barcelona, Spain; Max Planck Institute for Foreign and International Criminal Law, Freiburg, Germany; and National Defense University (NDU), William J. Perry Center for Hemispheric Defense Studies, Washington, DC, United States.

Katalina Barreiro Santana holds a PhD in Political Science from the University of Cuyo, PhD in Law from the Pontifical Catholic University of Ecuador, with a master's degree in International Relations from FLACSO. Academically, she has been a professor at the San Francisco de Quito University, Catholic University of Ecuador, and an associate researcher at FLACSO. In her professional life, she has worked as a career diplomat, ministerial advisor, and consultant on security, intelligence, and international relations for UNDP and IDB.

At the regional level, she served as Secretary for the High-Level Group for Border Integration of the Andean Community. In her professional experience, she also served as Deputy Secretary of Administration and Finance at the Ministry of Economy and Finance. Currently, she is the Dean of the School of Doctoral Studies at Instituto de Altos Estudios Nacionales—IAEN.

Antonio dos Santos is a master's degree holder and specialist in International Security and Defense from the Superior War School—ESG. He is an analyst in Geopolitics, Security, and Defense at the Strategic Studies Center of ESG, Rio de Janeiro (Brazil) and a researcher at the Laboratory of Simulations and Scenarios of the Brazilian Naval War College.

Sandro Sarkis holds a bachelor's degree in Law at Nilton Lins University, specializing both in Criminal Justice and Criminal Procedure at the Federal University of Amazonas, and in Public Security and Human Rights at Nilton Lins University. He was a professor at the Nilton Lins University Center and the Fametro University Center (Manaus). He has been a civil police officer since 2000, working as Head Delegate of the Environmental Police Department, Consumer Police Department, and Counter-Intelligence Department. Besides, he commanded the Organized Crime Repression Department at the Amazonas Civil Police and the Executive Intelligence Secretariat of the Amazonas government. He also held the position of Executive Secretary of Justice, Citizenship, and Human Rights in the State of Amazonas.

Jean Carlo Silva dos Santos holds a bachelor's degree in Administration from the Federal University of Rondônia (UNIR—1994), a master's degree in Public Administration from the Brazilian School of Public and Business Administration of Fundação Getúlio Vargas—EBAPE-FGV (2007), and a PhD in Administration from UFRGS-EA (2013). He has served as Secretary of People Management, Administrative Secretary, Director of the Human Resources Department, Planning Coordinator, and Administrative Modernization Coordinator of the Court of Justice of the State of Rondônia. His research interests are the daily life of public and private organizations, organizational modeling processes and their relationships with leadership roles, knowledge management and change strategies, governance applied to people management in the public sector, and public policies in the context of the Legal Amazon.

Carlos Alfredo Lazary Teixeira is former Executive Director of the Amazon Cooperation Treaty Organization (ACTO) and a former diplomat with a law degree. He was the Ambassador of Brazil in Ecuador (2015–2018) and in Peru (2011–2015). During his career as a diplomat, he was Deputy Chief of Mission in Washington, DC; Consul General in Atlanta and Deputy Consul General in Miami (United States); and Consul General in Ciudad del Este (Paraguay) and Head of the Political Sector of the Embassy of Brazil in Buenos Aires (Argentina). He was also a substitute representative in the Coordinating Intergovernmental Committee of the River Plate Basin and member of the Brazilian Delegation for the Negotiations of the Paraguay—Paraná Waterway. In Brazil, he worked at the General Secretariat of the National Security Council (Amazon Issues: Calha Norte and Nossa Natureza programs) and was Special Advisor to the President's Chief of Staff (biofuels program, atomic energy program, health industrial complex program, representative at COFIG and CAMEX), member of the President's Protocol team, and head of the Trade Promotion Division of the Ministry of Foreign Affairs.

Jean-Philippe Vauthier is a lecturer in private law and criminal sciences at the University of French Guiana and a member of MINEA research laboratory (Migration, Interculturality and Education in Amazonia, UR 7485). His work focuses on criminal law and health law. He also develops research on environmental criminal law.

INTRODUCTION

Why the Rule of Law?

Vicente Riccio and Guilherme Lopes da Cunha

The Amazon region is unique and attracts worldwide attention due to its valuable natural resources. It is composed of remarkable biodiversity and huge mineral stocks, forming the largest rainforest in the world and 20% of the planet's potable water. Furthermore, the region comprises indigenous people from many different cultures and traditions. This vast ecosystem covers nine countries: Bolivia, Brazil, Colombia, Ecuador, Guyana, French Guyana, Peru, Suriname, and Venezuela, with an area of approximately 7.7 million square kilometers (Le Tourneau, 2019). Since the European colonization started in the 16th century, the region has undergone many changes. The occupation of the area led to the exploitation of its original populations and richness, and its territory has been divided by frontiers established by the colonial powers.[1]

Since then, the socioeconomic landscape of the region has changed. Notably, in the 20th century, Amazon saw an economic model of development based on exploitative practices of its natural resources. This model led to many changes, such as the opening of roads, the development of large agricultural and cattle farms, the spurring of rubber and mining activities, and the construction of dams, among other realms. These processes resulted in increasing and inconsistent urbanization, contributing to adopting new modes of living distinct from the traditional ones. Despite these changes, the persistence of poverty, violence, deforestation, and inadequate care for the environment is a reality.

During the 20th century, all countries in the region, except French Guyana, faced authoritarian governments. They imposed development strategies based on the appropriation of land and its natural resources, undermining traditional communities and enlarging infrastructure projects without concerns about the legitimacy of its practices. This model of development, as described, impacted the ways of living and led to predatory practices toward the environment. This precarious situation led to the raising of violence in different forms: land conflicts, guerrillas, narcotics production, organized crime, and urban violence, among others.

For instance, the long-lasting conflict in the Western Hemisphere—the Colombian Civil War—has been fought since the 1960s, the main battleground being the Amazon rainforest. Other conflicts have been registered in the region, such as the Sendero Luminoso guerrilla and the Tupac Amaru's guerrillas in Peru. These conflicts were among the reasons for the raising of narcotics production in the region and the strengthening of cocaine exports for the global illicit market. More recently, the United Nations Office on Drugs and Crime (UNODC-SIMCI, 2022) has stated that deforestation areas of illegal crops in Colombia have increased, particularly in the Amazon region. According to this report, more than 50,000 hectares of forest have been cut off, and 12,939 hectares have been replaced by coca crops in 2020.

Violence problems occur in different countries in the Amazon. In Brazil, the homicide rates have decreased from their peak of 65,000 occurrences per year in 2017 (31.6 per 100,000 inhabitants) to 39,500 per year for 2023, according to the last report (19 per 100,000 inhabitants) from the Brazilian Forum of Public Security and the Institute of Applied Economic Policy (FBSP 204). The Amazon region has seen an increase in homicide, whereas in the other regions, its rates have decreased. The Brazilian hot spot, highlighting the most significant rate of homicides, is in the Amazon region, in which Amapá State concentrates a rate of 50 homicides per 100,000 inhabitants.

One example of the increase of violence in the region and the growing presence of criminal organizations in the daily lives of people was a massacre that occurred in the penitentiary "Complexo Anísio Jobim" in the city of Manaus during the 2017 New Year's Eve. A conflict between two criminal organizations inside the prison resulted in 56 inmate deaths. The register indicated that many of them had been tortured and killed in a cruel form. A criminal organization called "Família do Norte" (Northern Family) has decided to eliminate its competitors inside the prison system.[2] Then, the gangs issued an order for the massacre. This fact has attracted worldwide attention and has shown the deficiencies of the criminal justice system in the state of Amazonas.

Those examples depict a real and worrying situation in all countries in the Amazon: the fragilities in enforcing the law. They all face problems in this aspect, to a minor or more significant degree. There are problems in protecting the conservation units, the traditional peoples, the environmental assets, logistic routes, and the people in metropolitan areas. Thus, the capacity to uphold the law is a critical issue in the Amazon because governments have problems maintaining order, raising taxes, and providing public goods. If these problems occur, they indicate state fragility (Lindsey, 2021).

The World Bank report on Governance and The Law discussed its importance for improving the quality of life in different countries. The report leitmotiv is that without security, there is no possibility to enhance economic development because "growth requires an environment in which firms and individuals feel secure in investing their resources in productive activities" (World Bank, 2017, p. 5). Thus, the rule of law is crucial for the sustainable development of the Amazon.

There is great concern worldwide about conserving the rainforest, protecting its native population, and sustainable development. However, the concrete capacity to uphold the law is a central requirement to achieve these goals. The examples mentioned before are not exhaustive and depict the harsh reality of the region. Hence, this book aims to discuss how different States deal with the violence problem in the area, considering its complexities. For these reasons, the book covers various topics. The idea is to present multiple issues, such as environmental protection, indigenous population, organized crime, policing, urban violence, biopiracy, and the law.

In the field of social sciences, many studies have been done on Indigenous populations, the region's occupation processes, and the Amazon's economic strategies. However, studies concerning the capability of criminal justice institutions to uphold the law in the region are scarce. This book aims to fill this gap by discussing how criminal justice institutions deal with this problem. The authors are from different countries, such as Brazil, Colombia, Ecuador, French Guyana, Italy, and Peru. This diversity reflects the issues and intellectual approaches adopted. Finally, the book has three sections covering the following topics: (1) Crime, Violence, and the Rule of Law in the Amazon; (2) Policing Challenges in the Amazon; and (3) Law and Environmental Protection in the Amazon.

The first section, "Crime, Violence, and the Rule of Law," in the Amazon, opens with the chapter by Vicente Riccio, Giuseppe Giura, Deborah de Felice, Dorlí João Marques, and Antonio Gelson de Oliveira Nascimento titled "Rule of Law and Environmental Crimes in the Southern Amazonas," which discusses the capacity of police forces and criminal justice institutions to enforce the environmental law in the largest state of Brazil: Amazonas. This chapter presents the initial results of a research project to analyze the judicial decisions about environmental crimes in the cities of Apuí and Lábrea, ranked among the top ten places in Brazil for illegal logging and fires. This project has two axes: analysis of sentences and qualitative interviews with criminal justice professionals (attorneys, judges, police officers, prosecutors), environmental agents (federal and state levels), and civil society representatives. In this chapter, the authors present the results from qualitative interviews collected in Lábrea, Manaus (the capital of Amazonas State), and Porto Velho (the capital of Rondônia State).

The first results from the field depict the complex realities involving environmental law enforcement in Brazil. The chapter presents three issues that have emerged from the interviews: (1) the contextual scenario, (2) the cultural practices, and (3) the institutional resources. In the first category, the interviewees stress the socioeconomic characteristics of the region. For them, these are the central features that allow the occurrence of illegal logging and fires in the region. The second category describes the standard cultural practices observed in the area and how they legitimize a system of land trade based on informality without respecting legal requirements. Further, the chapter discusses the relationship between the landowners and local political power.

The third category depicts the problems faced by the criminal justice system and state agencies responsible for protecting the environment, which have limited resources to fulfill their mission. Finally, the chapter concludes that this fragility is persistent in the Southern Amazonas region, and there is no room for change shortly.

The second chapter, which was composed by Oscar Espinosa and titled "The State, Indigenous Communities, and Illicit Economic Activities in the Peruvian Amazon," discusses the impact of organized crime activities on the Indigenous population. First, the author analyses the constitution of the Amazon as a frontier region and how the Peruvian State has exploited the area since the 19th century. After this introduction, the chapter stresses the presence of illicit activities such as illegal logging, unauthorized gold mining, cocaine production, and smuggling. These activities impact indigenous communities that have adopted some activities to stop them. Lastly, the author discusses the Peruvian State's capacity to uphold the region's law.

In this case, the fragility of the Peruvian State varies. It alternates between a lack of equipment, resources, and qualified personnel to deal with organized crime in the region and the incidence of corruption among public officials that is not limited to the remote areas of the Amazon but includes the police, the military, the judicial system, and elected officials. As a result, there are few perspectives on change.

The third chapter, co-authored by Juan Carlos Ruiz-Vázquez and Rubén Sánchez David, is titled "Devastating Devastation: Impact of Crime in the Colombian Amazon," aims to understand the impact of organized crime and guerrilla groups' illegal activities in the region. The first section discusses the main crimes affecting the Colombian Amazon, and the second section analyses the strategies at the national and international levels to deal with these problems.

In the Colombian scenario, the challenges are related to the limited state presence. This panorama coexists with non-state actors, the territory's peculiar characteristics, and the corruption of public officials. Moreover, unexpected results from the peace agreement between the Colombian State and "Fuerzas Armadas Revolucionárias de Colombia" (FARC) guerrillas do not provide the required stability for protecting the Amazon.

Thus, these elements provide the conditions for the continuing devastation of the Colombian Amazon. The estimate is that the devastation will reach the tipping point by 2030. This process is aggravated by the involvement of guerrilla groups, criminal organizations, local populations, and economic interests in the illicit exploitation of natural resources. Lastly, the authors do not foresee real changes or improvements for the future.

The chapter by Rodrigo Costa Yehia Castro, Giuseppe Giura, Fabio Licata, Sandro Sarkis, and Vicente Riccio titled "The Use of Intelligence for Mapping the Activities of Criminal Organizations in the Amazon" aims to analyze, from a socio-legal perspective, the activities of criminal organizations in the region. Additionally, the authors discuss a national intelligence plan according to the Brazilian constitutional tenets that could solve criminal organizations' problems. The chapter sections present the following issues: the security in the Amazonian border space, the notion of criminal organization, the violence in the Amazonian territory, and the security and defense competencies in the Brazilian Constitution.

The authors stress the need for a national intelligence plan to guarantee Amazon's security. The plan must be able to hear the region's population, criminal justice professionals (judges, police officers, and prosecutors), and other public agents. It must also integrate the different stakeholders in the security field and adopt new practices and technology.

The chapter by Katalina Barreiro Santana and Diego Pérez Enríquez, "Ecuador's Presence in the Amazon: Security, Weak Institutions, Questioned Capabilities, and Strategic Opportunities," analyses Ecuadorean policies toward its Amazon territory. Traditional communities and natural resources such as minerals, oil, wood, and biodiversity mark this territory. They registered the conflict with Peru over disputed lands that almost led the two countries into war in 1992. Thus, the Ecuadorean Amazon is a strategic location left unprotected by the State.

They conclude that the policy for the Ecuadorean Amazon has deepened the voids in the region. It is worrying because the area is vast and holds strategic resources that increase the risk of predatory activities and distrust among the people living in the region. The authors point out that "despite a long-going presence of Ecuador in the Amazon, it might seem that the Amazon has not reached Ecuador yet." They affirm that Ecuador needs a severe policy to reinforce the region's protection. Otherwise, the critical situation observed will worsen for sure.

Milton Reyes Herrera and Patricio Trujillo Montalvo's chapter, "Strategic Resources, Border Economies, Transnational Dynamics, and Threats in the Amazon: The Case of Lago Agrio in Ecuador," discusses the impact of crime in the Sucumbios province in Ecuador. This region has a huge oil reservoir; nonetheless, illegal activities generated mainly by drug trafficking exert an impact on the Indigenous population. In this scenario, security problems arise, and the State response is generally insufficient and inadequate.

Second, these actors' articulation level will expand the problems outside Ecuador's borders with inflections in Peru and the Brazilian Amazon.

The authors conclude that integrating the National States is the right path to curb the actions of criminal organizations in the Lago Agrio region. South American countries must develop intelligence strategies that include the local population because this is the only way to create economic opportunities that can increase the local population's living standard.

The chapter by Rafael Ademir Oliveira de Andrade, Artur de Souza Moret, and Jean Carlo Silva dos Santos titled "Policing Indigenous Lands Impacted by Hydroelectrical Dams in the Brazilian State of Rondônia" refers to an area elevated from Territory to State in 1981. Rondônia is a state on the Brazilian agricultural frontier with extensive soybeans, corn, and cattle production. More recently, two hydroelectrical dams have been built in the Madeira River: Santo Antonio and Jirau. The former is the fifth-largest in the country, and the latter ranks in the seventh place. The construction of the dams was controversial, and it has been contested by indigenous and traditional communities living in the region.

The indigenous population is a victim of different crimes such as illegal logging, land grabbing, and illegal mining in their lands. In many cases, criminal groups expel these populations using threats and violence. The authors stress the scarce capacity of State institutions to control these territories. Hence, the actions that take place are punctual and occur to contain more critical situations. There are sustainable policies to promote a more permanent and efficient protection of the environment and the indigenous populations. The construction of the dams in Rondônia has increased the illegal actions of criminal gangs inside the indigenous lands, and the State's response to these events has not been able to curb it.

The authors conclude that the lack of coordination among the police forces, criminal justice institutions, and environmental agencies contributes to the low level of protection for indigenous communities. Additionally, the Brazilian State is also responsible for the problems caused by the loosening of environmental legislation in the region.

The chapter by Carlos Alfredo Lazary Teixeira, Guilherme Lopes da Cunha, and Fábio Albergaria, analyses the cooperation between the Amazon States through the Amazon Cooperation Treaty Organization (ACTO) to deal with the security problems in the region. They stress the instability and lack of security in the area and hypothesize that this scenario affects Statecraft Strategies in the region. Hence, they propose that ACTO is a potential space to bring together initiatives to foster the States' capabilities to counter organized crime in the area. The institutional framework of the ACTO can be an essential instrument to improve the rule of law and sponsor collective action in the region.

The authors conclude that ACTO can be essential in discussing standard policies to tackle transnational crime in the region. The implementation of the Amazon Regional Observatory (ORA) in 2019 has started this process with a focus on environmental matters. They propose that its scope can be broadened to include issues like biopiracy that are linked to criminal organizations and money laundering. Thus, this observatory, conceived initially to monitor natural assets, could be an essential tool to support policies against organized crime in the region. Finally, they propose that ACTO could create a special secretariat to deal with security issues.

The second section of the book, "Policing Challenges in the Amazon," opens with the chapter by Ludmila Ribeiro and Alexandre M.A. Martins titled "Being a Policewoman in the Amazon: Motivations and Everyday Routines," which aims to analyze the profile, motivations, and working conditions faced by the policewomen working in northern Brazil (the so-called Legal Amazonia). Due to the region's particularities, the authors analyze the conditions of the policewomen in their daily routine. To do so, they have used primary data gathered in 2015, when 11,982 policewomen officers (about 2% of all those performing police duties throughout Brazil) participated in a survey carried out by the Brazilian Forum on Public Security (FBSP) and the Center for Studies on Organizations and People (NEOP) of the Getulio Vargas Foundation (FGV), with support from Brazil's Ministry of Justice and the Center for Crime and Public Safety (CRISP) of UFMG (Federal University of Minas Gerais) to understand gender relations in Brazilian Police Institutions. The survey respondents from Northern Brazil are over 9% of the sample's universe, comprising 1,237 police officers.

The chapter presents interesting findings on different topics, such as ethnicity, education, and job satisfaction. According to the data, most policewomen in Amazonia identify themselves as brown (59%), and there are three times more indigenous women working in the region compared to those stationed in other Brazilian states (0.30% vs. 0.10%). Another interesting finding is the percentage of policewomen with graduate education (stricto sensu or lato sensu) in Legal Amazonia. It is higher than in the rest of Brazil. It is also related to the fact that a public career provides stability.

Additionally, there is a perception that women are in positions similar to men who have passed a public context. This is also reflected in the higher percentages of women in leadership and managerial positions in Amazon than in the rest of Brazil. These findings defy common sense about the region and suggest possibilities of changes in the context of criminal justice in the Amazon.

The chapter by Eduardo Magrone, Vicente Riccio, Wagner Silveira Rezende, Mario Aufiero titled "Procedural Justice Perceptions and Use of Force at the Civil Police of Amazonas" analyzes the perceptions of a sample of civil police officers from the state of Amazonas on the most relevant procedural justice issues. The respondents belong to the police force responsible for conducting investigations at the state level. The state of Amazonas is the largest in Brazil in terms of territorial extension, with more than 1.5 million square kilometers. Therefore, an internet questionnaire was used to gather the data. To this end, the questionnaire applied by Skogan in Chicago in 2015 was adapted to the Brazilian context. The questions covered the following subjects: (a) the demographic profile of police officers; (b) their views on violence, justice, and crime; (c) their perceptions about their relationships with the community; (d) their opinion on the use of force; (e) assessment of the structure of the Civil Police; (f) reports on relationships with other actors in the criminal justice system; and (g) measures of job satisfaction. The response rate was 12%. Out of a population of 2,465 police officers, 287 responded to the questionnaire.

The hypothesis that guided the research establishes a positive correlation between the use of force and community appreciation. Thus, the larger the resistance to the use of force by the police, the greater the importance attributed to community relations. After analyzing the data using a regression model, the conclusion is that support for the use of force by police officers is partially explained by their perception of the importance of community relations.

The chapter by Janaína de Mendonça Fernandes titled "Pressure on the Brazilian Amazon Border and State Discretion in Granting Asylum to Venezuelans" describes the influx of Venezuelans on the northern border of the country, the Amazon border, considering the Asylum Law. Such a law is still restrictive and would not account for two critical flows of migrants to Brazil, the Venezuelans and the Haitians, for which it is necessary to issue normative resolutions. The administrative process involving the entry of foreigners into Brazil, specifically the entry of refugees, is long.

In recent years, the increase in the granting of refugee status to citizens of Venezuela may reflect a political option for recognizing these citizens as refugees. This article aims to observe the pressure of the influx of Venezuelans on the Amazon border, trying to draw a parallel between discretion in response to pressure on the border and observing this fact about the lengthy administrative process of granting asylum. It also depicts the limited resources (material and personnel) of the Brazilian Federal Police to process the refugees' applications in the Amazon region. As the competent force to deal with the borders, it cannot fulfill its mission.

The third section of the book "Law and Environmental Protection in the Amazon" starts with the chapter by Marcos Vinício Chein Feres titled "Intellectual Property Rights Legislation as a Source of Inequality: A Case Study Based on Natural Genetic Resources From the Amazon Region." In this contribution, the author seeks to analyze intellectual property rights legislation as a source of inequality and as an instrument to boost the legalization of monopolies and the appropriation of genetic resources from the Amazon region. The chapter analyzes the international regulations on intellectual property concerning the TRIPS Agreement.

Hence, empirical evidence related to Brazilian natural genetic resources and their treatment under the regime of international property rights is available on the Patentscope database. The author affirms that the international patent regulatory system promotes inequality among developed and developing countries. This is the scenario for Amazon genetic resources, especially those used by local tribes in the region. The author concludes from the analysis of the codified and categorized data extracted from the patent scope database that there is an unequal distribution of intellectual property rights between developed and developing countries concerning the genetic resources of the Brazilian Amazon.

The chapter by Frédéric Bondil, Carole Hassoun, Mathilde Kamal-Girard, and Jean-Philippe Vauthier titled "The Environmental Protection in French Guiana: Normative Scheme and Stakes" analyses how the French state is able to uphold its legal commands in an overseas territory. The 1958 French Constitution establishes that "statutes and regulations shall be automatically applicable" but also that "they may be adapted in the light of the specific characteristics and constraints of such communities." Due to the rich environmental resources of French Guyana, its protection is a strategic objective for the French State. Then, legal norms protecting the region need the support of police and criminal justice officers to enforce them.

Thus, the authors discuss the general tools of environmental protection and the specific means of protecting the Guianese environment. The comprehension of the protection means in the French Amazon requires looking at the normative framework (A) and then considering the judicial judge's role, particularly regarding ecological damage (B). In their conclusion, the authors suggest a conciliation between different norms (constitutional, criminal, and environmental) that can complement each other. Remarkably, these legal norms will have more efficacy with a more profound intervention from the judge because he is responsible for enforcing them.

The chapter by Raimundo Pontes Filho discusses adopting the concept of "Logospiracy" as a form of appropriation of traditional knowledge and resources in the Amazon, and its harmful impacts in the region. This essay analyses international and Brazilian legislation to understand "Logospiracy," official data on patent registration, and the impacts generated by Amazon's interventions and activities that exploit resources, knowledge, and workforce.

In the conclusion, the author stresses the limitation of the institutional means at the disposal of Amazon states. Additionally, he points out the widespread lack of political will to face the impacts of "Logospiracy." Overcoming this process requires the integration of the knowledge embedded in the local communities with the scientific one. Without this regard, the protection of the resources or the Amazon in all spheres will not be achieved.

The book closes with the chapter by Guilherme Sandoval Góes and Antonio dos Santos titled "The Brazilian Amazon between Geopolitics and the Law." The authors discuss the hypothesis of the scientific connection between geopolitics and law as the founding basis of the sustainable development of the Amazon. In this sense, the geopolitical development of the Amazon region must depart from the democratic principles of the Brazilian Constitution in association with the values of environmental protection of public international law. Thus, it will allow the legal protection of the local populations that live in the most remote areas.

In this sense, the development of a new branch of constitutional theory, Geolaw, is suggested. This dynamic stresses the reciprocal influence of law and geopolitics and forms an epistemological whole, focusing on national development as a factor guaranteeing the dignity of the human person. Fragile states will not achieve this goal. Then, the reinforcement of states' capabilities is crucial for the region.

As previously exposed, this book discusses how the rule of law is a relevant tool for understanding the future of Amazon. According to this perspective, comprehending the context in which state institutions act in the region is central to drafting policies. The Amazon is no longer an untouched area but a space affected by human interactions on a global scale. The problems of the rainforest are related to those from the urban areas. State agents such as police officers, prosecutors, judges, environmental agents, public officials, and civil society activists fulfill their mission in a complex and risky context. For those reasons, this book aims to contribute to the debate about the importance of the protection of the Amazon.

Notes

1 Portugal and Spain have conquered and controlled the largest part of the Amazon's territory. France, the Netherlands, and the United Kingdom have managed to gain control in smaller parts in the Guyana's plateau.
2 Available at https://www.acritica.com/manaus/vitimas-do-massacre-no-compaj-foram-forcadas-a-comer-olho-humano-1.174150 at 03/15/24.

References

Fórum Brasileiro de Segurança Pública (FBSP). (2024). *Anuário Brasileiro de Segurança Pública*. São Paulo: FBSP.
Le Tourneau, F.M. (2019). *L'Amazonie, histoire, géographie, environnement*. Paris: CNRS Éditions.
Lindsey, Brink. (2021). *State Capacity: What is it, how we lost it, and how to get it back?* Washington, DC: Niskannen Center, 1–25.
Oficina de las Naciones Unidas contra la Droga y el Delito (UNODC)-Sistema Integrado de Monitoreo de Cultivos Ilícitos (SIMCI). (2022). *Monitoreo de territorios afectados por cultivos ilícitos 2021*. Bogotá: UNODC-SIMCI.

PART I

Crime, Violence, and the Rule of Law in the Amazon

1
RULE OF LAW AND ENVIRONMENTAL CRIMES IN THE SOUTHERN AMAZONAS

Vicente Riccio, Giuseppe Giura, Deborah De Felice, Dorlí João Marques, and Antonio Gelson de Oliveira Nascimento

Justification/Characterization of the Problem

The Amazon region has been an object of national and international interest for a long time. Holder of the largest forest reserve on the planet and its biodiversity, the region also holds great patrimony of natural resources, such as the largest reserve of fresh water in the world and essential minerals. Such a feature draws attention to the preservation of the region globally. Thus, the protection of the Amazon rainforest and its biodiversity is ensured by the Brazilian Federal Constitution of 1988, which also protects traditional peoples established in the region.

There are many issues concerning the Amazon, namely poverty, low levels of economic development, the misuse of natural resources (Ramos de Castro and Castro, 2022), illegal logging (Prado Capanema et al., 2022), fires, deforestation, and other environmental and social risks (Pacheco Farias and Szlafsztein, 2023).

Fires and illegal logging are the most visible problems in the region, and they attract attention worldwide. The incidence of those problems is not new and poses challenges for the Brazilian government on internal and external fronts. Criticism arises from non-governmental institutions, academia, and foreign governments. Considering the latter, pressures to halt commercial agreements with Brazil or even impose sanctions have been openly discussed.

Thus, this is a relevant problem that needs to be dealt with by Brazilian authorities.

Due to the vastness of the Amazon, especially in Brazil, governmental actions face obstacles to being implemented. Among them, the capacity to uphold the law is a critical one. However, there are few studies about the rule of law in the region, despite the growing problem of crime. It reflects the weakness of different nation-states in the region to enforce the law in a context marked by the presence of organized crime acting through global networks (Arnaud, 1998; Castells, 1996; Faria, 1997; Varese, 2010).

The deficiencies of law enforcement institutions and the judicial power in the region have been documented before lack of personnel, forensics experts, and equipment such as boats, airplanes, and off-road vehicles are common. Besides, there is no stable flow of resources to sustain operations (Riccio et al., 2016; Pontes, 2020). In general, the conditions to uphold the law in the region are scarce.

Environmental crimes are embedded in this context. Thus, the enforcement of environmental laws in the Amazon needs to be studied not only in a pure and abstract mode, but it must consider the context in which it is applied. In this sense, it is important to understand how law enforcement institutions and judicial authorities deal with the occurrence of fires and deforestation.

Due to the geographic characteristics of the Amazon, technology is essential to improve the capacity of legal institutions to uphold the law. Environmental crimes are complex, and the support of technology is essential for the investigation and trial phases. For those reasons, this chapter aims to discuss the relationship between the use of satellite technology and the capacity to uphold the law in the State of Amazonas, the largest in the country. The focus will be on the municipalities of Apuí and Lábrea, which are among the most cities affected by illegal fires and deforestation in the Brazilian Amazon.

These initial results are part of a research project that aims to analyze the capabilities of the Brazilian criminal justice system at federal and state levels, and other environmental agencies, to respond to environmental crimes in the State of Amazonas. This is mixed-method research that will analyze judicial decisions regarding environmental crimes in both cities and will be completed with semi-structured interviews. State agents such as police officers, attorneys, judges, and environmental agents will be interviewed. For the purposes of this chapter, only some interviews with public agents will be analyzed.

Rule of Law and the Amazon Context

The State as an institution has a basic feature: the monopoly of creating and imposing the law (Weber, 1995). This unique feature is a product of the Modern State that has emerged in Europe and has been exported throughout the world, mainly by conquest and colonization. Thus, it is commonly accepted that the international arena is organized through sovereign states since the Westphalia peace (1648). This is the landmark for the actual international system observed today in which countries are organized in this way.

After the end of World War II, the decolonization process in Africa and Asia, and the collapse of the Soviet Union gave birth to a huge number of independent states. However, the existence of these new States has been characterized in many cases by instability and weakness to enforce the law (Fukuyama, 2004). This is relevant because a basic tenet of any Modern State is the monopoly of promulgating and enforcing the law.

Thus, the debate about the lack of capacity of some states to maintain order or to enforce the law has gained prominence. The problems observed in the 1990s of the last century have sparked a discussion about the capacity of some states to fulfill their basic tasks: a central government, a functioning judiciary, a working legislative branch, and legitimate law enforcement institutions (Bayley, 2005). In this context, the instability in the Balkans, or in impoverished countries such as Haiti, Somalia, or Afghanistan, has raised the concept of failed States (Thürer, 1999, pp. 731–733). This concept originally advocated that some states were not able to maintain order and were doomed to fail.

The criticisms over the idea of failed states have emerged on the basis of the assumptions that it is centered on specific situations mainly affected by wars. Other problems related to State weaknesses can be observed without being in a war-like situation. The concept has evolved from "failed" to "fragile" states. In this sense, "fragile statehood is characterized by a wide range of dysfunctional state-society relations—states not being able to control their territory, states not being able to support their population that they have legitimate claims to dominate a given territory" (Grävingholt et al., 2015, p. 1284).

In this sense, state fragility is a multidimensional concept that involves three axes: violence control, implementation capacity, and empirical legitimacy. The first is the classical attribute of the state to impose order to exercise the monopoly of violence in a specific territory. The second is the ability to provide services for the population such as health, education, or pensions and infrastructures in general (Diniz, 2013). The last one refers to the acceptance of state order by a specific population. These dimensions are not isolated and interact with each other. Thus, the understanding of the state fragility must consider these aspects.

One interesting point is taxing, because it is related to the coercive power of the state to raise resources through imposition. For this reason, a fragile state cannot be able to collect taxes that are required to fund institutions responsible for maintaining order and protecting rights. It also impacts the capacity to implement social policies, especially for the population in need (Di Maro et al., 2021). Legitimacy from the population is a requirement of consent from the population to exercise its power (Ziaja et al., 2019).

All these elements are interrelated and depending on the country, it is possible to observe the presence of one failure compared to different ones. Those problems can be observed also inside a country with huge disparities. Some regions have more capacity to enforce the law than others. Or some countries have a lower ability to collect taxes.

These differences among states led to comparative studies between countries. Thus, indicators have been established to capture the levels of strength and weakness among states.

In general, indicators try to grasp the degree of statehood in each country. Versteeg and Ginsburg (2017) have analyzed different indicators developed to capture the quality of institutions, legal systems, and governance. It is important because the rule of law is a central element in the development process. Thus, in the literature, it is possible to identify at least 150 governance indicators, some of them with a stress on the rule of law.

Due to the huge number of indicators, Versteeg and Ginsburg (2017) discuss four indicators that deal with the rule of law (RoL): (1) the Heritage Foundation, (2) Freedom House, (3) World Governance Index (World Bank), and (4) World Justice Project. Those indexes deal with different variables but aim to measure how the rule impacts different countries and fosters development. Indicators are not exempt from criticism, and a common one is the reduction of complex phenomena to simple variables. Further, "some indicators measure formal institutions, others measure behavior, while yet others measure beliefs" (101).

Rule of law indicators can be built under "thin" or "thick" perspectives. For example, the first one stresses formal or procedural values, and the second one on substantial elements, such as the quality of the law. Additionally, it is possible to consider the adoption of experts or layperson perspectives in a specific indicator. These elements show how multilayered is the concept of the rule of law.

The authors have compared the four indexes with the concepts of "(1) democracy, (2) human rights, (3) constitutionalism, (4) judicial independence, (5) GDP per capita, and (6) corruption" (Versteeg and Ginsburg 2017: 113). They found a correlation of the small significance of the rule of law with democracy, human rights, judicial independence, and GDP per capita. However, they found a significant correlation between the four indexes with corruption. They also discuss the differences between experts' and ordinary people's perceptions of elements of the rule of law. The latter do not have the same level of information as the experts in core issues related to the rule of law. Thus, the experts' perceptions are a central element of convergence among the indicators. Besides, they found that "measurement strategy, rather than conceptualization, seems to be the dominant factor determining RoL indicators" (124).

It is not the objective of this chapter to discuss the indicators of the rule of law in depth, but it is important to observe how the indicators try to grasp their relevance to understanding developmental processes. Despite the diversity of perspectives and methods of analysis, "the rule of law has come to be associated—and occasionally identified—with a diverse range of values, including individual rights, social justice, democratic self-determination, free markets, judicial independence, and good governance" (Fatovic, 2019, p. 2). Moreover, the rule of law is crucial to curb authoritarianism and to provide stability to a given country.

However, there is a tendency to assume that societies will follow the path of liberal societies. This perspective based only on institutional elements does not consider broader contexts and the relationship between state and society. Lottholz and Lemay-Hébert (2016) criticize this approach based on the assumption that "a state is considered legitimate when its institutions can secure the monopoly of violence over a given territory" (1472). This perspective forgets one central tenet of Max Weber's thought: reflexivity. Hence, it is necessary to recognize the state as a product of human relationships embedded in a particular context. For these reasons, "the focus of inquiry should be on how and why people 'do', or enact, the state by practicing behavior" (1474).

In this reflexive perspective, the analysis does not fall exclusively upon the institutional structures of the state but also in the context in which they are built. In this sense, elements such as culture, tradition, economic levels, and historical processes are considered in shaping the State. For instance, Charron et al. (2012) analyzed the formation of States in Europe and consider their formation processes much more relevant in determining the characteristics of these societies—patrimonial or bureaucratic, than the legal tradition.

At the same pace, Börzel et al. (2018) criticize the "failed" or "fragile" States approach because it does not consider the fact that areas of limited statehood can be found everywhere, even in developed countries, and the deficit in upholding the law does not mean complete absence of governance. Hence, the concept of limited statehood is more adequate to deal with this problem in as much as not normative-oriented and exclusively focused on the Western experience. In this sense, "areas of limited statehood then constitute those parts of a country in which central authorities (governments) lack the ability to implement and enforce rules and decisions and/or in which they do not command a legitimate monopoly of the means of violence (2018, p. 6)." Through this perspective, it is possible to analyze the distinct layers in which governance is exerted in a given state.

The rule of law is central to the stability of any society. Thus, it is relevant to set the perspective in which this analysis will be conducted. The Amazonian context is very complex due to the vastness of its territory, and the difficulties faced by the States in the region to protect their territory, their indigenous populations, their urban population, and their natural assets. Additionally, the States face the development problem, because the persistence of poverty and low levels of living exert considerable pressure on governments. Therefore, the politics in the region reinforces traditional practices of clientelism, patrimonialism, and corruption.

This context faces the presence of organized crime, which is a phenomenon common to different countries and realities. Despite these particularities, some features are recurrent: hierarchical structure, high amounts of money obtained through illegal activities, transnational networks, weakening of civil society, and corruption of public officials. The list of illegal activities is long and ranges from drug trafficking, human trafficking, arms smuggling, money laundering, corruption of public officials, racketing, and biopiracy, among others. The literature has registered more than 150 definitions of organized crime, but those characteristics cited before are found in all of them (Varese, 2010).

Criminal organizations need to establish control over territories, or parts of them, to profit and avoid putting them in danger of their activities. To guarantee its interests, the use of force is a common resource, as well as corruption (Campana and Varese, 2018). In some cases, those organizations directly challenge the state authority with terror acts or establish de facto control over some areas (urban or rural). In Brazil, it is a reality in many "favelas," border areas, inhabited regions or using military tactics to attack banks in countryside cities (Loureiro and Guimarães, 2017; Abadinsky, 2010; Riccio and Skogan, 2018; Magaloni et al., 2020; Feitosa, 2022).

Hence, criminal organizations always target something valuable, such as natural resources. In the Amazon, there is great pressure on environmental assets due to the illegal economic activities in the region. Deforestation, illegal logging, fires, and illegal public land appropriation are common in the region. Another problem in the Amazon is the registration of lands. The great majority of lands in the region belong to the Federal Government, but they are not properly registered. As stated by Sant'Anna and Young (2010),

> deforestation is a way of obtaining property rights over an area of forested land with property rights undefined or poorly protected, with the expectation of subsequent sale to other economic agents who are only interested in advancing after the conditions basic institutionalization measures are guaranteed.
>
> (p. 385)

The authors have shown that there is a correlation between violence and deforestation due to poor protection of property rights after analyzing data from 575 municipalities in the region.

According to this scenario, an analysis of the rule of law must consider the societal conditions on which the institutional arrangements are built. Thus, how do criminal justice institutions enforce environmental laws in the context of rural Amazon? How does the local society react to the laws imposed by the central government? What are the main obstacles for state institutions to achieve effectiveness in enforcing environmental laws in the Amazon? These questions try to grasp in which measure the rule of law is exerted in the region. For the purposes of the research, one municipality of the State of Amazonas will be analyzed: Lábrea, because data has been gathered there. The city is among those with the highest levels of illegal logging and fires in the State and is one of the ten cities most affected by illegal logging and fires in Brazil.

If we look at the vastness of Amazonas State, and particularly the municipalities of Lábrea and Apuí, it is possible to figure out how difficult is to enforce the law in the region. Apuí will be analyzed in the future steps of this project. However, it is worth picturing the incidence of the problem. According to the most recent data from the Brazilian Institute of Geography and Statistics (IBGE), Lábrea has an area of 68.266,68 km^2 a population is 45,448 inhabitants, a demographic density of 0.67 inhabitants per km^2, and an HDI index of 0.57. The city relies basically on the primary sector for its economy (95%).

Apuí located on the border of the Transamazonic Highway has an area of 54.240,545 km^2, and a population of 20.647 inhabitants, a demographic density of 0.38 hab/sq2, and an HDI index of 0.637, according to IBGE. The city is the only one in the State of Amazonas that has not been formed on the banks of a river but alongside the highway. The economics is mainly based on cattle raising and agriculture, and Apuí has also attracted many migrants from the Southern region of Brazil in the 1980s in search of land. Since then agricultural activities have been developed there, and the city is the main food producer in the State.

Illegal deforestation in the Amazon, on the one hand, stands as the most critical issue on Brazil's environmental agenda, and the lack of data concerning these kinds of crimes makes it difficult to develop fitting public policies (Souza Ferreira and Veludo Watanabe, 2020); on the other hand, it is a great environmental problem in Brazil, because the largest emissions of CO_2 in the atmosphere are registered in the region (Pivetta, 2020, 2021a, 2021b). These levels are monitored by the National Institute of Scientific Research through the PRODES program.[2] It was created in 1988 to monitor the levels of deforestation through satellite imagery. Each year a report is issued with the data concerning the situation of deforestation. The data are used for certification in (a) agricultural chains, especially the soya beans moratorium and Livestock Conduct Adjustment Term—Meat TAC; (b) to inform the National Greenhouse Gas Emissions Inventory Reports; and (c) a reference for the policies of the Amazon Fund.[3] Hence, PRODES' data[4] are the reference for the policies concerning deforestation in the region.

Table 1.1 depicts the evolution of deforestation in Brazil using aggregate data.

This table shows the evolution of deforestation in the Brazilian Legal Amazon since the start of measurement. The peak was in 2004, with 27,772 km^2 deforested, and the lowest rate was in 2012 with 4571 km^2. After this year, it is possible to observe the growth of deforestation rates, which increased from 2018 to 2022. From 2021 a new decrease started.

From the data, it is possible to observe that Pará (second-largest in Brazil) is mainly responsible for deforestation in the country (39.9%), followed by Amazonas (the largest Brazilian State), which ranks 17.13%. The state of Amazonas is the most important in the region due to its economic importance. Manaus is an industrial hub in the Northern part of Brazil, for its centrality in the Brazilian Amazon. The State borders also three countries: Colombia, Peru, and Venezuela, and suffers pressure from the agricultural frontier. In 2022 Lábrea was responsible for 540.25 km^2 (4th place) and Apuí 329.88 km^2 (7th place).

Table 1.2 depicts the evolution of deforestation in the municipalities of Apuí and Labrea based on PRODES' data:

In the tables, the deforested areas in both municipalities have grown in the last ten years. For those reasons, the cities, as mentioned earlier, have been selected for the purposes of this research. This ongoing research aims to analyze judicial decisions regarding environmental crimes related to Apuí and Lábrea, and the perceptions of criminal justice professionals, environmental agents, and local leaders about the incidence of these problems in the region. For the sake of this paper, the first qualitative results will be presented. These data allow us to understand the nature of the problem faced by those who are responsible for law enforcement in the areas of high levels of illegal logging and fires. In this stage of the research, the data has been gathered in Manaus, Porto Velho, and Lábrea. Thus, it will be the focus of the present chapter.

TABLE 1.1 PRODES rates 1998–2021 (Legal Amazon km^2)

Year/State	AC	AM	AP	MA	MT	PA	RO	RR	TO	Legal Amazon
1988	620	1510	60	2450	5140	6990	2340	290	1650	21,050
1989	540	1180	130	1420	5960	5750	1430	630	730	17,770
1990	550	520	250	1100	4020	4890	1670	150	580	13,730
1991	380	980	410	670	2840	3780	1110	420	440	11,030
1992	400	799	36	1135	4674	3787	2265	281	409	13,786
1993	482	370	0	372	6220	4284	2595	240	333	14,896
1994	482	370	0	372	6220	4284	2595	240	333	14,896
1995	1208	2114	9	1745	10,391	7845	4730	220	797	29,059
1996	433	1023	0	1061	6543	6135	2432	214	320	18,161
1997	358	589	18	409	5271	4139	1986	184	273	13,227
1998	536	670	30	1012	6466	5829	2041	223	576	17,383
1999	441	720	0	1230	6963	5111	2358	220	216	17,259
2000	547	612	0	1065	6369	6671	2465	253	244	18,226
2001	419	634	7	958	7703	5237	2673	345	189	18,165
2002	883	885	0	1085	7892	7510	3099	84	212	21,651
2003	1078	1558	25	993	10,405	7145	3597	439	156	25,396
2004	728	1232	46	755	11,814	8870	3858	311	158	27,772
2005	592	775	33	922	7145	5899	3244	133	271	19,014
2006	398	788	30	674	4333	5659	2049	231	124	14,286
2007	184	610	39	631	2678	5526	1611	309	63	11,651
2008	254	604	100	1271	3258	5607	1136	574	107	12,911
2009	167	405	70	828	1049	4281	482	121	61	7464
2010	259	595	53	712	871	3770	435	256	49	7000
2011	280	502	66	396	1120	3008	865	141	40	6418
2012	305	523	27	269	757	1741	773	124	52	4571
2013	221	583	23	403	1139	2346	932	170	74	5891
2014	309	500	31	257	1075	1887	684	219	50	5012
2015	264	712	25	209	1601	2153	1030	156	57	6207
2016	372	1129	17	258	1489	2992	1376	202	58	7893
2017	257	1001	24	265	1561	2433	1243	132	31	6947
2018	444	1045	24	253	1490	2744	1316	195	25	7536
2019	682	1434	32	237	1702	4172	1257	590	23	10,129
2020	706	1512	24	336	1779	4899	1273	297	25	10,851
2021	889	2306	17	350	2213	5238	1673	315	37	13,038
2022*	847	2607	6	282	1906	4141	1512	240	27	11,568
Var. 2022–2021*	−5%	13%	−65%	−19%	−14%	−21%	−10%	−24%	−27%	−11%

TABLE 1.2 Deforestation rates Apuí and Lábrea

PRODES Year	Apuí Deforestation rate (%)	Deforested area (km²)	Lábrea Deforestation rate (%)	Deforested area (km²)
2012	0.14	73.88	0.12	83.61
2013	0.16	86.11	0.17	116.83
2014	0.15	80.04	0.19	132.54
2015	0.20	107.01	0.35	236.80
2016	0.30	161.35	0.45	310.24
2017	0.31	169.54	0.41	276.87
2018	0.29	158.19	0.46	315.52
2019	0.53	287.69	0.56	381.76
2020	0.48	259.63	0.56	382.87
2021	0.61	329.88	0.79	540.23
2022	1.35	731.72	1.03	699.59

Source: Prodes (http://www.obt.inpe.br/OBT/assuntos/programas/amazonia/prodes)

In this context of persisting pressures on the environment, some questions arise: (1) how do criminal justice institutions enforce environmental laws in the context of rural Amazon? (2) How does the local society react to the laws imposed by the central government? (3) What are the main obstacles for state institutions to achieve effectiveness in enforcing environmental laws in the Amazon? These questions try to grasp in which measure the rule of law is exerted in the region.

Methodology

This chapter adopts a qualitative analysis of interviews with criminal justice professionals and environmental agents who have worked with environmental crimes related to the city of Lábrea.[5] These are the initial results of a broader research project that aims to understand the capacity of enforcing the law in the Amazon. One step is the quantitative analysis of environmental crime decisions from the mentioned cities; the second step is the qualitative analysis of interviews with criminal justice professionals, environmental agents, public authorities, and civil society activists. The interviews were conducted in the cities of Manaus (capital of the State of Amazonas), Lábrea, and Porto Velho (capital of the State of Rondônia) and through face-to-face, video, and phone interview from January to August 2023.

Qualitative research allows the understanding of a social phenomenon, considering the particularities of the context that are not grasped by generalist methods. This perspective focuses on the study of problems aimed at understanding the meanings constructed by the subjects (Denzin and Lincoln, 1998). The articulation of quantitative and qualitative methods is also possible (Creswell, 2014), but this study will center its attention on the interviews gathered until now.

The interviewees were chosen due to their work in the criminal justice system related to environmental law enforcement in the region. The interviewees were contacted initially through the Association of Police Commissars of Amazonas and the State University of Amazonas. After these initial contacts, the research team was able to get access to professionals who have indicated other colleagues (snowball technique). The first contact aimed to explain the research project and its scientific nature. This initial approach to gain trust was required because the interviewees dealt with sensitive positions in their daily work.

All the interviews were recorded with the consent of the interviewees and later transcribed. Their names have been changed as determined by the research protocol. The transcriptions were coded using Ligre Software, and the initial categories were established. A content analysis has been performed. This sample is composed of the interviews of one high-rank officer from the Military Police of Amazonas serving in Lábrea, two State Judges from Amazonas State, one Federal Prosecutor from Amazonas, one Federal Judge from Amazonas, one State Prosecutor from Amazonas, one Federal Police Commissar from Amazonas, and two Agents from the Amazonas Environmental Agency.

Discussion

As exposed before, from the general argument of "State Capacity to Uphold the Law," there are three categories: (1) the context, (2) the cultural practices, and (3) the institutional resources. From these categories, other subcategories have been grouped due to their adherence to the issue. Despite this grouping, all the themes are interrelated in some manner. Table 1.3 describes how the categories have been organized.

The contextual dimension comprises the problems related to the Southern region of the Amazonas State, where Lábrea and Apuí are located. These issues have emerged from the interviews and refer to the socioeconomic characteristics of the region. For the interviewees, these are the core elements responsible for the persistent occurrence of illegal logging and fires in the region. In the first place, the geographical vastness of the Amazon Forest is emphasized by the interviewees. This topic is common to all of them and stresses the limitations of the Brazilian institutions to exert control and uphold the law in the region.

TABLE 1.3 State capacity to uphold the law

State capacity to uphold the law

(1) The context	(2) The cultural practices	(3) Institutional resources
• Local economic development • Political power and clientelism • Land legalization • Territorial extension and logistics • Economic power • Organized crime • Low level of land legalization	• Cultural practices and land commerce • Naturalization of logging and fire practices • Frontier logic	• Scarcity of personnel in public institutions • Scarcity of equipment • Limited investigation capabilities of criminal justice system institutions • Competencies conflicts among public institutions • Support of satellite imagery in environmental protection

22 Policing the Amazon

This territory does not allow real control by the criminal justice institutions, and it makes it easy for illegal lodgers, "grileiros" (people who take possession of public lands), and cattle farmers.

State failure is seen in different areas, such as the registration of public and private lands, the incapacity of promoting environmental policies, and the controlling of areas in the region. Due to the particularities of the region, these problems are aggravated. This excerpt from the interview with a federal judge sheds light on the problem.

> It's a complex response, I would say it's a complete failure of environmental policy, agrarian policy, the presence of the state, effective cadastral controls, control over the occupation of federal public areas, real control over federal territories, and these municipalities, most of them, are federal territories, so there is great resentment among the population, including, for them, conservation units and indigenous lands because they are federal. It is an obstacle to the growth they want, they want this development, are areas of violent conflict.
> *(Maria Silva, Federal Judge)*

An agent from the Environmental Agency of the Amazonas State presents a similar description of the problem. This fragility is compared to a "war zone" in which there is a force taking control of the territory. This metaphor depicts the harsh situation in the region and the limitations perceived by public officials. The following is the transcription:

> I would say fragile, the word would be fragile, especially because of vulnerability and access. Lábrea, I take the name Lábrea, but if we take it, it is not the center of the municipality, right, it is the territory of the municipality of Lábrea, which is already the border with the state of Rondônia. Apuí is the border with the state of Pará, so If I include Humaitá in this scenario, and that entire southern region there, as if it were a war zone, we are being invaded, in a reading like that.
> *(Antonio Carlos, IPAAM)*

This problem has also been raised by a Federal Police Commissar working in Manaus with a long experience in the region. The State of Amazonas is so large that the Federal Police does not have the capacity to respond to all the events. In the case of the municipality of Lábrea, they are dealt with by the Federal Police Precinct located in the city of Porto Velho, the capital of Rondônia State. This is an exception because the Federal Police headquarters located in one state is responsible for the events inside its territory. In this case, the police officers serving in Porto Velho constantly are called to deal with problems in the Southern Amazonas region. According to the Federal Constitution, the competency for dealing with federal crimes rests on the Federal Judicial Power (articles 108 and 109), and the Federal Police is responsible for investigating those crimes. The largest number of lands and forests in the State of Amazonas belongs to the Federal Government. Thus, it is responsible for the control of the area and for the investigation of federal crimes. The commissar stresses emphatically the low capacity of exerting control and the ad hoc solutions commonly adopted by public officials. As described next:

> Lábrea does not even belong to the superintendency of the Federal Police of Amazonas, right? The crimes committed in the municipality of Lábrea are investigated by Rondônia, taking into account the land proximity to get to Porto Velho and here it is much further

away. Apuí, despite being in our district, is very distant. So, this is the difficulty, you know, normally we already have a limit of federal police officers here.

(Ernesto, Federal Police Commissar)

This problem of resources in the region is also stressed by a Federal Prosecutor who reinforces the role of the Federal Police and the Federal Attorney Office from Porto Velho in dealing with those crimes. Despite this attribution, the resources to carry out diligence are limited. The availability of resources occurs when there is an ongoing operation authorized by a Federal Police Director or a Judge. It allows the operation in the field to arrest people, apprehend illegal stuff, or gather evidence. They need this authorization due to the high economic cost. This limitation does not allow checking warnings of crimes potentially harmful.

As you know, the south of Lábrea is isolated from the municipality's headquarters. So, we need to access it through Porto Velho. . . . The Federal Police responsible for Lábrea are the Federal Police located in Rondônia. Eventually, they need to carry out due diligence in these locations. The ideal would be, each relevant case has to have due diligence in the field. . . . For example, it is a deforestation notice of 1000 hectares, but it is not an operation, it is not possible to carry out due diligence. Because due diligence is restricted to cases considered operations, which are deeper investigations and such. (Fernanda Moura Federal Prosecutor)

Additionally, the connection between environmental crime and organized crime makes it harder for public officials to work in the region. Criminal organizations dispose of many resources to carry out their activities. It is a contrast in comparison with the lack of resources faced by the criminal justice institutions acting in the area.

And there's a connection, right? Environmental crime and organized crime—No doubt, because whoever is going to finance a risky activity, whoever is going to finance it, you are going to take your savings where you worked lawfully, buy ten dredgers, each dredger costs a 100 thousand reals? If they spend 1 million reals knowing that tomorrow Ibama, the Federal Police, and the military police could arrive there, it is too risky. (Ernesto, Federal Police Commissar).

Another problem observed is the risk for public officials to work in the area. The power of those who benefit from the illegal activities and their connections with the local political power pose a threat to them. It was stressed by a judge from the State of Amazonas:

There is, for sure. There is a friend of mine who works in Boca do Acre, and he carries a gun because he knows the reality there concerning illegal logging, understand? Thus, in Lábrea and Boca do Acre they can act freely. Political and economic influence are everywhere, especially in the South of Amazonas concerning environmental crimes. So, a judge must be careful, but he needs to do everything that doesn't interfere with his way of deciding. Of course, some judges have already been threatened.

(Flavio, Judge of the Court of Justice of Amazonas)

Land regulation is another relevant problem related to the State's fragility in the area. There is no effective regulation of property titles, and the practice of invading public forest areas is common. These people are commonly called "grileiros," who use illegal methods to occupy this land and to legalize it. The following excerpt stresses it:

What really caught my attention is the deficiency in property registries in the state of Amazonas. There is no legal certainty and no assurance that a certificate matches reality.

> So, sometimes you have to carry out an expert analysis, and you have to ask for proof, and sometimes two or more people present the same ownership certificate. So, I see a lot of this agrarian conflict of repossession here in the state of Amazonas.
>
> *(Flavio, Judge of the Court of Justice of Amazonas)*

The registration situation is so precarious that is taken for granted by the people who live in the region and public officials working there. This excerpt from the Public Prosecutor's interview reinforces this "acceptance" of reality by the officials designated to the region:

> Who are the public bodies in the region? The public registry office of real estate and Incra (National Institute of Colonization and Agrarian Reform), and we questioned this thing that there was no registration, and according to these local authorities was: nothing here really has registration. That's it! We just negotiate ownership and everything is fine, everyone does it.
>
> *(Fernanda Moura, Federal Prosecutor)*

The problems described here depict the problem observed in the Southern Amazonas State in a broader way. The interviewees stress the particularities of the region how the capacity of the State to enforce the law is limited by these constraints, and how difficult the change is. The other categories (cultural practices and institutional resources) are embedded in these contextual phenomena.

The second category pictures the cultural practices observed in the region, and how they naturalize the way in which the land is acquired, bought, and sold. Moreover, it stresses the relationship between those practices and the local political power. Finally, the frontier logic is present in Brazilian perceptions about the Amazon region, and in the country's vast hinterland. The expansion of agricultural activities after the construction of Brasilia and the occupation of areas in the Cerrado and in the Amazon are part of this imaginary. Many cities in these regions have been built in the past 50 years.

In the case of the Southern State of Amazonas, Lábrea is the final spot of the Transamazônica highway built between 1969 and 1974. The road has an extension of 4260 kilometers and goes from east to west. There is also the BR319 that links Manaus to Porto Velho. On the edge of these roads, many settlers have established small farms and then attracted people from different places in Brazil. Thus, there is a predominant logic of frontier in the region, that attracts settlers searching for low or no-cost lands. Amazonas State has not been "touched" as the States of Pará or Rondônia, but now there is a movement in its direction. A Federal Judge from Amazonas affirms:

> Amazonas is the last frontier, so the state of Pará has already experienced many phases of criminal dynamics that start small, go big, and become more sophisticated. It has already gone through these stages, and Rondônia as well, and now these people arrive in Amazonas. This is very clear for me because the biggest illegal lodgers do not live in Amazonas. They live in Ariquemes (Rondônia), in Itaituba (Pará). They are coming from neighboring states, entering through the state's borders with this practice of deforestation, and livestock exploitation. Thus, many slaughterhouses have been opened in recent years in

the South of Amazonas. Additionally, logging companies are also advancing, especially those from Rondônia.

(Maria Silva, Federal Judge)

An agent from the Environmental Protection Agency of Amazonas State stresses the impact of the demand for wood in this frontier region as the main reason for the land's demand. This statement is important because he works directly with the satellite imagery system responsible for monitoring illegal fires and logging. It can be observed:

It is due to the law of demand and supply. So, there is a demand for the wood. There is a demand for the land. There is a demand for speculation in these areas, and there are people who want a piece of land. They will tear it down and subdivide it. They will sell it, even by illegal means, but it will exist. So, the last frontier of land, of forest, is the Amazon, right? It is the Amazon, but mainly, today, the state of Amazonas. Unfortunately, in a few years, we will be the first in deforestation rates.

(Antonio IPAAM)

In this frontier logic, the local power has its own dynamics and exerts control of local institutions with practices based on clientelism. In this sense, the "Colonel" (a local leader) provides support for disadvantaged people in exchange for political favors. In this sense, if these people violate environmental laws, it is part of the game. This behavior is "naturalized," because they "help people" and the social practices in the region are legitimized, despite being contrary to the official law. It is clearly exposed by a Federal Prosecutor:

There is social recognition of these people, so I've heard in an audience several times that so-and-so is a great deforester, but he is an excellent person, who helps the community a lot, and he donates basic food baskets. When there is no transportation to the municipal hospital, he is the one who helps, and a wonderful person. And in fact, he does what the state should be doing.

(Fernanda Moura, Federal Prosecutor)

In this common perception, the local leaders provide protection, but there is no mention of the harm caused by their actions. This practice beyond the law causes many problems for the local communities, including the use of violence to settle disputes. The following excerpt reinforces it:

So he is the colonel and the owner of everything here, and he is the one who helps people here when necessary. He is a good guy, but also, eventually, he is the one who harms the people in the place. So . . . we also have violent conflicts, and violence has increased a lot in the interior of Amazonas, and in the State as a whole in recent years. People kind of leave this aside and naturalize it.

(Fernanda Moura, Federal Prosecutor)

The cultural practices embedded in the region strengthen patterns of behavior beyond the formal legality. For these reasons, the commerce of lands based on documents not fully legal is a constant in the region. It is related to the feeble system of registration observed throughout the Southern Amazonas. Moreover, these practices are reinforced by the local clientelism linked to the political interests in the region.

The third category of analysis is "Institutional Resources," which deals with problems related to the capabilities of criminal justice institutions and environmental agencies (federal and state levels) to handle the enforcement of law in the region. In this category, the management issues are discussed ranging from lack of personnel, adequate hardware, and the relationship between the public institutions. The following excerpt from a Military Police Officer depicts the limitations faced in the region. The size of the municipality and the scarcity observed on a daily basis do not allow it to reach the places in which environmental crimes occur:

> The logistics situation is a real problem. Today we have vehicles, and we can travel but I don't have fuel, I won't have fuel anymore. If I go to those places, in the southern region of Lábrea I won't have the logistics of accommodation, food, because it's a very sensitive topic, the state doesn't pay me per diem. I'm going to travel around the state, I enter the state of Rondônia, I enter the state of Acre and I go back to the state of Amazonas. At first, I don't have the logistics for the military police to maintain themselves on these missions, due to not having a base there, it's far away. Besides, there is the river issue, only last year that we managed to repair our boat. The same logistics issue, I don't have enough fuel. Each vehicle of mine has a daily fuel quota. It is impossible for me to leave here and go to Curuquetê village, it's practically 1200 km.
> *(Major Tavares, Military Police of Amazonas Officer)*

Environmental crimes are complex ones, and the investigation requires not only police officers but forensics support to produce scientific evidence for the investigation. There are limited resources to produce this kind of proof. It directly impacts the capacity of conducting investigations and attributing responsibility for the crimes. This excerpt from a State Prosecutor sheds light on the situation:

> For example, I need environmental forensics report so that I can request compensation for moral and environmental damages in a class action. Then, the sentence can revert to a fund to promote environmental protection, and often I can't get an expert report. Sometimes, I need environmental forensics report to attribute criminal responsibility to someone, and to prove the materiality of the crime. I can't get a report.
> *(Renan, Amazonas State Public Prosecutor)*

This situation leads to another problem, which is the unbalance between the moment of evidence gathering and use in the courts. As pointed out by a State Judge, when the evidence is analyzed by the judiciary there is a new reality. It makes it difficult to judge environmental crimes. Thus, evidence is central to judicial decisions, and the lack of forensic evidence reduces the capacity to enforce the law.

> When the evidence reaches the judiciary, the reality is different. Then we will need expert evidence to work with something that no longer exists. I believe, from my experience, that the timing of the incident and the state's analysis is the main problem of the state's system as a whole to protect this legal asset, which is the environment.
> *(Flavio, Judge of the Court of Justice of Amazonas)*

Despite the problems observed in the institutional resources, the development of a system to monitor illegal logging and fires allows for monitoring deforestation and fires with precision. The information from the environmental agency is available on a website:

> When I mention the embargoing of an area, I do not refer to a name or an identification tag. I consider an embargo in a polygon that has these geographic coordinates. I took precautions to identify who the offender was. The embargo can halt the possibility of seeking financing. If the bank has access to this information, illegal deforestation, or the absence of a license from the environmental agency, the credit will not be granted. It is written here on the environmental agency's page that you deforested illegally. This service will be available until the end of the month, it's called geoportal,[6] and we will be uploading all this information that is here on the dashboard for public consultation, both by control bodies and civil society in general.
>
> *(Leandro, IPAAM)*

Satellite imagery has allowed us to monitor the fires and illegal logging in the region, but the technology is inefficient in the rainy season, which ranges from November to March each year. Due to the intense rains, the system is not able to monitor properly the region. Thus, illegal lodgers take this opportunity to deforest. The fires come later in the dry season:

> Why have these spikes happened here? It is because we can't monitor it. We don't have good coverage of multispectral images, and it becomes an excellent camouflage for them to act. This is another aspect we are working on, we are looking for resources to contract radar images.
>
> *(Leandro IPAAM)*

The monitoring represents an advancement in fighting illegal logging and fires, but the limitations of institutions reduce the efficacy of operating in the field. Thus, the capacity to respond to the events is quite low:

> The purpose now is to avoid this conversion of forests. If we can get the team in the field to send, for example, this polygon was identified on 01/22/23, and today is 01/26/23, we have four days of delay in this deforestation, depending on the magnitude of this polygon I could still find people in the field, with machinery, with fuel, people with chainsaws and prevent the advancement of this deforestation.
>
> *(Leandro, IPAAM)*

The satellite system is an important instrument for capturing the advances of illegal logging and fires in the region. As the interviewee remarked: "Before (the system), we used in the past to run after rotten wood (Leandro, IPAAM)." The meaning of this statement is that now it is possible to know an illicit fact before its occurrence. However, there is a great limited capability to put the boots on the ground.

Conclusion

This chapter aimed to discuss the initial results of an ongoing research project. This text focuses on the city of Lábrea located in the Southern region of Amazonas. As observed, the rule of law in the region is embedded in a complex context in which the economic logic prevailing in the area confronts the legal commands established by the Brazilian State. This dynamic is reinforced by the prevailing political clientelism, the low level of land legalization in the area, and the cultural practices that naturalize illegal logging, fires, and the transaction of lands based on precarious documents (Sundström, 2016). This reality is constantly reproduced and does not seem to change in the near future.

The criminal justice and environmental agents must act to fight environmental crimes in this social reality. They face many difficulties, especially due to the institutional resources at their disposal, such as the scarcity of personnel and equipment to cover a vast rainforest region and the limited capability to conduct investigations and produce scientific evidence concerning environmental crimes. Despite the use of satellite technology to monitor illegal logging and fires that have been proven useful in determining the location of these crimes, the capability to "put boots on the ground" is weak.

Hence, it is possible to affirm, from these initial results, that in the Southern Region of Amazonas prevails a fragile statehood in which a very limited capacity to enforce the law is observed. Due to the circumstances, criminal justice and environmental agencies have little room to act. It is done in an *ad hoc* manner without any insertion into a larger strategy. The future development of this research will dig deeper into the problems related to the enforcement of environmental laws in the region, but these initial results provide a strong picture of the problems under study.

Notes

1 The authors would like to thank the financial support from the National Council of Scientific and Technological Development (CNPQ—Brazil—Grant 407241/2021–3) and the Gerda Henkel Stiftung (Germany—Grant AZ 13/KF/22) that allowed the data gathering.
2 "The PRODES project carries out satellite monitoring of deforestation through clear-cutting in the Legal Amazon and has produced, since 1988, annual deforestation rates in the region, which are used by the Brazilian government to establish public policies. Annual rates are estimated based on deforestation increments identified in each satellite image covering the Legal Amazon. The first presentation of data is carried out by December of each year, in the form of an estimate, when approximately 50% of the images covering the Legal Amazon are normally processed. Consolidated data is presented in the first half of the following year." Available at http://www.obt.inpe.br/OBT/assuntos/programas/amazonia/prodes 09/16/23.
3 "The Amazon Fund is a REDD+ mechanism created to raise donations for non-reimbursable investments in efforts to prevent, monitor and combat deforestation, as well as to promote the preservation and sustainable use in the Brazilian Amazon." Available at https://www.amazonfund.gov.br/en/home/ 09/16/23.
4 A description of PRODES program with English subtitles can be found at https://www.youtube.com/watch?v=l5YP1FHyqg4. Available at 09/18/23.
5 This research Project has been approved by the Ethical Committee from the Federal University of Juiz de Fora (Protocol Number 59249522.7.0000.5147).
6 Available at https://gis.ipaam.am.gov.br/geoportal/ on 06/12/23.

References

Abadinsky, H., 2010. *Organized Crime* (9th ed.). Belmont: Wadsworth.
Arnaud, A.J., 1998. *Entre Modernité et Mondialisation: Cinq leçons d'histoire de la philosophie du droit et de l'État*. Paris: LGDJ.
Bayley, D., 2005. *Changing the Guard: Developing Democratic Policing Abroad*. Oxford: Oxford University Press.

Börzel, T.A., Risse, T., Drande, A., 2018. Governance in Areas of Limited Statehood: Conceptual Clarifications and Major Contributions of the Handbook. In: Thomas Risse, Tanja A. Börzel, Anke Drande, eds. *The Oxford Handbook of Governance and Limited Governance*, 3–25. Oxford: Oxford University Press.

Campana, P., Varese, F., 2018. Organized Crime in the United Kingdom: Illegal Governance of Markets and Communities. *British Journal of Criminology*, 58, 1381–1400.

Castells, M., 1996. *The Rise of Network Society*. London: Blakewell.

Charron, N., Dahlström, C., Lapuente, V., 2012. No Law Without a State. *Journal of Comparative Economics*, 40(2), 176–193.

Creswell, J.W., 2014. *Research Design: Qualitative, Quantitative and Mixed Methods Approaches* (4th ed.). Thousand Oaks, CA: Sage.

Denzin, N.K., Lincoln, Y., 1998. *Collecting and Interpreting Qualitative Materials*. London: Sage.

Di Maro, V., Evans, D.K., Khemani, S., Arruda, T.G.S., 2021. Building State Capacity: What Is the Impact of Development Projects? *Policy Research Working Paper 9875*. Washington, DC: World Bank Group.

Diniz, E., 2013. Desenvolvimento e Estado desenvolvimentista: tensões e desafios da construção de um novo modelo para o Brasil do século XXI. *Revista De Sociologia E Política*, 21(47), 9–20. https://doi.org/10.1590/S0104-44782013000300002

Faria, J.E., 1997. Direitos humanos e globalização econômica: notas para uma discussão. *Estudos Avançados*, 11(30), 43–53.

Fatovic, C., 2019. *Emergencies and the Rule of Law*. Oxford: Oxford Research Encyclopedia of Politics, 1–20.

Feitosa, N.A., 2022. Não existe "Novo Cangaço". *Revista Brasileira de Inteligência*, 17, 143–161.

Fukuyama, F., 2004. The Imperative of State Building. *Journal of Democracy*, 15(2), 17–31.

Grävingholt, J., Ziaja, S., Kreibaum, M., 2015. Disaggregating State Fragility: A Method to Establish a Multidimensional Empirical Typology. *Third World Quarterly*, 36(7), 1281–1298.

Lottholz, P., Lemay-Hébert, N., 2016. Re-Reading Weber, Re-Conceptualizing State-Building: From Neo-Weberian to Post-Weberian Approaches to State, Legitimacy and State-Building. *Cambridge Review of International Affairs*, 29(4), 1467–1485.

Loureiro, V., Guimarães, E.C., 2007. Reflexões sobre a Pistolagem e a Violência na Amazônia. *Revista Direito GV*, 3(1), 221–246.

Magaloni, B., Franco-Vivanco, E., Melo, V., 2020. Killing in the Slums: Social Order, Criminal Governance, and Police Violence in Rio de Janeiro. *American Political Science Review*, 114(2), 1–21.

Pacheco Farias, R.É., Szlafsztein, C.F., 2023. Sacrificação ambiental da Amazônia brasileira, a partir do método DPSIR. *Novos Cadernos NAEA*, [S.l.], 25(3), 201–228. http://doi.org/10.18542/ncn.v25i3.12667.

Pivetta, M., 2020. *Amazônia, agora, é fonte de COO2*. Revista Pesquisa FAPESP. 2(287), fev. 2021. São Paulo: FAPESP. Available at: https://revistapesquisa.fapesp.br/mazonia-agora-e-fonte-de-co2/

Pivetta, M., 2021a. *A Amazônia perde o gás*. Revista Pesquisa FAPESP. 8(306). São Paulo: FAPESP, August. Available at: https://revistapesquisa.fapesp.br/a-amazonia-perde-o-gas/

Pivetta, M., 2021b. *Leste da Amazônia vira fonte de carbono e passa a emitir mais CO2 do qui absorve*. Revista Pesquisa FAPESP. 2(287), fev. 2021. São Paulo: FAPESP. Available at: https://revistapesquisa.fapesp.br/leste-da-amazonia-vira-fonte-de-carbono-e-passa-a-emitir-mais-co2-do-que-absorver/

Pontes, J., 2020. *Guerreiros da Natureza: a história do combate aos crimes ambientais na Polícia Federal*. Rio de Janeiro: Mapalab.

Prado Capanema, V., Sobral Escada, M.I., Andrade, P.R., Landini, L.G., 2022. Assessing Logging Legislation Parameters and Forest Growth Dissimilarities in the Brazilian Amazon. *Forest Ecology and Management*, 513, 1–8. https://doi.org/10.1016/j.foreco.2022.120170

Ramos de Castro, E.M., Castro, C.P., 2022. Desmatamento na Amazônia, desregulação socioambiental e financeirização do mercado de terras e de commodities. *Novos Cadernos NAEA* [S.l.], 25(1), 11–36. http://doi.org/10.18542/ncn.v25i1.12189.

Riccio, V., Fraga, P., Zogahib, A., Aufiero, M. 2016. Crime and Insecurity in Amazonas: Citizens and Officers' Views. *Sortuz. Oñati Journal of Emergent Socio-legal Studies*, 8(1), 35–50.

Riccio, V., Skogan, W., 2018. Gangs, Drugs and UPPs in Rio. In: Vicente Riccio and Wesley Skogan, eds. *Police and Society in Brazil*, 135–150. New York and London: Routledge.

Sant'Anna, A.A. and Young, C.E.F., 2010. Direitos de Propriedade, Desmatamento e Conflitos Rurais na Amazônia. *Economia Aplicada*, 14(3), 381–393.

Souza Ferreira, J.C., Yukari Veludo Watanabe, C., 2020. Rondônia: Crime Florestal Em Números (2013–2018). *Revista de Administração e Negócios da Amazônia*, 12(1), 321–376. https://doi.org/10.18361/2176-8366/rara.v12n1p321-376

Sundström, A., 2016. Understanding Illegality and Corruption in Forest Governance. *Journal of Environmental Management*, 181, 779–790.

Thürer, D., 1999. The "Failed State" and International Law. *International Review of the Red Cross*, 81(836), 731–761.

Varese, F., 2010. *What Is Organized Crime?* London: Routledge.

Versteeg, M., Ginsburg, T., 2017. Measuring the Rule of Law: A Comparison of Indicators. *Law and Social Inquiry*, 42, 100–137.

Weber, M., 1995. *Essays on Sociology*. London: Routledge.

Ziaja, S., Grävingholt, J., Kreibaum, M., 2019. Constellations of Fragility: An Empirical Typology of States. *Studies in Comparative International Development*, 54, 299–301.

2
THE STATE, INDIGENOUS COMMUNITIES, AND ILLICIT ECONOMIC ACTIVITIES IN THE PERUVIAN AMAZON

Oscar Espinosa[1]

The Peruvian Amazon is probably the only region within the country where almost all forms of illegal economies coexist. These are controlled by mafias and organized crime organizations that operate in the midst of violence and impunity: drug trafficking, human trafficking, smuggling, illegal logging, illegal mining, wildlife trafficking, etc. These illicit activities, in addition, are imposed on the indigenous communities, who have been suffering mistreatment and marginalization for decades. Moreover, during the COVID-19 pandemic quarantine, these activities were not interrupted but in some cases even increased.

The existence of illegal activities and the exercise of violence in this region are not a new phenomenon. For centuries, the Amazonia has been considered a frontier region in which violent relationships have been routinized. From the State's perspective, the control over the territory and of its "natural resources" has been prioritized over the people who have been living there for centuries. For the State, these indigenous peoples needed to be "civilized," or even "eliminated" if they became an obstacle for progress, as Commander Herndon, a US Navy exploring the Amazon in the 19th century, candidly expressed. Herndon, a close friend of Peruvian high-ranking politicians with whom he explicitly claimed to share a same worldview, concluded that: "Civilization must advance, though it treads on the neck of the savage, or even tramples him out of existence" (Herndon, 1854, p. 228).

The State's territorial control of the Amazon region was obtained through a violent process. It established military garrisons to accompany the arrival of settlers, and gave them firearms to legally use them against the "savages." Faced with the violent logic of conquest, the indigenous peoples reacted by defending their lands and families in various ways, sometimes also with violence. John W. Nyström, a Swedish engineer hired by the Peruvian State in the 19th century, after witnessing the assault of the official postal courier made by an armed group of Asháninka men, exclaimed:

What living creature, from the lowest animal to the most civilized man, would endure outrages similar to those that have been committed against these Indians, without seeking revenge and the defense of their homes where they were born and raised?
(Nyström, 1868, pp. 55–56)

DOI: 10.4324/9781003330653-4

The use of violence in this region continued during the 20th and 21st centuries, and although the social actors may have changed through time (rubber barons, plantation owners, drug traffickers, illegal miners, etc.), the indigenous peoples have remained struggling to defend their lives and lands.

In the following pages, I will first discuss the constitution of the Amazon as a frontier region and briefly sketch the history of the relationship between the Peruvian State and the Amazon region. I will then address some of the main illicit activities—the production of coca and drug trafficking, illegal logging and gold mining, and human trafficking—and their impacts on the indigenous communities, as well as the position and initiatives of some indigenous organizations to combat them. Finally, as concluding remarks, I will discuss the capability of the Peruvian State to exercise a regime of law and order in this region.

The Amazonia as Frontier Region

The "frontier" could be defined as a place located at the margins of the state and as a space open to violence. Etymologically, the word "frontier" refers to something that is "in front"; to "an area that is part of the whole that is ahead in the hinterland or in a foreign location. A frontier is outward-oriented (i.e., directed towards outlying areas that are both a source of danger and a desired prize)" (Ioris, 2020).

The frontier is located, located not only in the margins of the State but also in the margins of "civilization," and, therefore, it becomes a contested space characterized by violence. As Ana Maria Alonso (1995, p. 15) has stated:

> [I]n the New World the frontier is conceived as a liminal space, betwixt and between savagery and civilization, a place where the struggle of human beings against the wilderness assumes a particularly harsh form, where society's domestication of nature is always contingent and threatened. As an outpost of the civilized *polis*, the frontier is viewed as lying at the margins of state power.

In the Amazon, as in other "natural" frontiers, the violence has been directed mainly against the harsh environment, which through a mirror-like reflection is also seen as violent. The images of the forest devouring people, wild animals roaming around villages or settlements, snakes suddenly snapping at some innocent traveler, unknown diseases, and, of course, savage Indians hidden behind the bushes and ready to attack have abounded in the representations of Amazonia throughout history. This has been particularly true for the fictional representation of this region, both in literature and in film, as in Rivera's *La Vorágine*, or in Hollywood action-packed films from *Five Came Back* or *The Naked Jungle*, to *Anaconda*, or *The Green Inferno* (Rodríguez, 1997; Rueda, 2003; Nugent, 2007).

The representation of the indigenous peoples as "savage" and "violent" has been particularly important since the arrival of the first Europeans in the Americas, or even before, as can be found in the descriptions made by the main Andean chroniclers, such as Garcilaso de la Vega, who affirms that: they eat human flesh, they are fiercer than tigers, they have no god or law, nor do they know what virtue is (1991, vol. 1, p. 32). This extreme form of "savagery" represented by the figure of the cannibal has been used worldwide to justify the domination of other peoples (Arens, 1979; Barker et al., 1998). This practice continued afterward, and in the early 20th century, the supposed cannibalism of the Amazonian peoples was used by *caucheros* and rubber barons to justify the enslavement of the indigenous communities (Stanfield, 1998; Chirif & Cornejo, 2009).

In frontier situations, the settlers or colonizers project their own violence and fears to the "other," who then becomes objectified and thus subject of manipulation, control, or elimination. The settler thus appears as a force of civilization in the middle of the wilderness, but at the same time, as susceptible of also becoming wild. To overcome this ambiguous characteristic, settlers emphasize their role as "civilizing heroes." In this way, the use of violence is legitimized: they have the right to employ violence against anyone hindering their efforts, especially against the indigenous peoples who constitute an obstacle to their plans, and therefore a menace. Moreover, for settlers and State agents, the latter form part of the world they are trying to transform; they are considered as belonging to the realm of nature, and therefore in need of civilization. The State agents were often complicit with this violence. The settlers benefited from a more lenient attitude from the State authorities and the legal apparatuses. In a certain way, this attitude was considered as the way in which the State supported the "civilizing work" of the settlers.

The Peruvian State and the Amazon region

Since its origins in the early 19th century, the Peruvian State established a relationship with the Amazon region based mainly on the exploitation of its natural resources. The perception of Amazonia as a land of exploitable resources—and in a much lesser degree as a land for agriculture and settlement—was further reinforced during the period of the "rubber boom" (1880–1914). Since then, the history of the region can be interpreted as a continuous series of cycles of exploitation, marked by the demand of different commodities by national or international markets.

In the 19th century, several explorers followed the steps of the 16th- and 17th-century conquistadores, but this time they were not searching for *El Dorado* but were rather looking for different natural products to be commodified. At this time, most of the commodities traded in the Peruvian Amazonia were vegetable products such as sarsaparilla, quinine, copaiba balm, vegetable ivory, and vanilla. These products were usually collected by the indigenous communities and exchanged for metal axes and knives or for *tocuyo* (a coarse cotton fabric). Thus, the interest in these resources soon established unequal terms of exchange between the indigenous peoples and traders, and in many cases, it also implied the use of forced labor and of violence (Espinosa, 2022).

Amazonian lands were also considered open territory for colonization and for expansion of the agricultural frontier. As soon as 1828, only a few years after the declaration of Peruvian independence, the first laws to promote the colonization of the Amazonia were passed, and for decades the State policies promoted the settlement of European immigrants in this region. Between 1845 and 1869 almost a dozen laws were passed with this objective, and in 1872 the State crowned these efforts with the creation of the "Society for European Immigration" (Ballón, 1991; García Jordán, 1995, 2001).

One of the main arguments used by Peruvian authorities for the settlement of *colonos* made reference to a supposed incapability of the indigenous peoples. These ideas were clearly expressed in an official document of 1835, signed by Luciano Cano as Minister of Government and Foreign Relations, where he argued the need to do something about the Amazonian peoples, who "own vast, rich, and productive lands," but "do not know how to profit from them" (Larrabure y Correa, 1905, vol. 1, p. 225). In 1832, two senators from northern Peru, Del Campo Redondo and De la Vega, argued in a similar vein:

> [T]he inhabitants of these provinces . . . will leave behind the abyss of misery in order to live with decency and comfort. The savage tribes that live in their margins will establish civilized settlements; and the cultivator, the merchant, and the artist will find a place where to develop their talent, industry and capital.
> *(Larrabure y Correa, 1905, vol. 8, pp. 114–124)*

Evidently, both of these documents share a common racist discourse that has often been repeated throughout Peruvian history, even until now. In this version of the "white man's burden," the Peruvian State needs to provide for the well-being of the Amazonian peoples due to their incapacity. Therefore, the progress of the region and the improvement of its peoples has to come from outside, through the work of "cultivators, merchants or artists."

After 1940, the Peruvian State promoted more aggressive plans of colonization and territorial control. Of course, this process was linked to the expansion of capitalism and the development of an internal market in Peru (Barclay et al., 1991; Santos Granero & Barclay, 2000). In these years, the Peruvian State also needed to secure its territorial limits, especially those redefined by armed conflicts—and its correspondent peace treatises—with Colombia (1922, 1938) and Ecuador (1941, 1943). The context of World War II also opened the international market for some strategic Amazonian products, mainly rubber, timber, and oil.

In the second half of the 20th century, the relationship between the State and the Amazonian indigenous peoples underwent important changes. The presence of the State was intensified through the creation of schools, and especially through the constitution of a new form of territorial organization—the "native communities"—and the regulation of indigenous politics through the establishment of formal indigenous organizations. Thus, a new civilizational process was established through education, health, and agricultural development programs; which, in the 21st century, have been complemented with the implementation of social programs and new bureaucratic procedures, such as prior consultation processes (Espinosa, 2022).

In these same decades, the indigenous societies have also undergone important changes, especially in their forms of political organization and representation. The form of indigenous resistance was transformed, abandoning violent resistance and replacing it with the means established by the State itself, such as the creation of indigenous organizations, their participation in different instances of dialogue and negotiation with the State, and their struggle to defend their rights to their autonomy and self-determination within their own territories (Espinosa, 2022).

Coca Production and Drug Trafficking

The cultivation of the coca leaf has a long tradition in Peru. Since the time of the ancient pre-Columbian settlers, the coca leaf has had numerous uses, especially in ritual and medicinal contexts. There is archaeological evidence showing coca consumption, especially of coca-chewing, since 2,500 B.C. or even before (Gade, 1979; Stolberg, 2011). However, coca bushes cannot grow anywhere. One of the main production sites, since ancestral times, has been the warm valleys located on the Eastern slope of the Andes, in the Amazon region.

During Colonial times, although coca commerce grew in comparison to previous times, it was nonetheless limited, although highly lucrative, and it implied the exploitation and death of a large number of Andean natives (Hemming, 1973; Stolberg, 2011). Although coca was consumed widely among the indigenous population, its use was promoted so they could work for longer periods of time and in harsher conditions, especially in the mines. Until the 1970s, coca was still being used, along with alcohol, in the haciendas as a retribution for the work of the Andean peasants for the same reasons.

It was only in the 19th century when cocaine, one of the 14 alkaloids found in coca leaves, began to be commercialized, especially for medicinal purposes. As Paul Gootenberg (2003) has established, the history of cocaine as a commodity can be summarized in three phases. According to this periodization, the first phase corresponds to the decades between 1860 and 1910, and it was characterized by an international effort to convert cocaine into a modern and global medical commodity. There are several well-known examples of the expanded belief in cocaine's medical qualities at this time, including the recommendations made by Pope Leon XIII or Sigmund Freud.

The fascination with cocaine began to be questioned at the turn of the century, especially by different interest-groups in the United States, and, thus, a second phase can be placed between 1910 to 1940. In this new period, an intense crusade against cocaine activated both social fears and imaginaries and sought scientific support through formal medical discourses. In the United Stated new laws brought restrictions and prohibitions, although in other parts of the world, including most of the European countries and in Peru, this process appeared later.

According to Gootenberg (2003), the third and final phase began in 1940. In this period, the prohibitions against cocaine turned into worldwide policies. World War II brought an end to many licit commercial enterprises. However, the role played by the United Nations became crucial to these changes. In 1947 the U.N. Council on Narcotic Drugs decided to promote coca eradication and established a special Commission of Enquiry on the Coca Leaf, which presented its final report in 1950. Finally, in 1961, the United Nations' Single Convention on Narcotic Drugs was signed, and coca leaves were forbidden everywhere.

The United Nations decision added to the United States' pressure for the eradication of coca leaves led to the creation of illicit international networks of drug trafficking, and thus, also to the consolidation of organized crime, corruption, and the exercise of violence. Therefore, it was only in the last decades of the 20th century that coca cultivation changed its destination from medical purposes and traditional use, and became a prime commodity in the illegal drug trafficking circuits.

From a local perspective, the changes brought by the illegal drug trade of coca leaves and its byproducts (basic paste and cocaine) can be fully appreciated by following the history of coca production in Huallaga valley, located in the Peruvian Amazon region. The development of coca cultivation in this region began in the late 19th and early 20th centuries when there still was a legal demand, especially from the medical industry. In 1938, an extension of the Peruvian central highway was carried out, and the town of Tingo María grew due to the arrival of new settlers from other parts of the country, especially from the Andean regions of Junín, Cerro de Pasco, Huánuco, and La Libertad. These *colonos* discovered the environmental advantages and suitability of these lands for the cultivation of high-quality coca leaves, expanding their production. By the 1940s, as mentioned before, the legal international demand started to drop but not the internal demand for the traditional use of coca-chewing.

By the early 1970s, the illicit markets also began to demand coca leaves, and its production extended to other parts of the Huallaga valley, downriver from Tingo Maria, in what became known as the Upper Huallaga region. By 1975 the number of cultivated hectares went from one thousand to three thousand and reached six thousand by 1980. The ease with which the plant grew, yielding three harvests a year, and the quality of the leaf—the highest alkaloid index worldwide—drew the attention of local and Colombian drug traffickers, who used to import cocaine paste from Bolivia and from the traditional cultivation zones in La Convención and Lares valleys in the Peruvian region of Cusco (Espinosa & Tubino, 1992).

During the past 50 years, drug trafficking linked to the production of coca leaf, and its derivatives has been one of the worst scourges faced by the Amazon region throughout history. In these decades, the illegal production of coca, instead of being reduced, expanded to other areas within the Amazon region. Since colonial times, there were two zones particularly important for coca cultivation: the previously mentioned valleys of La Convención and Lares in Cusco, and the areas adjacent to Huánuco. However, during the second half of the 20th century, the international demand for cocaine led to its expansion to new areas, especially to the Upper Huallaga region, and to the valleys of the Apurimac, Ene, and Mantaro Rivers, more known by its acrostic "VRAEM," which comprises the Amazonian jungles shared by the Ayacucho, Junín, and Cusco regions.

During the Peruvian internal armed conflict, both Shining Path (*Sendero Luminoso*) and the Tupac Amaru Revolutionary Movement–MRTA, although in a lesser degree, established alliances with drug mafias in the Peruvian Amazon, thus financing their purchase of military weapons and exchanging it for armed protection (CVR, 2003). These alliances allowed the survival of a small Shining Path remnant in the VRAEM region, which continues to be active until now, periodically demonstrating their presence through armed attacks, such as the one that took place during the electoral campaign of 2021 in which 18 persons were murdered.

In these decades, the Amazonian peoples have tried to prevent drug trafficking from entering their communities, but this task is becoming increasingly difficult. There have been interesting experiences, such as the initiative of the Aguaruna and Huambisa Council (*Consejo Aguaruna Huambisa*), which at the beginning of the 1990s managed to prevent the advance of coca and poppy cultivation in its territory, or the case of the Shipibo-Konibo and Kakataibo communities that prevented the advance of drug trafficking in their territories during the internal armed conflict (Espinosa, 1995; CVR, 2003).

However, despite these attempts, drug trafficking has spread throughout almost all the Peruvian Amazonia. In the south, it has spread from the valleys of Cusco to the jungle areas of Puno, and more recently to the Madre de Dios region, up to the point of affecting the indigenous communities near the Manu National Park. In the central Amazonian region, it has spread from the Upper Huallaga to the province of Aguaytía, in Ucayali, affecting Kakataibo communities and resulting in the assassination of several of their leaders, including Herasmo García and Yenes Ríos in 2021. From the VRAEM region, it has spread throughout the Ucayali and its tributaries, especially impacting the communities located in the valleys of the Pachitea, Palcazu, and Pichis rivers, where in the last three years several Yánesha and Ashaninka leaders have been assassinated, including

Arbildo Melendez, Lucio Pascual, Cornelio Sharisho, Jesús Antaihua, Nusat Parisada, and Gemerson Pizango.

In the northern region of Loreto, the expansion has been considerable, multiplying its presence in different provinces, especially in those near the borders with Colombia and Brazil, affecting different indigenous peoples, especially the Tikuna. The impact of drug trafficking in these communities has been extremely serious, including human trafficking, mainly of young women, but also of young men, who are sexually exploited in the main regional cities and abroad. But it also has meant a general increase in violent acts, including domestic and gender violence, as well as an increase in suicide cases among Tikuna women and youth (Núñez et al., 2019).

This augmentation of violence is increasingly worrying the native communities that do not have the resources to defend themselves. Moreover, they fear that there is no decisive action from the State to protect them. In general, the Peruvian State's priority in recent decades has been the eradication of coca bushes and the implementation of crop substitution programs. These have been relatively successful in some regions, as in the case of the San Martín, where, thanks to a series of conjunctural, political, climatic, and geographical conditions, it has managed to substitute coca production with coffee and cocoa plantations (Manrique, 2017, 2018). However, the so-called miracle of San Martin has not been able to reproduce itself in other regions, nor has it been able to completely eliminate coca production, which continues as complementary income to coffee and cocoa commercialization.

The efforts deployed by the Peruvian State for the eradication and substitution of crops, however, have not had, in general, the desired impact. In the year 2021, Peru continued to be the second-largest producer of coca leaf in the world. The director of the National Commission for Development and Life without Drugs (DEVIDA), Ricardo Soberón, has publicly expressed that, although the Peruvian State has been fulfilling its "commitments for more than 50 years," it cannot control coca trafficking if the "international society, mainly Europe and North America, are unable to reduce the demand for cocaine from 20 million users" (La República, May 25, 2022).

As several former presidents of Latin America—along with other public figures in international public figures—have indicated, the solution to the scourge of drug trafficking does not lie in the repression of peasant producers or in crop substitution. This is one of the conclusions forwarded by the 2013 Report of the Latin American Commission on Drugs and Democracy (*Comisión Latinoamericana sobre Drogas y Democracia*), which was widely disseminated through the international media. The main problem of drug trafficking is the existence of organized crime and powerful mafias that use bribery and violence to impose themselves on the States, and only with the legalization of cocaine—and other illegal drugs—and with complex supervision measures could they be controlled or eliminated (Global Commission on Drug Policy, 2014).

However, the international political community has failed to make progress in this direction. On the contrary, they forward arguments made by specialists—mainly from the fields of medicine, psychiatry, psychology, and education—who approach the problem of drug legalization only from the perspective of health, consumption, and drug addiction. Meanwhile, the postponement of coca legalization continues to breed corruption, violence, destruction, and death.

Finally, coca trafficking indirectly affects the lives of indigenous communities through its negative impact on the environment. The cultivation of the coca bush, in itself, promotes deforestation and deteriorates the soil due to an unbalanced intake of nutrients (Bradley & Millington, 2008; Dávalos et al., 2011; Bedoya, 2016). But, in addition, the transformation of coca leaves into basic paste and cocaine implies the use of different chemicals: kerosene, acetone, etc., which are later thrown into the soil or rivers and streams, generating significant pollution, and which are rarely evaluated or considered in relation to coca trafficking. Nonetheless, the current worst impact on the life of indigenous communities is the violence it exerts and promotes, including the assassination of their leaders, as has been mentioned before.

Illegal Logging

Since the early 20th century, timber was exploited as commodity in the Peruvian Amazon region, especially fine woods such as mahogany and cedar. In 1918, the first foreign firm began exporting timber to the US market. In these first decades, entire logs were exported, but since 1930 there was a ban to export wood in the rough. Thus, by the 1960s, an important timber industry was booming in the major cities of the Peruvian Amazon, mainly Iquitos and Pucallpa (San Román, 1994). A few decades later, the extraction of fine woods led to practically its total depredation, and the State issued different laws limiting and controlling the extraction of timber from the Amazonian forests, especially from natural protected areas and indigenous territories.

As in the case of the illicit coca economy, illegal logging—and also illegal gold mining—do not only contribute to the destruction and degradation of the environment, but they also generate violence and corruption, as they involve powerful criminal groups associated with international mafias or cartels (AIDESEP, 2007; Bernales, 2008; Neuman & Zárate, 2013). An important study published by the United Nations Environment Program (UNEP), in coordination with Interpol (International Criminal Police Organization), warned precisely about this extremely dangerous link between illegal logging and corruption in the countries that have tropical forests, including Peru (Nellemann, 2012). A Shipibo leader, and former councilor from the Municipal Government of Coronel Portillo, shared with me his frustration—and the frustration of other indigenous leaders—since they could not enforce control measures to hinder illegal logging in their region because the main authorities, such as the Governor or the Provincial Mayor, were directly involved with companies extracting timber illegally, information that has been confirmed by journalistic reports (Jiménez, 2014).

Illegal logging also generates unjust labor conditions. Various reports from the International Labor Organization (ILO) have denounced, since the beginning of this century, the system of *"habilitación"* or compulsory indebtedness, used by illegal loggers. This practice directly affects the freedom of both indigenous and non-indigenous people in different parts of the Amazon region (Bedoya & Bedoya, 2005). The mafias dedicated to illegal logging, usually employ sophisticated weapons, and there are numerous testimonies of timber workers who were assassinated while trying to flee forced labor. The murder of indigenous peoples in isolation is common. So, the illegal loggers can extract wood from their traditional territories (Survival, 2008).

Illegal Gold Mining

Gold mining in the Amazon began also relatively early in the 20th century. Around 1930, numerous immigrants from the Andean highlands arrived to the Inambari valley, in the Madre de Dios region, with the city of Quincemil as the economic and logistic center for this activity. By the 1950s, there was a sharp decline in gold production due to the depletion of this resource in the area and the economic life in Quincemil languished. However, gold mining did not stop but rather moved to other parts of the region, bringing new waves of immigration. From an estimated 300 miners in 1975, the number increased to 8,000 in 1978, and to approximately 20,000 in 1980 (García Morcillo, 1982).

In the 21st century, the sustained increase in the international price of metals generated an increase in mining extraction in Peru, not only on a large scale, but it also boosted small-scale informal and illegal gold mining. Much of this latter activity takes place in alluvial plain deposits in the Amazon region, mainly in the Madre de Dios region, as mentioned before, but it has also spread to other regions such as Loreto and Amazonas. In these northern regions of Peru, it has brought problems to the Awajún and Wampis communities located in the provinces of Condorcanqui and Datem del Marañón. Faced with this situation, the Territorial Government of the Wampis Nation managed to expel an important group of illegal miners from its territory in 2017.

In the context of the mining boom, the Peruvian State passed a new law in 2002 to establish some regulations for small-scale and artisanal mining. However, it did not have the desired results, and thus illegal gold mining continued to multiply in the last decades, as can be appreciated by the exponential growth of deforested areas. According to official figures presented by the Ministry of the Environment, there has been an increase from approximately six thousand hectares deforested by mining in 2000 to almost thirty-three thousand hectares by 2011 and to more than fifty thousand by 2016 (De Echave, 2016).

One of the most pernicious effects of gold mining is the contamination of rivers with mercury, which is used to separate gold from other minerals. It is estimated that illegal mining discharges an average of 24 kilos of mercury per square kilometer. Only in the Brazilian Amazon, some 2,300 tons of mercury were dumped in streams and rivers until 1994; afterward, it has been increasing at the rate of approximately 150 tons per year (OTCA, 2018). The mercury thrown into the water is consumed by fish and also by humans, having devastating effects on their health. Children are especially affected, having long-term effects on their cognitive development and metabolism (Grandjean et al., 1999; Brack, 2011; Osores et al., 2012; Panduro et al., 2020). Contamination with mercury not only has a negative impact in communities near the mining places, but it also affects larger territories due to the fluid movement of water and fish through the complex network of Amazonian rivers. Faced with this serious health problem, the Peruvian State has not generated clear policies or procedures. The health personnel who work in Amazon towns and villages do not have the required knowledge or predetermined protocols to diagnose the presence of mercury, unlike other types of diseases, such as malaria or COVID today.

As in the case of illegal logging, the impact of illegal gold mining is not reduced to environmental destruction, as can be seen in some of the most devastated areas of Madre de Dios, such as Huepetuhe or La Pampa, but it also generates violence and other criminality activities. In Madre de Dios, for example, the Harakbut communities suffer the impact of gold mining not only due to the destruction of their forests and the contamination of their rivers but also through the impacts on their social and kinship relations. Finally, organized crime around gold mining not only controls its commercialization but also promotes sexual exploitation and traffic of women.

Human Trafficking and Sexual Exploitation

Since colonial times, and despite having been always prohibited, Amazonian peoples have suffered from human trafficking, slavery, and sexual exploitation (Espinosa, 2022). In recent decades, human trafficking has been acquiring increasingly dramatic dimensions, mainly due to its association with other criminal activities, such as drug trafficking, illegal logging, and especially, illegal gold mining (Novak & Namihas, 2009).

Despite the efforts made by the Peruvian State and by various initiatives from the Catholic church and other civil society institutions, the number of adult and teenage women victims of trafficking and sexual exploitation has continued to grow. For the period between 2016 and 2020, there is an estimate of more than five thousand victims in Peru. According to a report made by the Peruvian Prosecutor's Office (*Ministerio Público*) and published in October 2021, for the first ten months of that year, there were already twelve hundred victims officially registered; most of them women, and almost half of these, minors. These numbers are relatively conservative, due to the fact that a large number of victims are not reported and are not officially registered.

In the case of the Peruvian Amazon, the two regions most affected by human trafficking are Madre de Dios and Loreto (Garmendia, 2012). In the case of Madre de Dios, the majority of victims are brought from other regions, while in the case of Loreto, the victims come from indigenous communities and rural villages and towns within the region, including the city of Iquitos. In Loreto, the indigenous communities most affected are the same ones that are suffering from the impacts of drug trafficking and illegal logging, such as the Tikuna communities.

In most cases, indigenous girls, adolescents, and young women are offered jobs in houses, stores, or restaurants, but in reality, they are sexually exploited and forced to work in prostitution. There are also cases where children and adolescent boys are also sexually exploited. Some of these practices were described by a young Asháninka woman who was forced to work as a prostitute in bars and canteens in the city of Satipo to Fiorella Belli. According to this anthropologist:

> [She told me] how on days when there were few customers and they were unable to sell enough cases of beer (around five or seven cases), they were not given food. Likewise, if they resisted having sexual relations with a client, they were quickly subdued with the help of the employers, who did not seem to skimp on physical abuse as long as they complied. If any of them try to escape or start to disobey, she is confined and locked up without giving her food for a few days.
>
> *(Belli, 2014, p. 132)*

Both in 2013 and in 2020, the Peruvian Ombuds Office (Defensoría del Pueblo, 2013, 2020) published important reports demanding immediate attention and a more decisive response by the State in order to address this urgent issue. Thus, in 2021, the Peruvian State established a new policy for fighting against human trafficking (Ministerio del Interior, 2021). This new plan has three main objectives: strengthening prevention, penal prosecution, and victim reintegration. However, it is soon to determine its impact.

The Perspective of the Indigenous Organizations

Regarding the State's lack of real power in controlling these illicit activities, some indigenous organizations have taken some initiatives. One of these has been the aforementioned successful expulsion of illegal loggers and gold miners in the Santiago River by the Wampis Nation's Territorial Government in 2017. However, in more recent years there have been public death threats against Wampis leaders if they continue maintaining this interdiction (Vera, 2021; Chumpitaz, 2022).

Another initiative has come from the Asháninka organizations from the Peruvian *Selva Central*. A few years ago, they activated the "Arawak Army." This so-called "army" is constituted of the *ovayeriite* from different communities. *Ovayeri* (or *ovayeriite* in the plural) is the traditional name given to Asháninka warriors, but in the last decades is the name given to the members of communal organizations (*rondas* or self-defense committees) responsible for patrolling and protecting their territory. Usually, the *ovayeriite* are armed with shotguns or bows and arrows that have traditionally been used for hunting. The first time in which the Asháninka army was activated was in 1989, in the province of Oxapampa, to defend their lands from the Shining Path and MRTA guerrillas.

In the past decade, however, they have changed their name to the "Arawak Army," to include also the Yánesha, Nomatsiguenga, Yine, and Kakinte communities with whom they share the same linguistic family. Thus, in November 2012 and in July 2013, they made public pronouncements addressed to the Peruvian government, in which they described the vulnerable situation in which the indigenous communities of the region found themselves "in the face of the great threats we face such as the invasion of our territories, drug trafficking, terrorism and illegal logging." They also established that this situation was due to "the inability and irresponsibility of the [government] officials." Finally, they also expressed their "indignation" in face of the "inability of the government system" to solve these problems, "in many cases accompanied by corruption" (ARPI-SC, 2012; Espinosa, 2013).

Regarding the presence of drug trafficking and their links to terrorist groups in their territories, the Asháninka and the other Arawak communities have not only expressed their concern with the lack of an effective response from the government and civilian authorities, but they have also shown its mistrust in the Armed Forces and the National Police. In their second public statement, in July 2013, they declared that they were "ready to fight, in legitimate defense of their territories and will initiate actions for the recovery and control of their territories invaded by settlers, land traffickers, loggers and informal miners" (SIA-SEC, 2013).

In recent years, however, the problems encountered by the Asháninka communities in relationship with illicit activities have worsened. In September of 2021, after the assassination of several of their leaders, the Asháninka organization representing the communities located in the Pichis, Palcazu, and Pachitea valleys (ANAP) once again published a new official declaration regarding these issues. In this declaration, the ANAP leaders announced that the *ovayeri* were going to be summoned again so they could be "in charge of fighting these criminals and corruption." According to ANAP, these are desperate measures, because "the drug traffickers and the land traffickers shot at us first and murdered our people, if we continue to wait for the justice operators and the government officials, we will continue dying and disappearing" (ANAP, 2021).

A similar view is shared by the majority of indigenous communities in the Peruvian Amazon, who increasingly feel that the State is not capable of controlling the violence generated by these illicit activities, and they are especially worried about the increasing number of death threats and the assassination of their leaders.

Concluding Remarks: Can the Peruvian State Control the Illicit Economic Activities and Its Violence?

In the last decades, the different illicit activities in the Amazon region have been growing steadily, having a crucial impact on the lives of the indigenous communities, as well as on the rest of society and the environment. This is the case of coca drug trafficking, illegal logging, illegal gold mining, and human trafficking, as has been discussed in the previous pages. However, the Peruvian State's reaction to these scourges could be qualified as merely a mild response.

The primary form of State action has been to establish laws and a legal framework to dissuade, prevent, and eventually control these activities, such as the 2002 law regulating small-scale gold mining activities, the 2011 Forest and Wildlife law, or the 2021 policy against human trafficking. However, in legal terms there are also setbacks. In 2022, for example, a group of representatives in Congress have been trying to pass a new Forest and Wildlife law in order to facilitate timber extraction in the Amazon region, and different attempts to promote anti-corruption laws and policies have not succeeded either.

In general, the State faces important challenges to enforce these laws or to implement these policies. In some cases, these challenges come from the lack of adequate personnel—in terms of both numbers and qualifications. For example, in the Madre de Dios region, the State office that supervises the commercialization of gasoline and other fuels used by these illicit activities has only two persons working there: a field agent and a desk assistant. In other cases, both the police and the offices controlling illegal logging or drug trafficking do not have enough fuel to move their boats or cars and to travel to the places where these activities have been denounced by the local population. As the police chief of the Madre Dios region told me a few years ago, the lack of human and economic resources makes any type of intervention impossible. Therefore, in general, it would be correct to subscribe to the conclusion made by De Echave (2016), that the Peruvian State has a limited capacity for control and inspection of its own territories. In this sense, the Amazon region continues to be a "frontier region" where violence predominates and where the State has only nominal control.

In the case of coca production and commercialization, for decades, the Peruvian State has combined legal commercialization through the *Empresa Nacional de la Coca* (ENACO) with interdiction, bush destruction, and alternative crop policies promoted by the United States and other international agencies. The latter, however, have not been really successful. There was a small positive achievement in the San Martin region, which led to consider it a "miracle"; however, the reasons for this success were unique and conjunctural and could not be easily reproduced elsewhere. Moreover, coca production did not disappear entirely from this region, although it was considerably reduced.

However, probably the most important obstacle to state action against these activities is the corruption bred by illicit economies and organized crime. This corruption affects different State institutions, not only at the local and regional levels, but it also includes the police, the military, the judicial system, and high-ranking officials and legislators, eroding any possibility for a successful action against them.

Note

1 Professor of Anthropology, Department of Social Sciences, Pontificia Universidad Católica del Perú-PUCP. Email: oespinosa@pucp.edu.pe

References

AIDESEP–Asociación Interétnica de Desarrollo de la Selva Peruana (2007). *La tala ilegal de la caoba en la Amazonía peruana y su comercialización al mercado exterior*. Lima: AIDESEP.
Alonso, A.M. (1995). *Thread of Blood: Colonialism, Revolution and Gender on Mexico's Northern Frontier*. Tucson: University of Arizona Press.
ANAP–Apatyawakaitzi Ashaninka Pichis (2021). *Pronunciamiento público: Si no somos nosotros, ¿quiénes lucharán por nosotros?*, September 29th, 2021. Available in: https://www.facebook.com/100909288391997/photos/a.109246477558278/356888659460724/
Arens, W. (1979). *The Man-Eating Myth: Anthropology & Anthropophagy*. New York: Oxford University Press.
ARPI-SC—Asociación Regional de Pueblos Indígenas de la Selva Central (2012). *Carta abierta al presidente constitucional de la República del Perú Ollanta Humala Taso*. Satipo: ARPI-SC. Available in the Internet: https://www.servindi.org/actualidad/77482
Ballón, F. (1991). *La Amazonía en la Norma Oficial Peruana: 1821–1990*. Lima: Centro de Investigación y Promoción Amazónica. 4 vols.
Barclay, F., et al. (1991). *Amazonía 1940–1990. El extravío de una ilusión*. Lima: Terra Nuova/CISEPA-PUCP.
Barker, F., Hulme, P. & Iversen, M. (eds.) (1998). *Cannibalism and the Colonial World*. New York: Cambridge University Press.
Bedoya, E. (2016). La deforestación y la tragedia de los comunes entre los cocaleros del VRAE: 2001–2004. *Espacio y Desarrollo*, 28, 75–101.
Bedoya, E. & Bedoya, A. (2005). *El Trabajo Forzoso en la extracción de la madera en la Amazonía peruana*. Working Paper. Ginebra: OIT.
Belli, F. (2014). *Asháninkas trabajando en la ciudad: dinámicas, estrategias y dilemas de la migración laboral indígena en Satipo*. Tesis de Licenciatura en Antropología. Lima: PUCP.
Bernales, M. (2008). *Informe sobre la tala ilegal en el Perú*. Lima: PNUD y CONAM.
Brack, A., et al. (2011). *Minería aurífera en Madre de Dios y contaminación con mercurio: Una bomba de tiempo*. Lima: Ministerio del Ambiente.
Bradley, A. & Millington, A. (2008). Coca and colonists: Quantifying and explaining forest clearance under coca and anti-narcotics policy regimes. *Ecology and Society*, 13(1), 31.
Chirif, A. & Cornejo, M. (eds.) (2009). *Imaginario e imágenes de la época del caucho: Los sucesos del Putumayo*. Lima: Centro Amazónico de Antropología y Aplicación Práctica–CAAAP, International Workgroup for Indigenous Affairs–IWGIA, Universidad Científica del Perú.
Chumpitaz, O. (2022). Amazonas: taladores y mineros ilegales tienen en la mira a líderes wampis. *Diario La República*, June 20th, 2022.
Comisión Latinoamericana sobre Drogas y Democracia (2013). *Drogas y Democracia: hacia un cambio de paradigma*. https://www.globalcommissionondrugs.org/wp-content/uploads/2016/06/drugs-and-democracy_book_ES.pdf. Available 12th October 2024.
CVR–Comisión de la Verdad y Reconciliación (2003). *Informe Final*. Lima. 9 vols. https://www.cverdad.org.pe/ifinal/. Available 12th October 2024.
Dávalos, L., Bejarano, A.C. & Hall, M.A. (2011). Forests and drugs: Coca-driven deforestation in tropical biodiversity hotspots. *Environmental Science & Technology*, 45(4), 1219–1227.
De Echave, J. (2016). La minería ilegal en Perú: Entre la informalidad y el delito. *Nueva Sociedad*, 263, 131–144.
Defensoría del Pueblo (2013). *Informe N°158: La trata de personas en agravio de niños, niñas y adolescentes*. Lima: Defensoría del Pueblo.

Defensoría del Pueblo (2020). *Abordaje Judicial de la Trata de Personas. Informe N° 001–2020-DP/ADHPD*. Lima: Defensoría del Pueblo, Capital Humano y Social Alternativo.

Espinosa, O. (1995). *Rondas Campesinas y Nativas en la Amazonía Peruana*. Lima: Centro Amazónico de Antropología y Aplicación Práctica-CAAAP. https://repositorio.pucp.edu.pe/index/bitstream/handle/123456789/179028/Historias%20violencias%20y%20memorias%20en%20la%20amazonia.pdf;jsessionid=E289F20893B75380179F4264F6941422?sequence=1. Available 12th Otober 2024.

Espinosa, O. (2013). *El terror que no termina: la persistente amenaza a la vida y seguridad de las comunidades Asháninka de los ríos Ene y Tambo, Idéele*, 233.

Espinosa, O. (2022). *El nudo amazónico. El Perú y sus pueblos indígenas*. Lima: Ministerio de Cultura–Proyecto Especial Bicentenario de la Independencia del Perú.

Espinosa, O. & Tubino, F. (1992). *Violencia y Narcotráfico en la Amazonía*. Working Paper. Lima: Centro Amazónico de Antropología y Aplicación Práctica-CAAAP.

Gade, D. W. (1979). Inca and colonial settlement, coca cultivation and endemic disease in the tropical forest. *Journal of Historical Geography*, 5(3), 263–279.

García Jordán, P. (ed.) (1995). *La construcción de la Amazonía Andina (Siglos XIX–XX). Procesos de ocupación y transformación de la Amazonía peruana y ecuatoriana entre 1820 y 1960*. Quito: Abya Yala.

García Jordán, P. (2001). *Cruz y arado, fusiles y discursos. La construcción de los Orientes en el Perú y Bolivia, 1820–1940*. Lima: Instituto Francés de Estudios Andinos-IFEA, Instituto de Estudios Peruanos-IEP.

García Morcillo, J. (1982). Del caucho al oro: El proceso colonizador de Madre de Dios. *Revista Española de Antropología Americana*, 12, 255–271.

Garcilaso de la Vega, Inca (1991). *Comentarios Reales de los Incas*. 2 vols. Lima: Fondo de Cultura Económica.

Garmendia, R. (2012). *La trata de personas en Madre de Dios*. Lima: Capital Humano y Social Alternativo.

Global Commission on Drug Policy–GCDP (2014). *Taking Control: Pathways to Drug Policies that Work*. Geneva: GCDP.

Gootenberg, P. (2003). Between coca and cocaine: A century or more of US-Peruvian drug paradoxes, 1860–1980. *Hispanic American Historical Review*, 83(1), 119–150.

Grandjean, Philippe, et al. (1999). Methylmercury neurotoxicity in Amazonian children downstream from gold mining. *Environmental Health Perspectives*, 107(7), 587–591.

Hemming, J. (1973). *The Conquest of the Incas*. New York: Harcourt Brace.

Herndon, W.L. (1854). *Exploration of the Valley of the Amazon*. Washington, DC: Taylor & Maury.

Ioris, A. (2020). *Frontier Making in the Amazon. Economic, Political and Socioecological Conversion*. Cham: Springer.

Jiménez, B. (2014). Vicepresidente de Ucayali blanquea madera de la tala ilegal. *Diario La República*, October 2nd, 2014.

Larrabure y Correa, C. (ed.) (1905). *Colecciones de leyes, decretos, resoluciones y otros documentos oficiales referentes al departamento de Loreto*. Lima: Imprenta de La Opinión Nacional. 18 vols.

Manrique, H. (2017). El largo camino hacia la economía lícita: Estado y estrategias de desarrollo alternativo en el "milagro de San Martín". *Revista de Ciencia Política y Gobierno*, 4(7), 161–189.

Manrique, H. (2018). Auge y caída del tráfico ilícito de drogas en la selva alta peruana: un análisis desde el enfoque de relaciones Estado-sociedad. *Debates en Sociología*, 47, 131–156.

Ministerio del Interior (2021). *Política Nacional frente a la Trata de Personas y sus formas de explotación*. Lima: Ministerio del Interior.

Nellemann, C. (2012). *Carbono limpio, negocio sucio: tala ilegal, blanqueo y fraude fiscal en los bosques tropicales del mundo*. Programa de Naciones Unidas para el Medio Ambiente-PNUMA. INTERPOL. https://cld.bz/bookdata/Pm2rqje/basic-html/page-1.html#. Available 12th October 2024.

Neuman, W. & Zárate, A. (2013). Corruption in Peru Aids Cutting of Rain Forest. *The New York Times*, October 18th, 2013.

Novak, F. & Namihas, S. (2009). *La trata de personas con fines de explotación laboral. El caso de la minería aurífera y tala ilegal de madera en Madre de Dios*. Lima: OIM/IDEI-PUCP.

Nugent, S. (2007). *Scoping the Amazon: Image, Icon, and Ethnography*. Walnut Creek, CA: Left Coast Press.

Núñez, C., et al. (2019). Suicidios en los tiempos de coca: género, violencia y cambios sociales en comunidades Ticuna de la Amazonía peruana. En Hernández, W. (ed.) *Violencias contra las mujeres: la necesidad de un doble plural*. Lima: GRADE, pp. 299–326.

Nyström, J.G. (1868). *Informe al supremo gobierno del Perú sobre una expedición al interior de la República*. Lima: Imp. y Lit. de E. Prugue.

Osores, F., et al. (2012). Minería informal e ilegal y contaminación con mercurio en Madre de Dios: Un problema de salud pública. *Acta médica peruana*, 29(1), 38–42.

OTCA-Organización del Tratado de Cooperación Amazónica (2018). *Análisis de Diagnóstico Transfronterizo Regional de la Cuenca Amazónica*. Brasilia: OTCA-Organización del Tratado de Cooperación Amazónica.

Panduro, G., et al. (2020). Bioacumulación por mercurio en peces y riesgo por ingesta en una comunidad nativa en la amazonia peruana. *Revista de Investigaciones Veterinarias del Perú*, 31(3), e18177.

Rivera, J.E. (1976 [1924]). *La vorágine*. Caracas: Biblioteca Ayacucho. Available on https://www.ellibrototal.com/ltotal/ at 21st october 2024.

Rodríguez, I. (1997). Naturaleza/nación: lo salvaje/civil escribiendo Amazonia. *Revista de Crítica Literaria Latinoamericana*, 23(45), 27–42.

Rueda, M.H. (2003). La selva en las novelas de la selva. *Revista de Crítica Literaria Latinoamericana*, 29(57), 31–43.

San Román, J. (1994). *Perfiles históricos de la Amazonía peruana*. Lima & Iquitos: Centro Amazónico de Antropología y Aplicación Práctica–CAAAP, Centro de Estudios Teológicos de la Amazonía–CETA, Instituto de Investigaciones de la Amazonía Peruana. 2a ed.

Santos Granero, F. & Barclay, F. (2000). *Tamed Frontiers: Economy, Society, and Civil Rights in Upper Amazonia*. Boulder: Westview Press.

SIA-SEC–Seguridad Indígena Amazónica Selva Central (2013). *Pronunciamiento del Ejército Arawak*. Satipo: SIA-SEC–Seguridad Indígena Amazónica Selva Central.

Stanfield, M.E. (1998). *Red Rubber, Bleeding Trees: Violence, Slavery, and Empire in Northwest Amazonia, 1850–1933*. Albuquerque: University of New Mexico Press.

Stolberg, V.B. (2011). The use of coca: Prehistory, history, and ethnography. *Journal of Ethnicity in Substance Abuse*, 10(2), 126–146.

Survival (2008). Madereros asesinan a indígenas aislados. *Survival*. Available in the Internet: https://www.survival.es/noticias/3439

Vera, E. (2021). Frontera caliente: líderes wampís se enfrentan a madereros ecuatorianos para evitar tala indiscriminada de balsa. *Mongabay*, January 28th, 2021. Available in the Internet: https://es.mongabay.com/2021/01/tala-ilegal-balsa-topa-amazonas-peru-ecuador-bosques/

3
DEVASTATING DEVASTATION

Impact of Crime in the Colombian Amazon

Juan Carlos Ruiz-Vásquez[1] and Rubén Sánchez David[2]

Colombia has long neglected its vast Amazon region, spanning an area of 476,000 km², comparable in size to Germany, Belgium, the Netherlands, and Switzerland combined. Despite this expansive jungle, the presence of the state is nearly nonexistent in terms of governance, social investment, and effective protection of its biodiversity and tropical forests. Although this territory represents only 6.4% of the entire Amazon basin, six Colombian departments—Caquetá, Guainía, Guaviare, Putumayo, Amazonas, and Vaupés—constitute a critical part of the Colombian Amazon, encompassing 41.8% of its land.

Traditionally, Colombia, its government, and its inhabitants have primarily focused on the large urban centers in the central, western, and northern regions of the country, where political, economic, and social activities thrive, disregarding the environmental wealth of the southeastern Amazon.

Historically, the Amazon has been a hotbed of criminal activities. José E. Rivera's seminal novel, *La Vorágine*, published in 1924, vividly portrayed how the impenetrable "black forest" suffered from the exploitative extraction of natural resources, human enslavement, and violence intertwined within the jungle, from which few emerged unscathed. For Rivera (2024), the jungle devoured everything. During that time, rubber exploitation brought profits to European governments and the infamous Casa Arana, which enslaved indigenous populations and caused a genocide estimated to have claimed the lives of 100,000 individuals (Potafolio, August 8, 2008).

Today, the Colombian Amazon provides a conducive environment for criminal activities, enabling the actions of criminal gangs and the commission of crimes such as illegal logging, wood trafficking, coca leaf cultivation, land encroachment, illegal mining, arson, and wildlife and flora smuggling. These criminal activities are not solely the work of transnational criminal gangs and guerrillas but are also perpetrated by local inhabitants, settlers, artisanal miners, and legal companies.

This chapter aims to comprehend the reasons behind the increased destruction of the Colombian Amazon over the past decade, primarily driven by criminal activities and guerrilla groups that profit from these highly lucrative extractive activities. The first section provides a comprehensive analysis of the main crimes devastating the Colombian Amazon and their impact on ethnic communities. The second section evaluates the national and international strategies implemented to address these issues, assessing their effectiveness and outcomes

Colombian Amazon: No Man's Land, Violence, and Weak State

The Colombian Amazon confronts significant challenges resulting from the convergence of factors such as the unintended consequences of the peace agreement with the FARC guerrillas, the dominance of non-state actors, limited state presence, geographic obstacles, and corruption. Addressing these complex issues requires comprehensive strategies that involve coordinated efforts between national and regional authorities, as well as international cooperation, to establish effective governance, strengthen law enforcement, and combat corruption. Only through such measures can the Colombian Amazon region restore stability, protect its natural resources, and ensure the well-being of its inhabitants.

In accordance with a report disseminated by the Economic Commission for Latin America and the Caribbean (ECLAC), the Colombian Amazon region comprises an extensive expanse measuring 48 million hectares. Within the bounds of this territory, three discernible modalities of territorial organization dominate. First and foremost, the conserved area encompasses an astounding expanse of 38 million hectares, serving as a habitat for a network of 178 indigenous reservations dispersed over 25 million hectares, alongside the inclusion of 12 natural national parks that span an approximate 8 million hectares. Furthermore, a designated allocation of around 8 million hectares is earmarked as forest reserve zones. Concomitantly, a supplementary 8 million hectares have undergone prior intervention (CEPAL, June 2013).

Five Pivots That Enhance Crime

The Colombian Amazon region has experienced significant challenges in recent years due to the presence of guerrilla groups and criminal gangs. This part sheds light on five key aspects that have facilitated the proliferation of violence and the weakened state authority in the region.

Impact of the Peace Agreement With FARC Guerrillas

In 2016, the Colombian government signed a peace agreement with the FARC guerrillas, marking an important milestone in the resolution of a 50-year violent conflict. However, unintended consequences emerged in the Amazon region. The government failed to develop a comprehensive strategy to assume control over the territories vacated by the demobilized guerrillas. Consequently, dissident factions within the FARC swiftly seized control of these areas, seeking alternative revenue streams through illicit activities such as coca cultivation and illegal mining (Guio Rodríguez y Rojas Suárez, December 2019). Presently, five former FARC fronts, namely 1, 7, 16, 48, and 62, remain active across eight Colombian departments with influence in the Amazon basin.

Non-State Actors as Political and Criminal Entities

Colombia stands apart from other countries in the Amazon basin due to the presence of guerrilla groups and criminal gangs that effectively replace the state's role and govern with impunity. These heavily armed groups not only engage in criminal activities but also assume significant political influence, acting as *de facto* warlords and imposing their own set of laws on local populations. Their illicit activities serve as a source of financing for their ongoing conflicts. Moreover, the ease of movement across porous borders within the region poses challenges for capturing these groups and dismantling their operations (Insight Crime, 2022).

Weak State Presence in the Colombian Amazon

The Colombian Amazon suffers from a dearth of state institutions and a fragile presence of law enforcement agencies. The fractured topography, characterized by three mountain ranges and vast stretches of jungle and intricate vegetation, provides a favorable environment for criminal gangs, right-wing paramilitary groups, and leftist guerrilla organizations. The Colombian authorities face significant difficulties in deploying adequate personnel and resources to cover such an extensive and geographically challenging territory. The porous borders shared with Brazil, Peru, and Ecuador further exacerbate the situation, enabling a wide range of illegal activities, including arms trafficking, drug smuggling, human trafficking, illegal logging, and the illicit trade of flora, fauna, and gold.

Corruption as a Hindrance to Combatting Crime

Corruption and collusion within the public force pose significant challenges to effective law enforcement and state oversight in the Colombian Amazon region. Addressing these issues requires comprehensive efforts, including thorough investigations into corruption levels within the defense apparatus, improved accountability mechanisms, and enhanced oversight strategies in remote jungle environments. By combating corruption and strengthening state control, the Colombian government can bolster the rule of law, enhance security, and restore public trust in the Amazon region.

A critical impediment to effectively combatting crime in the Colombian Amazon is the issue of corruption among public officials. It has been observed that civil servants receive bribes from both criminal gangs and legal enterprises in exchange for turning a blind eye to environmental crimes. Regional Autonomous Corporations (CARs), the primary environmental authorities in various Colombian regions, including the Amazon Corpoamazonía, have been identified as patronage organizations beholden to local politicians. Reports indicate that corrupt CAR officials enable illegal trafficking and issue permits for logging and the transportation of timber without adequate verification of compliance with quantity and location restrictions (Insight Crime, September 22, 2021).

Corruption poses a significant obstacle to effective law enforcement and state oversight in the Colombian Amazon region. Collusion between criminal elements and members of the public force challenges hierarchical superiors in overseeing soldiers and police officers deployed in remote areas characterized by dense jungle, which hampers contact and accountability.

Assessing corruption levels in the Colombian defense apparatus is a complex task. Transparency International acknowledges a moderate risk of corruption within the entire Colombian defense apparatus, but their surveys do not explicitly consider the bribery of police officers and soldiers (Transparency International, 2020). This highlights the need for more comprehensive investigations into corruption within the public force.

Instances of collusion between criminals and members of the police force and military have been observed in the Colombian Amazon region. A notable example occurred in the Chocó jungle, located in the northern region and distinct from the Amazon. In this case, the police commander of the department was apprehended and accused of receiving a monthly salary of $1,500 from criminal gangs involved in illegal mining activities. This incident illustrates the potential for collusion between law enforcement personnel and criminal elements in the profound rainforest (Osorio, February 29, 2023).

The dense jungle terrain of the Amazon presents formidable challenges to hierarchical superiors responsible for overseeing soldiers and police officers stationed in remote areas. Limited access by boat, often requiring several days of navigation, hampers direct contact and supervision. This physical isolation creates opportunities for misconduct and corruption to thrive, as hierarchical superiors struggle to maintain regular oversight (Osorio, February 29, 2023).

Fragmented Social Fabric and Lack of Community Control

The social fabric that empowers local communities to regulate extractive activities and illegal revenue is severely lacking. On the one hand, social leaders have been subjected to intimidation, while on the other hand, local residents benefit from these illicit practices. The sparsely populated region, with its minimal population density, further hampers the ability of residents to convene and organize around common concerns.

Deforestation, illegal land appropriation, pollution-causing mining, and wildlife trafficking are perpetrated not only by criminal gangs but also by legitimate companies that corrupt local civil servants to exploit land and facilitate the trade of timber, gold, and endangered species.

The Amazon has become an unsafe place for environmental activists and defenders of ethnic groups. A shocking international incident occurred in June 2022, when British journalist Dom Phillips and Brazilian indigenous expert Bruno Pereira were tragically murdered during their travel through the Brazilian western Amazon. According to *The Guardian*, they fell victim to a Colombian criminal engaged in deforestation along the Brazil-Colombia-Peru tri-border region of the Amazon (Tom, December 5, 2022). This incident serves as a grim reminder of the assassination of environmental activist Chico Mendes in 1988, perpetrated by Brazilian landowners in response to his campaign against the colonization of the Amazon (Cappa, December 23, 2013).

In the absence of community leaders, social control is virtually nonexistent across much of the Amazon. Moreover, pervasive corruption renders the already scarce state presence ineffectual.

Species Trafficking

The illegal trafficking of species in Colombia, ranking as the third-most profitable illegal activity, has severe ecological consequences. The diverse Colombian fauna is under constant threat, with various species falling victim to this trade. While highly organized networks do exist, local involvement plays a significant role in perpetuating the problem. Enhancing awareness, implementing stricter regulations, and fostering community engagement are critical steps toward addressing this multifaceted issue. By working collectively to combat species trafficking, Colombia can protect its rich biodiversity and contribute to global conservation efforts.

Illegal wildlife trafficking has emerged as one of Colombia's most profitable illegal activities, ranking third after drug and arms trafficking, with an estimated benefit of $23 billion. Colombia boasts a remarkable biodiversity, with approximately 67,000 species, making it one of the most diverse countries in the world in terms of birds, amphibians, butterflies, fish, and more. Unfortunately, around 234 bird species, 76 mammals, 27 reptiles, and 9 amphibians are subjected to illegal trafficking within Colombia, positioning the country as the second-largest hub for species trafficking globally.

The illegal trafficking of animals encompasses a range of motives, including display, extraction of teeth, feathers, and fur, use in traditional medicines, and even consumption as food. However, there is a concerning lack of awareness regarding the scale of the crime and the resulting damage inflicted on natural populations and ecosystems. This unregulated trade disrupts ecological balances and leads to the extinction of various species.

Insight Crime (September 15, 2021) reveals that wildlife trafficking in the Colombian Amazon does not primarily involve highly organized networks but rather opportunistic actions by local farmers seeking quick monetary gains through the hunting and sale of certain easily marketable species. Animals are trafficked either alive or as body parts. In some instances, they are processed into products locally or transported alive with falsified documentation via legal breeding farms. As with the deforestation of the Amazon, responsibility for this crime extends beyond illegal gangs to include legal companies.

Contrary to popular perception, the illegal wildlife trade in Colombia is closely intertwined with local communities rather than being solely orchestrated by sophisticated criminal networks. InsightCrime emphasizes the active role of local residents, who engage in opportunistic trapping and trading. This highlights the complex dynamics at play, where socioeconomic factors drive individuals to participate in the illicit trade of species (Insight Crime, September 15, 2021).

Deforestation

The extensive deforestation of the Amazon, the largest tropical forest on Earth, and its subsequent destruction represent a primary factor contributing to the global decline in biodiversity, climate change, water cycle disruption, and soil degradation. The consequences of these changes are linked to the detrimental effects of tree felling and burning, which not only endanger the survival of the region but also give rise to conflicts resulting from the presence of illegal actors and the displacement of the agricultural frontier.

The magnitude of this problem has elevated it to the status of a national security concern. Colombia possesses approximately 60 million hectares of natural forests, and an alarming 64% of the country's deforestation occurs in its Amazon region. Large-scale fires have become the preferred tool of land settlers to clear the jungle and seize vast tracts of land for agricultural cultivation, livestock rearing, and land speculation. Moreover, deforestation, accomplished through logging and deliberate fires, is carried out by legal companies and traffickers seeking to profit from the timber trade, by small-scale farmers and drug cartels clearing land for coca cultivation, by legal mining companies and illegal miners engaged in extraction activities, particularly for gold, and by guerrilla groups constructing roads to connect their vanguard and rear-guard forces and facilitate various illicit activities.

According to Captain Édgar Obando, the head of rural environmental control at the Carabineros Police, there are six key drivers of deforestation: land grabbing, illicit crop cultivation, infrastructure development and road construction, forest fires, extensive cattle ranching, and illegal mining operations. Conflict has played a pivotal role in these events. Presently, illegal armed groups that have taken over areas vacated by the FARC guerrillas have grown in strength and are engaged in territorial disputes that coincide with areas under threat of deforestation. The United Nations Office on Drugs and Crime (UNODC) latest report reveals that coca crops, which reached 143,000 hectares in 2020, expanded by 43% between 2020 and 2021, reaching an estimated 204,000 hectares nationwide.

The creation of illegal pathways into jungle areas is intricately linked to the colonization of territories orchestrated by individuals seeking to seize extensive land tracts. According to Rodrigo Botero, the director of the Foundation for Conservation and Sustainable Development (FCDS), the construction of roads and the acquisition of inexpensive land are policies that fuel unchecked territorial interventions, often commencing with cattle ranching activities. It is estimated that over 2 million cattle grazes in the region. Botero identifies three key factors contributing to the construction of illegal roads associated with the settlement of the region and the expansion of the Amazonian frontier. He explains,

> The Amazon experiences an unregulated colonization process, where populations migrate to areas lacking river navigation, necessitating overland travel. Additionally, the presence of illegal economies facilitates the movement of people. Finally, large-scale land grabs utilize these roads as access points to new territories.
>
> *(Jaimes Vargas, November 12, 2020)*

Cattle ranching represents one of the simplest and most prevalent methods employed to appropriate deforested areas. Furthermore, it is crucial to recognize the vital role of the Amazon in the illicit activities of illegal groups, particularly due to its abundant water sources, including rivers such as Guaviare, Inírida, Vaupés, Apaporis, and Caquetá. These rivers also serve as natural conduits to neighboring countries such as Venezuela and Brazil.

Studies conducted by Mongabay Latam have illustrated how FARC dissidents, in collaboration with local authorities, distribute government-owned lands as if they were their own, perpetuating the strategy of certain landowners to acquire these lands at low prices from settlers and subsequently legalizing their claims before the courts (Paz Cardona, 2021).

Land hoarding occurs for various reasons, including the economic incentives resulting from the construction of roads like the Marginal de la Selva, which would connect the regions of Macarena in Meta and San José in Guaviare, strategic routes for various forms of trafficking. Another factor driving land hoarding is the government's promotion of agricultural development projects, such as the Zones of Interest for Rural Economic and Social Development (Zidres), introduced during President Iván Duque's administration (2018–2022).

In general, according to the Colombian Institute of Hydrology, Meteorology, and Environmental Studies, the proportion of natural forest area in Colombia relative to the country's total area has gradually decreased since the implementation of the Monitoring Forests Program in 1990. The Andean and Pacific regions also harbor significant forest coverage, accounting for 17.8% and 8.9% of the national total, respectively (Insight Crime, September 1, 2021; IDEAM, 2021).

As shown in Table 3.1, deforestation throughout Colombia and its Amazon region had its highest peak in 2016, with 219,718 and 74,796 hectares of forest destroyed, respectively. Between 2001 and 2021, 3,182,876 hectares have been deforested throughout Colombia, more than half, 1,858,285 of the Colombian Amazon. This means that in the last decade approximately between 4% to 4.6% of the total area of the Colombian Amazon has been destroyed (Ministerio de Ambiente y Desarrollo Sostenible, September 7, 2022).

IDEAM employs two levels of estimation to assess deforestation in Colombia. The first level involves generating early deforestation warnings through the digital processing of images with a resolution of 250 meters, allowing for the identification of active hotspots. The second level utilizes digital processing of medium-resolution images to generate information at a scale of 1:100,000. The official publication of this information occurs through annual indicators. However, the time lag in consolidating data means that consolidated figures for a given year are typically only available by the middle of the following year. Consequently, the current state of deforestation, for instance, will only be fully measurable in about 18 months, around mid-2023. This highlights the crucial role of early warnings, which on the ground manifest as fires and burnings, reducing extensive areas that were once dense jungle to ashes (IDEAM, 2021).

Between 1990 and 2021, Colombia experienced the clearance of forests, resulting in a loss of 6.1 million hectares. Furthermore, the average deforestation between 2016 and 2021 reached 384,000 hectares annually. If this trend continues, it is projected that by 2030, approximately 20% of the country's forests will be affected, leading to severe environmental consequences, and incurring a significant social cost (Fernández & Ariel, November 27, 2022).

According to the United Nations Office on Drugs and Crime (UNODC), the Amazonian departments of Guaviare, Casanare, Vaupés, Amazonas, Caquetá, and Putumayo accounted for approximately 40,000 hectares of coca cultivation in 2016, particularly concentrated in the Putumayo-Caquetá region. The Foundation for Conservation and Sustainable Development (FCSD) reports a 7% increase in deforestation in the same region in 2021, equivalent to 92,399 hectares.

One of the key contributing factors to deforestation in the Amazon and the consequent threat to numerous ecosystems is the presence of road infrastructure. According to the Colombian Institute of Hydrology, Meteorology, and Environmental Studies (IDEAM), a report published in 2018 revealed that 48% of forest loss in the Amazon occurred within a kilometer of a road (Jaimes Vargas, November 12, 2020).

For Corpoamazonía, the damage inflicted by road construction can be irreparable. They state,

> The construction of illegal roads in an environmentally sensitive area such as the Amazon means the gateway for the radical and irreversible transformation of the landscape and land use, that is, it is a seriously impactful activity that has dire consequences not only for local ecosystems, but also has serious planetary implications.
>
> *(Jaimes Vargas, November 12, 2020)*

Nature Reserves and Indigenous Reservations Threatened

The destruction of the Amazon rainforest not only contributes to climate change and biodiversity loss but also leads to the eradication of ancient indigenous cultures and a significant

TABLE 3.1 Deforestation in Colombia and in the Colombian Amazon, 2012–2020

Years	Hrs	Amazon
2012–2013	120,724	41,566
2013–2014	140,249	42,049
2014–2015	123,986	34,272
2015–2016	178,574	39,555
2016–2017	219,718	74,796
2017–2018	197,175	59,118
2019	158,894	
2020	171,685	

Source: (IDEAM, 2021)

portion of humanity's heritage. Deforestation, driven by land-grabbing mafias, armed groups, and landowners, results in the closure of nature reserves and indigenous territories, perpetuating a cycle of conflict and dispossession.

Colombia is home to 59 natural national parks, which encompass 17 million hectares and represent 64.5% of the country's ecosystems. However, the 2021 report by Parques Nacionales Cómo Vamos revealed that deforestation occurred in 32 of these parks, with 45 out of the 59 parks facing varying degrees of ecosystem threat (NP).

Deforestation is particularly concentrated in environmentally valuable areas such as the Amazon, which accounted for 70% of the total in 2018. Furthermore, within National Natural Parks, the impact of deforestation was reported to be 12,000 protected hectares in 2017, representing 5.5% of the national total for that year. This figure doubled in 2018 to reach 12% of the total deforested hectares, before dropping to 7% of the national total in 2019.

The deterioration of natural forests has severe consequences, including soil degradation, the jeopardization of entire ecosystems, disruption in climate regulation, and extensive geographical impacts. It is crucial to emphasize the reliance on the water supply of the Sabana de Bogotá and other areas of the Eastern Cordillera on the rain patterns in the forests of Guaviare and the southern region of Meta.

The presence of criminal gangs in jungle areas poses a significant threat to indigenous communities, particularly in Putumayo and Guaviare, where disputes over control of illicit crop cultivation and illegal mining encroach upon indigenous reservations. The deforestation that affects national parks is primarily driven by the accelerated colonization process promoted by criminal mafias and the reconfiguration of organized armed groups.

The recognition of the rights of indigenous peoples began in the mid-20th century, with the promotion of indigenous reserves as a form of provisional collective land tenure starting in 1966. In 1977, these reserves gained legal protection status. Reservations are territorial divisions that provide indigenous groups with title-based ownership of traditionally inhabited territories. Currently, there are approximately 120 reservations in the Amazon, housing 56 indigenous peoples belonging to linguistic families such as Tucano, Arawak, Huitoto, Guahibo, Makú, Puinave, Quechua, Bora, Sáliba-Piaroa, Chocó, and Caribe. Most of these reservations fall under the jurisdiction of Corpoamazonia.

Despite the existence of organized communities represented by various organizations, the survival of indigenous communities is under threat due to continuous encroachment on their territories by outsiders and the loss of control over their lands. At the regional level, the Organization of Indigenous Peoples of the Amazon (OPIAC) brings together communities in the region, while at the national level, the National Indigenous Organization of Colombia (ONIC) represents these communities.

The trails that were once used by the former FARC guerrilla have now become pathways that bring about significant transformations. The FARC strategically restricted access to the dense jungles of the Amazon. However, following the signing of the 2016 Peace Agreement and the withdrawal of combatants from the territory, control of these areas has fallen into the hands of dissident factions of the former guerrilla group. Unfortunately, these dissidents have not prevented deforestation, road construction, or the expansion of coca cultivation.

Highways are cutting through the Amazonian jungle, sometimes outside the bounds of legal authority, creating a network aimed at connecting specific regions with the rest of the country. For instance, La Marginal de la Selva is a road that has sought to traverse the northern Amazon region for years. In close proximity, an illegal road crosses the Sierra de La Macarena Natural Park, linking the municipalities of Vistahermosa and La Macarena, serving as an important ecological corridor.

The construction of roads not only poses a threat to biodiversity but also endangers the survival of several indigenous communities whose voices are often ignored by the State. One such example is the Yaguará II reservation, which is home to indigenous communities of Pijao, Tucano, and Pirayacuyo. This reservation is intersected by multiple illegal roads, facilitated by individuals with significant economic resources and heavy machinery. The network of roads within the reservation enables agricultural and livestock exploitation, transforms forests into pastures, facilitates the extraction of natural resources, and encourages the influx of outsiders. Unfortunately, amidst an atmosphere of oppressive silence, any attempt to speak out can result in death. The indigenous people of the reservation were previously displaced by armed actors, and while they have reclaimed their lands, which are still in the process of characterization and registration, they have only been granted preventive measures for their properties. The Colombian government, despite ordering a halt to deforestation and the guarantee of citizen security, has failed to effectively enforce its decisions.

Another illustration of the absence of national institutions and the questionable actions of certain local authorities can be seen in the case of Nebio Echeverry, former governor of Guaviare, an Amazonian department. In 2018, Echeverry requested the construction of a road connecting the municipalities of Calamar and Miraflores to the Nukak Nature Reserve, a protected area. Additionally, the Departmental Road Plan, approved during Echeverry's tenure, included various roads within the infrastructure investment program that cut through the forest reserve area.

The Nukak people have endured continuous dispossession and displacement at the hands of peasants and armed groups who operate as adversaries within their 932,463-hectare territory. This area holds significant environmental importance as it serves as a corridor connecting the Serranía National Natural Parks of Chiribiquete and the Serranía de La Macarena.

In 1997, the government officially recognized the Nukak people as the exclusive owners of the reservation through a resolution issued by the now-defunct Colombian Institute for Agrarian Reform (INCORA). However, a portion of the reservation coincides with a peasant reserve area, another form of collective land ownership. This overlap has sparked a conflict over land ownership. Presently, a judge from the Land Restitution Unit is overseeing the case to determine rightful ownership and enable the Nukak people to fully reclaim their reservation. If the peasants can provide legitimate evidence of property rights, the judge may order compensation in their favor, which could range from monetary compensation to the allocation of alternative farms in a different area of the country.

Illegal Minery

Between 100,000 and 200,000 illegal miners are estimated to be operating in the Colombian Amazon. The indiscriminate exploitation of gold, accompanied by the dumping of mercury and heavy metals, has had severe consequences for riverside communities. Large-scale mining operations utilizing heavy machinery, bulldozers, dredgers, and drills cause significant damage to rivers altering their natural course and causing erosion (OTCA, 2018),

This type of criminal activity is challenging to detect, as some miners employ mobile boats that stop, explore, and continue their search upstream. These mining rafts, accommodating up to ten individuals, allow for extended stays of several months, providing the necessary mobility to avoid detection while navigating through a complex network of rivers and tributaries within the dense jungle.

The governments of Brazil, Peru, and Colombia have made efforts to control border points and land crossings. However, the extensive river systems in the region make effective surveillance by the police and armies of these countries difficult. These operations could potentially expose criminal gangs involved in illegal mining. However, the pervasive levels of corruption within the public forces of these countries often allow such operations to continue for months, resulting in significant ecological harm. Occasionally, the public forces may intervene by destroying heavy machinery using explosives. However, arrests are generally few, and by the time police operations are conducted, the illegal miners have typically vacated the site. Furthermore, the transportation and trade of gasoline and mercury from small towns and distant cities in the Colombian Amazon to the miners are largely unregulated, raising concerns about the integrity of national and local authorities.

The mercury used to extract gold is subsequently released into the water, leaving a trail of contamination that can extend for several kilometers. Satellite images have identified mercury discharges in rivers such as Apaporis, Guainía, Caquetá, Putumayo, Puré, Cotué, and Inírida, resulting in severe environmental contamination. Mercury levels in humans have been found to be twice the acceptable limits. The consumption of contaminated fish has led to an unprecedented health crisis, with serious implications for human well-being (Lizarazo, 2022)

In the Colombian Amazon, a total of 119 extraction zones have been identified, out of nearly 2,000 in the entire basin, with a concentration in the Putumayo River and the Caquetá River basin. Mining activities are encroaching upon areas designated as indigenous reserves, even disrupting the lives of voluntarily isolated indigenous peoples within national parks and forest reserves. This situation has led to the expulsion of guards under threats and intimidation. Shockingly, it is estimated that approximately 80% of indigenous people in the region are contaminated with mercury, highlighting the grave environmental and health consequences of such mining practices (Minería Ilegal, 2020; Sierra, January 7, 2019).

In the Amazon region, the problem is not solely generated by illicit crops and illegal mining. According to Brigitte Baptiste, former director of the Humboldt Institute, there exists a well-structured mafia within the Amazon territory, involving not only armed groups but also "corrupt accomplices" within the government. This is exemplified by the National Mining Agency, which has granted over 150 mining titles for the extraction of precious and construction minerals. One of the contributing factors to deforestation is the construction of roads, which facilitate tree logging and the export of wood. Furthermore, large-scale investors acquire land for peasants to colonize further inland, thereby expanding the agricultural frontier (UNODC, 2021).

Mining activities extend into environmentally sensitive regions such as wetlands, which have been recognized as areas of international importance for the conservation and sustainable use of water resources and biodiversity. Forest reserves, national natural parks, and protection zones are also impacted. The use of mercury in alluvial gold mining contaminates water sources and the fish that local populations rely on for sustenance, through both rural aqueducts and daily food consumption. This has resulted in a slow poisoning of local populations, particularly affecting children. Illegal mining has emerged as a new environmental crime with far-reaching consequences across Colombia. In 2020, it is estimated that alluvial exploitation covered approximately 100,000 hectares across ten Colombian departments (UNODC, 2021).

Regulations and Results

Strategies to Combat Crime and Devastation

In recent years, there has been a proliferation of regulations, international agreements, and strategies aimed at combating crime in the Colombian Amazon. The defense of the environment and its connection to national security has become a top priority in government agendas. Military operations to combat crime in the region have become more frequent, and it is expected that they will continue indefinitely as a means to confront illegal armed groups involved in criminal activities. Some high-profile cases, covered extensively by the national media, have shed light on the threats posed to Amazonian species by well-known personalities in Colombia. These incidents may have increased public awareness and made urban dwellers more conscious of the significance of the Amazon and the need for its preservation. The Amazon fires have begun to impact the air quality of major urban areas in Colombia, including its capital, Bogotá, to the extent that local authorities have had to declare environmental emergencies. The devastation of the Amazon is starting to affect the inhabitants of these urban areas, which could lead to a heightened understanding of the irreversible consequences of such destruction.

However, the practical results of these efforts have been limited. Deforestation, river pollution, and species trafficking have increased in the past three years. The number of individuals apprehended for these crimes remains small, and major criminal organizations have not been dismantled. Similarly, those responsible for large-scale forest fires, often intended to expand the agricultural frontier legally or illegally or to acquire vacant land through usurpation, have not been brought to justice.

Policies aimed at coca eradication have also contributed to a reduction in the number of hectares dedicated to coca cultivation. Paradoxically, however, these policies have also contributed to the degradation of the Amazon. The use of glyphosate sprays, while intended to destroy coca crops, has caused harm to human beings, soil, bodies of water, and wildlife. Additionally, it has resulted in the displacement of coca cultivation.

The Environmental Crimes Law of 2009 in Colombia establishes the necessary measures to prevent, control, and penalize environmental crimes in the country, while also promoting the restoration of the affected environment. This law represents one of the primary tools available to the Colombian government to safeguard the environment, protect biodiversity, and prevent contamination and degradation of natural resources.

In 2022, this law was strengthened through the incorporation of new offenses and increased penalties for crimes such as deforestation, wildlife trafficking, financing the invasion of protected areas, appropriation of public lands, illegal hunting and fishing, and environmental pollution. The amendments to the law have reinforced the sanctions associated with these offenses (Ministerio de Ambiente y Desarrollo Sostenible, May 10, 2022).

The Law of Environmental Crimes in Colombia establishes sanctions and punitive measures against individuals, companies, or organizations that cause damage or harm to the environment. It sets penalties, such as imprisonment ranging from 60 to 135 months and fines ranging from 300 to 40,000 times the legal minimum salaries, for offenses such as wildlife trafficking. The Law on Environmental Crimes promotes collaboration among various entities and agencies responsible for environmental protection, justice, and security, which enhances the effectiveness of preventing and punishing environmental crimes (WWF, 2022).

Regarding illegal mining and mercury contamination, Colombia did not ratify the UN Minamata Convention in 2013, which aims to protect human health and the environment from the adverse effects of mercury. This convention has been ratified by 101 countries. Instead, Colombia has chosen to "legalize" artisanal miners to remove them from the criminal sphere, enabling their registration, location, and assistance in mitigating their environmental impact (Sierra, January 7, 2019).

Law 2250 of 2022 was enacted to formalize traditional mining activities that lack a registered title in the National Mining Registry, considering an environmental perspective (Pure Earth, 2022a, 2022b).

The Colombian government, in an effort to avoid criminalizing the relationship between local inhabitants and their environment as a source of resources, has opted to grant permits. However, this approach has inadvertently become a means of "legalizing" trafficking. Even the Colombian state, through its environmental defense corporation Corpoamazonía, has participated in the "legalization" of species trafficking and deforestation by issuing permits. Animals trafficked from Peru, where such permits are not issued, are brought to Colombia so that individuals holding these permits can legally reclaim, transport, and trade them without encountering obstacles.

Colombia, as a signatory to the Convention on International Trade in Endangered Species of Wild Fauna and Flora (CITES), along with 182 other countries, has endeavored to regulate international trade in endangered species. In Colombia, the Ministry of Environment and Sustainable Development, through its CITES Scientific and Administrative Authority, is responsible for implementing CITES. This has enabled Colombia to exercise control over the import and export of species of wild fauna and flora by issuing CITES permits and certificates. These measures may have contributed to reducing illegal trade in threatened species and preserving certain endangered populations (Metropolitano Ambiental, May 23, 2019).

The landmark ruling in Sentence 4360 of April 2018 by the Supreme Court of Justice recognized the Amazon as a legal entity, acknowledging its significance as a crucial ecosystem for the survival of humanity. As a subject of law, the Amazon is entitled to protection, conservation, and restoration. This recognition also entails ensuring its integrity, existence, and restoration in the face of activities that may jeopardize its survival. Consequently, concrete measures must be taken to safeguard the Amazon and the communities that depend on it, and policies promoting conservation and sustainable use of natural resources must be implemented.

The Colombian government has pursued greater interagency integration, with the assistance of the Ministry of Environment and Sustainable Development and the Ministry of Defense, to establish "environmental bubbles." This strategy aims to mitigate the impact of deforestation, illegal wildlife and flora trafficking, mining, and illegal hunting. By imposing exemplary judicial sanctions on environmental criminals, this approach seeks to deter environmental devastation (Guio Rodríguez & Rojas Suárez, December 2019).

In October 2022, the Colombian Congress ratified the Escazú Agreement. However, it is premature to determine the agreement's specific effects on guaranteeing the protection of human rights related to the environment, promoting citizen participation in environmental decision-making, and enhancing transparency in environmental management. Future developments will shed light on the application of the agreement in combating ecocide when local inhabitants are not consistently aligned with environmental protection (Cardona, January 24, 2023).

The issue of species trafficking in the Colombian Amazon gained prominence in 2014 when renowned scientist Manuel Elkin Patarroyo was accused of "illegally trafficking" the Aotus Nancymae monkey for malaria vaccine experiments. Eventually, a Colombian high court ruled in favor of the scientist, requiring a permit for the extraction of the monkeys (Rojas, October 13, 2020). Another significant event that raised public awareness of environmental issues in Colombian urban areas was the capture and subsequent extradition to the United States of a well-known Colombian designer accused of illegally trafficking protected species to produce fashion items.

Military Operation Artemis

In response to ongoing complaints and pressure from environmental groups, the government of Iván Duque (2018–2022) implemented certain measures in 2019 to combat deforestation. One of these initiatives was the launch of Operation Artemisa, a military operation with a budget of $700,000 aimed at recovering the jungle and prosecuting those responsible for forest clearance, particularly in the Amazon region encompassing 20 forest parks and reserves.

The government's strategy, which primarily focused on combating the cultivation of coca plants as the main driver of deforestation, involved key institutional actors such as the Office of the Attorney General of the Nation, the Mobile Carabineros Squad, the Police, the National Army, and the Ministries of Defense and Environment and Sustainable Development.

However, the results of Operation Artemisa have been modest, with the number of recovered forest hectares significantly lower than the number of hectares deforested in various regions. Furthermore, the operation has failed to effectively halt deforestation within protected areas, including indigenous reserves.

This military intervention has had adverse effects on communities, particularly indigenous peoples and peasants, and it has not appeared to target large-scale land grabbers. Reports from residents indicate the persecution of minority leaders and arbitrary arrests. Paradoxically, Operation Artemisa, in addition to falling short of its objectives, has exacerbated violations of the rights of indigenous peoples, who have been excluded from the planning, execution, and monitoring of projects aimed at reducing deforestation in the Amazon.

The government's actions have not only disregarded agreements with indigenous communities but also fostered discourses that stigmatize indigenous leaders and expose them to violent actions. Dispossession and the lack of security in their territories have forced entire communities to migrate to urban areas where they become vulnerable to child sexual exploitation when their social structures are disrupted. According to the Ombudsman's Office, between January and August 2022, 136 social leaders, including 31 indigenous leaders, were assassinated.

While the number of murders of environmental leaders in Colombia has decreased, with 65 reported homicides in 2020, the data remains alarming. According to the latest report by the NGO Global Witness, Colombia ranked second in the number of assassinations of environmental leaders in 2021, with 33 cases, following Mexico, which had the highest count with 54 cases.

This joint operation has highlighted the challenges of adapting the military apparatus and strategy to combat eco-criminals and recover forests. The results have failed to halt or reverse the deforestation trend of the past decade. The campaign managed to recover between 23,000 and 27,000 hectares, representing only 12% to 15% of the national annual deforestation in 2022. Unfortunately, specific figures for the Colombian Amazon are not available, but the military intervention only managed to preserve 8% of the estimated 10% of forests that were at risk of being cleared.

Ultimately, the operation resulted in the arrest of 113 individuals, with only 13 convictions. This outcome is meager considering the high cost of the operation, which involved ten high-mountain battalions, an anti-narcotics brigade, and an anti-illegal mining brigade.

Moreover, it remains unclear how the Colombian government determined the extent to which the intervention saved portions of the jungle. The number of "recovered" hectares and the ratio of arrests to the operation's cost and time invested reveal a relatively inefficient campaign (Tarazona & Parra, December 6, 2022)

Final Remarks

Crime continues to ravage the Colombian Amazon, with the government struggling to find a real and effective solution in the short term. A weak state presence in the territory, corruption among civil servants, excessive economic interests, and the impenetrable nature of the jungle have created the conditions for environmental devastation that are rapidly approaching a tipping point by 2030. The involvement of guerrilla groups, sophisticated criminal gangs, as well as local inhabitants and legal companies in the extraction of environmental resources, has further complicated efforts to halt the destruction. If this trend of devastation persists, Colombia could witness the disappearance of approximately 2.1 million hectares of forest by 2040, a figure that could double if human activity related to environmental crimes intensifies (López Zuleta, March 7, 2023).

Only through determined regional and multilateral cooperation, encompassing both social and law enforcement components, can this trend be halted and reversed. Thus far, predominantly bi-national agreements have prevailed, with some negotiations underway between governments (Ministry of Environment and Sustainable Development, 2023). Collaborative efforts involving multiple countries or multilateral cooperation hold the potential to effectively address this devastation. Isolated police and military campaigns confined to a single country are likely to fail, given the vast territory that needs monitoring and the extent of the devastation.

In the decades to come, as global warming intensifies, it is plausible that the international community will begin to consider high-impact environmental crimes as crimes against humanity, similar to how international pacts during the interwar period made acts of aggression between countries illegal as crimes against peace and humanity. However, at present, it appears that the international community is passively waiting for action to be taken.

Notes

1 Associate Professor, Universidad del Rosario, Bogotá, Colombia.
2 Expert on security and defense.

References

Cappa, Maria. December 23, 2013. "Se cumplen 25 años del asesinato del activista ambientalista Chico Mendes." https://www.lamarea.com/2013/12/23/chico-mendes/#:~:text=Mendes%20fue%20asesinado%20en%201988,las%20empresas%20mineras%20y%20forestales

Cardona, Antonio. January 24, 2023. "Desafíos ambientales en Colombia para el 2023: seguridad a líderes y detener la deforestación." *Mongabay Latam/Redprensaverde*. https://redprensaverde.org/2023/01/24/desafios-ambientales-en-colombia-para-el-2023-seguridad-a-lideres-y-detener-la-deforestacion/.

CEPAL. June 2013. "Amazonía: posible y sostenible." https://www.cepal.org/sites/default/files/news/files/folleto_amazonia_posible_y_sostenible.pdf

Fernández, Eduardo y Cifuentes Ariel. November 27, 2022. "El combate contra la deforestación: un esfuerzo insuficiente." *Razón Pública*. https://razonpublica.com/combate-la-deforestacion-esfuerzo-insuficiente/.

Guio Rodríguez, Andrés y Adriana Rojas Suárez. December 2019. "Amazonia colombiana. Dinámicas territoriales." *Heinrich Böll Stiftung*. https://co.boell.org/sites/default/files/2020-01/IDEAS%20VERDES%20web%20_1.pdf. Available 12th October 2024.

IDEAM. 2021. "Resultados del monitoreo de deforestación: Año 2020 y primer trimestre año 2021." http://www.ideam.gov.co/documents/10182/113437783/Presentacion_Deforestacion2020_SMByC-IDEAM.pdf/8ea7473e-3393-4942-8b75-88967ac12a19

Insight Crime. September 1, 2021. "Las raíces de los delitos ambientales en la Amazonía colombiana." https://es.insightcrime.org/investigaciones/raices-delitos-ambientales-amazonia-colombiana/.

Insight Crime. September 15, 2021. "Un comercio voraz: el tráfico de vida silvestre en la Amazonía colombiana." https://es.insightcrime.org/investigaciones/comercio-voraz-trafico-vida-silvestre-amazonia-colombiana/

Insight Crime. September 22, 2021. "Corrupción en todas las etapas: la confluencia de actores legales y redes criminales." https://es.insightcrime.org/investigaciones/corrupcion-confluencia-actores-legales-redes-criminales-colombia-amazonia/

Insight Crime. 2022. "Ex-FARC Mafia." https://insightcrime.org/colombia-organized-crime-news/ex-farc-mafia/.

Jaimes Vargas, Juliana. November 12, 2020. "Trochas en el Caquetá, una vía libre hacia la deforestación." *El Espectador*. https://www.elespectador.com/ambiente/trochas-en-el-caqueta-una-via-libre-hacia-la-deforestacion-article/

Lizarazo, María Paila. 2022. "Minería ilegal en el Amazonas: otro fenómeno que agudizó la pandemia." *El Espectadpr*. https://www.elespectador.com/ambiente/amazonas/mineria-ilegal-en-el-amazonas-otro-fenomeno-que-agudizo-la-pandemia-noticias-colombia/

López Zuleta, Diana. March 7, 2023. "La Amazonia colombiana perderá bosques del tamaño de El Salvador si nada cambia." *El País*. https://elpais.com/america-colombia/2023-03-07/la-amazonia-perdera-bosques-del-tamano-de-el-salvador-si-nada-cambia.html.

Metropolitano Ambiental. May 23, 2019. "Así se nueven las mafias del tráfico internacional de especies." https://www.metropol.gov.co/Paginas/Noticias/elmetropolitano-ambiental/asi-se-mueven-las-mafias-del-trafico-internacional-de-especies.aspx

Minería Ilegal. 2020. "Datos actualizados 2020." https://mineria.amazoniasocioambiental.org/

Ministerio de Ambiente y Desarrollo Sostenible. May 10, 2022. "Ley de Delitos Ambientales, la norma que protege los ecosistemas de los colombianos." https://www.minambiente.gov.co/bosques-biodiversidad-y-servicios-ecosistemicos/ley-de-delitos-ambientales-la-norma-que-protege-los-ecosistemas-de-los-colombianos/#:%20~:text=may%2010%2C%202022-,Law%20of%20Environmental%20Crimes%2C%20the%20regulation%20that%20protects%20%20ecosystems,may%20of%202022%20%2DMADS%2D.

Ministerio de Ambiente y Desarrollo Sostenible. September 7, 2022. "En Colombia se han deforestado más de tres millones de hectáreas de bosque en las últimas dos décadas." https://www.minambiente.gov.co/uncategorized/en-colombia-se-han-deforestado-mas-de-tres-millones-de-hectareas-de-bosque-en-las-ultimas-dos-decadas/

Osorio, Camila. February 29, 2023. "La policía captura a la policía: detenido el comandante en Chocó por tres delitos." *El País*. https://elpais.com/america-colombia/2023-02-09/la-policia-captura-a-la-policia-detenido-el-comandante-en-choco-por-tres-delitos.html.

OTCA. 2018. "Análisis dagnóstico transfronterizo regional de la Cuenca Amazónica." http://otca.org/wp-content/uploads/2021/02/Analisis-Diagnostico-Transfronterizo-Regional-de-la-Cuenca-Amazonica-ADT.pdf

Paz Cardona, Antonio. 2021. "Las deudas ambientales de Colombia en 2020: defensores asesinados, más deforestación y la polémica sobre el glifosato." *Mongabay*. https://es.mongabay.com/2021/01/balance-deforestacion-asesianto-lideres-colombia-2020/

Potafolio. August 8, 2008. "La Casa Arana tiene en su interior crímenes que perduran." https://www.portafolio.co/tendencias/casa-arana-interior-crimenes-perduran-137812

Pure Earth. 2022a. "Nuevo marco jurídico para la legalización y formalización minera en Colombia." https://www.pureearth.org/nuevo-marco-juridico-para-la-legalizacion-y-formalizacion-minera-en-colombia/

Pure Earth. 2022b. "Promoting the recovery and responsible management of mercury in contaminated tailings from artisanal gold mining in Colombia." https://www.pureearth.org/colombia-proyecto-de-recuperacion-de-mercurio-en-relaves/

Rojas, Tatiana. October 13, 2020. "Primatóloga que denunció a Patarroyo fue premiada por su trabajo." *El Tiempo*. https://www.eltiempo.com/vida/medio-ambiente/medio-ambiente-angela-maldonado-primatologa-que-denuncio-a-patarroyo-premiada-por-su-trabajo-542550

Sierra, Yvette. January 7, 2019. "Minería ilegal: la peor devastación en la historia de la Amazonía." *Mongabay*. https://es.mongabay.com/2019/01/mapa-mineria-ilegal-amazonia/

Tarazona, David y Julián Parra. December 6, 2022. "Artemisa: radiografía de una operación gubernamental que no frenó la deforestación en Colombia." *Mpngabay*. https://es.mongabay.com/2022/12/artemisa-radiografia-de-una-operacion-que-no-freno-la-deforestacion-en-colombia/

Tom, Phillips. December 5, 2022. "Six months after Dom Phillips and Bruno Pereira were murdered, the Amazon remains unsafe for activists." *The Guardian*. https://www.theguardian.com/world/2022/dec/05/six-months-after-dom-phillips-and-bruno-pereira-were-murdered-the-amazon-remains-unsafe-for-activists

Transparency International. 2020. "Government defence integrity index." https://ti-defence.org/gdi/

UNODC. 2021. "Colombia Explotación de oro de aluvión." https://www.unodc.org/documents/colombia/2021/Agosto/Colombia_Explotacion_de_Oro_de_Aluvion_EVOA_Evidencias_a_partir_de_percepcion_remota_2020.pdf

WWF. 2022. "Estos son algunos de los animales más traficados en colombia." https://www.wwf.co/?379192/Estos-son-algunos-de-los-animales-mas-traficados-en-Colombia#:~:text=Entre%20los%20animales%20m%C3%A1s%20traficados,%2C%20serpientes%2C%20monos%2-0y%20felinos.. Available 12th October 2024.

4

THE USE OF INTELLIGENCE FOR MAPPING THE ACTIVITIES OF CRIMINAL ORGANIZATIONS IN THE AMAZON

Rodrigo Costa Yehia Castro, Giuseppe Giura, Fabio Licata, Sandro Sarkis, and Vicente Riccio

Introduction

The security and defense of the Brazilian Amazon is one of the main problems the Brazilian State faced over time. Interest in the region, considered the "lung of the world", transcends Brazil's limits, and the proper confrontation of organized crime installed in that place will increasingly be a topic on the agenda of international geopolitics. Still, it is impossible to talk about the Amazon without mentioning the issue of Brazilian borders (Becker, 2005), since their gigantism often explains their permeability.

Thus, to establish the foundations of the security framework in the Amazon region, it is necessary to start with an analysis of criminal organizations. Their performance is something that directly affects the State's ability to maintain order in different places worldwide. In a place like the Brazilian Amazon, where state power is already little perceived by the population, all of this is enhanced. All this is within a framework in which competencies are established in the Federal Constitution itself to deal with the issue of security and defense in border areas, for example. Only a national plan, which has integration, technology, training, and investment promotion as its axes, which involves the solid use of intelligence, which includes both that of the Stateb – regulated by Law 9883/199-, and that of Public Security Intelligence Subsytem – (SISP), regulated by Decree 3695/2000 (Cepik, Antunes, 2003) and their problematic colaboration and integration (Kraemer 2015) in the fight against organized crime (OC) installed in the Amazon, will be able to change the current situation substantially.

Hence, the objective of this chapter is to demonstrate, from a socio-legal perspective, what the issue of public security is like in the Amazon and the activities of criminal organizations in the area. Furthermore, considering the Brazilian constitutional model, formulating a national plan, in which the use of intelligence is highlighted, can be a viable solution to the issue. This chapter is divided in the following sections: a. The Issue of Security in the Space of the Amazonian Border: Overview of the Territory; b. The Notion of Criminal Organization; c. Violence in the Amazon territory: An Approach to the Performance of Organized Crime in Northern Brazil and the Amazon; d. Defense, Intelligence, and Security in the Brazilian Constitution. Finally, the conclusion summarizes the discussions carried out in the work, its findings, and future questions.

The Issue of Security in the Space of the Amazonian Border: Overview of the Territory

Many states that comprise the Brazilian federation and correspond to a considerable space of the national territory are located in border areas, including the Amazon, the object of this study. Brazil has one of the most extensive dry borders on the planet, with almost 17,000 kilometers. Border zones are always sensitive places that work as hard as possible to implement actions to guarantee local security. This is within a framework in which, national defense interests are ensured by protecting such areas (regional aspect).

The states that make up the Brazilian Legal Amazon border the following countries or possessions: French Guiana (France's overseas possession), Suriname, Republic of Guyana, Venezuela, Colombia, Peru, and Bolivia. That central position makes the Amazon the principal route of cocaine flow to Europe and Africa. Brazil has a double function as an area of transit and market (Couto, 2018). Another feature of the Amazon context directly connected to globalizatoin is the rise and consolidation of criminal networks (Varese, 2020). Although the Amazon is the focus of global debates, especially on environmental issues, given its notable relevance for the balance of life forms on the planet, investment in security and defense in the region is still developing. As will be discussed later, by constitutional imposition, The Union is the federative entity established as primarily responsible for promoting security and defense actions in border locations. This impacts the preponderance of the wealthiest and most capitalized entity in the federation in ensuring that the Amazon is as immune as possible to the actions of organized criminal groups.

An article in the newspaper Valor Econômico from June 2022 brought the following headline, accompanied by a lead: Amazon lost border protection funds—resources from the military surveillance program fell from R$30 million in 2016 to R$12 million in 2021 (Fernandes, 2022). In other words, the institutional framework for security and defense in the Amazon region should be better refined so that adequate means of controlling the activity of criminal organizations and other agents that could destabilize the integrity of the place can be implemented.

The vastness of the territory (Le Torneau, 2019, pp. 16–20) the low population, (Le Torneau, 2019, p. 300) and the fragile infrastructure are deemed the main reasons for a weak capability to uphold the law in the region. In this sense, a peculiarity constantly cited as a "commonplace" about the Amazon is the fact that "the roads are rivers." It is explained: the main navigable rivers in the Amazon region are the Solimões/Amazonas, the Negro, the Branco, the Madeira, the Purus, and the Juruá, and waterway navigation untill a while ago was the primary access to several of the municipalities in the region (Ribeiro, 1998, Oliveira Neto, 2014). In other words, there is a culture of water transport within local societies (Olivera Neto, 2023; Castro et al., 2023).

Sometimes, taking advantage of this navigability, parts of the Amazon territory are used as routes for the outflow of drug trafficking and other illegal activities carried out by organized criminal groups. (Couto, 2018). Drug trafficing in Brazil does indeed not only by river but also by land and air, and ports and airports not only in the Amazon but in all Brazilian regions are also used in criminal enterprises. However, the geographical aspects of the area, marked by forests and abundant water, favor its use in criminal enterprises, to the point that it makes it difficult for the State to act in its repression. For all these reasons, we use the word "frontier" as a synonym for space that undergoes or is subject to continuous modifications, "something that maintains two or more different ideas, one that does not exclude the other" (Zanini, 1997, p. XVII), as opposed to border (frontier, boundary), measured-stabilized space, characterized by the presence of tangible signs that make it that way: an expression and symbol of the connection between the legal system and location (Schmitt, 1998 [1974]). Looking closer, criminal organizations operate close to the border, while institutional apparatuses are forced within borders.

An example of this is the triple border between Letícia, in Colombia; Santa Rosa, in Peru; and Tabatinga, which has the highest homicide rate in the Amazonas State (Santos, Cunha, 2024). The place has fewer than 150000 inhabitants (if the three cities are considered), in approximate values. In an initial plan, one imagines that it would not be of great difficulty for the security and defense forces to carry out the control of criminal activities promoted in a place like this, where there is not a large installed population (unlike, for example, on the outskirts of large cities Brazilian, overpopulated). It so happens that the vastness of the aforementioned triple border territory, combined with the natural factors that make its protection difficult, potentiated by the disarticulation between countries and the low investment in security and defense, forms the "perfect storm" for the practices of transnational criminal organizations (Paiva, 2019).

There is an explanation for why illicit activities, especially those related to drug trafficking, are carried out with such profusion in Brazil. Although it cannot be considered a producer of a refined drug such as cocaine, such as in Bolivia, Colombia, and Peru (Couto, 2017, p. 812; Nunes Dia et al., 2022, p. 227), the value of purchasing already refined hydrochloride in the country is considerably lower than in Europe and other countries (affluent) drug users. Thus, even via the airport, which is notably more expensive, exploring the activity is still economically rewarding, given the scale of profitability for operators of the illicit act. Thus, even in a context in which it is not a notorious producer of cocaine, nor does it have a "primordial target" of producers and dealers in its Brazilian consumer market (since for a long time it was a drug used by people with greater purchasing power, primarily concentrated in rich countries), the "negative balance" of the exploitation of the drug trade for Brazil and, above all, for the Amazon is remarkable. This is due to the increase in violence resulting from the use of the Amazon routes for the exploitation of cocaine and other drugs, impacting border towns and large cities in the region (Couto, 2017).

One of the one factor that helps to understand the maintenance of such a scenario is that the (already restricted) state response to such activities often occurs only through the repression of the so-called top workers. Such people, in general, are the "local" inhabitants of regions with a high incidence of trafficking and who provide services—sometimes sporadically, sometimes regularly—to criminal groups. These are genuinely organized (Fraga, Nascimento Silva, 2018).

The picture drawn so far makes it clear that there is a security problem in the Amazon and, as will be shown later, this has as one of the factors (among several others) the enormous disarticulation of Brazilian border security. The Amazon frontier, above all, is highly unguarded and, given its territorial size, the use of intelligence to identify and control criminal groups will become increasingly necessary. To continue to this point and talk about intelligence in the control of organizations, it is required to make a brief digression and talk about what a criminal organization means in the current context.

The Notion of a Criminal Organization

Having presented the security issue in the Amazon, it is necessary to draw an overview of what criminal organizations are. This is because the presence of such groups in the territory under analysis was referred to as a striking factor in the description of the public security situation in the region. The activity of criminal organizations is one of the significant security and public order problems faced by States today. The structure used for the criminal enterprise, the existence of a hierarchy, the movement of financial resources, in some cases, the transnational character of the organization, the use of violence, and the corruption of public agents characterize their actions, challenging the traditional logic of repression of criminality (Castro et al., 2020, p. 78).

Varese (2010, p. 11), when analyzing the definitions of organized crime present in the specialized literature on the subject, recorded more than 150 existing concepts; as von Lampe specifies. However, a point that can be highlighted is that organized crime is not configured through an exclusively individual undertaking, adopting complex organizational elements to achieve its objectives (Castro et al., 2020, p. 78). Organized crime, in general, aims to illegally control the production of some good or commodity in a given area (von Lampe, 2001). This modus operandi generates conflicts with state institutions and, sometimes, with other criminal groups. Conflicts with state institutions and civil society arise at this juncture and can take different forms. Organized crime is a response to a specific type of government failure, its inability to prevent coordinated actions aimed at enrichment through predatory activities or the exploitation of illegal markets (Reuter, Tonry, 202, p. 5), the corruption of public and private sectors, the use of violence to ensure domination over a given territory (Abadinsky, 2010). In the world of criminal organizations, it is often necessary to delimit and control territories and spaces through threats and force (Campana, Varese, 2018, p. 1.383).

Such a territorial dispute can even be observed in the Amazon, where the issue of public security is addressed in the present. In this sense, an article published in the Spanish newspaper *El Pais* on April 28, 2021, stands out, which had the following headline: Frontline in the war between factions in Amazonas, the *Compensa* neighborhood in Manaus is experiencing bloody days. The lead of the article above read as follows: "Authorities are investigating an alliance between the Northern Family and the Pure Third Command against the *Comando Vermelho*, which partially dominates the region. A new group, the Northern Cartel, may also be involved in the killings." The monopoly in specific businesses and the control of territories, also characterizing elements of organized crime (Riccio, Skogan, 2018), are factors that can be observed in events such as the aforementioned, which demonstrates the dispute for space between factions in northern Brazil (where the Amazon is located).

The State's response to the action of organized crime occurred over time through the development of specific legislation to combat it. The concept of organized crime has been discussed in recent decades until its inclusion in the legislation in several countries. The Palermo Convention reinforced this concern at the international level. Ratified by the UN General Assembly on November 15, 2000, to provide legal parameters for the actions of states in the containment of organized crime, this convention brought a definition of what would be an "Organized Criminal Group," with the inherent conceptual insufficiencies to such a thorny topic (Abadinsky, 2010).

The definition in question, of a fluid nature, disregards other elements, such as the model of organizations (Atuesta, Pérez-Dávila, 2018, p. 238), the nature of their economic action, and the insertion with formal businesses (Dugato et al., 2015, p. 945). It is relevant to understand that no concept is free of values, with organized crime also being strongly influenced, especially in its genesis, by factors such as aversion to being different and xenophobia (Castro et al., 2020, p. 81). In any case, it cannot be ignored that despite the difficulties of conceptualization, the phenomenon of organized crime is a concrete reality that generates negative impacts in different spheres such as government institutions, the business world, and socially vulnerable groups, among others.

Notably, the conventional criminal, not associated with groups that provide him with material resources to carry out the task, would not be able, by himself, to act in a territory as vast as the Amazon. This is because it has already explored, of the vastness of its territory and the conditions of trafficability and navigability through the place. Several inputs are needed, such as vessels, aircraft, and vehicles for transporting drugs, accompanied by teams for their handling, as well as fuel and other products that guarantee the operation. Furthermore, a group without the condition to enter into and articulate business with organized crime from other neighboring countries would not have access to various products that are produced across the border. Thus, through the exposition of the characterizing elements of criminal organizations, it is seen that several of the factors that make up such a concept can be observed in the works carried out in the Amazon, highlighting their transnational character, the movement of significant financial resources for the realization of the enterprise and even the use of violence.

Violence in the Amazon territory: An Approach to the Performance of Organized Crime in Northern Brazil and the Amazon

The Legal Amazon is a region comprising an area of 5.2 million square kilometers, comprising nine Brazilian states in the North, Midwest, and Northeast regions, distributed in 772 municipalities and with an estimated population of 28 million inhabitants (Salomão et al., 2020). Such complexities are explained, in part, by the natural aspects of the region. Since large portions of the territory are covered by water and forests, sparsely populated and, at the same time, one of the largest industrial centers in the country is located in this region, which is Manaus, where more than two million people live. The region's complexity also stems from the fact that it corresponds to 40% of the national territory and has the largest tropical forest and biodiversity on the planet (Riccio et al., 2016).

The Brazilian Amazon has a severe problem with illicit activities (as demonstrated in the preceding chapters). Its territory suffers pressure, specifically, from large drug trafficking networks, linked to criminal organizations with solid operations in Andean countries, preferably (Bolivia, Colombia, and Peru). Such countries can be considered the largest cocaine producers in the world (Couto, 2014, p. 809). This information demonstrates that the degraded institutional framework of South America is highly correlated with the fact that the continent is a prominent producer of narcotics, especially cocaine. This illicit product is mainly used by rich countries (in Europe and elsewhere).

An even more recent study on the subject was published in February 2022 by the Brazilian Public Security Forum (Fórum Brasileiro de Segurança Pública), entitled Cartographies of Violence in the Amazon Region: Final Report. The study brings much information about the spread of organized crime and drug trafficking factions in the region, concluding that the Amazon is a place where many of the relationships were established from the global market of drug and arms trafficking. This is in a true global confluence of organized crime, highlighting several elements that characterize organized crime already discussed here: transnationality, use of violence, and others.

The analysis of the performance of organized crime in the Amazon region and even the illegal activities that operate there must be seen in a broader context, contemplating factors such as the forms of occupation and use of its territory in such illicit undertakings (FBSP, 2022, p. 38). An example is the use of the Amazon River and its tributaries. This river is a significant drug (mainly cocaine) outflow corridor between producing and consuming poles, whether nationally or across borders. This is because it is interconnected with several others, in an intertwined water network that spreads over large portions of the territory. Furthermore, because of this, the widespread distribution of narcotics through this means is facilitated (Forum Brasileiro De Segurança Pública (FBSP), 2022, pp. 38–39). In other words, criminal groups use vast local natural resources to achieve their illicit objectives.

It is also true that security problems derive from violent and opaque occupation processes that were conducted outside of state supervision (Riccio et al., 2016, p. 38). Waves of migration to the Amazon region were promoted over time without much planning, stirring up disputes between traditional populations and groups from other places. This situation led to the following picture: the regions of the great Amazonian metropolises such as Manaus and Belém present problems typical of different areas of the country; on the other hand, the agricultural frontier regions present conflicts over land ownership, such as falsification of property titles, expulsion of traditional populations, and assassinations of political and union leaders. Moreover, as already discussed in the present, the border regions comprise crimes mainly related to international drug trafficking (DATI).

The most relevant Brazilian criminal organizations were intertwined in the region, in addition to the groups that already operated there in their illicit endeavors. The Primeiro Comando da Capital (PCC) and the Comando Vermelho (CV), prominent Brazilian criminal organizations aware of the importance of the region for the domain of the drug exploitation chain, soon flew to the Amazon region (FBSP, 2022, p. 42). As well as regional groups, no less violent and worrying for authorities involved in public safety, began to organize themselves to gain control of the reagion's leading distribution and consumption routes.

In this sense, the Northern Family (FDN) stands out, as it emerged in Amazonas in 2007 within the penitentiary system. This organization gained control of the main route for cocaine entry into the Amazon, which is the Solimões River, an area of geostrategic interest for the PCC generating a bloody conflict with each other(Ferreira, Framento, 2019, pp. 99, 105). More recently, however, we have witnessed the dissolution of the FDN with the strength of the CV and the formation of new groups, such as the Cartel of the North (CDN) and the Revolutionaries of Amazonas (RDA) (Nunes Dias, 2024, p. 67). Until 2017, the FDN and the CV were allies. Currently, the groups are rivals, as the CV managed to control Manaus after a long war with the FDN (FBSP, 2022, p. 42). In 2017, the First Northern Command (PCN) was created in Pará, with links to the São Paulo PCC, which would have come from the latter faction's strategy to expand its domains in the chains of Northern Brazil and, at the same time, control the market and drug trafficking routes in Altamira and Marabá. Several other groups with the same intention emerged in the region, each with its own interests, but with the same objective: territorial control for the exploitation of trafficking and other undertakings, in addition to controlling the Amazon routes for transport.

Therefore, the picture of public security in the Brazilian Amazon: highly equipped and active organized crime takes advantage of the territory's vastness and operates in the place, due to the high financial returns resulting from the exploration of the routes. There are even disputes over the dominance of the routes between organizations with interests beyond Brazilian borders. Thus, it is necessary to rethink what is being promoted in terms of security for the space of the Brazilian Amazon. Therefore, below, we will examine who is responsible, according to the Federal Constitution of Brazil, for the defense of the areas that touch the Amazon and why it is necessary to promote an effective security plan that pervades the use of intelligence.

Defense, Intelligence, and Security in the Brazilian Constitution

To understand the problem concerning the expansion of criminal organizations in the Amazon region, it is essential to outline the federated entities' legal/institutional framework of the competencies. This is so that it is possible to attribute to each entity its responsibility for the repression of groups organized in the place and to do so through the most modern intelligence practices. In this axis, the focus on the Amazon will be on the competence to protect not only the forest and its resources and the borders, which correspond (as seen) to a large part of the territory.

The Brazilian Constitution establishes as Union assets the rivers, lakes, and all sources of water inside the territory, the indigenous lands, and the vacant lands. The last are lands belonging to the Federal government that are irregularly occupied. As it is possible to observe, the Union is responsible for most of the Amazon lands but has limited resources to protect them. It is legally established by the article:

Art. 20. The following are assets of the Union:

. . .

II—vacant lands essential for the defense of frontiers, fortifications, and military constructions, federal means of communication and environmental preservation, as defined by law;
III—lakes, rivers and any streams of water in lands under its domain or that bathe more than one State, serve as boundaries with other countries, or extend to foreign territory or come from it, as well as marginal lands and beaches rivers;
XI—the lands traditionally occupied by the Indians . . . .
The article also stresses the relevance of border areas in matters of national defense. The Constitution clearly states that border areas are the federal government's responsibility. Moreover, it establishes the Federal Police as the force responsible for controlling the borders (terrestrial, maritime, and airports).
Art. 144. Public security, duty of the State, right and responsibility of all, is exercised for the preservation of public order and the safety of persons and property, through the following bodies:
. . .
§ 1 The federal police, established by law as a permanent body, organized and maintained by the Union and structured in a career, is intended to:
. . .
III—exercise the functions of maritime, airport and border police; . . . .

At the same pace, the Constitution defines the National Defense Council as a consultive branch of the President of the Republic. Among its tasks, is to counsel in border matters.
§ 1 It is incumbent upon the National Defense Council:
. . .
III—propose the criteria and conditions for the use of areas essential to the security of the national territory and give an opinion on their effective use, especially in the border area and those related to the preservation and exploitation of natural resources of any type; . . . .

The constitutional articles (exposed earlier) show how much the 1988 constituent was concerned with maintaining the security of national. Both from the national defense and public security in such areas. Moreover, he bequeathed this obligation, primarily, to the Federal Union, the most capitalized and structured entity. Thus, it is a fact that national defense itself is carried out through security control of neighboring areas. Moreover, the clear objective of the Constitution was to ensure that such areas were more porous than they are (given what has already been exposed in the present).

This is because the spread of criminality practiced in the Amazon region, especially in border areas, reaches the entire national territory. The control of such routes and their commercial exploitation for the promotion of international drug trafficking is not restricted to groups that explore the Amazon regions but concerns groups that operate in the main cities of the Center-South of Brazil (as shown in the previous chapter). In other words: to relegate what happens in the Amazon to a distance from everyday life in the large centers of the Southeast would be "turning a blind eye" to a reality that affects the very need to promote national defense since the articulation of groups that exploit organized crime is increasingly more prominent and their networks are increasingly intertwined.

Despite the competence of the Union, already reputed as the federal entity with the most significant capacity to spend resources to achieve the objective of promoting security in border areas, rivers, and indigenous areas (which adds a considerable part of the Amazon region), there is no effective strategic planning carried out by such an entity on security and defense in that region (which, as explained earlier, are closely linked). Over time, several projects have been made, originating from security and defense agencies but without proper integration in such a sensitive matter. In this sense, the Amazon Protection System (SIPAM) and the Amazon Surveillance System (SIVAM) stand out, which did not fully fulfill their objectives. This is because, even though these programs are in force, organized criminal groups that use Amazon for illicit activities continue their activities in total.

To develop a truly effective plan for the security of the Amazon, covering the border regions, it is necessary to promote the hearing of populations affected by crime in those border regions. It is also required to listen to the professionals who work or have worked in the localities on the most diverse fronts: whether these are military personnel, agents (lato sensu) of the Revenue and Federal Police, and other members of the Union's defense and security forces. Nor should they be forgotten, in formulating an effective plan, local security forces, because, although they are not constitutionally legitimized to promote security on site, they end up suffering the consequences of the actions of organized crime in cities in the North of Brazil. The plan must be carried out with a focus on integrating the different security segments and mechanisms must be added to promote the due periodic review of its compliance and effectiveness.

The repression of organized groups must aim to control the financial activity of groups involved in organized crime. What is happening, in the current situation, is that accountability occurs, above all, in the face of smaller agents in the organization, often coming from local, impoverished populations and who merely carry out localized actions without great relevance to the whole of the organization—operation (as discussed in a previous topic). Thus, the axes of a lasting policy, to be promoted by the Union, but taking into account other federated entities, must be integration, technology, and training of professionals involved in Amazonian security and defense and the massive promotion of investments in the area.

In this sense, for a national plan for greater surveillance of the vast Amazonian territory to be implemented, the use of intelligence is vital (Rider, 2023, p. 18). Furthermore, intelligence may assist in identifying and securing pieces of evidence, but itself has no evidential value (Rider, 2023, p. 18). Hence, protecting the Amazon region requires considerable effort in intelligence gathering and articulation among all criminal justice system institutions to curb the presence of criminal organizations, also creating a legislative framework regulating informational interoperability exchange between the Brazilian intelligence system and the Public Prosecutor's Office (Queiroz Rodrigues, 2022, p. 83).

Everything highlighted above already has interesting, but not systematic, foundations (Gomes, 2022; Amorim, 2021).In a territory where "there is a lack of human resources from institutions, mainly in the security area, and a poor communications infrastructure, which provides a low level of dialogue between the different organizations, federations, and states, which take place in the region." (Amorim, 2021, p. 23), a comprehensive effort is needed to strengthen cooperation, increase human resources significantly, and implement technical and logistical resources.

It is a question of taking the good practices developed in recent years with the "Agata operations" to a higher level, learning from the mistakes made in their organizations (Amorim, 2021, pp. 28–33). However, we need to imagine a streamlined and linear decision-making structure; we need to remodel that rhetorical process of producing centers with similar functions, the results of which would be worth questioning, to define a participatory structure for interinstitutional cooperation (Hiath da Silva et al., 2023) also through the integration of the computerized systems used by the Law enforcement with those of the armed forces (Gomes, 2022, pp. 324–325), in which both the hierarchy and the functions are clearly defined. A structure capable of collecting data and processing valuable information to contrast and prevent criminal organizations' activities. Great attention must also be paid to both internal and, above all, external communication regarding the results obtained to strengthen accountability (Cepik, Antunes, 2003; Matei, Bruneau, 2011; Cepik, 2021; Miranda, 2023). An example of how it is already possible to use the available resources for environmental crimes is the technical cooperation project launched by the public ministry of Parà to prevent and combat illegal deforestation (Coelho Amaral et al., 2024). In this model, the relational resource seems to play a predominant role; trust between the various actors involved, the speed with which they exchange information, the security of the latter, their continuous updating, and the awareness of what is being discussed are fundamental. Likewise, for the fight against organized crime, "to ensure good management of the plan [...] among the interoperations, at the operational level, it is important to establish an organizational structure with greater cooperation between the agencies, considering the problem of being prevented and the available resources to optimize the situation processes of decision making" (Amorim, 2021, p. 17).

Conclusion

One of the main issues about the Brazilian state is maintaining the security and defense of the Amazon space, which includes areas of forest, and rivers, generally located in border areas. Given its geographic factors, organized crime constantly uses the Amazon region to dispose of narcotics, in general, those produced in countries neighboring Brazil. Organized groups also use the region to pursue their interests at the local level, mobilizing significant resources to do so.

The performance of such organizations in the region directly affects the Brazilian State's capacity to maintain order, radiating effects far beyond the vast space of the Amazon. In this sense, the Brazilian Federal Constitution brings the Union, entitled with the largest share of tax revenues, as the competent one to provide security and defense in border areas, where a considerable part of the illicit activities promoted in the Amazon are practiced. It is concluded that only a national plan, which has as its axes the integration of the agents involved in the security and defense of the Amazon, the wide use of technology, and the training of personnel will be able to control the issue of organized crime activity in the place. This happens by promoting investments and contemplating the use of effective intelligence mechanisms in such an endeavor.

References

Abadinsky, H., 2010. *Organized Crime* . 9th ed. Belmont: Wadsworth.

Amaral, P.H.C., Costa de Mattos, M. Alves, A., Texeira, A.M., D., 2024. Cooperação técnica como estratégia de fortalecimento da atuação do ministério Público estadual do Pará, na prevenção e no combate ao desmatamento ilegal. In: Folly, M., Amaral Viera, F., *Crimes ambientais na Amazônia: Lições e desafios da linha de frente*, pp. 128–149. Rio de Janeiro: Plataforma Cipó.

Amorim, C. R., 2021. *Operações Interagências Na Amazônia: uma nova concepção de planejamento militar em apoio à repressão aos crimes ambientais e transnacionais nos rios transfronteiriços da região*. Dissertação apresentada à Escola de Guerra Naval, como requisito parcial para a conclusãodo Curso de Estado-Maior para Oficiais Superiores. Rio de Janeiro: Escola de Guerra Naval.

Atuesta, L. H.; Pérez-Dávila, Y. S., 2018. Fragmentation and Cooperation: The Evolution of Organized Crime in Mexico. *Trends in Organized Crime*, 21 (3), 235–261. https://doi.org/10.1007/s12117-017-9301-z

Becker, B., 2005. Geopolítica da Amazônia. *Estudos Avançados*, 19 (53), 71–86.

Brasil, 2016. *Constituição da República Federativa do Brasil*. Brasília, DF: Senado Federal, 2016, 496 p. Disponível em: https://www2.senado.leg.br/bdsf/bitstream/handle/id/518231/CF88_Livro_EC91_2016.pdf. Acesso em: 12 janeiro 2023.

Campana, P.; Varese, F., 2018. Organized Crime in the United Kingdom: Illegal Governance of Markets and Communities. *The BritishJournal of Criminology*, 58, 1381–1400. Oxford University Press.

Castro, R. C. Y.; Giura, G.; Riccio, V., 2020. O crime organizado no Brasil e na Itália: análise de decisões. *Revista de Informação Legislativa: RIL*, Brasília, DF, 57 (228), 77–92, out./dez. Disponível em: https://www12.senado.leg.br/ril/edicoes/57/228/ril_v57_n228_p77

Castro De Jesus, A. B.; Oliveira Neto, T.; Araújo Da Silva, F. B., 2023. Periodização Da Rede Urbana Na Faixa Pioneira Amazônica: Os Casos Do Sul Do Amazonas E No Oeste Do Acre. Boletim De Conjuntura (Boca), Boa Vista, 15 (44), 182–203. Doi: 10.5281/Zenodo.8231887. Disponível Em: https://Revista.Ioles.Com.Br/Boca/Index.Php/Revista/Article/View/1848.

Cepik, M., 2021 Intelligence and Security Services in Brazil Reappraising Institutional Flaws and Political dynamics. *The International Journal of Intelligence, Security, and Public Affairs*, 23 (1), 81–102. https://doi.org/10.1080/23800992.2020.1868784

Cepik, M., Antunes, P., 2003. Brazil's New Intelligence System: An Institutional Assessment. *International Journal of Intelligence and CounterIntelligence*, 16, 349–373.

Couto, A.C., 2018. Ameaça e caráter transnacional do narcotráfico na Amazônia brasileira. *Revista do Instituto Histórico e Geográfico do Pará*, 5 (2), 64-81. Available at https://ihgp.net.br/revistaojs/index.php/revihgp/download/140/109/337 – Acesso em: 15 set. 2024.

Couto, A. C., 2017. A geografia do narcotráfico na Amazônia – *Geographia Opportuno Tempore, Londrina*, 3 (1), 52–64. Disponível em: http://www.uel.br/revistas/uel/index.php/Geographia/article/view/31774 – Acesso em: 22 fev. 2023.

Couto, A. C., 2014. Geopolítica, Fronteira e Redes Ilegal Na Amazônia. In: *Anais do I Congresso Brasileiro de Geografia Política, Geopolítica e Gestão do Território*, pp. 807–815. Rio de Janeiro. Porto Alegre: Editora Letra1.

Dugato, M.; Favarin, S.; Giommoni, L., 2015. The Risks and Rewards of Organized Crime Investments in Real Estate. *The BritishJournal of Criminology*, 55, 944–965. Oxford University Press.

Ferreira, M., Framento, R., 2019. Degradação da Paz no Norte do Brasil: o conflito entre Primeiro Comando da Capital (PCC) e Família do Norte (FDN). *Revista Brasileira de Políticas Públicas e Internacionais*, João Pessoa, 4 (2), 91–114. https://doi.org/10.22478/ufpb.2525-5584.2019v4n2.48617

Fernandes, M. C., 2022. Amazônia perdeu verba de proteção de fronteira. *Valor Econômico, São Paulo*, 15 jun. Disponível em: https://valor.globo.com/brasil/noticia/2022/06/15/amazonia-perdeu-verba-de-protecao-de-fronteira.ghtml. Acesso em: 28 jan. 2023.

Forum Brasileiro De Segurança Pública (FBSP). 2022. *Cartografias das Das Violências Na Região Amazônica: Relatório Final*. https://publicacoes.forumseguranca.org.br/items/e006ea2f-652e-4bee-846a-3df69ac0b0bd. Available at 12th october 2024.

Fraga, P.; Nascimento Silva, J. K., 2018. Police Action and the Drug Business in Brazil. In: V. Riccio, W. Skogan, eds., *Police and Society in Brazil*, pp. 135–150. New York and London: Routledge.

Gomes, R. C., 2022. A Inteligência Policial e a Cooperação Interagências no Combate ao Crime Organizado nas Fronteiras. *Revista Brasileira de Ciências Policiais*, 13 (8), 287–331. https://doi.org.br/10.31412/rbcp.v13i8.938

Hiath da Silva, M.P.H., Oliveira Junior, A., Mendonça Leimos Ribeiro, A. C., 2023. Uma visão crítica sobre a ausência de protocolo geral de integração de agências na inteligência em segurança pública. *Revista Brasileira de Inteligência*, n. 18, 167–186. doi: https://doi.org/10.58960/rbi.2023.18.228

Kraemer, R., 2015. Incompreensão do conceito de Inteligência na Segurança Pública. *Revista Brasileira de Inteligência*, n. 10, 73–82. doi:10.58960/rbi.2015.10.128

Le Tourneau, F. M., 2019. *L'Amazonie*, Paris: CNR Éditions.

Matei, F.L., Bruneau, T., 2011. Intelligence reform in new democracies: factors supporting or arresting progress. *Democratization*, 18 (3), 602–630. https://hdl.handle.net/10945/43281

Miranda, J.R.Y., 2023. The Role Of The Media And Civil Society In Intelligence Accountability: The Cases Of Spain And Brazil. *The Journal of Intelligence, Conflict, and Warfare*, 5 (3), 23–57.

Nunes Dias, C. C., 2024. Dinâmica da Violência e do Crime na Macrorregião Norte do Brasil: o efeitodas facções criminais. *Boletim de Análise Político-Institucional*, n. 36, 59–69. http://dx.doi.org/10.38116/bapi36art4

Nunes Dias, C. C., Paiva, L. F. S., 2022. Facções prisionais em dois territórios fronteiriços. *Tempo Social*, 34 (2), 217–238. https://doi.org/10.11606/0103-2070.ts.2022.191220

Oliveira Neto, T., Nogueira, R. J. B., 2014. Geopolítica Rodoviária Na Amazônia. Anais do I Congresso Brasileiro de Geografia Política, Geopolítica e Gestão do Território, Rio de Janeiro. Porto Alegre: Letra1, 229–240.

Oliveira Neto, T., 2022. Infraestruturas, circulação e transportes na Amazônia: impactos multiescalares. Ar@cne, 26, 1–29. https://doi.org/10.1344/ara2022.272.34612

Paiva, L. F. S., 2019. As dinâmicas do mercado ilegal de cocaína no tríplice Fronteira entre Brasil, Colômbia e Peru. *Revista Brasileira de Ciências Sociais*, São Paulo, 34 (99), 1–19. https://doi.org/10.1590/349902/2019

Queiroz Rodrigues, L. C., 2022. Interoperabilidade informacional entre Sisbin e Ministério Público e aplicação pelo órgão ministerial de conhecimentos oriundos da Atividade de Inteligência – estágio atual e desafios. *Revista Brasileira de Inteligência*, n. 17, 65–87.

Ribeiro, M. A. C., 1998. *A complexidade da rede urbana amazônica: três dimensões de análise* (Tese de Doutorado). Rio de Janeiro: UFRJ.
Riccio, V.; Fraga, P. P.; Zogahib, A.; Aufiero, M., 2016. Crime and Insecurity in Amazonas: Citizens and Officers' Views. *Sortuz: Oñati Journal of Emergent Socio-Legal Studies*, 8 (1), 35–50.
Riccio, V.; Skogan, W., 2018. Gangs, Drugs and Urban Pacification Squads in Rio. In: V. Riccio, W. Skogan, eds., *Police and Society in Brazil*, pp. 135–150. New York and London: Routledge.
Rider, B., 2023. Organised crime – what we know and what we think we know! In B., Rider, eds, *A Research Agenda for Organised Crime*, Cheltenham (UK) – Northampton (USA): Edward Elgar Pub., pp. 1–56.
Rider, B., 2013. Intelligent investigations: the use and misuse of intelligence – a personal perspective, *Journal of Financial Crime*, 20 (3), 293–311.
Reuter, P., Tonry, M., 2020. Organized Crime: Less Than Meets the Eye. *Crime And Justice*, 49 (1), 1–16.
Salomão, R.; Gomes, I.; Pinto, A.; Amaral, P.; Cunha, C.; Figueiredo, L., 2020. *Situação territorial, desmatamento e focos de calor em 60 municípios daAmazônia Legal*. Belém: Imazon.
Santos, M. P., Cunha, V. H., 2024,[2023]. Dinâmicas da violência no território brasileiro: Amazonas. In Maria Paula Gomes dos Santos, eds, *Dinâmicas Da Violência E Da Criminalidade Na Região Norte Do Brasil*, pp. 121–166. Brasília: Ipea. http://dx.doi.org/10.38116/978-65-5635-072-1/capitulo4
Schmitt, C., 1998 [1974]. *Il Nomos della Terra*, 2nd ed. Milano: Adelphi.
Varese, F., 2010. *What Is Organized Crime?* London: Routledge.
von Lampe, K., 2001. Not a Process of Enlightenment: The Conceptual History of Organized Crime in Germany and the United States of America. In: *Forum on Crime and Society*, pp. 99–116, Vol. 1, No. 2. New York: United Nations.
Zanini, P., 1997. *Significati del confine*. Milano: B. Mondadori.

5
ECUADOR'S PRESENCE IN THE AMAZON

Security, Weak Institutions, Questioned Capabilities, and Strategic Opportunities

Katalina Barreiro Santana and Diego Pérez Enríquez

Introduction

This chapter reviews Ecuador's historical and political relationship with its Amazon Region, popularly known as the "*oriente.*" The "east," "*el oriente*" in Ecuadorian jargon, is the way the Amazon is generally referred to. The term loses its historical and cultural essence when presented in English, for in Ecuadorian history "el oriente" has always been a geographical location, as well as a historical geopolitical element around which a large part of the national being has been built.

As discussed in the following pages, Ecuador's 20th-century history has a central scenario in this part of the country, due to its historically unresolved border dispute with Perú. That meant that the country's defense and foreign policy had this issue as the key element; in practical terms, such an emphasis reduced or even eliminated broader considerations. Politically and economically, decision-makers deepened such perspective after rich oil reserves were found in the country's Amazon region. The 1972–1979 dictatorships considered their main responsibility to preserve all the oil extraction and distribution infrastructure as strategic for the country's future. Such a view gave way to setting up institutions (formal as well as informal), policies, and political and socioeconomic arrangements that have guided every decision-maker ever since.

After the peace agreements with Perú were signed in late 1998, several other problems became evident for the country. Whereas in the 20th century the agenda for the Ecuadorian Amazon seemed to be summarized in full control of the territory while containing Peru's agenda toward the region, as soon as the agreements were reached, the country was forced to deal with unknown phenomena.

Thus, the 21st century meant dealing with security risks that came from the uneasy neighborhood formed by Colombian terrorist and drug trafficking organizations, as well as that country's own actions—or lack of them—and its consequences in Ecuador. Also, in a global context where stronger environmental commitments are demanded upon the countries' policies in oil extraction, as well as their responsibilities toward indigenous populations in the Amazon, decisions may face a harder scenario.

Finally, the country's institutions are set on a path that is quite difficult to redirect. That means larger voids in policy for the Amazon region, as well as practical situations of incapability to deal with this area. Consequently, Ecuador's relationship with the Amazon is not only difficult but also built upon a deficit of State presence and public policy aimed at effectively including this region in the country's agenda.

Such are the issues and state problems reviewed in the following pages. A historical institutional approach is considered as an explanatory way for the facts described. It is clear that Ecuador's academia must delve deeper into these issues, considering all of the natural resources, high inequalities, high vulnerability, and quite light attention and decision-making politicians have regarding this region.

20th Century: Wealth, Disputes, and Borders

It is important to notice that 43% of Ecuador's territory belongs to the Amazon basin, with riverbanks and ports on the Pacific and neighboring countries Colombia and Peru. The Amazonian provinces currently include Sucumbíos, Orellana, Napo, Pastaza, Morona Santiago, and Zamora Chinchipe. Despite being a small segment of the vast Amazon, each kilometer of it presents unique characteristics and different activities.

The construction of Ecuador's frontier imaginary has its origins in the country's founding as a Republic in 1830. The most contentious area was the Amazonian territory, which led to conflicts that were resolved with the Itamaraty Peace Declaration in 1998. The complex definition in geographical, human, and potential terms meant that for a large part of Ecuador's republican history, this region represented the greatest vulnerability in the face of the threat posed by its neighbor, Peru, and the claim for a riverine access to the Marañón River. This shaped a defense and foreign policy that revolved around the major threat to national security, which was the possibility of war and the potential dismemberment of the national territory (Kisic, 2009).

In a way, the possibility of territorial loss led to the establishment of a fundamental strategy involving a certain presence and social investment by the Armed Forces in the border provinces. The goal was to emphasize the geopolitical notion that a vacuum could result in the complete loss of these territories due to enemy occupation (Saltos, 2020). In addition to this looming threat, the Ecuadorian Amazon held significant export potential for the country. By the late 1960s, the northern Amazonian provinces, Sucumbíos and Orellana Pastaza, became the site of major oil reserves and the most crucial resource for Ecuador's trade balance.

While the "oil boom" of the 1970s facilitated a leap in development for Ecuador due to the nationalization of oil production and nationalist regimes, the northern Amazonian border of Ecuador also shared boundaries not only with Colombia but also with an emerging conflict, involving nascent guerrilla groups and criminal organizations linked to the drug trade. These circumstances, during the final decades of the Cold War, were more associated with anti-communist struggles than with the plague that would later deeply affect the region as organized crime.

On the other hand, in the southern Amazonian provinces, Zamora Chinchipe and Morona Santiago, the situation was different. The majority of crises and military confrontations between Ecuador and Peru were concentrated in these territories, which lacked clear delineation. This was the case during the Paquisha War (1980) and the Alto Cenepa conflict

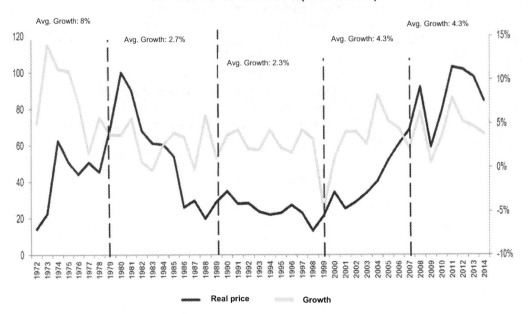

FIGURE 5.1   GDP growth and oil price
Source: (Foro Economía Ecuador, 2014)

(1995). Two particularities added to these circumstances. In the 1980s, the reactivation of gold and copper mines in Nambija, Zamora Chinchipe, led to illegal mining becoming the primary economic activity in the southern provinces of Ecuador. This was due to the closure of the Portovelo mines (Heck & Tranca, 2014) and the movement of indigenous communities such as the Shuar and Ashuar peoples, who were settled in the Cordillera del Cóndor but were divided by imaginary boundaries.

The end of the Cold War and the beginning of the last decade of the 20th century brought about the unipolarity of the United States, which imposed the need to expand a model of liberal democracy aimed at a free-market economy. However, traditional conflicts like the ones Ecuador had with Peru hindered the consolidation of a free market in the Andean region (Barreiro, 2018). In addition to the concern for global economic revival, a new threat emerged. This was the period of the most intensified phase of the Colombian conflict, which managed to bring together irregular armed forces and drug trafficking activities, all occurring in the southern departments of Colombia bordering the province of Sucumbíos in the Ecuadorian Amazon.

Efforts were made to promote mechanisms of commercial integration, such as the case of the Andean Community of Nations (CAN). This led to the establishment of the Colombia-Ecuador Neighborhood Commission in 1989, signed by Presidents Borja and Barco, with the goal of creating a continental free trade area (Barreiro, 2002). However, in less than a year, the level of violence in Colombia and a conflict in its departments of Nariño, Cauca, and Putumayo forced President Gaviria to acknowledge that the Colombian conflict had surpassed its domestic boundaries and had become a transnational global threat.

The shift in Ecuador's national security during this decade was influenced by two key factors: the resolution of the conflict with Peru and the potential to confront a new threat. This new threat had shifted from the disputed provinces on the southern border to those in the north. Unlike traditional state actors, this threat was now posed by armed and criminal groups (Barreiro, 2018).

The year 1996 was crucial for understanding the Colombian-Ecuadorian Amazon, as it revealed two fundamental issues. On the Colombian side, there was a low presence of state institutions and military forces along the border, in contrast to the high operational capacity of irregular groups. On the Ecuadorian side, there was a geographically extensive border guarded by limited military resources, aimed at preventing and containing the potential expansion of internal conflict onto its territory (Bustamante, 1996).

As a result of this new dimension of national security, a binational mechanism was created on November 21, 1996, between Ecuador and Colombia as a proposal for collective security. This mechanism was called the Binational Border Commission (COMBIFRON in Spanish). The fundamental strategies included the exchange of information between the intelligence services of both countries, coordination, monitoring, and evaluation of agreements and security issues in border areas, organized crime, drug trafficking, illicit arms, ammunition and explosives trade, and irregular groups, following the mechanisms established in the United States' National Security Strategy (Castillo, 2009).

For Ecuador, in 1998 several shifts took place in its binational relations. The country signed Peace Agreements with Peru on October 26 and immediately had to redirect its national security agenda toward the new threats of combating drug trafficking and the Colombian conflict. In November, President Pastrana of Colombia proposed a negotiation process with Manuel Marulanda, representing the Revolutionary Armed Forces of Colombia (FARC) (López, 2011). As part of the peace process guarantees, he withdrew police and military forces from the Caguán area in the south-central part of Colombia, which was referred to as the "zone of distension." This area was situated right on the northern border of Ecuador.

The final year of the decade and the 20th century concludes with a defining moment for the northern border of Ecuador and the Southern border of Colombia. The US Drug Czar, Secretary Barry McCaffrey, designates the Colombian conflict as a matter of US national security, thus framing the war between narco-guerrillas (Barreiro, 2002). This declaration solidified with the unveiling of Plan Colombia in the same year. The initial strategy of this plan was social-economic development to counteract the illegal economies fueled by guerrilla groups and drug trafficking. It included a significant military cooperation component, with the focus being the Putumayo department bordering the Ecuadorian provinces of Sucumbíos and Orellana in the Amazon region. This delineated a territory of routes intertwined with illegality, trafficking, violence, and a lack of institutional resources.

21st Century: Organized Crime, Violence, and Migration

By the beginning of the 21st century, Ecuador had resolved its greatest conflict in the history of national defense with Peru. The Ecuadorian Armed Forces were undergoing a reconfiguration under parameters such as democracy, strengthened civil-military relations, transparency, and an apparent doctrinal transformation from a traditional realist and national security approach to a multidimensional one. The previously disputed territory, the

Ecuadorian Amazonian provinces, became a prime example of regional integration. Indigenous bi-nationality was recognized in the area, infrastructure was developed to align with the South American Regional Infrastructure Initiative (IIRSA), Binational Border Attention Centers were established as mechanisms of the Andean Community of Nations (CAN), and efforts were made toward demining, river trade, among other initiatives (National Secretariat of Planning and Development (SENPLADES), 2011).

In contrast, the United States' War on Drugs and the effects of the Colombian armed conflict changed the nature of the relationship between Ecuador and Colombia. Key aspects included issues such as aerial fumigations, displacement, migrants, refugees, and the Colombian government's military engagement with "hot pursuit" strategies against irregular groups in areas near the Ecuadorian border. This period was marked by ongoing disputes, disagreements, and long periods of silence between the two countries.

The Development Plan "Change to Build Peace" or "Plan Colombia," proposed by President Pastrana, failed to yield significant results. Despite the recognition of the importance of incorporating strategies for alternative economic development, addressing displaced populations, implementing control mechanisms, reducing violence, and tactics to combat the operations of drug trafficking groups (García, 2001), the outcomes were a reinforcement of military strategies to address the presence of irregular and criminal groups. The period from 1998 to 2001 could be considered the phase of the greatest expansion of paramilitary forces, increasing from 4,000 to 12,000 men, and a surge in kidnappings by the FARC, with around 1,500 reported cases of kidnappings per year (Handel, 2005). Military combat strategies intensified during this period.

In the case of Ecuador's northern border, specifically in the province of Sucumbíos, the period from 2000 to 2001 saw a series of events. These included kidnappings of both national and foreign personnel from oil companies operating in the area, an explosion at a military outpost in the region, bombings of the Ecuadorian oil pipeline, mass killings, discovery of cocaine laboratories in the border area, and displacement of indigenous populations and settlers due to guerrilla threats. Ecuador consistently maintained the principle of non-intervention in the internal affairs of other states in its official documents. The idea of any involvement in military strategies or the possibility of its territory becoming a combat scenario was never entertained. The best mechanism was to fortify Ecuador's northern border using military and police forces to shield against the effects of the Colombian conflict, which manifested as the flourishing of illegal economies and an increase in violence (A. Suárez, personal communication, October 11, 2014).

In the final months of 2000, the Colombian government implemented crop eradication operations in the Putumayo department, adjacent to Ecuador's province of Sucumbíos. This involved aerial spraying to eliminate opium poppy and cocaine crops, resulting in the dispersion of chemicals onto Ecuadorian territories and border populations. The report "Impact on Ecuador of Aerial Spraying Conducted in Putumayo as Part of the Plan Colombia," carried out by a verification mission, indicated that the toxic effects of the glyphosate used in these operations had resulted in the deaths of 16 Ecuadorians, skin allergies, respiratory issues, disruption of the ecosystem due to animal and species deaths, and significant negative impacts on crop productivity in the area (Barreiro, 2018).

In response to these circumstances, Ecuadorian President Gustavo Noboa, with financial assistance from the United States Agency for International Development (USAID), established the Executive Unit for Northern Development (UDENOR) in the year 2000. This was based on the development versus criminality logic. The main objective was to create a Comprehensive Border Development Plan covering the northern provinces of Ecuador. In the official creation document, Official Registry No. 134 of the year 2000, the justification for its establishment was the region's vulnerability and underdevelopment in the face of the Colombian conflict and drug trafficking activities, "which make it a fragile area and threaten and disrupt its security" (Official Registro No. 134, 2000).

By 2002, Ecuador presented its Defense White Paper, marking an important post-conflict milestone following the resolution of issues with Peru. This document outlined the new threats to Ecuador's security, with the most evident one being related to the impacts of the Colombian conflict on Ecuadorian territory, as well as the intertwining issues of drug trafficking and organized crime. These consequences necessarily involved the northern provinces of Ecuador, especially those in the Amazon region. The main variables of this new threat were:

1. Weakness in the Colombian state's presence in the southern departments, leading to significant vulnerability along the Ecuadorian border.
2. Escalation of the conflict resulting in many displaced people and refugees seeking safety in Ecuadorian border communities that lacked the infrastructure to handle this situation.
3. Increase in violent and criminal activities in Ecuadorian border territories due to the presence of armed illegal groups and organized crime.

On August 7, 2002, Álvaro Uribe was inaugurated as the President of Colombia amid significant dissatisfaction with the policies of his predecessor, Pastrana. These policies, both economic and in terms of the escalating violence, had resulted in around 2 million displaced individuals throughout the country. The early 21st century depicted a Colombia with high levels of violence, where threats and armed actors forced many Colombians into forced displacement. During this same year, Ecuador experienced its first significant wave of refugees, averaging around 3,500 annual asylum applications, which rose to 11,463 in 2003 (Rivera, 2012). For the first time, Ecuador faced a large refugee population seeking safety within its territory, mainly in cities and border towns that lacked sufficient basic services to accommodate this group.

Ecuador maintained its stance of viewing Colombia's lack of control over its southern departments as well as considering Colombia's conflict to be of an internal nature. Despite this, President Uribe believed that the strategy should be regional in combatting irregular groups, internationally labeling them as terrorists (Barreiro, 2018). In both 2005 and 2006, Ecuador lodged continual complaints about the aerial fumigation activities targeting coca plantations that were affecting agricultural activities and the population of Sucumbíos province. In 2006, Colombia agreed to suspend fumigation activities within 10 kilometers of its border, but this suspension lasted only until 2007. Following the resumption of aerial spraying operations by the Colombian government, citing the emergence of 10,000 new hectares of coca on the Colombian side of the border (Bermeo Lara & Pabón Ayala, 2008), without notifying Ecuador, a diplomatic tension arose, leading to the withdrawal of the Ecuadorian ambassador in Bogotá.

By March 2008, within the framework of the Democratic Security Consolidation Plan of Minister Santos, the intelligence and military operation "Fénix" was implemented. Its objective was to dismantle the top leadership of the FARC. The opportune scenario was the

"II Bolivarian Camp for Our America," which was scheduled to take place in Quito, Ecuador. The event included the presence of Raúl Reyes and other individuals linked to irregular groups. Through extensive monitoring and cooperation in police intelligence between both countries, it was known that for this event, Raúl Reyes would be in the Angostura area in Ecuador. Geographically, this area is characterized by its proximity to the Amazonian border with Colombia and the Putumayo River. Despite clear violations of Ecuador's sovereignty and the brutal attack on the FARC camp in Angostura, this incident was internationally justified as part of Colombian operations against the global drug threat. Regionally, a prohibition on preemptive attacks was established in response.

Through Rafael Correa's term, from 2007 to 2017, going beyond the attack in Angostura, the conceptualization of the "Amazon" was directed toward its rich biodiversity, petroleum, and mineral resources, and the control of drug trafficking routes. Concerning drug trafficking, the northern provinces of the country, especially Sucumbíos, became the central focus of national security. This involved military and police intelligence operations related to controlling illegal crossings and potential trafficking routes. However, in the environmental aspect, a different path was taken. During Correa's first presidency (2007–2013), the Yasuní-ITT Initiative was launched. This initiative aimed to commit to not exploiting 845 million barrels of oil in the Ishpingo, Tambococha, and Tiputini oil fields located in the provinces of Orellana and Pastaza. In exchange, international sale of oxygen and avoiding the emission of 407 million tons of CO_2 was proposed. Unfortunately, this initiative did not gain international traction, and petroleum activities continued.

For the presidency of Lenin Moreno in 2018, the focus shifted toward petroleum resources as the primary source for renegotiating the debt, which amounted to 6 billion dollars with China, and acquiring 2 billion dollars through Global bonds (Infobae, 2018), as well as funding from the International Monetary Fund (IMF). This was aimed at strengthening Ecuador's engagement with multilateral banks. By 2019 and 2020, the public debt from multilateral banks and bonds offered to private debt holders reached approximately 58 billion dollars (El Universo, 2019). This maintained Orellana and Pastaza provinces as the main sources of exploitation.

While petroleum became intertwined with the traditional image of Amazonian wealth and nature, Moreno's presidency was compelled to address the threat of organized crime and uncontrolled Venezuelan migration passing through the Andean region to the south. In March 2018, when three Ecuadorian journalists were killed on the Colombia border by members of the Oliver Sinisterra Front, an unusual event for Ecuador, this prompted a reassessment of defense policy and an alliance with the United States. This alliance encompassed three fundamental aspects: cooperation in national security, Venezuela as a symbol of a population exodus, and the potential for Ecuadorian exports to enter the US market (Reyes Herrera et al., 2021).

The presidency of Guillermo Lasso, which started on May 24, 2021, and has ended by November 30, 2023,[1] began with a strong focus on economic reactivation and trade promotion, including a successful vaccination plan. However, the administration once again positioned the Amazon region as the country's primary resource zone and, simultaneously, the area with the greatest potential security threat due to the operations of organized crime. As a result, Lasso's discourse shifted away from the possibility of an environmental agenda in favor of promoting tourism, increasing oil exploitation from 530,000 barrels to 1 million, controlling illegal mining in the provinces of Zamora Chinchipe and Morona Santiago through foreign mining investment, and harnessing river resources for 4,000 megawatts of annual industrial conversion, transitioning away from oil as a fuel source (Primicias, 2021). Additionally, there has been investment and an alliance with the United States in terms of military and police intelligence equipment to combat drug trafficking along the Colombian border.

Institutional Influences and Weaknesses

A discussion about Ecuador's policy in the Amazon region requires the identification of certain theoretical elements. This calls for conceptualizing institutions from two perspectives:

1) A functional perspective, which views institutions as mechanisms for addressing specific problems (Dahl, 2000; Downs, 2001; Schumpeter, 1986).
2) An interrelation perspective that examines the actors operating at a more personal level, particularly focusing on individual leadership (Burns, 2010; French & Raven, 1986).

When identifying the system, one must distinguish its actors and map out their interests. Adding a historical perspective can reveal patterns and turning points in these interactions, facilitating a more structural understanding while distancing from mere contingencies. It is acknowledged that there are multiple interactions among actors of diverse nature, each guided by individual or collective, current, or historical pursuits that shape their agendas. This "political life" constitutes a "system of interrelated activities" (Easton, 1957, p. 384), in which each actor seeks its interests.

The focus will be on developing a long-term perspective that identifies regularities in certain relationships deemed crucial to understanding institutional dynamics in the country. This involves interpreting Ecuadorian policy in relation to significant interactions for the design of strategic policy regarding the Amazon, drawing from historical institutionalism and systems theory. The primary actors in this context are the Executive branch and the Armed Forces, on one hand, and the interactions occurring between individuals—referred to here as leaders—and diffuse actors falling within the generic category of international organized crime (IOC) operating in Ecuadorian Amazon territories. Naturally, not all interactions can be fully discerned, but the primary intention is to discern the operations that constitute an institution (North, 1991).

The Political System and Its Connection With the Amazon

Going along Easton's (2001) and Luhmann's (2013) perspectives, the totality of possible interactions is delimited to those that are significant and capable of producing concrete impacts on how the State presents itself in the specified territory. Considering the country's traditional political dynamics (Pérez Enríquez, 2012, 2018) and aligned with the argument developed by Loveman (1999), the Armed Forces became a sort of backbone in the configuration of the recently liberated nations toward the end of the colonial era. This vocation began with the action, typically Westphalian, of consolidating national borders. As mentioned, Ecuador's history with the Amazon region was always schizophrenic. On the one hand, there was a sense of distance imposed by a country that centralized political and economic life in its two main cities while making very meager contributions to the infrastructure that would enable their interconnection (Ayala Mora, 2003). On the other hand, in a paradoxical manner, the distant Amazon constituted one of the fundamental elements in the construction of the Ecuadorian identity (Ayala Mora, 2018; Espinosa, 2010; Maiguashca, 2012). In both dimensions, the Armed Forces represented the main presence of the state in these distant territories, where the notion of nationality/homeland was constructed in opposition to the "dangerous" neighbor, Peru. Thus, in this context, the Armed Forces became a predominant actor, maintaining a specific agenda and interests that guided their positions in relation to other actors.

The executive branch, as the holder of civilian power, held political responsibility and a historically fundamental role in making decisions for the control of the eastern territory of the country. However, prevailing conditions are characterized by the tension between the political-economic bipolarity of the country (Quito—Guayaquil) and the physical distance and complex topography of the Amazon territory. These factors regularly led political decision-makers to overlook the necessity of developing state presence through state infrastructure and mechanisms to guarantee rights.

The war with Peru in 1941 highlighted those distances and tensions. While the military attempted to contain the Peruvian troops' advance into Ecuadorian territory, political leaders were engaged in a series of disputes and attempts to provoke changes in the administration of power. Ultimately, the war was lost with consequences that would be resolved more than five decades later (Bonilla, 1999; López, 2012; Orquera Polanco, 2020). This experience made it clear how uncertainty stemmed from political tension and the costs of the distance between the central areas and the eastern territories. The revival of the foundational myth of the Amazon became a crucial element in defining Ecuadorian identity from that point on. This element became interwoven in the military's relationship with all political actors, but particularly with the executive.

During the military dictatorship (1972–1979), the notion of the Armed Forces as the predominantly responsible institution for ensuring national sovereignty and state security was solidified. This approach took the form of an institution under the structure of the National Security Council (COSENA), which concentrated within a single entity the military capabilities to address various threats the state might face. In this institution, functions such as national mobilization, intelligence, civil defense, academic reflection, and system administration were consolidated under a specialized secretariat responsible for compiling and processing inputs and proposing necessary courses of action to the executive (Barreiro Santana et al., 2019).

The predominant advisory role adopted by the armed forces, along with their central role in designing national defense policy, which was almost exclusively focused on the border issue with Peru (Bonilla, 1999), led to a reinforced Westphalian conception of the country's relationship with the Amazon. This resulted in a significant military deployment, particularly in the border areas with Peru, where Ecuador argued the inapplicability of the Rio de Janeiro Protocol of 1942. This constructed "two" Amazon regions: those in dispute that needed protection from potential Peruvian invasion, and those in the northern region, which housed the main oil wells and constituted the country's wealth base.

It's crucial to note that there were no state development plans related to either of these territories, and state policy focused on maintaining the status quo. Despite this, some peculiarities can be highlighted. Following the earlier classification, the provinces of Morona Santiago and Zamora Chinchipe dealt with tensions arising from the thesis of the non-executability of the Rio de Janeiro Protocol of 1942 for much of the 20th century. This had implications from the perspective of national security, as the entire state institutional framework revolved around territorial claims through diplomatic means and anticipation of new confrontations on the uncertain border (Adrianzen, 1999; García Gallegos, 2018; Luna Tobar, 1981).

On the other hand, the provinces of Sucumbios (bordering Colombia and Peru), Orellana (bordering Peru), and Napo (without international borders) are where the oil exploitation is concentrated. They were not subject to the same pressures as the other provinces, and their security situation was not a major concern, except for occasional incidents like the occupation of oil wells by indigenous populations demanding certain improvements or sporadic cases of kidnapping of employees from oil companies (Célleri & Pérez Enríquez, 2019).

In any case, the provinces of the Ecuadorian Amazon were distant from the dynamics of national development, evidenced by their poor levels of human development (Vélez-Tamay et al., 2021) and the increasingly polarized positions demonstrated by indigenous organizations toward a distant and deficient state that fails to guarantee even basic rights, as proven by the protests in 2019 and 2022.

A key issue to consider is that:

> From the perspective of national security and the imagery of the east as the stage where Ecuadorian identity was played out, the demarcation of borders and the subsequent peace agreement with Peru in 1998 implied a change in the historical conditions of power organization, particularly in the relationship between the military and political power.
> *(García Gallegos, 2018, p. 44)*[2]

The resolution of the classic border tensions with Peru did not eliminate any threats to the country; it simply shifted the geographical location to the border with Colombia. The rapid spread of activities by Colombian guerrilla groups in Ecuador challenged the country's ability to respond effectively.

In the 21st century, with an advanced peace process in Colombia, Ecuadorian decision-makers formulated a security agenda based on the assumption that Colombian demobilization and disarmament would be comprehensive, covering all actors and leading to a more secure border. However, the opposite occurred: insecurity conditions for the country multiplied, and they also incorporated another actor for which there was no preparedness—international organized crime.

Institutions and Regimes in the Ecuadorian Amazon

The dynamics that have been evident since 1998, and whose consequences are observed in the current difficulties the country faces in ensuring security in its northern territory, highlight the need to look at Colombia and all its internal events as the main source of impact on state sovereignty in contemporary times. This is particularly the case when the type of control exerted by the neighboring country is intermittent, and large stretches of the border are dominated by organizations linked to guerrilla groups and drug trafficking.

The peace process in Colombia in 2016 led to a dispersion of illegal activity into areas with weaker state presence. From Ecuador's perspective, this exacerbated the problems that had initially arisen due to the lack of strategic foresight during the development of that process. Thus, Ecuador's policy at the beginning of the 21st century, which was focused on consistently criticizing Colombia's decision to eradicate illegal crops through glyphosate spraying, shifted to another approach in which the lack of control, especially in the eastern zone, seemed to have deepened.

Schultze-Kraft (2016, 2018) argues that there is a significant presence of regimes of criminal origin that, taking advantage of the voids left by the state, have established conditions of quasi-legality in their interaction with the civilian population. They deploy conflict resolution mechanisms and ensure a certain order in exchange for their criminal activities being respected and supported. These criminal-legal regimes are active in territories where the absence of state institutions has left large populations in need of channeling responses to their daily social needs through some socially recognized mechanism—and from that perspective, legitimate—that allows for effective conflict resolution.

In this context, the deployment of criminal organizations operating in these territories has gained a certain degree of legitimacy in the absence of state presence. When such efforts to establish order have proven insufficient, the use of violence has been the mechanism employed to ensure a type of social cohesion that facilitates illegal operations, including recruitment, drug and arms trafficking, and transit.

The similarities between the Colombian Putumayo and the province of Sucumbios lie precisely in the weak presence of the state, which has resulted in a relationship where Ecuadorian territory has been used for provisioning, medical treatment, and rest for individuals and groups linked to these organizations. Perhaps the most notable case of this relationship was observed in the 2008 attack on Angostura, when the top leader of the FARC was bombed by Colombian Armed Forces on Ecuadorian territory. This case was not exceptional but rather the most visible instance. The proximity to the border, economic activity, Ecuador's acceptance of refugees displaced by the internal Colombian conflict, and the provision of healthcare services, among other factors, have facilitated the overflow of these types of regimes into Ecuadorian territory.

While Ecuador has sought to contain this overflow, the volume of exchanges and the absence of state presence have rendered the border area extremely vulnerable. The vast expanses, primarily within jungle areas, greatly hinder the possibility of control over illegal activities taking place in this complex border region. As argued, this elevates the likelihood of the establishment of a regime that, founded on criminality, could consolidate itself on Ecuadorian soil.

Conclusion

Despite the long-going presence of Ecuador in the Amazon, it might seem that the Amazon has not reached Ecuador yet. The sort of problems this region faces are of different and urgent nature, and yet, public officials' attention to them is only circumstantial, mostly when problems arise. Considering such a priori conditions, from a security perspective, to strengthen the country's response capabilities in the region is key to avoiding generating wider social contempt toward the State, and consequently, a higher incidence of ICO operating in the area.

The country has emptied several of the spaces it held before 1998 due to policy reforms that do not, necessarily, consider the risks behind creating voids in decision making and state's presence, especially when a relationship with society is thinning.

To pursue the traditional approach toward the Amazon would mean that the voids would multiply, making it even harder for the state to cover and solve anything about them. Being such a vast and unguarded territory, but also one that holds strategic resources, and it is inserted in a wider, regional, complex of high geopolitical relevance, the Amazon basin needs to be incorporated into the state, in a manner that furthers the country's prospective advantages.

Finally, academia has a key responsibility in bringing the "oriente" closer to society and especially decision-makers, in order to move beyond the mystical, historical, and functional considerations of the region's value for the country.

Notes

1 On May 17, 2023, Ecuador's president, Guillermo Lasso, enabled a constitutional mechanism that allowed him to disband the country's legislative branch, and moving forward the electoral scheduled, six months after such decree was issued. Although he had the legal possibility to be a candidate, he chose not to run, which means his term will officially finish in the aforementioned date.
2 Translation by the authors.

References

Adrianzen, A. (1999). Perú y Ecuador. Enemigos intimos. En A. Bonilla (Ed.), *Ecuador—Perú. Horizontes de la negociación y el conflicto* (pp. 83–88). FLACSO Sede Ecuador.
Ayala Mora, E. (2003). Centralismo y descentralización en la historia del Ecuador del pasado a la situación actual (Estudios). *Procesos. Revista Ecuatoriana de Historia*, 19, 203–221.
Ayala Mora, E. (2018). *Resumen de Historia del Ecuador (Sexta)*. Universidad Andina Simón Bolívar—Corporación Editora Nacional.
Barreiro Santana, K. (2002). La agenda de política exterior Ecuador-Estados Unidos. En A. Bonilla (Ed.), *Orfeo en el infierno una agenda de política exterior ecuatoriana* (pp. 231–330). FLACSO—CAF—Academia Diplomática. http://flacso.com.ec/docs/sforfeoinfierno.pdf#page=231
Barreiro Santana, K. (2018). *Angostura: La Inteligencia, el espejo oscuro de la seguridad*. IAEN.
Barreiro Santana, K., Reyes Herrera, M., & Pérez Enríquez, D. (2019). The Role of the Ecuadorian Armed Forces: Historical Structure and Changing Security Environments. *REPATS—Journal Studies and Advanced Researches on Third Sector, Special Issue*, 2, 50–72.
Bermeo Lara, D., & Pabón Ayala, N. (2008). *Las relaciones de seguridad entre Colombia y Ecuador: Una nueva construcción de confianza*. RESDAL. http://www.resdal.org/jovenes/investigacion-pabon-bermeo.pdf
Bonilla, A. (1999). Fuerza, conflicto y negociación. Proceso político de la relación entre Ecuador y Perú. En A. Bonilla (Ed.), *Ecuador—Perú. Horizontes de la negociación y el conflicto.* (pp. 13–30). FLACSO Sede Ecuador.
Burns, J. M. (2010). *Leadership*. Harper Perennial Political Classics.
Bustamante, F. (1996). La cuestión de las medidas de confianza mutua en el contexto de la subregión andina. En F. Rojas Aravena (Ed.), *Balance estratégico y medidas de confianza mutua* (pp. 195–216). FLACSO Chile.
Castillo, J. (2009). La influencia en la estructura de inteligencia nacional en el Ecuador. En R. Swenson & S. Lemozy (Eds.), *Democratización de la función de inteligencia* (pp. 91–109). NCDI Press.
Célleri, D., & Pérez Enríquez, D. (2019). Problemas globales de la seguridad en Ecuador. Una reflexión desde los vacíos y tensiones globales, regionales y locales. En *¿Cómo se posiciona la región frente a los cambios globales en materia de seguridad?* KAS, PUCEP, IDEI.
Dahl, R. (2000). *On democracy*. Yale University Press.
Downs, A. (2001). Teoría económica de la acción política en una democracia. En A. Battle (Ed.), *Diez textos básicos de ciencia política.* (pp. 93–111). Ariel.
Easton, D. (1957). An approach to the analysis of political systems. *World Politics*, 9(3), 383–400.
Easton, D. (2001). Categorías para el análisis sistémico de la política. En A. Battle (Ed.), *Diez textos básicos de ciencia política* (pp. 221–230). Ariel.

El Universo. (2019, junio 7). *Deuda total sube a 49,17% del PIB con nuevo cálculo.* https://www.eluniverso.com/noticias/2019/06/07/nota/7366671/deuda-total-sube-4917-pib-nuevo-calculo

Espinosa, C. (2010). *Historia del Ecuador. El contexto regional y global.* Lexus Editores.

Foro Economía Ecuador. (2014). *Crecimiento del PIB y precio del petróleo.* http://foroeconomiaecuador.com/fee/wp-content/uploads/2015/04/Crecimiento-del-PIB-y-Precio-del-Petróleo2.png

French, J., & Raven, B. (1986). The bases of social power. En B. Kellerman (Ed.), *Political Leadership. A Sourcebook.* University of Pittsburgh Press.

García, A. (2001). *Plan Colombia y ayuda estadounidense. El Plan Colombia y la Internacionalización del Conflicto.* Editorial Planeta.

García Gallegos, B. (2018). La formación histórica de la Defensa en Ecuador. *Estudios en Seguridad y Defensa,* 13(26), 23–46.

Handel, M. (2005). Leaders and Intelligence. En M. Handel (Ed.), *Leaders and Intelligence* (pp. 3–39). Frank Cass.

Heck, C., & Tranca, J. (2014). *La realidad de la minería ilegal en los países amazónicos.* Sociedad Peruana de Derecho Ambiental. https://hdl.handle.net/20.500.12823/274

Infobae. (2018, noviembre 26). Ecuador, muy cerca de pedir un salvataje al Fondo Monetario para enfrentar la crisis. *Infobae.* https://www.infobae.com/america/america-latina/2018/11/26/ecuador-muy-cerca-de-pedir-un-salvataje-al-fondo-monetario-para-enfrentar-la-crisis/

Kisic, D. (2009). Impactos y retos futuros de los Acuerdos de paz en el desarrollo económico binacional. En C. Donoso (Ed.), *Ecuador-Perú: Evaluación de una década de paz y desarrollo* (pp. 93–114). FLACSO—CAF.

López, C. A. (2012). Memorias de la guerra de 1941. *Procesos. Revista Ecuatoriana de Historia.,* II Semestre, 36, 193–201.

López, G. (2011). *The Colombian Civil War* (Potential for Justice in a Culture of Violence) [Policy Briefing]. Jackson School Journal of International Studies. http://depts.washington.edu/jsjweb/wp-content/uploads/2011/05/JSJPRINTv1n2.-Lopez-G.pdf

Loveman, B. (1999). *For la Patria: Politics and the Armed Forces in Latin America.* Rowman & Littlefield Publishers.

Luhmann, N. (2013). *Introduction to Systems Theory.* Polity Press.

Luna Tobar, A. (1981). La inejecutabilidad del protocolo de rio. En *La Cordillera del Cóndor y el Río Cenepa, causas de la inejecutabilidad del Protocolo de 1942* (pp. 13–17). Casa de la Cultura Ecuatoriana. http://repositorio.casadelacultura.gob.ec/bitstream/34000/19069/2/CCE-CDE-N30-1981.pdf

Maiguashca, J. (2012). La incorporación del cacao ecuatoriano al mercado mundial entre 1840 y 1925, según los informes consulares. *Procesos. Revista Ecuatoriana de Historia,* 35, 67–98.

North, D. C. (1991). Institutions. *Journal of Economic Perspectives,* 5(1), 97–112. https://doi.org/10.1257/jep.5.1.97

Orquera Polanco, K. (2020). La representación de la Guerra de 1941 en diario El Comercio. *Textos y Contextos,* 21, 63–74. https://doi.org/10.29166/tyc.v1i21.2476

Pérez Enríquez, D. (2012). Liderazgo político y transformaciones institucionales. Revisar las transiciones con ocasión del bicentenario. En *Reflexiones del Bicentenario de la Independencia de los Países Iberoamericanos* (pp. 319–383). Ediciones Escuela Superior de Guerra.

Pérez Enríquez, D. (2018). *Liderazgo político y transformaciones institucionales. Relaciones ejecutivo—Partidos políticos—Fuerzas Armadas (1996—2006).* Instituto de Altos Estudios Nacionales.

Primicias. (2021, mayo 24). Lasso apostará por petróleo, minería y más participación del sector privado. *Primicias.* https://www.primicias.ec/noticias/politica/lasso-petroleo-mineria-participacion-sector-privado/

Registro Official No. 134, 134 (2000). Decreto No. 640, 134 Registro Oficial § Segundo Suplemento (2000). Available at https://derechoecuador.com/registro-oficial-3-de-agosto-del-2000-suplemento/ on 22nd October 2024.

Reyes Herrera, M., Pérez Enríquez, D., & Barreiro Santana, K. (2021). El reposicionamiento del Ecuador: Competencia intraestatal y coyuntura en la administración 2017-2019. *Desafíos,* 33(1), 1–32. https://doi.org/10.12804/revistas.urosario.edu.co/desafios/a.9056

Rivera, F. (2012). *La seguridad perversa.* FLACSO Sede Ecuador.

Saltos, N. (2020). Cenepa: La última guerra Territorial. *Revista de la Academia de Guerra del Ejército Ecuatoriano,* 13(1), 20–27. https://doi.org/10.24133/age.n13.2020.02

Schultze-Kraft, M. (2016). Órdenes crimilegales: Repensando el poder político del crimen organizado. *Íconos—Revista de Ciencias Sociales,* 55, 25–44. https://doi.org/10.17141/iconos.55.2016.1899

Schultze-Kraft, M. (2018). Making Peace in Seas of Crime: Crimilegal Order and Armed Conflict Termination in Colombia. *Crime, Law & Social Change*, 69, 475–496. https://doi.org/10.1007/s10611-017-9759-2

Schumpeter, J. (1986). Democracy as Competition for Leadership. En B. Kellerman (Ed.), *Political Leadership. A Sourcebook* (pp. 199–203). University of Pittsburgh Press.

Secretaria Nacional de Planificación y Desarrollo (SENPLADES). (2011). *Programa Plan Binacional de Desarrollo Fronterizo de la Región Fronteriza, Capítulo Ecuador 2011–2017*. SENPLADES.

Suárez, A. (2014, octubre 11). *Embajador del Ecuador ante el Gobierno colombiano entre 2006 y 2008. Subsecretario de Soberanía Nacional en la Cancillería del Ecuador entre 2000 y 2006* K. Barreiro [Comunicación personal].

Vélez-Tamay, A., Carriel, V., & Castillo-Ortega, Y. (2021). Índice de Desarrollo Local para Ecuador con datos del 2010. *Revista Desarrollo y Sociedad*, 88(Segundo Cuatrimestre), 83–127. https://doi.org/10.13043/DYS.88.3

6
STRATEGIC RESOURCES, BORDER ECONOMIES, TRANSNATIONAL DYNAMICS, AND THREATS IN THE AMAZON

The Case of Lago Agrio in Ecuador

Milton Reyes Herrera and Patricio Trujillo Montalvo

Introduction

This chapter, based on an interdisciplinary and intertextual approach, and historical review, articulates a contribution of ethnographic sources[1] with a geopolitical and social characterization of different constituent moments of the Ecuadorian Amazon, focusing on Sucumbíos, a province in northeastern Ecuador, specifically on the Lago Agrio canton. It analyzes how the social world is interwoven, in a porous and permeable border where strategic resources (oil), illegal economies (trafficking), urbanization of the indigenous population, and transnational threats (narco industry) converge, in order to understand the particularities of the urban phenomenon in a border region and possible scenarios within the field of security and defense, through a delimited case study.

Lago Agrio or Nueva Loja for many years was imagined as the capital of the oil subregion in Ecuador. Located on the northern border, it borders the Sierra provinces (Ecuadorian Andes) of Carchi, Imbabura, and Pichincha; has influence from and on the Putumayo River, and the area of Tres Fronteras (shared by Ecuador, Colombia, and Peru); and is a "global city," crossed by violence, illegal economy, poverty, and marginality (Trujillo, 2009). The name of the city comes from the first oil well found by the Texaco company in this region in 1970. With the migration and colonization toward the northern area of the Ecuadorian Amazon, an oil sub-region was formed with some peculiarities. First, the formation of a singular identity of settlers-migrants (settlers-peasants); second, the appearance of towns distributed along the roads, wells, and oil camps; third, a region that went from rural to urban tinged with violence. Violence generated by its own dynamics, by the Colombian internal historical conflict; and where the emergence of armed conflicts and the drug trafficking industry have been escalating. All this has been generating a border area linked to illegal work (Trujillo, 2013).

Development Models in the Ecuadorian Amazon

The model of extraction of natural resources (oil, mining, agro-industrial) represented, for the Amazon Region of Ecuador (RAE, in Spanish), the main development project executed by the State since the 1970s. Trujillo (2009) considers that this economic and political strategy integrated the region with local and global economic markets, and represented the ideal project of well-being, modernity, and progress, for the migrant workers, peasants, and indigenous people who settled in the area, as well as for the rest of the urban population, as they are direct or indirect co-participants in the oil income.

Oil exploration began under the revolutionary nationalist government of General Rodríguez Lara, who articulated a developmental and nationalist discourse with a modernizing one related to defense. However, with the deepening and expansion of the extractivist process and the oil frontier, the way of imagining the Amazon forests and their inhabitants legitimized practices, implementations, and interventions of models that violate the rights of the native populations and nature. There was a chaotic territorial occupation related to the extraction of resources, guaranteed, in time and space, by the State.

The development model imposed for the RAE is configured in the following indicators:

- A spatial and human construction linked to the discovery and development of oil fields that design a characteristic form of development resulting from the correlation of social forces concerning the administration or the intermediary role of the State, in relation to the local economy and in relation to worldwide order (Cox, 1993), where the (dis) occupation of space resulted in (a) the commercial exploration of hydrocarbons, and complementary, (b) the founding of permanent settlements.
- The scheme of appropriation of the Amazon rainforest was governed by an essentially extractivist spirit (Trujillo, 2009) that formed three sub-regions with their own characteristics, with historical, social, and economic differences, as follows: the Northern Amazon (the border, the oil company, and colonist); the central Amazon (configured by the presence of high biodiversity areas, with the majority presence of indigenous nationalities); and the Southern Amazon (mining).

This can be observed more deeply when exploration was delegated to private sectors and transnational companies, where the State "extended the delegation" of part of its action and responsibility to the oil companies and service providers themselves, to different NGOs and other organizations in spaces influenced by oil exploration. After the developmentalist attempts—generated in the 1970s until the presidential period of Jaime Roldós (1979–1981, died in a plane accident)—a gradual dismantling of such orientation began. This occurred initially under a period of structural adjustment, coinciding with the Latin American debt crisis, and since the second half of the 1980s; to finally, and in the Ecuadorian case especially since 1992, culminate in the establishment of a liberal economic proposal. Thus, the organizations, built in the Bretton Woods order, such as the World Bank or the International Monetary Fund, under the new "flexible dollar international monetary system," proposed but also coincided with the block of social forces in charge of the administration of the State in the need to shrink and reorganize the State (North et al., 2008)—"necessity" that converged with its image as inefficient and corrupt, contrasting the ethical and dynamic model of the private company, in order to control and privatize all strategic resources (Escobar, 1993).

This discourse delegitimized the intermediation of the State and built a monopolistic response under the image of delegation to the "free market," which impacted the control of oil resources and revenues, but also in the areas of development. Transformation that gradually managed to introduce new social and productive relations in rural areas and old original and ancestral spaces; logics that were rhetorically linked to (a) the idealization of the market space as separate from the State (without considering that it is built according to the concrete dynamics of the State-society complex, and to the economic, social and cultural particularities of the space) and (b) a way of conceiving, representing and imagining progress and development, as intrinsic to modernization articulated to the "West" (North et al., 2008).

Here, as in other Amazonian countries, the State did not consolidate an efficient action to "integrate rather than deliver" (following Terezinha de Castro), nor did it reduce the asymmetries *vis-à-vis* the main cities of the Sierra and the Coast, generating basic geopolitical problems such as that of social cohesion in the population within a certain territorial political unit (as in Friedrich Ratzel *apud* Costa, 2005), and even worse a lack of unity and continuity between the economic, political, and identity dimensions—the national State-economy (Fiori, 2009).

In the past 40 years, a rapid urbanization process has been generated with the creation of different neighborhoods, precincts, communes, parishes, cantons, and cities. The original matrix that was the pre-rural cooperative or the commune changed to settlements nucleated along a complex and well-supplied road system that are now linked to cities such as Nueva Loja (Lago Agrio), La Joya de los Sachas, Shushufindi, Francisco de Orellana (Coca), Tena, Puyo, Macas, Sucua, Gualaquiza, Yantzantza, Pangui, and Zamora (Trujillo, 2009).

A rapidly consolidated, but chaotic, urbanization becomes the characteristic of local development, forming a largely colonial-mestizo and increasingly nucleated region, presenting new future challenges such as contamination of water sources, drinking water supply, environmental sanitation and basic services, garbage collection and waste management—all linked to an inadequate urban planning proposal.

Currently, the Ecuadorian Amazon would represent 5% of the country's population (739,874 inhabitants) with a population density of 6.36 inhabitants per km^2. The most populated province is Sucumbíos, with 176,472 inhabitants. In all these provinces, the rural population is larger than the urban population and represents 61.19% of the total. These are considered dispersed areas and present different planning challenges from urban or consolidated areas, which only represent 38.81%.

The population growth of the region does not follow the same pattern of growth at the national level—from 1962 to the present rate of 2.51% and the RAE a higher growth rate, 4.8%. The RAE presents variations in its growth rate and does not maintain a constant growth trend. This shows the increase in the population in 1962 as a result of the migrations produced by the Agrarian Reform. The second peak of growth occurred between 1971 and 1982 as a product of oil exploration, which due to the demand for services generated the opening of roads and attracted new migrants.

The growth of the Amazonian population is also a result of population growth (births and deaths) (SENPLADES, 2015).

The ethnic composition of the Amazon is very diverse; in the 2010 census, 59.3% of the population self-identified as mestizo and 33% as indigenous. To a lesser extent, there is a white, Afro-descendant, and Montubia population.

Strategic Resources, Border Economies, and Threats in the Amazon 91

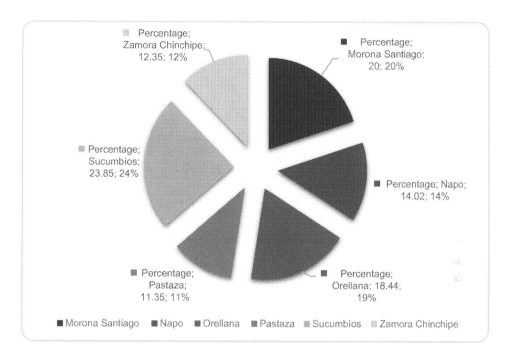

FIGURE 6.1 Percentage of population in each Amazon province
Source: INEC (2010). Elaboration: SENPLADES (2015)

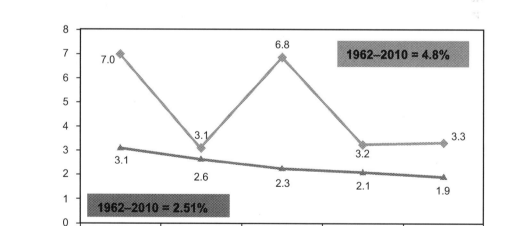

FIGURE 6.2 National and Amazon annual intercensal growth rates
Source: INEC, Population census, 1990, 2001 and 2010. Elaboration: SENPLADES (2015)

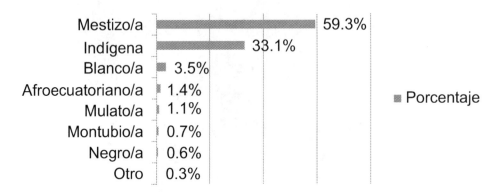

FIGURE 6.3   Ethnic self-identification in the RAE
Source: INEC (2010). Elaboration: SENPLADES (2015)

Here, 245,014 inhabitants are projected, self-represented as part of the peoples and nationalities, which means around 33% of the total Amazonian population. The largest indigenous population stands out in Morona Santiago, with 48.3%, and in Napo with 56.74% of the total population, and a lower percentage in the province of Zamora Chinchipe, with 15.6%.

The provinces where there is the greatest presence of mestizos by self-identification are Zamora Chinchipe (75.26%), Sucumbíos (82.46%), and Orellana (56.81%). From this point on, the percentages of most of the population lean toward self-identification as indigenous in Morona Santiago (54.22%), Napo (49.96%), and Pastaza (47.32%). The dynamic of identity self-ascription has not been a trigger in specific problems of violence among the population (besides cases concerning relatively recent people originating from the Amazon forced to integrate into the imaginary territory of the State).

Finally, in this characterization, it should be noted that there are also interests related to the mining sector in addition to the oil sector but that as an activity it is not yet fully projected in Sucumbíos. In any case, the pressure of these two activities and the expansion of the agricultural frontier and interests in the extraction of timber resources, among others, have generated a scenario of high pressure in conservation areas.

LAGO AGRIO: AMAZONIAN BORDERS, BACKGROUND, AND GEOPOLITICAL CHARACTERIZATION

Lago Agrio: Land of Hope

Lago Agrio is an urban space that was born as a result of the expansion of the exploration of oil resources. This is how the so-called East has been imagined, a complex word that combines different meanings in the Ecuadorian narrative. For example: while, from urban, and even academic perspectives and experiences, *going to the Ecuadorian jungle was classified as a mixture of adventure and enthusiasm,* for the State, the understanding was only given as lands with abundant resources to be explored. And, finally, for its inhabitants, this territory is seen almost exclusively as a living space. Between 1970 and 1990, the myth of the East was linked to the image of the land of hope, an uninhabited

TABLE 6.1 Indigenous population, nationalities, and peoples in the Amazon by provinces as of 2012

Province	Indigenous	Afro-descendent	Black	Mulatto	Montubio	Mestizo	White	Other
Sucumbíos	23,684	4281	2269	3801	1682	132,354	8015	386
Napo	58,845	846	184	654	606	39,515	2824	223
Orellana	43,329	2619	1663	2430	1647	78,390	5998	320
Pastaza	33,399	574	151	506	346	46,383	2448	126
Morona Santiago	71,538	1081	184	580	329	68,905	4566	757
Zamora Chinchipe	14,219	802	233	286	210	73,397	1909	320
TOTAL	245,014	10,203	4684	8257	4820	438,944	25,760	2132

Source: ECORAE, 2012. Plan Integral De La Circunscripción Territorial Especial Amazónica. Informe Técnico. Instituto de Ecodesarrollo de la Región Amazónica del Ecuador.

region where everyone could find work, land, and wealth. Hope, too, because the East was a land to colonize. People could go and get land *freely*. It should be noted that this was possible even in the 1990s, when there were still remote lands (territories) to be colonized.

Another reason for the "hope" image was because of the economic *boom* that oil brought. With its exploration, there was a great demand for workers who would receive high salaries. And, finally, *"Ecuadorians saw hope in the East, because now there was a place to emigrate and start a new life"* (Trujillo, 2009, 2013).

Hope centered on Lago Agrio, which was for many years the capital of the East, and where all the images described earlier were condensed. Its name is related to the first oil well that the Texaco Company found in 1972, near a lake called "Agrio," despite the fact that the formally and institutionally recognized name of the city is Nueva Loja.

Here, it should be noted that Loja is the name of the original province where most of the colonizers came from. Oral history indicates that when the first family of settlers[2] founded the town, its members decided to baptize the place with the name of their homeland to remember the place of their birth. At the same time, they wanted to transcribe their worldview, emotions, and stories. In short, they wanted to reproduce their cultural identity in a completely different ecosystem: the Amazon rainforest.

Lago Agrio is part of the so-called border areas—spaces that, in addition to being characterized by a geopolitical approach, are here understood from a sociological and anthropological reading. This allows us to identify an imagination referring to spaces of colonization, where there are deep social conflicts, and as a border of invisible people—this, especially, from the perspective of the authorities of the Ecuadorian State. These are areas also seen as a distant land where populations coexist under harsh economic conditions, with health problems, poverty, and violence, and a jungle region with high levels of crime, delinquency, prostitution, and drug trafficking—all perceptions that reproduce some erroneous representations built under moral prejudices.

The East in general and Lago Agrio, as one of the first specific oil exploration and exploitation, also represented part of the main project of modernity[3] in the border regions within the vision of the Ecuadorian State.

Since 1970, Ecuador applied one of the most ambitious modernizing projects in this area: the colonization and settlement of the then-distant Eastern region and the massive and commercial use of its natural resources. In previous years, Ecuador focused its economy on agricultural production. However, the implementation of the modernizing project meant that the national economy was based on the exploitation of large-scale natural resources (oil in the first place) as a basis of support in the revolutionary nationalist project of the sustainability of fiscal resources for said modernization. This was the main strategy that integrated the Amazon region with modernity, development, and local and international markets, later including the expansion of more extensive exploitation of other resources (such as gold and wood) (Taussig, 1987).

Modernization also deployed strategies of States and societies still informed by representations of their colonial past: "*domesticating*" the indigenous people and the jungle. These, and later the colonists, should cultivate the land and explore all possible resources. Such actions were the main paradigm of the State in search of modernization that intrinsically linked discourses on the capitalist market, modernization, civilization, and well-being (Escobar, 1993). The result was the demographic, ecological, and symbolic transformation of the region. Natives were colonized, the forest was devastated, and the original and new populations were stigmatized.

Lago Agrio as Human Geographic Space

The Ecuadorian northeast was populated or colonized by migrant populations that formed a region of borders that are living spaces (Camille Vallaux, *apud* Costa, 2005) and where resources and population are not monopolistically assigned to only one specific political unit or nation-state.

However, at the institutional level, the geographical limits of our study unit can be observed as follows:

- North: Colombia, at a formal level; however, for several years the territory was de facto occupied by Frente 48 of the Revolutionary Armed Forces of Colombia (FARC); and, currently, the situation in the specific territorial space is confusing, with remnants or dissidents of that group, after the peace agreements.
- South: Shushufindi and Cuyabeno cantons, neighbors of the same province of Sucumbíos; and also the province of Orellana, specifically the La Joya de los Sachas canton in the same province.
- East: Putumayo canton, which borders Colombia through the Putumayo River, and Cuyabeno canton, within which is the Cuyabeno National Park, a natural reserve and living cultural heritage; both belonging to the province of Sucumbíos
- West: Cáscales canton, within the same province of Sucumbíos.

According to the 2010 population census (INEC 2010), the canton of Lago Agrio had a population of 66,788 inhabitants. Of this number, 25,556 were in the rural area, while the majority of the population, 40,045, lives in the city. These data demonstrated that the population quickly changed to urban with the highest concentration in the city of Lago Agrio. In a comparative reference, in the 1990 census, the city of Lago Agrio had a population of 13,165 inhabitants. However, a decade later, in the 2001 national census, the same city showed a population of 34,106 inhabitants. The growth variation was 259.06%. The inhabitants in the city represent 85.17% of the urban population in the entire province.

There is also an additional peculiarity since in this canton there is an Afro-Ecuadorian population of mestizo origin and self-representation, populations of Kichwa origin, and three nationalities (minority): Kofan-Ai, Sieokopai, and Siona. Although between nationalities originating from the region and other residents of the area, there is a kinship relation and socio-cultural dynamics typical of border areas. In the case of the Kofan-Ai, Sieokopai, and Siona, they can be characterized as a binational population continuum, since their inhabitants are distributed between the borders of Ecuador and Colombia. Curiously, it is observed that, in the Colombian case, these nationalities, as a result of the dynamics of war and production economy related to drug trafficking, were linked to the "business" as *"raspachines"* (coca collectors) (Trujillo, 2009; Jansson, 2008).

The growth of Lago Agrio has been constant since 1997 and is linked to two main events: the first is related to the coffee crisis, as a result of the decrease in international and regional prices, in addition to the lack of modernization of agriculture. This crisis caused a deep economic depression in rural areas. The populations impacted by the debacle of their farms migrated to the city in search of better opportunities. Lago Agrio began to attract a population that saw the possibility of monetary success in the city.

The second process is related to the increased armed conflict in the neighboring country to the north and the beginning of the Colombia plan in 2000, as well as the beginning of glyphosate fumigation that impacted both sides of the border. Whether it is due to the increase in violence in Colombia, and the need for refuge, as well as the loss of access to resources for subsistence (legal agricultural activities and/or related to the coca leaf production chain), the city and the canton were the recipient spaces of this new migration.

In this process, Lago Agrio has been the largest receptacle of this human exodus. Between the 1990 and 2001 censuses, the province of Sucumbíos grew at a rate of 4.67. The canton grew 4.38 and its capital grew at a rate of 8.65. The city had an exceptional growth of almost double compared to the canton and the province (INEC, 2001).

With the coffee crisis and the aerial fumigation of Plan Colombia we are poorer . . . we sell some products to merchants on the river . . . some animals when we need money to go to the city . . . our children must go to the other side to work there . . . we know it is dangerous . . . but between the mountain people, the police and the army . . . there is not much option.

(Trujillo, 2009, 2013)

After a complex process of population consolidation in the past 20 years, there was a rapid urbanization in Sucumbíos that created different precincts, communes, parishes, cantons, and cities. The original matrix that was the pre-cooperative or the commune changed to settlements nucleated along the multiple roads in the sector. Thus, old pre-cooperatives and cooperatives no longer exist, and gave rise to small urban settlements and cities. The urban and rural plot is now linked to cities such as Nueva Loja, La Joya de los Sachas, and Coca, and to population centers, such as Enokanki, Santa Cecilia, and General Farfán (La Punta)—places that have become commercial, services, and political representation centers.

On the other hand, the Lago Agrio canton and even the areas interrelated with its activity, the deepening of liberal globalization—beyond the specific profits of oil companies and national and international private service providers, and its "multiplier effect" in the formal and informal tertiary sector related especially to the city—have deepened the crisis within families and local economies in rural and suburban sectors (Ong, 2005).

Here, describing (a) the daily life of the inhabitants of a political but also globalized border and (b) the construction of a particular geographical imaginary by actors of the socio-economic dynamics of such space, we find that the aforementioned is inscribed in a scenario where forms of transnational economy and global actors have shaped a particular social and cultural context where violence and conflict are social references of identity (Trujillo, 2013). That is to say, as images and representations, there is a cyclical vision of violence or eternal return, given the social, political, and cultural context and the daily life of the Putumayo region (of course with emphasis on the Ecuadorian side), its adaptation and social conflicts, and its relationship with the war and violence that occurs on the other side—the Colombian Putumayo.

The conflict and its most violent expression—war—have been recurring manifestations in the cultures of the Amazon regions. Despite this, it seems that violence in the Ecuadorian-Colombian border region has been present as a new regional characteristic around different stages of economic, political, and social development: from the imposition of colonialism to the development of a capitalist economy. From the exploitation of gold to that of rubber, passing through the oil era, until today (which we could characterize as the era of "warlords" and drug trafficking), people have had to adapt their daily lives to these conflictive conditions in the region.

Lago Agrio: "But Also a Global City"

Lago Agrio is a typical global frontier city. Using the concepts of global assemblages (Collier and Ong, 2005), it is a perfect example where the local and global are expressed together. Forty years ago, it was just an insignificant town with small houses around a large camp owned by a transnational oil company. The settlers lived in rustic wooden houses, depending on the profit from the oil industry. In contrast, the oil technicians lived in luxurious chalets with air conditioning, satellite television, a restaurant, and a bar. The center and the periphery were clearly drawn in this microspace. Transportation, basic services (electricity, health, and education), and manpower were supplied by the global oil industry, which at that time helped the settlers to survive in the rainforest ecology while their farms began to be productive.

Lago Agrio was the oil capital of Ecuador. With important international oil camps, residents lived and worked around this economic activity. The economy of the oil subregion is based solely on what oil and international companies could or could not do. It was the time when everyone benefited directly or indirectly from the wealth produced by the "black gold": transportation, hotels, restaurants, and employment places (Trujillo, 2009).

Oil gave this region an economic well-being never imagined. The workers had the highest salaries in the country. Lago Agrio encompassed the most evident representation of the meaning of globalization and global economy. The transnational oil companies represented the "global," especially the image of the negative impact of the deregulation of the economy in the "localities": luxury camps, security, and above all, norms of living within the camps. Meanwhile, the local population (with limited basic services, many economic problems and needs) was the periphery, where there was a delimitation by a metal fence border. The border between the modern—rich—global and the poor periphery was clearly expressed in that image.

In the late 20th century (1995–2000), the population of Eastern Ecuador had the perception that Lago Agrio was the city where they could obtain wealth and well-being. This imaginary contributed to a sustained migration of peasants to the city, creating slums and neighborhoods without planning, order, or public services. However, after 2000 a new oil boom began in the southern region of the provinces of Sucumbíos and Orellana, and Lago Agrio lost its economic dynamics, since the main operations moved to the city of El Coca. Despite this, a new and much more powerful economic phenomenon was consolidating in the region, now linked to the illegal economy: drug trafficking and arms smuggling.

The commercial exchange on the border had generated wealth and prosperity for many families on the Ecuadorian and Colombian sides. Lago Agrio became a city dependent on commerce. Every weekend the city markets became large fairs waiting for people from Colombia to come to buy, drink, and eat in the town. The city was full of bars, restaurants, and shopping centers; an immense commercial movement had dramatically changed this city in the last ten years. Many local residents were very proud of the new economic situation of the city:

> [N]ow Lago Agrio is a real city, we have large shopping centers, appliance stores, private hospitals . . . here many people from Colombia come to buy . . . spend their money . . . they have a lot . . . you know that they work with the *cocoroco* . . . on the left . . . on the other side . . . they come on Saturday, Sunday . . . here they are offered good food . . . good drinks and good girls, too . . . then people come, spend the money and on the weekend they disappear again . . . they return to the mountains again.
>
> *(Trujillo, 2009)*

On the other hand, in the past three decades, the internal migration of people from Sucumbíos who worked on Colombian plantations controlled by armed groups gave an illusory well-being to the border region. Drug trafficking fueled a parallel economy and a dynamic monetary circuit where many people work directly or indirectly. The explosive demographic growth is an example of this new economic dynamic, the population increase related to the new *boom* of the illegal economy. "Now there are more people from Colombia here than Ecuador . . . the city is a place of business for both right-wing and left-wing businesses." This situation of prosperity increased commercial exchange and therefore internal migration. Thousands of people came looking for work and well-being on the border, on the "other side of the Putumayo River" (Trujillo, 2013).

Lago Agrio: Border of Borders and Center of Multidimensional Interconnection

From a perspective of everyday life, Lago Agrio is perceived as a border city of social violence. Now, from our perspective, Lago Agrio as a continuity of this region and as a particularity—due to its geographical position—is a symbolic reference in the interstice of the global and the local, and where illegality and legality share common spaces. This implies that several human groups have to adapt and negotiate their social spaces affected by levels of conflict of different order and form. Oil exploitation, coca crops, drug trafficking, and smuggling of chemicals and weapons, together with symbolic images of war and violence, have been ingredients for the construction of a particular political identity in relation to the figure of the State and on both sides of the border.

Local and global city and border articulated with the Putumayo region (binational expanded zone), where a combination of clan groups, local political identities, intermingled with postmodern guerrillas and transnational or global corporations, NGOs, local environmentalists, radical environmentalists funded (in some cases by power-state foundations), missionaries, local and global adventurers, etc., occupy the ecological and symbolic space. Both socially and culturally, the population, throughout its history, has been impacted by several factors: first by colonialism and later by the application of aggressive extractive projects, where resources, population, and ecology have been seen only as entities to be exploited from a rentier and predatory perspective (Taussig, 1987).

Lago Agrio represents, due to the importance of its location (in the sense proposed by Ratzel, 1975), a last populated space in the northeastern area of Ecuador, as a border between civilization and jungle. Jungle that contains multiple meanings:

- Jungle as a natural resource and guardian of ancestral wisdom (even *exoticized*, such as the Cuyabeno);
- Jungle as an exploitation space (from oil, wood, etc.);
- Jungle as a space for material reproduction or a complement for the survival of native populations and settlers;
- Jungle as an opportunity to be domesticated and used.

Here, it is also worth mentioning that it is the border between a space with full presence of the State and one with a diffuse presence. Curiously, even though oil resources are dispersed, there are no conflicts over this specific resource, and there is full command capacity of the State, which differs from non-legalized activities and resources, where serious conflicts are reproduced with a marginal presence of State power—following the characterization of conflict over dispersed resources by Le Billon (2004).

Thus, when trying to decipher how the social and cultural dynamics of the population have been impacted by the illegal economy (coca crops and drug-industry) and the presence of various armed actors—who, as we know, have controlled the region in the last two decades—we can state that this complex combination of scenarios has generated diverse political and symbolic imaginaries of war, conflict, and violence related to the construction of a particular identity of the natives (settlers-peasants and *Kichwas*), the ethnic groups predominant in the Ecuadorian Putumayo, a region that has long been imagined as "the frontier of social violence" (Trujillo, 2013).

In the Putumayo region (as a geographical, spatial, and social space of continuity between Ecuador and Colombia), the deepening of the open economy model added to the inability of structural solutions during the reformist and neo-developmentalist has increased the daily crisis within families and the local economy. Many of the population live in structural poverty and without imagining themselves represented by any of the different governments.

On the other hand, *Lago Agrio is a central space for the interconnection* of several spaces relevant to the production, economy, and security of Ecuador and the Region. Thus, as a *multidimensional interconnection center*, it is vital to understand the location of the canton and its urban area, as a logistical space, road interconnection, market, service provider, place of transit, etc.

First, there is a long road interconnection between Lago Agrio and Quito, and specifically in the section through Baeza. Because this road has some complexities, such as the erosion of the "historic" road built for oil exploitation, work is being done on an alternative route. And in the current route, three key activities for the national economy converge at the level of infrastructure, road interconnection, and energy: highway, crude oil transportation, and hydroelectric power.

Also, by land, from the urban center of the canton to the town of General Farfán to the north, a town bordering Colombia, there is barely 19 km. For the last decade of the 20th century, the infrastructure was planned and built so that the binational connection became an important hub of commerce and exchange comparable to the Rumichaca International Bridge in the Ecuadorian highland province of Carchi, although with poor results. On the other hand, there are about 180 km between Lago Agrio and Puerto El Carmen, in the Ecuadorian province of Putumayo, by land. It is located in the northeastern area on the banks of the San Miguel River near the mouth of the Putumayo River, which marks the binational border with Colombia.

Toward the south-east, we can find a land road distance of approximately 59.2 km to Shushufindi, a town also linked to oil activity since its foundation, although in recent years it has lost relative importance in this activity.

Following the Amazon trunk road to the south is Coca, capital of the neighboring province of Orellana, 63 km away approximately. It is related to oil production, but also to the projected network articulated with the South American Regional Infrastructure Integration Initiative (IIRSA) for the Manta-Belém-Manaus (multimodal) connection, starting from here via river to the Amazon.

Finally, Lago Agrio, in addition to this multiplicity of multidimensional connections in Ecuador itself and even in the Putumayo region itself, can be considered not only a place of conflict due to its own interrelations but also as a space with strategic characteristics to be occupied by other actors in case the State does not occupy it efficiently. But likewise, it presents several opportunities to promote efficient regional integration (northern Ecuador) and maximize the potential of the northern region of the Ecuadorian Amazon. Even more so when it has installed capacities such as an airport with full projection of being expanded and interconnecting with the Amazons of Colombia, Peru, and Brazil. This topic is of interest for the interconnection of people, trade, and production but also for South American regional defense. Hence, the importance of relating the efforts and opportunities of the IIRSA and the state and regional projection for the multidimensional security of the northern Amazon and the whole of South America.

Final Considerations: Geopolitical Projection, Articulation to Integration and Security

As mentioned, Lago Agrio and associated spaces present structural challenges such as lack of social cohesion, violence, and armed actors also related to drug trafficking, just as the FARC and paramilitary groups were before, and as dissidents, haulm, etc.

However, from the above, the scenario could be even worse, considering that there are reports that "the heirs" of production and transportation in the Colombian Putumayo area, after the peace signings, maintain control of the "business" and "commercial relations with Mexican cartels. However, given the orientation and expansion capacity of the latter, two negative scenarios for the expanded binational Putumayo region could occur:

- An attempt to expand and occupy the space by said drug cartels, which would mean a violent armed conflict with serious consequences

- Deeper articulation between the actors mentioned earlier that represents a challenge of greater dimensions for the security systems, not only of Colombia and Ecuador but also of Peru and the Amazon region (also taking into account the dynamics of drug trafficking actors in the Atlantic and Brazilian Amazon)

Therefore, it is strategic to resume initiatives that integrate this region with their respective national States, and with the South American region. These States should understand the need for intelligent integration that includes the population, to rebuild social cohesion through the generation of opportunities at an economic level, enhanced by greater production, trade, and interrelation coordinated by the efforts of the Amazonian and, even better, South American states.

We do not propose as the only solution to resume the interconnection perspectives raised in IIRSA, promoting not only regional integration, investment in territory, and its multiplier effect, trade, productive chaining but also the interconnection with a bioceanic orientation that—in addition to the above—can be projected for spaces of multidimensional security and defense, both at the level of the states themselves and in an integration organization such as UNASUR, through its most efficient proposal, the South American Defense Council.

In this region, we find the IIRSA Waterway Putumayo project, which is multimodal: Tumaco-Pasto-Mocoa Road Corridor; and Puerto Asís-Belém do Pará waterway, which passes through Puerto Leguizamo and Manaus, also facing the Atlantic and to Natal in the southeast (the closest space between South America and the Americas) and Dakar, in Africa.

Furthermore, this route could also be complementary or, in the worst case, subsidiary to the IIRSA Manta-Manaus project, which could also be projected into the main bioceanic interconnection through its exit to Belem and the Atlantic Ocean.

Thus, Lago Agrio, as a site geographically articulated to the Ecuadorian capital and the Pacific Ocean, would also be a nodal point toward Puerto del Carmen on the San Miguel River, very close to the national Putumayo River, acting as a multidimensional logistical support that provides wealth, cohesion, but also defense for this important and strategic sector of the South American Amazon.

Notes

Note: The authors appreciate the cooperation of Diana Calero in the validation and editing of maps.

1 Based on field diaries mainly from researcher Patricio Trujillo, for more than 20 years in the Ecuadorian Amazon region and in the space analyzed here, accompanied by complementary field notes from researcher Milton Reyes, during the years 2000–2003 in the same area of the Province of Sucumbíos. In the first case, the validity of the "everyday life" methodology is also appealed (Caughey 1982). The confidentiality of some oral sources is maintained following the customary practice method.
2 *Colonos* [settlers] has been the word that condenses the way of self-identification of the migrant populations of the Oriente [East] (Trujillo 2009).
3 The concept of modern is taken here as the project that leads to "modernity." Arturo Escobar (1993) understands modern and modernity by relating it to the economic and political development projects of nation-states.

References

Caughey, John L. 1982. The Ethnography of Everyday Life: Theories and Methods for American Culture Studies. *American Quarterly*, 34(3):222–243.

Collier, S.J. and A. Ong. 2005. Global Assemblages, Anthropological Problems. In S.J. Collier and A. Ong (eds) *Global Assemblages: Technology, Politics, and Ethics as Anthropological Problems*. Malden, MA: Blackwell.

Costa, Wanderley Messias. 2005. *Geografia política e geopolítica: discursos sobre o território e o poder* [Political and Geopolitical Geography: Discourses on Territory and Power]. São Paulo: Edus/Hucitec.

Cox, Robert W. 1993. Fuerzas Sociales, Estado y Ordenes Mundiales: Más allá de las Relaciones Internacionales [Social Forces, State and World Orders: Beyond International Relations]. In Abelardo Morales (ed) *El Poder y el Orden Mundial*. Costa Rica: FLACSO.

Escobar, Arturo. 1993. *Encountering Development: The making and Unmaking of the Third World1945-1992*. Northampton: Dept. of Anthropology, Smith College.

Fiori, Jose Luís. 2009. O poder global e a nova geopolítica das nações [Global Power and the New Geopolitics of Nations]. *Crítica y Emancipación*, 2:157–183.

Instituto Nacional de Estadística y Censos—INEC. 2010. *Censo de población y Vivienda* [Population and Housing Census]. Quito, Ecuador.

Jansson, Oscar. 2008. *The Cursed Leaf. An Anthropology of the Political Economy of Cocaine Production in Southern Colombia*. PhD Thesis, Uppsala Universitet.

Le Billon, Philippe. 2004. *Geopolitics of Resource Wars*. London: Routledge.

North, Liisa, Wade A. Kit, y Robert B. Koep. 2008. Conflictos por tierras rurales y violación de derechos humanos en Ecuador [Conflicts Over Rural Lands and Violation of Human Rights in Ecuador]. In Liisa L. North and John D. Cameron (eds) *Desarrollo rural y neoliberalismo*. Quito: Universidad Andina Simón Bolívar (UASB), Sede Ecuador, y Corporación Editora Nacional (CEN).

Ong, Aihwa. 2005. Ecologies of Expertise: Assembling Flows, Managing Citizenship. In S.J. Collier and A. Ong (eds) *Global Assemblages: Technology, Politics and Ethics as Anthropological Problems*. Malden, MA: Blackwell.

Ratzel, Friedrich. 1975. Ubicación y Espacio [Location and Space]. In *Geopolítica* (pp. 12–52). Buenos Aires: Editorial Pleamar.

Secretaría Nacional de Desarrollo—SENPLADES. 2015. *Diagnóstico Amazónico* [Amazonian Diagnosis]. Quito, Ecuador.

Taussig, Michael. 1987. Culture of Terror-Space of Death. Roger Casement's Putumayo Report and the Explanation of Torture. *Comparative Studies in Society and History*, 26(3):467–497.

Trujillo, Patricio. 2009. *Everyday Life on the Ecuadorian Putumayo Frontier*. Quito: FIAAM.

Trujillo, Patricio. 2013. La construcción de la etnografía del día a día en la frontera amazónica del Putumayo ecuatoriano [The Construction of Everyday Ethnography on the Amazonian Border of Ecuadorian Putumayo]. In Chaumeil Correa y Pineda (eds) *El aliento de la memoria*. Antropología e historia en la Amazonia andina. Universidad Nacional de Colombia, Facultad Ciencias Humanas.

7

POLICING INDIGENOUS LANDS IMPACTED BY HYDROELECTRICAL DAMS IN THE BRAZILIAN STATE OF RONDÔNIA

Rafael Ademir Oliveira de Andrade, Artur de Souza Moret, and Jean Carlo Silva dos Santos

Violence and Necropolitics Against Indigenous People in the Amazon and Rondônia

The western Brazilian Amazon, made up of the states of Acre, Amazonas, Rondônia, and Roraima, is known for its social and biological diversity. However, its reality is marked by high rates of violence resulting from the forms of occupation of urban and especially rural territories. The aim is to present general data on violence in Rondônia and a specific section on violence in the countryside and against indigenous peoples. The intention is to present the context of the police forces' actions in the region.

Rondônia is a Brazilian state located in the northern region of the country and limited by the borders with the states of Amazonas, Acre, and Mato Grosso, in addition to having a border with Bolivia. The state is a region of recent colonization due to its location in the far west of the country. The Portuguese confirmed possession of the region through the Treaty of Madrid in 1750, based on the right bank of the Guaporé River. The state's borders were demarcated in 1871. Rubber exploration was a relevant economic activity and in 1943 the region was elevated to the category of national territory with the name Território do Guaporé, later called Rondônia in 1956. The territory was elevated to the category of state in 1981.

The occupation of the state intensified from that moment on with migratory flows in search of fertile land at a reduced cost. As a result, there was a great expansion of agricultural activities in the state, particularly livestock and soybeans, in addition to other crops. This advance occurred mainly in areas occupied by forests. Recently, the state received investment in two large hydroelectric plants, Santo Antônio and Jirau, which were heavily criticized for their social and environmental impacts. Jirau, in fact, is the third-largest hydroelectric plant in Brazil.

In summary, the state's occupation process and its development strategies resulted in security problems. Rondônia is one of the three most violent states in Brazil in crimes against sexual dignity and property, and its capital, Porto Velho, had the highest rates of rape and femicide, with a rate 600% higher than the national average (FBSP, 2018). The neighboring state of Rondônia, Acre, has the second-highest occurrence of violence against life, and its capital, Rio Branco, had the highest homicide rate in the country in 2017 and 2018 (IPEA, 2019). Another important fact that confirms Rondônia's historical relationship with violence is that according to the Violence Atlas (IPEA, 2019), Rondônia is in the fifth place among the most violent states in the historical series 1980–2017, being first place between 1980 and 1990 and later (between 1990 and 2010), giving way to another Amazonian state, Roraima.

In the debate between development, which builds lasting well-being networks, and economic growth, which causes a temporary increase in resources in the region, the Growth Acceleration Program (PAC) of the Lula and Dilma governments promoted several infrastructure works in the state, but even thus, there was an increase in violence in the region. According to data from the Pastoral Land Commission (CPT), in its Rural Violence Reports (2008–2018), in the years 2015 and 2016, the state of Rondônia recorded the highest number of deaths in land conflicts, as it had the highest number of murders of human rights activists in the country.

Still on urban and rural violence in Rondônia, IPEA (2019) points to an imminent dispute for control of international drug trafficking routes in the region, which is one of the factors behind the increase in violence rates. To a large extent, the presence of drug trafficking is related to the state's proximity to Bolivia, a drug-producing region, as well as Peru and Colombia. Such problems are constantly addressed in local media and social networks (FBSP, 2018).

In relation to environmental crimes, Rondônia is the fourth state with the highest incidence in Brazil. The action of local land regularization and environmental protection bodies has proven to be incompetent and ineffective, whether in relation to prevention and punishment operations, as well as in actions to raise awareness among the population regarding the relationship between man and nature (RondôniaDinâmica, 2023).

Understanding the problem of violence in Rondônia in urban, rural, and indigenous environments is related to several factors. Among them, it is possible to mention a low level of investments in the public security structure with reduced effectiveness, a strong presence of illegal markets for primary resources (biopiracy, drugs, minerals, wood, land), and weak training of human resources. Furthermore, there is a low allocation of federal and state resources to populations in situations of social vulnerability, such as peasants, extractive communities, indigenous people, quilombolas, and riverside communities. The absence of policies for such groups reinforces the precarious situation in which they find themselves and the possibility of victimization.

Violence, Hydroelectric Power Plants, and Police Action in Indigenous Lands in Rondônia

Violence against indigenous peoples has always been a common practice in their relationship with the Brazilian State. The spatial and temporal focus on the indigenous issue assumes that a specific look is needed for the organization of the forms of such violence. Large infrastructure projects, such as large hydroelectric plants, change local political, economic, and demographic compositions, and increase predatory action on indigenous lands. This section will analyze such dynamics using local examples.

There are many forms of violence against indigenous populations in Rondônia, the most common in Rondônia being illegal logging (Andrade, 2021). Wood is the most commonly used form, both due to the price of selling the raw material and because it is the first necessary action when seeking to carry out other forms of illegal action in the territory: land grabbing (*grilagem*[1]), cattle breeding, plantation, mining, among others.

There is great fragility in the government bodies of the executive and judiciary operating in the state, which do not have the capacity for permanent control over the territory. In this way, the protection of natural resources and indigenous populations occurs through episodic actions that act punctually. After carrying out these operations, the predatory process resumes. This problem affects all institutions directly or indirectly involved in the application of environmental law in the state, such as the Military Police, the Federal Police, the Public Ministry of Rondônia, the Federal Public Ministry (MPF), the National Indigenous Foundation (FUNAI), the Brazilian Institute of Environment and Renewable Natural Resources (IBAMA). This situation is a sign of the fragility of state bodies in the region.

Furthermore, labor relations in the region are precarious and several reports of exploitation are observed. The most common method is the "per diem" regime—a form of semi-slave labor where only the day worked is paid at a very low rate, with daily payments of several days being common without the worker receiving any rights—or acting in accordance with their own interests (CIMI, 2017). This context contributes to the incidence of violence in the region, as well as in relation to indigenous populations.

In relation to indigenous lands, there is intense activity by illegal groups such as loggers, land grabbers, and miners who constitute true criminal organizations, which have a network and protection for their actions (APOIKA, 2017). As the lawsuit filed by the Karipuna[2] says against the consortium that built the Madeira Complex Hydroelectric Power Plants (HPP):

> Scouts remain in strategic locations and warn about any movement outside the local routine and especially about the presence of representatives from inspection bodies. They use an efficient communication network with amateur radio devices, which cover the entire region. A survey carried out by CIMI based on statements from residents, who only speak anonymously, listed scout observation points in restaurants, bars, private homes and even churches.
> *(Amazônia Atual, 2023, p. 01)*

APOIKA (2017) points out that the construction of HPPs in the Madeira Complex[3] intensified the illegal actions of people within indigenous lands with the support of a "criminal organization" that mixes public and private agents with the intention of illegally exploiting indigenous lands and other units of conservation in the state of Rondônia.

The problems are not new and the Amazon Working Group (GTA) published in 2007 the document "Organized Crime and Environmental Terrorism in Protected Areas of Rondônia," which highlights a serious problem in the region: the appropriation and sale of public lands.

In fact, the annex to the document presents a report produced by the Military Police of Rondônia on an investigation into sales of public lands in Rondônia by organized private agents.

The report points to the participation of people in the illegal sale of land in the region, with those involved occupying positions as councilors, lawyers, local leaders of the landless movement, and civil police officers. These agents act in a structured manner with a view to repudiating the actions of military forces and indigenous protection agents on the bureaucratic and practical fronts of operations. Those accused of committing these crimes were farmers, settlers, elected councilors, and former councilors (already previously arrested for selling Union land) working in the region. Furthermore, the report identified 15 logging companies acting illegally in the municipality. The report concluded that there was a criminal organization made up of politicians, local loggers, and land grabbers who were responsible for threatening the work of public agents in the region. The purpose of the threats is to eliminate barriers to the illegal exploitation of the region's natural resources, especially environmental and indigenous reserves.

Analyzing the above context, it is possible to point out that impact actions on indigenous lands are difficult to contain and extinguish by police forces, as they are not the result of individual actions but of structured organizations that involve public and private agents. The following article (one of the hundreds we found when searching on content aggregator sites) highlights the contemporary nature of the action:

> Last Thursday, the Federal Police (PF) carried out an operation with around 80 men and support from Ibama and Funai to remove invading loggers from the Karipuna Indigenous Land, in Rondônia, located south of the capital Porto Velho. According to information from the PF itself, the action was the product of long intelligence work and preparatory actions began to be taken at the beginning of this year. In total, the agents reached 12 deforestation points within the indigenous land that supply approximately 20 companies, including logging companies and sawmills located around the territory.
>
> *(Sanz, 2023, p. 01)*

The material collected at these 12 deforestation points supplied 20 companies, which was later legalized through a corruption scheme in issuing deforestation notes. Such false legalization of timber has been practiced for a long time throughout the Amazon and has not yet been effectively attacked by the State, as some reports point out at different historical moments (Adário, Ávila, 1999; GTA, 2007; Sanz, 2023).

Another document produced by FUNAI in 2011 addresses this problem. In this case, the "Survey Report on the Environmental and Social Protection Situation of the Indigenous People URU EU Wau Wau—Aldeia Alto Jamari" reports a routine inspection in the village took place without the support of the Rondônia Military Police due to the lack of budgetary resources and personnel. This scenario points to an impact on different scales, causing vulnerability and risk to the team itself, in addition to the inability to remove, even temporarily, the aggressors/criminals from within the indigenous land.

The precariousness of military bodies (low financial and human resources) reappears in other documents, such as the report "Inspection in the Karitiana Land 2000" (Kanindé, 2000), which pointed out the recurrent return of illegal miners to indigenous land after inspection actions such as one of the region's constant problems. The state's inability to maintain security forces in these indigenous areas is a constant structural problem in Rondônia.

In other words, the problem of the lack of presence of police forces around indigenous lands is opposed to the large organization of criminal action, leading to inefficient action by the bodies involved. Additionally, the precariousness of FUNAI observed recently (Cardozo, 2009) also impacts the reduction of formal policing in indigenous areas, as the action of the federal agency is essential to bring other state bodies into environmental protection.

This problem is also observed with regard to the renovation and installation of support and protection bases in the Jatuarana territorial space, following a request from the Gavião

People in 2016. As stated by the head of FUNAI's environmental and territorial management service (SEGAT) in Rondônia, illegal logging in indigenous land is very dangerous due to the violent actions of the criminals who carry it out. Considering this, it points out that the missions carried out there should not be carried out by indigenous people but by police officers (Kanindé, 2016).

The problem in question was the direct conflict between the Gavião People[4] and the invaders due to the ineffectiveness of official bodies that should, by law and the objective of institutional existence, repress these actions. Due to this incapacity for the overt action of police forces, the invasion of indigenous peoples' land has happened. Besides, the treats against environmental activists have been registered too (Kanindé, 2016). The aforementioned documents (Kanindé, 2000; Kanindé, 2016) point out the damage caused by the episodic presence of public agents in relation to the Karitiana, Karipuana, and Uru Eu Wau Wau lands in Rondônia. This absence makes it possible to constantly violate the rights of these populations.

The discontinuity of police action is highlighted by the Federal Public Ministry when it points to the lack of resources for maintaining bases around indigenous lands as one of the factors that increase violence against indigenous people. Additionally, it reinforces the need to invest in intelligence actions, and technical and anthropological training of Federal Police agents as fundamental points to increase their effectiveness in traditional territories (Andrade, 2021). Kanindé (2016) points out that the greater the presence of state agents acting directly on indigenous lands, the lower the action of criminals in these areas.

The document "Studies on the impact of indigenous peoples along BR 429—Alvorada do Oeste stretch, Costa Marques (RO)" highlights the impact of violence on indigenous lands close to BR 429[5] in Rondônia. Invasions of public lands in this region have a peculiar modus operandi. Land occupants, also called "posseiros," obtain financing from loggers to cut down the forest and open small paths inside the forest. In this process, they deliver illegally obtained noble wood to their financiers. The practice of such environmental crimes is recurrent and mainly affects the Uru Eu Wau Wau Indigenous Lands (less than 2.5km from the highway), Rio Muqui (direct boundary), Rio Cautário (3.6 km from the highway), Rio Branco (15 km from the highway), and Massaco (54 km from the highway) (Andrade, 2021). Such lands are repeatedly preyed upon by such criminal organizations.

Considering the documents analyzed earlier, the construction of hydroelectric plants on the Madeira River increased the impact on indigenous lands in the state of Rondônia. In return, there was no increase in investment in state or even federal police forces. Furthermore, the federal agencies responsible for protecting the environment and indigenous populations did not have an increase in material and personnel resources. Infrastructure megaprojects in the Amazon generate impacts beyond their initial objectives. Despite this, the ability to mitigate these negative effects is extremely reduced.

Conclusion

As described in this chapter, Rondônia is a state in the Brazilian Amazon that is among the most violent in terms of environmental issues and human rights. This problem impacts organized civil society, police forces, environmental and indigenous agents, as well as other actors linked to the criminal justice system who deal with this context in their institutional and cultural missions.

It is necessary to understand which are the main agents causing such violence. In the private sphere, there is a relationship between small invaders and a denser organization that has intersections between private people and state public power. Agents seeking to prevent impacts and violence work in this network.

Thus, the main cause of impacts on indigenous lands is the Brazilian State, through action in two central ways. First, due to its inability to prevent/mitigate risks and vulnerabilities in indigenous populations in the face of large projects such as hydroelectric dams. This is because this lack of institutional coordination does not take into account the fair impact on indigenous, environmental, police, and criminal justice system protection institutions that operate in a situation of financial, technical, and personnel precariousness (Andrade et al., 2022).

Second, the Brazilian State is also an active agent of the impact, as by promoting the construction of large hydroelectric plants it allows the loosening of environmental legislation, grants land around (and even within) indigenous lands, enhances policies for the expansion of predatory agribusiness, and does not monitor how and where such expansions will be carried out effectively, among other actions already highlighted in other works (Andrade, 2021; Da Costa Silva et al., 2020).

One point to highlight is the positive action of the Federal Public Ministry in petitioning other public bodies to defend indigenous rights in various situations, such as in the case of the construction of hydroelectric plants. Another factor that interferes with the protection of indigenous rights is the power games of those interested in indigenous lands. The corruption of political and state agents directly interferes with this equation (DHESCA, 2011).

Therefore, it is essential to strengthen and restructure environmental and indigenous protection bodies, police forces, and the criminal justice system operating in these territories. Finally, the training process of these agents who work in these areas is fundamental to understanding the problem, particularly regarding the humanistic aspect. The problems related to the state's capacity to protect indigenous lands in Rondônia are little studied and constitute a promising field of study for the future.

Notes

1 The term *grilagem* refers to the illegal occupation of public lands and appropriation through fraud.
2 Threatened ethnic groups with territory located between Porto Velho and Nova Mamoré gathered in the Panorama village. Available at https://pib.socioambiental.org/pt/Povo:Karipuna_de_Rond%C3%B4nia on 01/30/24
3 It is important to note that the Madeira Complex is made up of two large plants installed on the Madeira River, the largest tributary of the Amazon, and with a generation capacity of 3300 MW at the Jirau Plant and 3150 MW at the Santo Antônio Plant. The Madeira River is crucial to the ecological balance of the entire Amazon region.
4 "The Ikolen, also known as Gavião, speak a language from the Tupi-Mondé family. They inhabit the basin of the Lourdes stream and other tributaries of the Machado (or Ji-Paraná) river, in the state of Rondônia, close to the border with Mato Grosso. Its population is distributed across six villages, all of them located within the Igarapé Lourdes Indigenous Land, which they share with another indigenous group: the Karo." Available at https://pib.socioambiental.org/pt/Povo:Ikolen#:~:text=Os%20Ikolen%2C%20tamb%C3%A9m%20conhecidos%20como,divisa%20com%20o%20Mato%20Grosso on the day 01/30/24.
5 BR-429 is a federal highway created by the National Road Plan by federal law n° 5,917 of September 10, 1973. Its length is 339 kilometers (km 41 to km 380) and covers the municipalities of Presidente Médici, Alvorada do Oeste, São Miguel do Guaporé, Seringueiras, São Francisco do Guaporé, and Costa Marques.

References

Adário, P., D'Ávila, N. (1999). *À margem da Lei: Relatório sobre o consumo de madeira por empresas de compensados e laminados do Amazonas e sua relação com fornecedores de matéria-prima.* Brasil: GREENPEACE (Relatório sobre o consumo). Available at https://www.greenpeace.com.br/amazonia/pdf/margemdalei.pdf. Access in 05/05/23.

Andrade, R. A. O. (2021). *Dimensões e articulações dos impactos, as relações dos poderes Público, Privado e Povos Indígenas em Rondônia.* Porto Velho: Programa de Pós-Graduação em Desenvolvimento Regional e Meio Ambiente, UNIR (P.HD. Dissertation Thesis).

Amazônia Atual. (2023). *Povo Karipuna vive iminência de genocídio em Rondônia, diz procurador.* Porto Velho: Jornal Amazônia Atual. Available at https://amazonasatual.com.br/povo-karipuna-vive-iminencia-de-genocidio-em-rondonia-diz-procurador/ Access in 8/05/2023.

Andrade, R. A. O. de, de Souza Moret, A., César Silva Moreira, R., & Krauze Lopes, R. (2022). Structures and Precautions of the Fundação Nacional do Índio: Analysis of National Management Reports 2008–2018. *International Journal for Innovation Education and Research*, 10(9), 79–94. https://doi.org/10.31686/ijier.vol10.iss9.3888

Associação Indígena do Povo Karipuna Abytucu (APOIKA). (2017). *Pedido de Tutela de Emergência—no Procedimento 1.31.000.001373/2019–94*, Documento 1.1, Página 1. Porto Velho.

Cardozo, I. B (2009). *A reestruturação da FUNAI: Promessa do Caos.* Porto Velho: Kanindé.

Conselho Indigenista Missionário (CIMI). (2017) *Relatório: violência contra os povos indígenas no Brasil—dados de 2017.* Brasília: CIMI, 2017. Disponível em: https://cimi.org.br/wpcontent/uploads/2018/09/Relatorio-violencia-contra-povos-indigenas_2017-Cimi.pdf. Access in 07/20/2020

DA Costa Silva, R. G., Cunha, G. D. O. B., DE Campos Ferreira, R. A. A. (2020). Hidrelétricas, Direitos Humanos e alienação do território na Amazônia: Estudo de caso da UHE Tabajara-Rondônia. *Monções: Revista de Relações Internacionais da UFGD*, 9(18), 404–434.

Fórum Brasileiro de Segurança Pública (FBSP). (2018) *12º Anuário Brasileiro de Segurança Pública.* São Paulo: Fórum Brasileiro de Segurança Pública.

Fundação Nacional do Índio (FUNAI). (2011). *Relatório de levantamento da situação de proteção ambiental e social do povo indígena URU EU Wau Wau—Aldeia Alto Jamari.* Porto Velho: Kanindé.

Grupo de Trabalho Amazônico (GTA). (2007). *O crime organizado e o terrorismo ambiental em áreas protegidas de Rondônia.* Porto Velho: GTA.

Instituto de Planejamento e Economia Aplicada (IPEA/FBSP). (2019). *Atlas da violência 2019.* Brasília: Instituto Brasileiro de Pequisa Econômica Aplicada e Fórum Brasileiro de Segurança Pública.

Kanindé (2000). *Relatório de fiscalização na terra indígena Karitiana.* Porto Velho: Kanindé.

Kanindé (2016). *Ata de reunião do dia 18 de agosto de 2016 sobre vigilância da TI Igarapé Lourdes.* Porto Velho: Kanindé.

Plataforma de Direitos Humanos (DHESCA). (2011). *Violações de Direitos Humanos nas Hidrelétricas do Rio Madeira.* Curitiba: Dhesca Brasil.

RondôniaDinâmica. (2023). *Em 2022, Rondônia foi o 4º estado com mais crimes ambientais autuados pelo Ibama; Porto Velho também surge no topo entre cidades.* Porto Velho: Rondoniadinamica. Available at https://www.rondoniadinamica.com/noticias/2023/05/em-2022-rondonia-foi-o-4-estado-com-mais-crimes-ambientais-autuados-pelo-ibama-porto-velho-tambem-surge-no-topo-entre-cidades,160617.shtml Access in 05/08/23.

Sanz, R. (2023). PF retira madeireiros da Terra Indígena Karipuna, em Rondônia. *Revista Fórum.* Disponível em https://revistaforum.com.br/meio-ambiente/2023/5/12/pf-retira-madeireiros-da-terra-indigena-karipuna-em-rondnia-135799.html. Access in 05/08/23.

8
A POLYCENTRIC GOVERNANCE MODEL THROUGH THE AMAZON COOPERATION TREATY ORGANIZATION

Capabilities for Tackling Transnational Threats[1]

Carlos Alfredo Lazary Teixeira, Guilherme Lopes da Cunha, and Fábio Albergaria de Queiroz

Introduction

Amazonia is known for being the largest tropical forest and home to one of Earth's largest and most important biodiversity. Other legitimate arguments comprise expectations to guarantee its biodiversity, water resources, climate conditions, and desire to preserve it for future generations. Nonetheless, Amazonian countries deal with a gloomy scenario related to the emergence of transnational threats, in which under-developing conditions contribute to the expansion of illegal activities. Grasping this outlook implies analyzing ACTO as an institutional initiative, its evolution, and the responses implemented.

In this context, we verify strong indications that point to the unwanted consolidation of an Arc of Instability in the North-Andean-Amazon region. Political-institutional weakness is one of the main factors contributing for the rising organized crime networks responsible for the insertion of the subregion in the world market of illicit activities. So, how could Amazonian countries improve their decision-making process? Does it demand innovative institutional architecture? Or can we redraw initiatives already into force or consolidate and update existing policies to tackle transnational issues? Considering this scenario, we support the premise that the Amazonian States' absence or insufficient presence facilitates the growth of transnational criminal activities. This has turned the Amazon shared by nine countries into a space where the most varied threats thrive, affecting statecraft strategies. As a result, it forms one of the central geopolitical puzzles in South America.

About the challenges in the Andean-Amazonian sub-region, according to the words of Buzan and Waever (2003, p. 331), would we witness "a weakening of states, increasing external involvement, and much violence at all levels of society?" Thus, given the region's systemic deficiencies, which include the Andean-Amazonian countries, the state-building process is an essential dimension of security and defense realms (Fukuyama, 2004). Thus, as a means to make it feasible, we propose that the Amazon Cooperation Treaty Organization (ACTO) can potentially (i) coordinate capabilities to counter organized crime and (ii) strengthen its Rule of Law (RoL) effectiveness through the institutional framework of the Amazon Cooperation Treaty (ACT). It is worth saying that neither RoL was an aim or proposal considered in the ACTO foundation, nor was it created to deal with transnational threats or to promote RoL.

According to these circumstances, we analyze ACTO's vocation to facilitate collective action to improve RoL and coordinate actions to support Amazonian countries in finding stability. In the near past, it was expected that the Union of South American Nations (UNASUR) would be able to balance and structure proposals to institutionalize action against illegal transnational networks. However, while changing moods in South American Politics, meanwhile UNASUR's fragile structure dealt with the unstable effects of political backlash expectations—alternating between obstructing or defending it—ACTO has stood out as a relevant tool to confront transnational networks through a polycentric governance model[2] based on three different dimensions: political-diplomatic, strategic, and technical, as described in the following causal chain.

Thus, we analyze aspects of the Amazon Cooperation Treaty (ACT) regulatory framework through a qualitative approach in the context of polycentric governance, a decision-making architecture that combines intergovernmental and some supranational characteristics. Using primary and secondary sources, we suggest causal propositions between the variables of the causal chain that justify ACTO as an actor capable of providing RoL standards and halting transnational crime networks in the Andean-Amazon region.

Is There an Andean North-Amazonian Arc of Instability?

Richard Haass (2017) states that we live in a highly interconnected world. In his words, we are in World Order 2.0, where almost anything—threats and people—can reach anywhere, thus establishing complex relationships of interdependence. In this context, characterized by disruptive challenges, some unprecedented, "what happens within a country can no longer be considered an exclusive issue of that country" (Haass, 2017, p. 2).

In other words, overlapping threats from outside and within a region—as in the case of South America—demands coordinated responses. It offers opportunities to protect the interests of those who, to a certain extent, are affected by externalities resulting from environmental degradation, climate change, and the proliferation of organized crime.

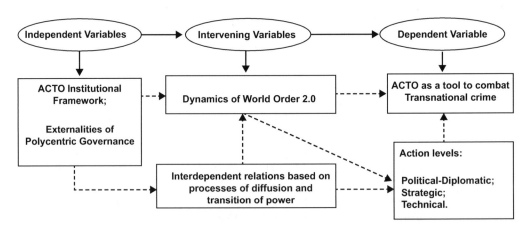

FIGURE 8.1 The causal chain[3]

That being said, we consider the understanding of Buzan and Waever (2003, p. 315) on disparities between the Northern and Southern parts of the South American continent. While the Southern Cone opted for the path of integration and the strengthening of mutual trust, having Mercosur as a pillar, the Andean North-Amazonian—our universe of analysis—in turn, keeps latent the reminiscences of a past of conflicts and rivalries in a scenario aggravated by endemic structural problems.

From a historical perspective, considering the specificities of each subregion, the facts point to the existence of two distinct areas of interaction in South America, both marked by instability of different natures. On the one hand, we have the Southern Cone, alternating between positive perceptions due to successful cooperative processes; nonetheless, domestic issues bring together skepticism about collective coordination through integrative entrepreneurial initiatives.

On the other hand, the Andean-Amazonian region shows a prevailing zone of instability, fueled by new threats that add to traditional issues on the subregional security agenda, all likely to cause "spillover effects." Because our analysis emphasizes Northern's Arc, this dilemma helps test the existence of a Polycephalic Geopolitical Model, in which each Amazonian State represents a head, underlining national interests; nonetheless, each one bonded to a standard body to protect the basin, the biome, the rainforest, its socio-biodiversity, and its strategic assets. Considering the ecosystem's integrity, critical topics in Amazonia's agenda—transnational threats and RoL—should be marked by common ground in the national interests to protect its natural resources and socioeconomic development.

Thus, it is worth highlighting that the Andean-Amazonian region encompasses countries with economic fragility, high levels of poverty, and a growing presence of criminal networks of varied nature and origin, especially drug production and trafficking:

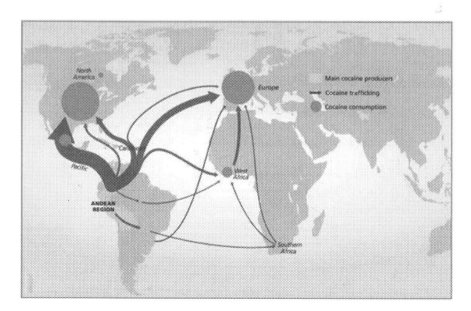

FIGURE 8.2 Cocaine flow routes from the Andean-Amazon axis

Source: https://www.oestadonet.com.br/noticia/11142/o-narcotrafico-ameacador/

These factors, in turn, encourage the corruption of Amazonian countries' local constituted powers. Consequently, they provoke the weakening of the capacity of the Amazonian States to deal with crimes that converge with the illicit drug economies, such as environmental devastation and the degradation of human rights,[4] especially in socially vulnerable groups (Naím, 2005). However, if, on the one hand, delinquency undermines local governments, the lack of governance also contributes to potentialize this dramatic scenario. As asserted by Ucko and Marks (2023, p. 93),

> wherever governments fail to deliver on human need, criminal actors capitalize on unmet desire or despair. For those excluded from the political economy, from patronage systems or elite bargains, organized crime can offer opportunity, possibly also protection. On aggregate, it amounts to an illicit form of governance, furnishing alternative services to a wide range of clients—be it the vulnerable and weak or a covetous elite. Reflecting the strength and resilience of this illicit order, those who stand in its way—individuals, institutions, even states—find themselves corrupted, co-opted, or violently eliminated.

Hence, poverty and organized crime spur each other, chiefly when the administration has difficulties exerting its clout to provide institutional weight. As Fukuyama (2004) states, these are catalytic events for instabilities capable of threatening security, in this case, at a regional level.

Therefore, there is a risk of the eventual presence of fragile or failed States[5] in this Amazonian scenario. The limited presence of effective multilateral instruments for repressing illicit activities in the Andean-Amazonian space leads us to reflect on Buzan and Waever's (2003) statement that the relationship between the nations of the North of the subcontinent presents an unstable interaction pattern. In turn, this context brings them closer to the definition of a security regime: a situation in which the States still consider some of their neighbors as potential threats; however, negotiated agreements are created to avoid the security dilemma in the area.

From UNASUR to ACTO

Based on different aims, purposes, and contexts, UNASUR and ACTO were designed to support specific political projects with few characteristics in common. They also differ in terms of historical context and geographic scope. Notwithstanding disparities, the political environment offers the opportunity to verify UNASUR's institutional fragility, which has been evinced since 2018, and henceforth compare it with ACTO. This is crucial in realizing how Amazonian countries could deal with transnational challenges.

As pointed out through the inferences, the threats and vulnerabilities in the Andean-Amazonian arc indicate a complex and diffuse agenda. These issues are marked both by transnational issues, attained to the endemic practices of illegal activities, and endogenic matters, derived from the profound structural fragility that characterizes some countries of the region (PCRS 2006, p. 2): some of them bring about prototypes of failed states "in which the institutions stopped working or were regimented for services of private interests, often illegal" (Naím, 2005, p. 57).

Still, in the context of efforts to build mutual and necessary trust, it is essential to mention that as a governance tool in South America, the signing of the treaty created UNASUR on May 23, 2008, in Brasília, Brazil. Congregating the 12 countries of South America (except French Guiana for being a French overseas territory, in an institutional conformation quite similar to ACTO), UNASUR emerged intending to promote its own strategic identity through South American integration in the economic, political, social, environment and infrastructure, as established in the Declarations of Cuzco and Ayacucho, both in December 2004.

In this sense, the creation of the South American Defense Council (CDS) should be highlighted in its structure. It was a strategic-military plan designed to promote, in the short and medium terms, a set of initiatives in the following thematic axes: (a) establishment of a network for the exchange of information on defense policy, (b) transparency in defense spending and economic indicators, (c) joint actions in cases of natural disasters, (d) exchange of knowledge acquired in peace missions, (e) preparation of a diagnosis of the defense industry of the member countries to promote complementarity in areas of strategic association, and (f) training and qualification of human resources through exchanges between military academies (Queiroz, 2012).

However, UNASUR suffered a severe blow in 2018. Under the argument of the entity's inefficacy, the foreign ministers of Peru, Colombia, Brazil, Argentina, Chile, and Paraguay—through a document addressed to the presidency of UNASUR, chaired by Bolivia, and represented by its Minister of Foreign Affairs, Fernando Huanacuni—announced that they would stop participating in the bloc's activities. In 2019, the host country, Ecuador, announced its withdrawal, considering that the regional entity had become a "political platform."[6]

From a geopolitical point of view, the scenario is complex and uncertain since the successful reconstruction of UNASUR depends on factors such as ensuring that a feeling of peace and stability in the regional environment is feasible. It is worth remembering that after 2018, under the denunciations of some countries, UNASUR became a "ghost organization" that formally existed but had no operational capacity.

Despite these setbacks, political voices are defending the renewal of UNASUR. For Nolte (2023), the report offered by Long and Suñé (2022) was an initiative since it proposed a broad analysis, considering socio-political and juridical approaches to justify a reactivation. This report encouraged other rounds of negotiation, paving the way for a meeting with 12 South American leaders held in Brazil on May 30, 2023.[7]

Despite regionalism under an incomplete construction, it is possible to verify the capabilities of ACTO, as an institution, to serve as an alternative for dealing with transnational threats in Northern South America's Arc of instability. In this scenario, we propose the instrumentalization, in the ACTO structure, of tools to combat organized crime through cooperation in three axes: political-diplomatic, strategic, and technical.

What Are the ACTO's Capabilities for Tackling Transnational Threats?

Located in North-Central South America, the Amazon region is immersed in countries with different vibrant cultures and united by common transnational dilemmas. It encompasses Brazil, Bolivia, Peru, Ecuador, Colombia, Venezuela, Guyana, Suriname, and French Guiana (French overseas territory). It occupies around 7,800.000 km^2, corresponding to 40% of the subcontinent's surface (Queiroz, 2012).

With 30% of the tropical forests, almost 20% of the available surface fresh water, and 1/3 of the planetary genetic stocks, the Amazon biome stands out in contemporary

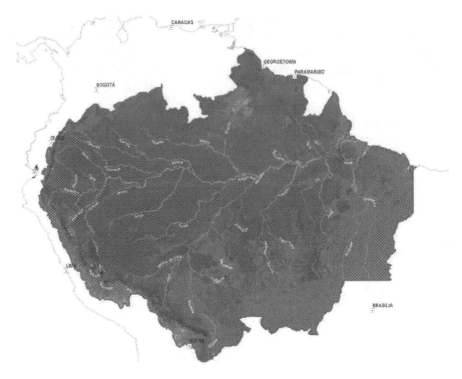

FIGURE 8.3. The Amazon rainforest
Fuente: http://otca.org/la-amazonia/

international debates for its incomparable natural resources and role in climate change and biodiversity. This motivates the idea that the Amazon is a vital issue and, therefore, many efforts led to the design of a governance mechanism, currently based on a Treaty (1978) and an Intergovernmental Organization (1998).

Thus, on July 3, 1978, the eight Amazonian countries signed the Amazon Cooperation Treaty (ACT). In summary, the ACT is oriented, through its 28 articles, to promote the harmonious development of the Amazonian territories so that joint actions produce mutually beneficial results for the region as a whole.

Over the years, ACTO's ability to meet its objectives has been much criticized, partly due to the great mistrust among the member countries (Queiroz et al., 2020). This normative framework, stemming from the images that the actors build of themselves and of those with whom they relate, shaped the Amazonian cooperative governance, as it is known, to mediate their mutual interactions. This represented an important step, though limited in scope and results.

Since 1988, due to substantial efforts, several institutional initiatives have strengthened collective entrepreneurship. Among the most prominent references, Special Commissions[8] paved the way to deal with topics such as Environment (CEMAA); Science and Technology (CECTA); Health (CESAM); Indigenous Affairs (CEAIA); Transport, Infrastructure and Communications (CETICAM); Tourism (CETURA); and Education in the Amazon

(CEEDA). Even though this institutional architecture was planned as a modern platform, these Special Commissions were not used as a unique tool for spurring proactive decision-making processes, as expected when they were created. The Belém Declaration (2023) recognizes the need to revitalize them and facilitates the creation of new commissions to promote effective Rule of Law.[9] However, notwithstanding efforts, it was not possible to create a Commission to deal with the problem of illegal menaces and correlated issues.

A milestone in Amazonian multilateralism was approving an amendment to the ACT, creating the Amazon Cooperation Treaty Organization (ACTO) in 1998. This constituted a new phase, reinforcing and strengthening the implementation of the aims established in the ACT. Within the framework of these efforts, the Permanent Secretariat was established in Brasília, Brazil, in 2002, with the objective of, according to the Amazonian Strategic Cooperation Agenda (ACSA), identifying the economic, political, environmental, and social priorities of the Amazon countries. In addition, for Teixeira et al. (2023, p. 83), the ACSA 2010–2018,[10] proposed in 2009, was the touchstone for launching the renewal of ACTO. According to Tigre (2017, p. 273):

> As such, eight years after the Permanent Secretariat (PS) was created, the organization went through a relaunch and strengthening phase . . . it welcomed emerging themes into the agenda, including climate change. Forests played a central role, with the discussion of policies that addressed several economic threats to the region, such as illegal deforestation, forest fires, and sustainable forest management policies.

This is how ACTO was born: an intergovernmental organization that is the only socio-environmental block in Latin America and that, through South-South Cooperation, seeks to establish synergies between governments, multilateral organizations, cooperation agencies, organized civil society, social movements, community science, productive sectors, and culture in the framework of the implementation of the ACT. In this sense, there is room for implementing ACT's articles VII and IX,[11] and converting socio-biodiversity in science, technology, and innovation assets, as asserted by Cunha et al. (2021, p. 155).

Meanwhile, it should be noted that in the institutional structure of ACTO, normative provision has yet to be formally established for the fight against transnational crime. In this sense, the political-institutional weaknesses observed in some Amazonian countries are one of the main factors responsible for turning the region into a kind of geopolitical black hole, or power vacuum, where organized crime networks and transnational illicit flourish: a topic of growing importance in International Relations and whose externalities are still not fully known.

According to Procópio (2007, 2010), due to these countries' common inability to fully exercise sovereignty and authority over their Amazonian territories, strengthening the Rule of Law in the region, which the author labeled as the "Periphery of the Periphery," assumes an important dimension of security, an essential component to maintaining regional order.

Then, faced with the complexity of a scenario in which the fate of its actors is inevitably intertwined, it urges us to reflect on factors capable of shaping the Amazonian geopolitical arena. For this reason, we underline ACTO's vision of the future that, in its breadth, in theory, allows the inclusion of the topic and, therefore, grounds our proposal for the institutional expansion of its capacities for action because it is:

> An Organization recognized within the Member Countries and internationally as a benchmark in regional cooperation, in discussion and positioning on issues on the international agenda related to the Amazon, and in the exchange of experiences, acting based on the principles of the whole exercise of sovereignty in the Amazon space, respect and harmony with nature, comprehensive sustainable development and the reduction of asymmetries of the States of the Region.[12]

A crucial step in this process is understanding the interests that unite the Amazonian countries around cooperative proposals. Besides, the effects and institutional mechanisms must be improved to face multidimensional challenges, including the exponential role of organized crime.

Final Remarks

As expressed in our causal chain, in World Order 2.0, externalities stemming from polycentric governance (independent variable) are necessary to face the contemporary challenges in the Andean-Amazon Arc of Instability. For this reason, the research design suggested that ACTO could combat transnational threats based on the three selected axes: political-diplomatic, technical, and strategic. Thus, as an example of verifiability—at the political-diplomatic and technical level—we highlight one of the main results achieved at the VIII Meeting of ACTO Foreign Ministers (2004): the inclusion of the topic "security and defense" in the field of Amazonian multilateralism.

This decision acquired a strong symbolism. It reflected a new reality, very different from the one that prevailed during the so-called defensive-protectionist period of ACT, notably marked by mistrust among the signatories of the treaty and which, as has been said, prevented the inclusion of sensitive issues in the negotiation process. Consequently, in the following Meeting of Ministers, held on November 25, 2005, in Iquitos, Peru, the Foreign Ministers reiterated their intention to discuss incorporating the issue as one of the vectors of Amazonian cooperation. Thus, on July 13, 2006, at Colombia's initiative, the First Ministerial Meeting on Defense and Comprehensive Security of the Amazon was held in Bogota (ACTO, 2005).

The Ministers of Defense and the delegations of the ACTO countries fostered a series of conversations to build cooperation mechanisms that would contribute to mitigating problems that could compromise the security of the Amazon countries. In this sense, two actions were highlighted: (1) the proposal made by the Peruvian delegation to create a Special Commission for the Defense and Comprehensive Security of the Amazon to support the sectoral policies of the strategic axes of ACTO and (2) the formal identification of the primary sources of threats that affect the region.

In this sense, due to its multidimensional nature and broad scope, transnational illicit activities were identified as a significant threat that affects the Amazon space and, therefore, would justify adopting emergency actions or special measures to solve the problems identified. As expressed by Camilo Ospina Bernal, then Minister of Defense of Colombia,

> in this context, the armed forces must be prepared to play a leading role in guaranteeing the integrity of the Amazon, especially in the extensive border areas where the action of the forces security is limited by the geopolitical singularities of the region.
> *(ACTO, 2006, p. 1)*

As a result, three central themes were established as a referential basis for the construction of a multilateral action agenda on security and defense matters: (1) counteract transnational organized crime, especially arms and drug trafficking; (2) develop a comprehensive surveillance and protection system for the Amazon; and (3) combat the trafficking of Amazonian flora and fauna species (ACTO 2006).

Finally, at the strategic level, the uncertain future of UNASUR activities reinforces ACTO as a possible alternative governance instrument to tackle transnational crime, even if in a complementary way or for a specific period. The implementation of the Amazon Regional Observatory (ORA) in 2019 has been the first step in this direction, albeit indirectly.

ORA promotes a great flow of information between institutions and intergovernmental authorities linked to the study of the Amazon, becoming a reference center for scientific-technological details on the topics established in the ACTO's Strategic Agenda. One of its tasks is collecting information on Amazonian biodiversity, such as the richness and abundance of species, endemism, degree of threat and vulnerability, and the illegal trafficking of species based on the Convention on International Trade in Endangered Species of Wild Fauna and Flora (CITES).[13]

Moreover, ORA is extending its monitoring capacity to dimensions other than the environmental one. This is partially realized through the creation of health modules (epidemiological surveillance, genomic mapping), indigenous peoples, commercial navigation, water resources (basic sanitation, drinking water, and solid waste), infrastructure (energy transition), and sustainable community tourism, among other subjects. So, through ORA, ACTO is blueprinting a progressive agenda in Amazonian affairs, which aims to encompass in its institutional structure the fight against biopiracy, frequently associated with other types of crimes such as money laundering or corruption.

ACTO builds the perception of an affirmative agenda in the Belém Summit and the XIV Meeting of Chancellors, held in Brasília on November 23, 2023. The creation of an International Police Cooperation Center (called CCPI Amazônia, supported by DAMAZ, the Brazilian Federal Police's Environment and Amazon Department) tends to bring together police officers from the eight countries to create and improve combined actions against cross-border illicit activities, such as the indiscriminate use of mercury, gold smuggling, and illegal trade of species under the aegis of CITES agreement.

These measures are being created to tackle the production chain and marketing cycle of cocaine base paste, from precursors to money laundering. Traceability, a way to track and monitor location, social conditions, and legal aspects of (licit or forbidden) Amazonian products, such as gold, coca leaf, and wood, is one of the leading technological improvements ACTO encourages to reach these goals.[14]

Other initiatives provided through the Belém Declaration (2023) unveil an avant-garde program. In addition to CCPI Amazônia, it deliberates the formation of an Integrated Air Traffic Control System between the State Parties, as well as convening a meeting of ministers and authorities from the public security sectors of the members. These three innovative topics prescribed in items 65 (CCPI Amazonia), 66 (Integrated Air Traffic Control System), and 67 (Public Security Meeting) of the Declaration reveal a collective action plan to combat transnational threats in the region through coordination and interoperability between States Parties' specialized bureaucracies (ACTO 2023).

A collaborative perspective between ACTO, NGOs, and partner institutions highlights the possibility for additional ORA monitoring modules, paving the way for generating important indicators for polycentric decision-making processes carried out jointly by public and private institutions and civil society. In cooperation with different partners,[15] efforts are being coordinated to combat illegal mining, as clarified in the 64th item of the Belém Declaration (ACTO 2023), besides the Technical Note on mercury contamination in the Amazon (WWF 2023).

Thus, ACTO operates with a positive agenda that employs strengthening and converging public policies to reduce the asymmetries between the TCA member countries in Amazon. In this context, creating a Special Commission on illicit acts is the natural path for a second stage. It is important to note that the Special Commissions have a deliberative character (accessory to chancellors) because they are conducted by representatives from the specific departments (thematic) of the governments of the member countries.

Finally, corroborating a polycephalic geopolitical model and recognizing the favorable moment in terms of opportunity and alignment of interests in an attempt to formulate a joint development strategy, the three axes mentioned in the causal chain must be in synergy, which implies two immediate measures: (1) the Permanent Secretariat to establish a Special Thematic Commission (STC), and (2), since ACTO's budget is limited, define a source of financing (funding) to support the activities of a working group in charge of proposing an action agenda for, then, the STC to be created.

Notes

1 Professor Fábio Albergaria de Queiroz initially developed this research during the 2022 Course on Combating Transnational Threat Networks (CTTN) held at the William J. Perry Center, Department of Defense, United States of America.
2 According to Elinor Ostrom (2010), polycentric governance is characterized by greater participation of sub-state and non-state actors in multilateral negotiation forums. As a counterpoint to the traditional and state-centric governance model, polycentrism has been highlighted (Ostrom 2010; Cole 2011) as capable of addressing problems characteristic of international regimes, such as the democratic deficit, lack of transparency, and low effectiveness of international agreements. The polycentrism proposed by Ostrom presents itself as a governance system focused on the collective management of common-use resources at different scales of interactions between the actors involved, especially when facing global challenges.
3 The variables selected for the study are listed in the causal chain. The so-called independent variable affects other variables: they are valuable phenomena to explain the characteristics or behavior of the object of study. Therefore, the dependent variable is what the researcher wants to explain regarding the influence of one or more independent variables. Finally, the intervening variable is

the one that, in a causal sequence, is located between the independent variable and the dependent variable, helping to explain the process by which the first influences the second.
4 Environmental crime constitutes nearly two-thirds of global illicit financing. It is one of the world's most destructive, fast-growing, and profitable criminal activities, including illegal logging, fishing, wildlife, and dumping of hazardous waste (FATF 2021; Earth League International & John Jay College of Criminal Justice 2023).
5 Gerald Helman and Steven Ratner published the paradigmatic article "Saving Failed States" in *Foreign Policy 1992*. This text is the starting point for discussing states considered "failed." At that time, it was noted that this typology of countries was proliferating in the International System. From then on, the academic debate on the topic discussed earlier took shape and gave rise to several other denominations, such as "Weak States" and "Rogue States."
6 Source: https://www1.folha.uol.com.br/mundo/2018/08/renuncia-de-chefe-expoe-situacao-de-penuria-da-unasul.shtml. Access on: December 15, 2023.
7 Consequently, expressing signs of collective dissent yet enjoying the opportunity for a leapfrog ahead, a contact group led by foreign ministers was proposed to analyze regionalism conditions. At the end of 2023, the contact group presented a favorable vote. However, without mentioning UNASUR, heralding, as stressed by Nolte (2023), is the end of magical regionalism based on speeches and ideological reciprocity, and it opens a window of opportunity for a pragmatic one.
8 As mentioned by Filippi and Vinicius Macedo (2022, p. 198), the Special Commission for Science and Technology in the Amazon (CECTA) and the Special Commission for Health in the Amazon (CESAM) were created during the 3rd Meeting of the Amazon Cooperation Council, in Brasília, in 1988. The Special Commission for the Amazon Environment (CEMAA) and Special Commission for Indigenous Affairs in the Amazon (CEAIA) were created during the 3rd Meeting of Ministers of Foreign Affairs of the TCA in Quito, Ecuador, in 1989. The Special Commission for Transport, Infrastructure and Communications for the Amazon (CETICAM) and the Special Commission for Tourism for the Amazon (CETURA) were created during the 4th Meeting of the Amazon Cooperation Council in Bogotá, Colombia, in 1990. Last, the Special Amazon Education Commission (CEEDA) was created at the 5th Meeting of Ministers of Foreign Affairs of the TCA in Lima, Peru, in 1995.
9 As reported in the fourth item of the Declaration of Belem (2023), Amazonian Countries expect to reactivate Special Commissions under the ACTO's platform and facilitate the creation of other subjects, such as in the public security sector. See ACTO (2023).
10 As mentioned in Brazil (2017), on January 1, 2017, The XIII Meeting of Foreign Affairs of Member Countries of the ACTO took place in Tena, Ecuador. According to ACTO (2017), it approved the Resolution RES/XIII MRE-OTCA/04, establishing that "The Declaration of the Heads of States of the Amazon Cooperation Treaty Organization (ACTO) adopted in Manaus on November 26, 2009, instructed the Permanent Secretariat to prepare a new Strategic Agenda of ACTO for the short, medium, and long terms in order to strengthen the cooperation process, to be implemented in a cycle of eight years. The process should end on December 31, 2018; The Amazonian Strategic Cooperation Agenda (ASCA) was approved by Resolution RES X/MRE-ACTO/05 of 30 November 2010, in order to build a comprehensive vision of the Amazonian regional cooperation, incorporating economic dimensions, as well as environmental, health, indigenous and tribal peoples, education, knowledge, science and technology, water resources, infrastructure, commercial navigation and its facilitation, tourism and communications and emerging issues, in order to promote the harmonious and sustainable development of the respective Amazonian environments. . . . [Therefore,] resolve to commend the success in the implementation of RES/X MRE-OTCA/05-Amazonian Strategic Cooperation Agenda 2010–2018."
11 Article VII defines rules for promoting scientific research and the exchange of information and technical personnel; on the other hand, article IX establishes standards for cooperation in scientific and technological research, aiming for the region's economic and social development. For consultation of the ACT Treaty (1978), see United Nations (1980).
12 Source: http://otca.org/quienes-somos/. Accessed on March 28, 2024.
13 The Convention was signed in 1973, came into force in 1975, and today has 184 members. According to Kilonzo et al. (2024, p. 1), "CITES is the main multilateral environmental agreement (MEA) created to protect at-risk species from unsustainable international trade."
14 It can be reached in different manners. In corporate accountability, as asserted by Schöneich et al. (2023, p. 954), "traceability allows companies, regulatory authorities, and right holders to

ensure and verify the accuracy of information related to a product's origin, composition, processing history, quality, safety, and labeling but also related to the compliance with environmental and social standards." In forensics analysis, using technological advances that can identify chemical signatures, among other methods, can be done through geochemical and isotopic traceability (Salvador 2023, p. 33), chemical and physical heterogeneity (Chapman et al. 2021, p. 1563), and X-ray Fluorescence Spectrometry (Ramos et al. 2023, p. 16).

15 The Igarapé Institute, Plataforma Cipó, WWF, the Institut de Récherches pour le Dévelopement, and the Federal Police of Brazil stand out.

References

ACTO—Amazon Cooperation Treaty Organization. 2005. *Declaración de Iquitos* [Declaration of Iquitos]. November 25. Retrieved from: https://otca.org/wp-content/uploads/2021/02/IX-Reunion-de-Ministros-de-Relaciones-Exteriores.pdf.

ACTO—Amazon Cooperation Treaty Organization. 2006. *Ata da Primeira Reunião de Ministros da Defesa sobre Defesa e Segurança Integral da Amazônia* [Minutes of the First Meeting of Defense Ministers on Defense and Comprehensive Security of the Amazon]. July 14. Retrieved from: https://www.resdal.org/ultimos-documentos/conf-min-sud.html.

ACTO—Amazon Cooperation Treaty Organization. 2017. *The XIII Meeting of Foreign Affairs of Member Countries of the Amazon Cooperation Treaty Organization: RES/XIII MRE-OTCA/04*. December 1. Retrieved from: https://otca.org/en/wp-content/uploads/2021/01/Resolutions-13TH-MEETING-OF-MINISTERS-OF-FOREIGN.pdf.

ACTO—Amazon Cooperation Treaty Organization. 2023. *Declaração Presidencial por ocasião da Cúpula da Amazônia—IV Reunião de Presidentes dos Estados Partes no Tratado de Cooperação Amazônica. Nota à imprensa nº 331* [Presidential Declaration on the occasion of the Amazon Summit—IV Meeting of Presidents of the States Parties to the Amazon Cooperation Treaty. Press release nº 331]. August 9. Retrieved from: https://www.gov.br/mre/pt-br/canais_atendimento/imprensa/notas-a-imprensa/declaracao-presidencial-por-ocasiao-da-cupula-da-amazonia-2013-iv-reuniao-de-presidentes-dos-estados-partes-no-tratado-de-cooperacao-amazonica.

Belém Declaration. 2023. Retrieved from: https://www.gov.br/planalto/pt-br/agenda-internacional/missoes-internacionais/cop28/declaracao-de-belem

Buzan, B. and Waever, O. 2003. *Regions and Powers: The Structure of International Security*. Cambridge: Cambridge University Press.

Chapman, R., Banks, D., Styles, M., Walshaw, R., Piazolo, S., Morgan, D., Grimshaw, M., Spence-Jones, C., Matthews, T. and Borovinskaya, O. 2021.Chemical and physical heterogeneity within native gold: Implications for the design of gold particle studies. *Mineralium Deposita*, 56, 1563–1588.

Cole, D. 2011. From global to polycentric climate governance. *Climate Law*, 2, 395–413.

Cunha, G., Queiroz, A. and Martínez, M. 2021. Biodiversidade, Biotecnologia e Poder: a Amazônia em meio às Estratégias de desenvolvimento da América do Sul [Biodiversity, Biotechnology, and Power: the Amazon amidst South American Development Strategies]. In: Buenafuente, S. and Gantos, M. (eds) *Políticas ambientais na Amazônia: sustentabilidade socioeconômica e povos indígenas* [Environmental Policies in the Amazon: Socioeconomic Sustainability and Indigenous Peoples], 142–160. Boa Vista: Editora da UFRR. ISBN: [978-65-5955-009-8]

Earth League International & John Jay College of Criminal Justice. 2023. *Environmental Crime Convergence 2023: Launching an Environmental Crime Convergence Paradigm Through Investigation of Transnational Organized Crime Operations*. Retrieved from: https://earthleagueinternational.org/wp-content/uploads/2023/06/ELI-Environmental-Crime-Convergence-Report-June-2023.pdf

FATF. 2021. *Money Laundering from Environmental Crime*. Retrieved from: https://www.fatfgafi.org/media/fatf/documents/reports/money-laundering-from-environmentalcrime.pdf

Filippi, E. and Vinicius Macedo, M. 2022. The conversion of the Amazon cooperation treaty into an international organization. *Revista Tempo do Mundo*, 27, 191–214.

Fukuyama, F. 2004. *State Building: Governance and World Order in the 21st*. London: Profile Books.

Haass, R. 2017. World order 2.0: The case for sovereign obligation. *Foreign Affairs*, 96(1), 1–9.

Kilonzo, N., Heinen, J. and Byakagaba, P. 2024. An assessment of the implementation of the convention on international trade in endangered species of Wild Fauna and Flora in Kenya, *Diversity*, 16(183), 1–13.

Long, G. and Suñé, N. 2022. *Hacia una nueva Unasur: Vías de reactivación para una integración suramericana permanente* [A New Unasur: Paths of Reactivation Towards Permanent South American Integration]. October 18. Retrieved from: https://cepr.net/report/hacia-una-nueva-unasur-vias-de-reactivacion-para-una-integracion-suramericana-permanente/.

Naím, M. 2005. *Illicit: How Smugglers, Traffickers and Copycats Are Hijacking the Global Economy*. New York: Anchor Books.

Nolte, D. 2023. *Unasul: do regionalismo mágico ao regionalismo pragmático* [Unasur: From Magical Regionalism to Pragmatic Regionalism]. October 22. Retrieved from: https://latinoamerica21.com/br/unasul-do-regionalismo-magico-ao-regionalismo-pragmatico/.

Ostrom, E. 2010. Beyond markets and states: Polycentric governance of complex economic systems. *American Economic Review*, 100(June), 641–672.

PCRS. 2006. Tendencias de Seguridad en América del Sur e Impactos en La Región Andina [Security Trends in South America and Impacts in the Andean Region], *Policy Paper*, 9, Mayo.

Procópio, A. 2007. *Subdesenvolvimento Sustentável* [Sustainable Underdevelopment]. Curitiba: Juruá.

Procópio, A. 2010. *Diplomacia e Desigualdade* [Diplomacy and Inequality]. Curitiba: Juruá.

Queiroz, F. 2012. *Hidropolítica e Segurança: As Bacias Platina e Amazônica em perspectiva comparada* [Hydropolitics and Security: The Platinum and Amazon Basins in a Comparative Perspective]. Brasília: Ministério das Relações Exteriores.

Queiroz, F., Cunha, G. and Oliveira, L. 2020. Reflexões sobre a construção de um Regime de Cooperação Amazônico: do Protecionismo Defensivo à Reinvenção Institucional (1978–2020) [Reflections on the construction of an Amazon cooperation regime: From defensive protectionism to institutional reinvention (1978–2020)]. In: Dias, J., Filho, J. and Araújo, J. (eds) *Direito e Desenvolvimento da Amazônia* [Law and Development of the Amazon], 517–534. Vol. 2. Florianópolis: Qualis.

Ramos, D., Ronchi, F., Geiser, G. and Adam, E. 2023. Programa Ouro Alvo [Target gold program]. *Revista Perícia Federal*, 19(52), 16–31.

Salvador, F. 2023. Rastreabilidade isotópica do ouro. Viável e promissora [Isotopic traceability of gold. Viable and promising], *Revista Perícia Federal*, 19(52), 33–37.

Schöneich, S., Saulich, C. and Müller, M. 2023. Traceability and foreign corporate accountability in mineral supply chains. *Regulation & Governance*, 17, 954–969.

Teixeira, C., Queiroz, F. and Cunha, G. 2023. Brazil in the geopolitics of Amazonia: Reflections on the construction of an international regime. In: Queiroz, F. and Cunha, G. and Barros-Platiau, A. (eds) *Brazil in the Geopolitics of Amazonia and Antarctica*, 69–92. Lanham: Lexington Books.

Tigre, M. 2017. Fifth period of cooperation within the ACT's framework (2009–2017): Revitalizing the ACTO. In: Tigre, M. (ed) *Regional Cooperation in Amazonia: A Comparative Environmental Law Analysis*, International Environmental Law Series. Vol. 13, 272–352. Leiden and Boston: Brill/Nijhoff.

Ucko, D. and Marks, T. 2023. Organized crime as irregular warfare: Strategic lessons for assessment and response. *PRISM*, 10(3), 93–117.

The United Nations. 1980. *Treaty for Amazonian Co-operation*, 70–76. Registered under v. 1202, 1–19194. July 3, 1978. Retrieved from: https://treaties.un.org/doc/Publication/UNTS/Volume%201202/volume-1202-I-19194-English.pdf

WWF. 2023. *Contaminação por mercúrio na Amazônia* [Mercury Contamination in the Amazon]. Technical Note. July 2023. Retrieved from: https://wwfbrnew.awsassets.panda.org/downloads/notatecnica_otca.pdf.

PART II
Policing Challenges in the Amazon

9
BEING A POLICEWOMAN IN THE AMAZON

Motivations and Everyday Routines

Ludmila Ribeiro and Alexandre M.A. Martins

Introduction

In recent years, attempts have been made to increase the number of women in law enforcement in Brazil and to address issues of gender discrimination within the profession. Some of these efforts have included training programs for women in leadership roles, as well as initiatives to encourage more women to join the police force. Nevertheless, police organizations are places where the "smart macho" is the most desirable profile, making gender discrimination part of daily life (Brown, 2007).

In Brazil, this process began in the first decades of the 20th century as a result of the impact of international feminist movements that began to reach the country, demanding greater freedom for women (Ribeiro, 2018). According to Mourelle et al. (2009, p. 1), the Women's Emancipation League (*Liga para a Emancipação da Mulher*), created in 1919 by Bertha Maria Júlia Lutz, the first woman to enter public service, had the objective of "expanding the civil and political rights of women, as well as increasing their valorization, through recognition of their space in society and their fundamental role in the private sphere, at the heart of the family." It is worth remembering that, at this time, black women were already inserted in the work market in a highly precarious form, in domestic occupations that were, in fact, vestiges of slavery (Oliveira Costa et al., 2019).

Soon, the feminist movement, led by Bertha Maria Júlia Lutz, would demand that middle-class white women be allowed to enter professions traditionally seen as a male preserve, such as those reserved for candidates with higher education (Carrington et al., 2022). It was, therefore, a movement that maintained a given social structure where sex (female) when combined with race (white/black) and social class (higher/lower) placed the woman either in a domestic environment in unremunerated positions or in spaces traditionally reserved for upper-class white men, just as the concept of intersectionality today proposes (Crenshaw, 2017).

This discussion has a direct bearing on the way in which police organizations became accessible to women in Brazil. From the outset, allowing the entry of women was conceived as a male benevolence to white women with higher education and, consequently, coming from higher social classes (Carrington et al., 2022). The police officer positions were, therefore, occupations intended for the daughters, sisters, and partners of some prominent men in the political field, given that the relations in the context of these institutions were eminently horizontal and marked by cronyism (Bonelli, 2003). The first organization to allow the entry of women was the Civil Police of São Paulo, which, in 1906, permitted women with a law degree to occupy the position of *delegada* or police chief (Bonelli, 2003).[1]

It was never a strategy intended to give opportunities for all women: few studied at law faculties (one or two women per intake, all white), and fewer still ended up practicing law since many were gradually forced to marry and eventually gave up the career. Bertolin (2017, p. 20) illustrates this situation when she notes that in 1930 just three women were registered with the Brazilian Bar Association of São Paulo, which did not represent even 1% of the total law graduates licensed to practice litigation in the locality.

According to Mott (2001), this situation began to change in 1934 when the Federal Constitution recognized the possibility of women entering public service, which started to include the police forces as a possible sphere of female work. In 1955, the Military Police of São Paulo allowed women to join its ranks, albeit very timidly and as a repercussion of the Second World War when professional organizations began to replace the men fighting on the battlefront with women holding university degrees (Grisoski, 2022). A virtual consensus exists in the literature here that it is only in the second half of the 20th century that women began "to be increasingly present in higher professions previously considered male bastions" (Bertolin, 2017, p. 19). This change included the legal professions in which women started to work as lawyers, prosecutors, and judges (Bonelli, 2003; Bonelli and Barbalho, 2008) and also the police forces, which opened their ranks a little more to women after the 1964–1985 civil-military dictatorship (Ribeiro, 2017).

The larger entry of women into Brazilian police forces from 1980 sought to respond to two specific demands. On one hand, the idea that women could assist in the transformation of the masculinity present in these organizations, making the police forces work less on the use of force and more on closer ties with the community, a strategy that requires skills that women supposedly "naturally" possessed, such as sensitivity and a capacity for communication (Ribeiro, 2017). On the other hand, the growing demand for police to intervene in gender-based conflicts, especially in the domestic sphere, to curb the female mortality rate, a task that would demand a specialized service, preferably coordinated by women (Carrington et al., 2022). The confluence of these demands became called the *lobby do batom*, the lipstick lobby, which enabled the "strategic articulation with diverse categories of rural and urban female laborers, domestic workers, healthcare professionals and police chiefs" (Pitanguy, 2019, p. 91) toward the inclusion of female issues in the 1988 Constitution of the Federal Republic of Brazil (CFRB/1988).

The inclusion of women as police officers in Amazonia responds to these pressures but also exhibits certain specificities. The process of migration to the Amazon region was especially intensified after the military dictatorship (Celentano and Veríssimo, 2007), making women a resource that could not be disregarded as a valuable asset for public institutions, including police officers. As some of the states today making up this area, like Acre, Amapá, Rondônia, and Roraima, were created by the CFRB/1988, their police institutions were already founded under a logic of prohibiting any sex discrimination on entry to the profession (Bonelli, 2003).

Considering that the police organizations in the Amazon region are more recent, which means that the paths involved in their institutionalization have differed from those observed in other states, the proposal in this chapter is to present (i) the women who perform the job of policing in Amazonia, (ii) their motivations for entering this occupation traditionally perceived as male, and (iii) challenges these women still face to practice an occupation that continues to be seen as male (Brown, 2007).

The Survey

To anchor this analysis, data will be used from a survey undertaken in 2015 on women in police institutions, conducted by the Brazilian Forum on Public Security (FBSP)[2] and the Center for Studies on Organizations and People (NEOP)[3] of the Getulio Vargas Foundation (FGV), with support from Brazil's Ministry of Justice and CRISP (Center for Studies on Crime and Public Security)[4] of UFMG (Federal University of Minas Gerais). The study aimed to understand how gender relations were constructed inside various police agencies.

The institutional arrangement of public security in Brazil is governed by article 144 of CRFB/1988. In 2015, the task of keeping order and combating crime was assigned to the following organizations: 3 Federal Police agencies, 27 Military Police organizations (performing ostensive policing duties), 27 Civil Police forces (the latter with judicial police power), and 181 Municipal Guards—formerly assigned to public asset protection and currently engaged in crime prevention (Table 9.1). Each type of agency follows a very distinct modus operandi, meaning that any research focused on individual officers and their gender relations must consider the specificities of these institutional frameworks.

In order to reach these different groups of officers, online questionnaires with password-controlled access were made available to all registered public security professionals listed in the Ministry of Justice's database. The use of the internet to conduct the survey is justified by Brazil's size, and our intention to reach the largest possible number of police officers, ranging from those working in state capitals to those based in the country's most remote locations. The resulting sample broadly reflects the wide diversity of policing in Brazil today. From the total number of questionnaires distributed, 13,055 valid returns were received, or about 2% of all those performing police duties throughout the country. The distribution of respondents was broadly in proportion to the distribution of organizations and the numbers of police officers—male and female—currently active in Brazil.

For the analysis presented here, the focus is on Legal Amazonia,[6] that is, an area equivalent to 59% of the Brazilian territory, which encompasses the entirety of the states of Acre, Amapá, Amazonas, Mato Grosso, Pará, Rondônia, Roraima, and Tocantins, as well as part of the state of Maranhão[7] (IPEA, 2008). The region also contains a large sociocultural diversity, home to no less than 60% of the 220 indigenous peoples living in Brazil (ISA, 2005). Of the total number of officers interviewed in 2015, 9% were stationed in Legal Amazonia, comprising 1,098 men and 290 women.

Area Under Study

Over the second half of the 20th century, the Brazilian state adopted a policy of providing incentives for the demographic and economic occupation of the Amazon region, which

TABLE 9.1 Police agencies and forces in Brazil: responsibilities and level of institutionalization in 2015[5]

Agency	Level of institutionalization	Responsibilities	Number of police forces in service in Brazil
Federal Police	Federal	To prevent and investigate federal offenses, which include crimes against the political and social order, and violations with interstate or international repercussions	1
Federal Highway Police	Federal	To perform ostensive patrolling of highways	1
Federal Railway Police	Federal	To perform ostensive patrolling of railways	1
Military Fire Brigades	State	To execute civil defense activities	27
Civil Police	State	To perform judicial police duties and to investigate criminal offenses, except federal crimes	27
Military Police	State	To perform ostensive policing and to maintain public order	27
Penal Police	State	To provide security inside penitentiary units	27
Municipal Guards	Municipality	To protect local assets, services, and facilities and to perform preventive policing	181

Source: Brazilian Forum on Public Security (FBSP 2015)

culminated in the transfer of thousands of migrants from other Brazilian regions, especially the Northeast. As an example of these policies, we can highlight the program espoused by President Médici (1969–1974), which concretized the territorial project of integrating Amazonia with the rest of Brazil.

Inspired by the slogan "landless men for lands without men," the National Integration Program (PIN)[8] was intended to create a solution to the problem of drought in the Northeast while simultaneously populating the Amazon. Based on the PIN, National Development Plans I and II (PND I and II) were implemented, which induced a mass migration of Northeastern workers in a context of the expansion of capitalism and the territorialization of capital (Dos Anjos, 2020).

In the 1980s and 1990s, there was a reduction in the flow of public investments in road and energy infrastructure projects in the region. However, the occupation of the agricultural frontier intensified due to the activities of logging companies combined with the expansion of cattle ranching, agribusiness, and speculation on federal land. For their part, the first decades of the 21st century have been marked by the increasing complexity of the actors and interests present in the region, which include significant investments with a large potential for intensifying deforestation: these include farming activities, the expansion of agrarian reform settlements, and the influx of private capital to meet the global market in the areas of mining, mixed farming, and timber extraction (Celentano and Veríssimo, 2007).

Today, Legal Amazonia is composed of 772 municipalities (IBGE, 2002), presenting a GDP equivalent to R$ 660 billion (9% of national GDP) and an estimated population of approximately 330 million inhabitants (14% of Brazil's total population) (Figure 9.1). Over

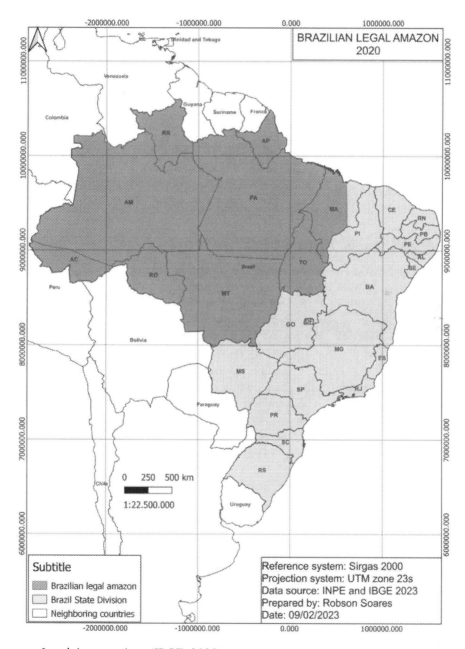

FIGURE 9.1 Legal Amazon Area (IBGE, 2020)

the past decade, the region grew 10.6% (in relation to 2012) while its share in relation to Brazil as a whole rose by 0.41% over the same period. As in other border regions, the male population is slightly higher than the female. The number of people identifying as brown (*pardo*) is around 70%, followed by approximately 18% white (Legal Amazonia, 2022). In relation to public security, the region stands out for the high rate of homicides in 2020 (31 per 100,000 inhabitants), second only to the Northeast region, which recorded a rate of 40.5/100,000 (FBSP, 2022). Legal Amazonia was also notable for the high rate of transport fatalities, presenting the highest incidence among Brazil's regions, with 20 deaths per 100,000 inhabitants in 2020 (Legal Amazonia, 2022).

In terms of policing activity in this area, women officers entered these organizations from 1980 onward. However, women are expected to present some similarities with their female colleagues working in the same organizations elsewhere (Ribeiro, 2017). At the same time, other skills are required of them in a region that entails a series of specificities when it comes to policing, given the extensive rural area, illegal wildcat mining, and the constant attempts to invade forest areas to transform them into pastureland for cattle ranching (FBSP, 2022). In the next sections, therefore, policewomen from across the country will be compared with those working in the Amazon region in order to determine whether differences exist between these police corps and the activities that they perform in terms of preventing and prosecuting crimes.

Women in the Brazilian and Amazonian Police Forces

In Brazil today women make up, on average, 1/5 of the total of police corps (FBSP, 2022). This number is higher than observed in other countries, especially in the Americas (Carrington et al. 2022). According to the review by Donohue Jr (2021), in the United States of America, policewomen represent approximately 18% of inducted recruits, a share that has remained relatively stable since 2007. According to UNODC (2018), the percentage of policewomen in the Americas countries varies 7% and among countries from 3% and 29% (Figure 9.2). Still, this figure of around 20% is far from being equal among the police forces and regions of Brazil as a whole.

Analyzing the difference between men and women stationed in the Amazon region and outside, it can be observed that the area had a slightly higher percentage of female police officers (18.5% vs. 20.9%—as shown by the average bar in Graph 9.1), a difference that is statistically significant ($\chi = 6.037$; DF = 1; $p < 0.050$). In part, this result can be explained by the prohibition introduced by CFRB/1988 on candidates being identified by name in public exams, which limited the elimination of female names before even ascertaining their knowledge (Bonelli, 2013). In the states created by the 1988 Federal Constitution, police organizations were already founded under the ideal of gender equality, which enabled a larger influx of women. Nevertheless, these organizations were perceived as places for "smart machos" (Brown, 2017), that is, for men capable of "running after criminals," but identifying them previously. This logic is reflected in the data organized in Graph 9.1, which indicates that in the majority of police organizations operating in Brazil there is a higher percentage of women working in the Amazon region compared to the rest of the country. This difference is especially relevant when we recall that there exists a higher proportion of men in the region compared to the overall Brazilian population.

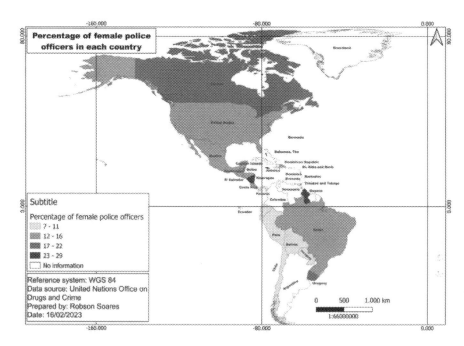

FIGURE 9.2 Percentage of female police officers in Americas (UNODC 2018)

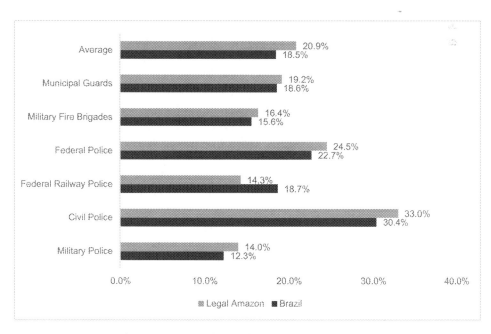

GRAPH 9.1 Percentage of women in Brazilian police organizations (Total and Amazon Region)—Brazil 2015

Source: Women in Police Institutions (2015)

According to the survey undertaken by Carrington et al. (2022), for it to be possible to create an environment in which gender discrimination is non-existent, the number of women in a force needs to be at least 25% of the total contingent. Following this criterion, only Brazil's civil police forces are moving rapidly in this direction, given that almost 1/3 of its officers are women, particularly in the Amazon region. To some extent, this result would be expected, given that the transformation of police organizations, in terms of a new openness to issues of crimes and violence that affect women especially, occurred through this institution with the creation of police stations specialized in providing assistance to women in 1985 (Debert and Gregori, 2008).[9] However, as Ribeiro (2017) problematizes, this opening did not signify a democratization of the service but a ghettoization by creating a captive location where women were expected to work irrespective of their education and training for the job.

Understanding the extent to which women who work in the Amazon region manage, within the context of their corporations, to construct some degree of gender equality, rather than reifying the experience of ghettoization as emerges when we focus on Brazil as a whole (Ribeiro, 2017, 2018), will be the objective of the next section. To this end, we will compare the women officers working in the nine states of Legal Amazonia (290 interviewees) with those performing their activities in other localities of the country (2119 interviewees).

Who Are the Policewomen in the Amazon Region?

The policewomen who work in the nine states making up Legal Amazonia are similar to the other participants of the survey in terms of age and children. The large majority are aged up to 45 years old and, reflecting the age range in which they are found, a little over half are also involved in childcare. On the other hand, the women differ substantially in terms of race and schooling, as indicated by the data summarized in Table 9.2.

The majority of women who work as police officers in Amazonia identify as brown (59%), with three times more indigenous women working in the region in comparison to the ones stationed in other Brazilian states (0.30% vs. 0.10%). According to Donohue Jr (2021), in localities where larger minority populations exist, the police forces tend to reflect this diversity, which would explain the enormous presence of brown women among the Amazonian police. As this region was colonized later, attracting poor migrants from different states of Brazil, above all from the Northeast, with the promise of better living conditions, it has ended up being a blacker region too than the wealthier states (like Minas Gerais and São Paulo).

The percentage of indigenous women working in the Amazon police agencies is far below the indigenous population in the region (0.30% vs. 1%), indicating that police forces do not reflect the Amazon's racial-ethnic diversity. It is worth noting that the Amazon area comprises 15.5% of the total number of indigenous people in the country (Legal Amazonia, 2020), and the small percentage of people considering themselves as indigenous is due to the strong miscegenation between the detribalized indigenous populations and the representatives of the various successive waves of national and foreign migrants who arrived in the region. Hence, the higher presence of brown (*pardos*) officers is not a great surprise even when, historically, police work has been dominated by white men (Carrington et al., 2022). It is rather a reflection of the racial structure that characterizes the female population living in the region (Legal Amazonia, 2022).

TABLE 9.2 Percentage distribution of women police officers according to age, skin color, marital status, children, and schooling, per region where they work

	Outside Legal Amazon (%)	Legal Amazon (%)
Age		
18 to 25	16.50	18.60
26 to 35	8.50	10.00
36 to 45	38.70	43.10
46 to 55	26.60	22.40
Above 56	9.70	5.90
Total	100.00	100.00
$\chi = 8.304$; DF = 4; p > 0.050		
Skin color		
White	52.90	29.70
Black	9.10	7.90
Brown	35.60	59.30
Yellow	1.40	1.70
Indigenous	0.10	0.30
Other	0.80	1.00
Total	100.00	100.00
$\chi = 66.049$; DF = 5; p < 0.001		
Marital status		
Single	32.20	28.60
Married/in steady union	57.10	61.70
Divorced	10.00	7.60
Widow(er)	0.70	2.10
Total	100.00	100.00
$\chi = 8.969$; DF = 3; p < 0.050		
Children		
Yes	51.50	55.90
No	48.50	44.10
Total	100.00	100.00
$\chi = 1.197$; DF = 1; p > 0.050		
Schooling		
First grade—completed	0.10	0.00
Second grade—incomplete	0.40	0.00
Second grade—completed	8.80	3.10
Higher education—incomplete	14.70	15.20
Higher education—completed	36.50	24.10
Post-graduation—lato sensu (specialization) complete or incomplete	34.40	50.00
Post-graduation—stricto sensu (MA/PhD) complete or incomplete	5.10	7.50
Total	100.00	100.00
$\chi = 46.716$; DF = 7; p < 0.001		

In the review by Donohue Jr (2021), it was possible to observe that police forces with a greater diversity in terms of sex and race were able to implement community policing programs more successfully, given that the greater diversity of the police corps reinforces the commitment to equality vis-à-vis local residents. Though, perhaps it is impossible to expect a revolution within the police organizations to which the surveyed women belong, since the majority of them (58.8% outside the Amazon region and 60% within the Amazon region) state that they have relatives in the police, a barrier to transformation of police forces, as Vilarouca et al. (2022) point out.

According to Bonelli (2003), depending on the type of family connection, the new recruit creates a prior expectation of what police work is about, which in Brazil is frequently associated with an authoritarian model of policing. The standard model of the latter is the excessive use of force against darker-skinned and poor people (Ribeiro et al., 2023). As a consequence, the announced expectations of more democratic patterns of policing based on the racial diversity found among Amazonian women tend to be undermined by the inhibiting factor that the presence of relatives in the police force possesses in terms of police reform.

The good news is that the percentage of policewomen with postgraduate education (stricto sensu or lato sensu) in Legal Amazonia is higher than that found in other regions of the country. A possible explanation for this pattern is that the entrance exams in this region tend to be highly competitive, meaning that the best-prepared women enter the corporation and, consequently, have greater chances of climbing to positions of power (Ribeiro, 2017, 2018). On the other hand, the high level of education among policewomen may be the result of a lack of other occupations that combine a steady income and the advantages of public service, especially with regard to stability (Musumeci and Soares, 2004). Understanding which of these options applies to the policewomen of the Amazon region will be the topic of the next section.

Why Be a Policewoman in Amazonia?

The third item investigated was related to the motivations that the women identified for joining the police force, inside and outside the Amazon region (Graph 9.2). The main reason acknowledged by all the interviewed women for pursuing a career in the police was the stability promised by public service, which also affects the possibility linked to maternity. This is a pattern noted by Musumeci and Soares (2004) in their studies about Female Military Police Officers. According to them, since the CFRB/1988 prescribes that all women in public service have the right to maternity leave, as well as other benefits, such as the possibility of a reduction in work hours while breastfeeding and assistance with creche fees, police work became a possibility among other civil servant positions available in the job market.

The second motive identified by the policewomen who participated in the survey was "opportunity." As the entrance exam for the police tends to be less competitive than those for other legal careers, many female law graduates joined the police forces because of the "opportunity" they offered. This pattern was also something noted by Bonelli (2003) when surveying Civil Police Officers at the end of the last century. As a result, the women who perform their work as police officers in Legal Amazonia diverged substantially from their

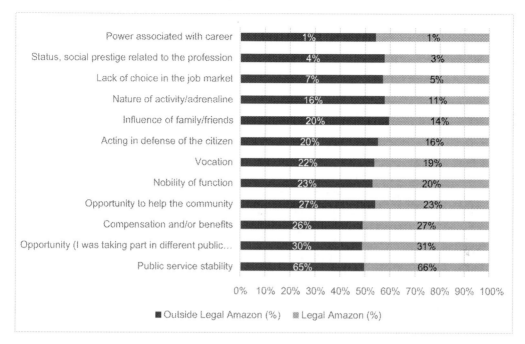

GRAPH 9.2 Chief motivations for women joining the police (inside and outside the Amazon region)
Source: Women in Police Institutions (2015)

colleagues in other states of the federation. Aspects such as the opportunity to help the community, or the nobility of acting in defense of citizens, which appeared as driving forces for the entry of women into the police in general (Ribeiro, 2017), were mentioned in substantially lower percentages by the policewomen working in the Amazon region. This finding indicates that typical dimensions of policing are overlooked by the women stationed in the Amazon region, which, according to Donohue Jr (2021), may further hinder the development of close relations between the police and the community. If women enter the police because they believe that outside the force they will experience greater difficulties, then it is reasonable to suppose that their relationship with citizens will also be neglected, generating tensions and conflicts with the public who they are supposed to serve (Vilarouca et al., 2022).

In this comparative analysis, attention is drawn to the 7% difference when it comes to the influence of family/friends in choosing a police career, with policewomen in Amazonia less susceptible to this pressure than the women active in other states. For Bonelli (2003), deciding to enter the police, as well as having family members working in the institution already, is related to the problems that this connection can cause in terms of work expectations or subordination. In the case of women, given the patriarchal culture, the presence of male relatives may signify the constant devalorization of the work they perform, comparisons, and a constant criticism of policewomen's performance as a whole.

What Are the Day-to-Day Activities of Policewomen in the Amazon Region?

One of the most problematized issues in terms of gender within police organizations is the "glass ceiling" (Ribeiro, 2017, p. 218). According to Brown (2007), the identity of the police profession is extremely masculinized, meaning that women are seen as "precarious" officers, since they were not born with the sex needed for good performance of the role. As a result, what is observed is the opening of these institutions to the recruitment of women, but their insertion in specific roles, such as those related to the administrative sector and the response to demands perceived as feminine (Ribeiro, 2017, 2018). This would represent what management studies call the "glass ceiling," that is, a barrier that appears invisible but prevents women from rising further in their careers because they are incapable of presenting themselves as "smart machos" (Brown, 2007).

According to Brown (2007), the "glass ceiling" will begin to shatter when women represent at least 35% of the total number of police officers. In the case under analysis here, even in the Amazon region, women represent on average 20% of all the professionals in active service who participated in the survey. In the view of Carrington et al. (2022), breaking the "glass ceiling" may be possible with percentages of around 25% if women can reverse the male tendency to pull them back from career promotions and positions of power.

Carrington et al. (2022) argue that some Latin American police organizations have, over recent years, begun to shatter this "glass ceiling" by resisting policies that take white men as the principal stereotype of the police officer. Among these changes is the removal of the maximum quota on women's entry, something that would help to increase the percentage of women working in the police forces. In Brazil, the "lipstick lobby" managed to overturn this veto in the civil and federal police, due to the presence of female police officers on the commissions that led to the Constituent Assembly (Pitanguy, 2019). However, the quotas remain in the military police and the military fire brigades analyzed here, but they were also included in the municipal guards, forces created after the CFRB/1988 indicating that "smart machos" are the stereotype of these police forces (Ribeiro, 2017).

The women interviewed in the survey confirmed this perception, reinforcing that "smart machos" are preferable to educated women in police forces (Ribeiro, 2017), especially the military police (Ribeiro 2018). However, among those located in the Amazon region, there is a greater perception that they are in positions similar to the men who passed the entrance exam at the same time as them (Graph 9.3), with this difference being statistically significant ($\chi = 9.450$; DF = 3; P < 0.050).

If there is a greater perception of equality, this may be due to the type of work that the women perform (Musumeci & Soares 2004). Since policewomen in the Amazon region have a better educational profile than those located in other regions of the country, it is to be expected that they are represented in higher percentages at the strategic and tactical levels rather than operational, which is closer to the frontline. As shown in Graph 9.4, this assertion is reflected in the data collected, with special emphasis on the higher percentages of women in leadership and managerial positions in the Amazon region compared to outside, with this difference being statistically significant ($\chi = 19.615$; DF = 7; P < 0.010). While almost one-third of policewomen outside the Amazon region are in an operational role—that is, actively policing in a strict sense, which frequently signifies dealing with women, children, and elderly people—in Amazonia, there are higher percentages of women directly running police departments.

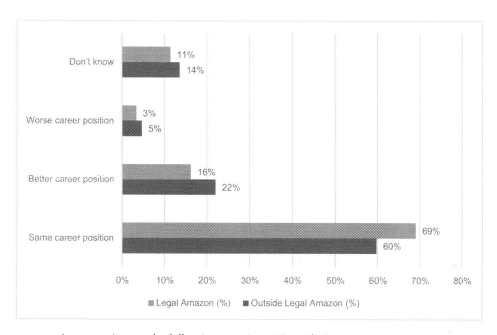

GRAPH 9.3 Answers given to the following question: "Considering your current career stage, compared to colleagues who entered the same competition, would you say that the men who passed the exam at the same time as you are now in the same career position?"

Source: Women in Police Institutions (2015)

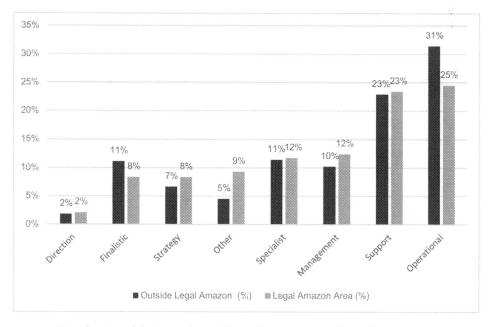

GRAPH 9.4 Distribution of duties performed by policewomen, inside and outside Legal Amazonia

Source: Women in Police Institutions (2015)

These findings are highly encouraging when we consider the challenges that the Amazon region poses in terms of processes of police reform. As Carrington et al. (2022) point out, the higher participation of women in managerial positions enables a more effective shift in police organizations toward prevention policies, especially when it comes to taking advantage of festivals and holidays to make the police presence in the community widely visible. Hence, the last point of our analysis involves understanding the difference between police work in the Amazon region and other parts of the country due to the place where this activity unfolds.

As emphasized earlier, the process of occupying the 11 states making up Legal Amazonia is still a challenge even today. Part of this region is occupied by dense tropical forest, constantly threatened by diverse illegal activities related to the extraction of natural resources from this territory (FBSP, 2022). Added to this is the absence of large metropolitan regions, which transforms the area of the state capitals into the center of all "civilized" life. This also gives rise to public order problems caused by the internal migration of people to these cities in search of better living conditions (Cardoso and Muller, 2008).

Women who work in the Amazon region are concentrated in two main areas: (i) the state capitals, which is necessary considering that the women occupy positions of command, whose structures tend to be concentrated in these localities; (ii) rural areas, which is also consistent with the specificities of the region, given the presence of huge rural areas in Legal Amazonia. On this point, the differences between these policewomen and those stationed outside the Amazon area are statistically significant (χ = 23.541; DF = 2; P < 0.001), confirming that this region has specificities that need to be considered in studies of policing.

The place of activity is a key component because it poses additional challenges for the exercise of an occupation that continues to be seen as a characteristic of the "smart macho" (Brown, 2007) or the "white man" (Donohue Jr., 2021). This occurs, in part, because the patriarchal system—in which men dominate women and what is deemed male is more highly valued than what is deemed female—is more visible in these areas (Chesney-Lind, 2006). In rural areas, this naturalization of women as the property of men could imply some barriers for an adequate exercise of police labor.

Policewomen in rural areas are also more susceptible to feelings of discomfort because of their gender, which immediately triggers the perception among their male counterparts (inside and outside the police) that they are incapable of performing the police role (Brown and Fielding, 1993). Consequently, women who work in the rural zone tend to suffer more sex discrimination or prejudice (Brown and Fielding, 1993), given that patriarchy functions here as a system of social stratification, which uses a wide range of policies and practices of social control to affirm male power and keep women subordinate to men. To balance police stereotypes and gender expectations, women stationed in rural areas can end up creating "women-only" spaces (Brown & Fielding 1993). However, this solution can result in the ghettoization of female police work as exclusively a gateway for cases of violence against women, reinforcing the very "glass ceiling" that needs to be broken (Carrington et al., 2022).

Final Considerations

If we consider the elements of the "glass ceiling" problematized by Connell (2006), it is possible to affirm, perhaps, that this barrier is less shatterproof in Amazonia than outside the region. The fact that the police organizations of these states were structured later, observing that Amapá and Tocantins, for example, were only constituted as states in the CFRB/1988, may have helped reduce discrimination against women, a possibility verified by the statistics showing higher access of women to police forces compared to outside the Amazon region. Although this does not mean the complete removal of the traditional stereotypes and preconceptions against women, the later institutionalization of these police forces may have afforced policewomen the opportunity for them to be more frequently represented in positions of authority (Bonelli, 2003).

The fact that more women are in positions of power in the police forces located in Amazonia compared to outside can be interpreted, from Connell's perspective (2006), as proof of the rationality of bureaucracy. Since these women possess high levels of education, with substantial percentages of them with specialization, masters' degrees or even doctorates, discrimination would be irrational, given that it would entail an underutilization of these women's talent. In the context of the Amazon region, therefore, the challenge appears to be the institutionalization of organizational measures that remove barriers to the advancement of women in their careers, such as eliminating prejudice and enforcing equal opportunity rules in the case of promotions. This challenge applies especially in the case of those women who perform their activities in the rural setting and who, perhaps, have not obtained the organizational recognition due to them.

It remains, though, to understand how schooling and race intersect in the Amazon region and to what extent black and indigenous women end up being overlooked for the higher levels of police work. Advancing in this debate means making effective use of an intersectionality approach (Crenshaw, 2017), a field in which police studies are still taking their first steps.

Notes

1 TN: In Brazil, the *delegado* or *delegada* is a chief in the civil or federal police, holding a law degree by requirement and acting as head of a *delegacia* or station, in the case of the civil police, or head of police inquiries, in the case of the federal police.
2 Fórum Brasileiro de Segurança Pública.
3 Núcleo de Estudos de Organizações e Pessoas.
4 Centro de Estudos de Criminalidade e Segurança Pública.
5 The Penal Police Force was created in 2019 following approval of Constitutional Amendment 104. This law recognized all correctional officers as police officers, charged with the duty of ensuring security inside penitentiary institutions. Presently the country has 27 Penal Police units, one in the Federal District and one in each of the 26 states. Together, they account for 12% of all police officers in service, a ratio of 45 officers per 100,000 inhabitants, making it the third-largest agency (Ribeiro, Oliveira & Diniz 2023).
6 Legal Amazonia was instituted in order to define the geographic limits of the policy region covered by the work of SUDAM (Superintendency of Development for the Amazon), created to promote the inclusive and sustainable development of the region and the competitive integration of the regional productive base in the national and international economy.
7 For the purposes of this research, the entire territory of Maranhão state was included.
8 *Programa de Integração Nacional*.
9 In Portuguese, *Delegacias Especializadas no Atendimento à Mulher* (DEAMs).

References

Bertolin, P. T. M. (2017). Feminização da advocacia e ascensão das mulheres nas sociedades de advogados. *Cadernos de Pesquisa*, 47(163), 16–42.

Bonelli, M. D. G. (2003). Perfil social e de carreira dos delegados de polícia. *Delegados de Polícia.* São Paulo: Sumaré, 31–68.

Bonelli, M. D. G. (2013). Profissionalismo, diferença e diversidade na advocacia e na magistratura paulistas. *Revista Brasileira de Ciências Sociais*, 28, 125–140.

Bonelli, M. D. G., & Barbalho, R. M. (2008). O profissionalismo e a construção do gênero na advocacia paulista. *Sociedade e Cultura*, 11(2), 275–284.

Brown, J. (2007). From cult of masculinity to smart macho: Gender perspectives on police occupational culture. *Sociology of Crime, Law and Deviance*, 8(1), 205–226.

Brown, J., & Fielding, J. (1993). Qualitative differences in men and women police officers' experience of occupational stress. *Work & Stress*, 7(4), 327–340.

Cardoso, F. H., & Müller, G. (2008). *Amazônia: expansão do capitalismo* [online]. Rio de Janeiro: Centro Edelstein de Pesquisas Sociais, pp. 40–54. A Amazônia de hoje. ISBN: 978-85-9966273-1. Available from SciELO Books: http://books.scielo.org.

Carrington, K., Sozzo, M., Ryan, V., & Rodgers, J. (2022). Women-led police stations: Reimagining the policing of gender violence in the twenty-first century. *Policing and Society*, 32(5), 577–597.

Celentano, D., & Veríssimo, A. (2007). *O avanço da fronteira na Amazônia: do boom ao colapso* (No. 338.9811 C149). Instituto do Homem e Meio Ambiente da Amazonia, Belém (Brasil).

Chesney-Lind, M. (2006). Patriarchy, crime, and justice: Feminist criminology in an era of backlash. *Feminist Criminology*, 1(1), 6–26.

Connell, R. (2006). Glass ceilings or gendered institutions? Mapping the gender regimes of public sector worksites. *Public Administration Review*, 66(6), 837–849.

Crenshaw, Kimberlé W. (2017). *On Intersectionality: Essential Writings*. New York: The New Press.

Debert, G. G., & Gregori, M. F. (2008). Violência e gênero: novas propostas, velhos dilemas. *Revista Brasileira de Ciências Sociais*, 23, 165–185.

Donohue Jr, R. H. (2021). Shades of Blue: A review of the hiring, recruitment, and selection of female and minority police officers. *The Social Science Journal*, 58(4), 484–498.

Dos Anjos, C. P. (2020). Migração Norte/Nordeste para a Amazônia Oriental/North/Northeast Migration to Eastern Amazonia. *Brazilian Journal of Development*, 6(10), 75526–75545.

FBSP. (2015). *9º Anuário do Fórum Brasileiro de Segurança Pública* [9th Annual Report Brazilian Security Forum]. São Paulo: Fórum Brasileiro de Segurança Pública.

FBSP. (2022). *16º Anuário do Fórum Brasileiro de Segurança Pública* [16th Annual Report Brazilian Security Forum]. São Paulo: Fórum Brasileiro de Segurança Pública.

Grisoski, D. C. (2022). Divisão sexual do trabalho no contexto da Polícia Militar: uma análise no campo da psicodinâmica do trabalho. *Psicologia Revista*, 31(2), 287–309.

Instituto Socioambiental (ISA). 2005. *Povos indígenas no Brasil*. Available at: http://www.socioambiental.org/pib/portugues/quonqua/ondeestao/indexon.shtm.

IPEA. (2008). Sistema de justiça criminal no Brasil: quadro institucional e um diagnóstico de sua atuação. Ferreira, H. R. S. A., & Fontoura, N. D. O (eds). Brasília: ipea.

Legal Amazonia. (2020). *Amazônia Legal, limites municipais e as posições das sedes dos municípios*. Rio de Janeiro: IBGE. Available at: https://www.ibge.gov.br/geociencias/cartas-e-mapas/redes-geograficas/15819-amazonia-legal.html

Legal Amazonia. (2022). *Amazônia Legal, limites municipais e as posições das sedes dos municípios*. Rio de Janeiro: IBGE. Available at: https://www.ibge.gov.br/geociencias/cartas-e-mapas/redes-geograficas/15819-amazonia-legal.html

Mott, M. L. (2001). Maternalismo, políticas públicas e benemerência no Brasil (1930–1945). *Cadernos Pagu*, 199–234.

Mourelle, R. C., Torres, A. C., Monteiro, B. M., de Oliveira, C., Fontes, L. A. S., & de Lima, S. M. (2009). A Federação Brasileira pelo Progresso Feminino e o governo de Getúlio Vargas na década de 1930: estratégias e paradoxos do movimento feminista no Brasil. *Colóquio Internacional Gênero, Feminismos e Ditaduras no Cone Sul*. Universidade Federal de Santa Catarina. https://www.coloquioconesul.ufsc.br/anais.html. Available at 12th October 2024

Musumeci, L., Soares, B.M., 2004. *Mulheres Policiais*, Rio de Janeiro: Civilização Brasileira.

Oliveira Costa, A., Arruda, A., Nascimento, B., Sorj, B., Alves, B. M., Barroso, C., & Carneiro, S. (2019). *Pensamento feminista brasileiro: formação e contexto*. Rio de Janeiro: Bazar do Tempo Produções e Empreendimentos Culturais LTDA.

Pitanguy, J. (2019). A carta das mulheres brasileiras aos constituintes: memórias para o futuro. In *Pensamento feminista brasileiro: formação e contexto*. Rio de Janeiro: Bazar do Tempo, 81–96.

Ribeiro, L. (2017). Managing gender relations in the Brazilian police. In *Police and Society in Brazil*. London and New York: Routledge, 89–108.

Ribeiro, L. (2018). Polícia Militar é lugar de mulher? *Revista Estudos Feministas*, 26.

Ribeiro, L., Oliveira, V. C., & Diniz, A. M. (2023). Are the Brazilian police forces lethal weapons?. In *Policing & firearms: New perspectives and insights* (pp. 33–56). Cham: Springer International Publishing.

UNODC. (2018). Booklet 5: Women and drugs: Drug use, drug supply and their consequences. *World Drug Report 2018*. Available at: https://www.unodc.org/wdr2018/prelaunch/WDR18_Booklet_5_WOMEN.pdf

Vilarouca, M. G., Ribeiro, L., & Menezes, P. (2022). Os policiais das UPPs e a crise permanente da segurança pública no Rio de Janeiro. *Revista Brasileira de Ciências Sociais*, 37, 108.

10

PROCEDURAL JUSTICE PERCEPTIONS AND USE OF FORCE AT THE CIVIL POLICE OF AMAZONAS

Eduardo Magrone, Vicente Riccio, Wagner Silveira Rezende, and Mario Aufiero

The Civil Police of the State of Amazonas

The organization of the Brazilian police is based on article 144 of the 1988 Federal Constitution and establishes the existence of police forces at federal and state levels, in addition to allowing municipalities to create Municipal Guards as support forces. The Union Police (Federal Police and Federal Highway Police) act in crimes of a federal nature and in patrolling federal highways. In turn, the aforementioned article establishes the competence of states to deal with the majority of crimes that occur in everyday life. Thus, the Military Police is responsible for the ostensible patrolling of the streets, and the Civil Police, also called the Judiciary Police, is responsible for investigating crimes (Lino, 2004; Sapori, 2018). In 2019, article 144 was amended and the criminal police were created with the responsibility to guarantee security in prisons.

Therefore, the Civil Police of the state of Amazonas is the State Government body responsible for criminal investigation. It was officially established only in 1922 (Law 3052/22) with the aim of adapting to the national requirements of the penal and criminal procedure code of the republican period. In the early days of the republic, it was not mandatory to have a degree in Law to hold the position of Commissar, as the lack of qualified professionals made it difficult to appoint graduates in remote and isolated regions of the country.

The current organization of the Civil Police of the state of Amazonas began with the promulgation of a constitutional amendment in 1971, which established the mandatory graduation to exercise the functions of Commissar. However, there were exceptions to that rule. This is the case of the so-called "provisioned" or "commissioners" who could perform functions in a specific location, in the absence of graduates. In the Amazon region, there are vast areas whose access is difficult, which is why provisions were widely used.

The 1988 Constitution abolished the employment of provisioned workers. After its promulgation, the police role of Commissar began to require a bachelor's degree in law and approval in a public examination (Dantas, 2009). In their organizational model, the civil police in Brazil have two entry careers with hierarchical divisions established between them. Thus, the Commissar, trained in law, is responsible for conducting the criminal

DOI: 10.4324/9781003330653-13

investigation. In a similar career situation are criminal experts tasked with carrying out scientific reports. The other career, hierarchically lower, is made up of investigators and clerks (administrative employees).

However, the most significant change in the organization of the Civil Police in the state of Amazonas occurred in 2009. From that year onward, a higher education requirement was established to work as an investigator and administrative officer. Thus, the Civil Police of Amazonas today has a greater number of professionals with higher education and not just in the Commissar and Expert careers. This hierarchical division generates conflicts between groups and for this reason, is the subject of criticism. This chapter addresses the perception of civil police officers in the state of Amazonas regarding the problem of procedural justice and the use of force.

Surveying the Civil Police of Amazonas

The data used in this research were collected in a survey carried out between November and December 2013 with the Civil Police of Amazonas. This is the only research carried out to date by this organization. The questionnaire was applied through a web survey as part of a project to discuss its operating strategy. The use of this means of data collection occurred due to the territorial extension of the state of Amazonas (1,559,167.87 km^2) and logistical difficulties, as the state is covered by tropical forests. According to the most updated estimate from the Brazilian Institute of Geography and Statistics (IBGE), the population of the state of Amazonas is 4,269,995 inhabitants. Due to the size of the state and budget restrictions, the questionnaire was administered via the Internet.

The instrument sent to members of the Civil Police of the state of Amazonas was based on a questionnaire prepared by Skogan (2015) for a survey of the Chicago Police Department. The focus of this research was on relations between the police and the community. Furthermore, it also involved attention to problems of procedural justice between police officers and their superiors. This questionnaire was translated into Portuguese and adjusted to the Brazilian reality. The final version of the questionnaire included questions about (a) the demographic profile of police officers; (b) their views on violence, justice, and crime; (c) their perceptions of their relationships with the community; (d) their view on the use of force; (e) assessment of the structure of the Civil Police; (f) reports on relationships with other actors in the criminal justice system; and (g) measures of career satisfaction.

After applying the questionnaire, 287 responses were recorded from 2,465 police officers, with a return rate of 12%. If evaluated based on the administrative database of the Civil Police of the state of Amazonas, the respondents are representative when it comes to characteristics of gender, function, and career length. Regarding the profile of the respondents, it can be said that the members of the Civil Police of the state of Amazonas are young. In general, 65% of respondents were under 40 years of age at the time the questionnaire was administered. Therefore, many respondents were at the beginning or mid-career. Among them, more than 90% had been working in the Civil Police for less than 15 years. This data is corroborated by the administrative database of the Civil Police of the state of Amazonas. Furthermore, there was a significant contingent of women, comprising 34% of respondents. As a result of the reforms mentioned earlier, 96% of respondents had completed a higher education course, and 80% had a postgraduate diploma. It is important to highlight that, in Brazil, a higher education or undergraduate course involves at least four years of study.

Regarding race, the majority, that is, 55%, declared themselves mixed race, and 39% were white. Those who identified themselves as Afro-Brazilian were 3%, Orientals 2%, and indigenous 11%. The ethnic classification used was based on IBGE criteria.

Procedural Justice and Developing Democracies

Currently, there is a wide variety of studies on procedural justice. The approaches encompass several themes, but the concern about how the law is applied is central. On this point, it can be said that most authors deserve to highlight the assessment of the exercise of authority and the influence on perceptions of fairness of procedures and the treatment given to citizens by state agents (Goldsmith, 2005). The interaction of citizens with state agents in courts of law or with the police is the focus of the analyses (Tyler, 1997; Eberhardt, 2016; Leben, 2019). Indeed, obedience and compliance with the law depend mostly on procedural justice (Hough, Ruuskanen and Jokinen, 2011; Terril, Paoline and Gau, 2016). Specifically, regarding police legitimacy, the studies bring together two analytical perspectives supported by social psychology and organizational institutionalism. In the first case, the approach prioritizes cooperation with the police and compliance with the law. In the second, the emphasis is on aspects related to the police organization and how external factors influence police officers' responses on a daily basis (Worden and Mclean, 2017).

There are four dimensions of procedural justice that are frequently highlighted by authors: participation (voice), neutrality, respect, and trust. Regarding participation, the concern is about the police's ability to allow citizens to express their demands. In turn, neutrality concerns the adoption of legitimate criteria for the exercise of power. Respect is associated with dignified treatment and the level of education of police officers on duty. Finally, trust is understood as the degree of consideration toward citizens and the well-being of the community (Tyler, 2004; Murphy and Tyler, 2017).

These four dimensions express the indispensable elements for establishing fair interactions between state agents and the population (Sunshine and Tyler, 2003; Tyler, 2011). The notion of procedural justice implies the adoption of a complex perspective regarding the conditions for the application of the law by state agents (Bradford, 2016). From this perspective, negative interactions tend to produce undesirable effects, such as the perception of humiliation, fear, and contempt. Similar feelings can be intensified in specific situations when there is a need to adopt "high-policing practices." In these cases, policing is directly or indirectly linked to national security issues and, therefore, tougher and more rigorous procedures are more frequently adopted. In such circumstances, the probability of illegitimate use of force increases enormously (Jonathan-Zamir, Hasisi and Margalioth, 2016). In fact, negative experiences with police forces produce unwanted effects whose variation is 4 to 14 times compared to positive experiences. In such cases, it matters little whether the encounter was initiated by the police or by citizens (Skogan, 2006). In short, "from a legitimacy perspective, every encounter that the public has with the police, the courts, and the law should be treated as a socializing experience that builds or undermines legitimacy" (Tyler, 2017, p. 257).

Studies on procedural justice direct their attention to the type of treatment that the police give to poor communities and ethnic minorities. Eberhardt (2016) studied police action in Oakland. There, the police stopped to check 20% of white people and 96% of black people. Police action displays the degree of social division. Tyler (2017) draws attention to the

Gallup poll in the United States, carried out between 2006 and 2014, on trust in the police. According to Gallup, two in three white people trusted the police, while only one in three black people had the same perception. In turn, Kang (2022) studied the repercussions of the Arizona state law (S.B. 1070), which forced members of the Hispanic community to present documents to immigration authorities. The law significantly diminished the perception of the legitimacy of local police in five American states: Alabama, Utah, Indiana, Georgia, and South Carolina. In Denmark, (Haller et al., 2020) found a negative perception of police action by young people from a ghetto whose origins were predominantly immigrants.

The organizational elements of the police began to be included in the research agenda on procedural justice. From interactions between citizens and police, studies began to address the positive effects of the application of procedural justice on police activity. In short, the objective was to explain how the application of procedural justice within police forces (IPJ) can lead to increased job satisfaction, alternation in jobs, increased commitment, and less repercussion of negative events (Haas et al., 2015; Van Craen and Skogan, 2017). Trinkner, Tyler, and Goof (2016) found manifestations of trust in superiors and reduced levels of stress, cynicism, and distrust in relation to life in general and the communities in which they operate due to the existence of internal procedural justice (IPJ). Van Craen and Skogan (2017) identified a positive correlation between the perception of procedural justice in the context of the organization and the appropriate use of force. A similar phenomenon was observed in Taiwan (Sun et al., 2018)

It is in Anglo-Saxon countries and North Atlantic democracies that most studies on procedural justice are located. However, some studies have already been carried out in Asian countries (Sun et al., 2018), Latin American and African countries (Hills, 2012) with varied research objects. Often, the organization of the criminal justice system occurs after violent conflicts. In fact, the fragility of state institutions, social inequality, high levels of corruption, human rights violations, and ineffectiveness of the criminal justice system tend to weaken the law enforcement power of the state (Frühling, 2009; Hinton and Newburn, 2009).

The legitimacy of the police is strongly influenced by the population's levels of trust. The relevance of such a consideration comes from the fact that the proper functioning of democracies depends on the functionality and equality of the criminal justice system. In this regard, the Brazilian case is exemplary, and one could even speak of a "Brazilian paradox," since the poorest population approves of police violence, while they are also the main victims of violent police (Caldeira, 2002). In turn, the perception of the police by the Mexican population as being highly corrupt and inefficient contrasts with the perception of the Federal Police, which is attributed to greater professionalism. A similar contrast arises from the predominance of patrimonial relations at the local level (Esparza and Uques Jr., 2020). Furthermore, the Argentine case reveals that the reduction in the effectiveness and legitimacy of the police may be the result of their weak professionalization and high political interference in their functioning (Flom, 2019). The implications of the perception of procedural justice for the assessment of police effectiveness and legitimacy were also observed by Tankebe (2008). In other words:

> In divided or authoritarian societies, sustained neglect and abuse of citizens is common as well as destructive of public regard for government. Government may take the form of a distant, often weak, state that has had little regular or positive contact with significant

sectors of civil society; their weakness typically makes them unable to perform basic state functions.

(Goldsmith, 2005, p. 449)

Studies on procedural justice are still scarce in Brazil. In research carried out among the population of the city of São Paulo, Zanetic (2017) observed that actions based on principles of procedural justice had a greater positive impact on the process of legitimizing the police. In short, the legitimacy of laws in association with procedural justice was more relevant than trust. Based on a survey carried out in the city of Porto Alegre, Rolim and Hermann (2018) observed low trust in the military and civil police. This survey also recorded lower confidence among young, poor, and black people in relation to police action, especially the action of the Military Police. Among the participants, 25.7% of black people were searched by the police at some point, while white people were 14.7%. In turn, Cubas et al. (2021) studied the perception of self-legitimacy in the São Paulo Military Police. In this study, effectiveness was considered the main predictor. By the way, organizational and distributive justice and the population's perception of police work were also positively highlighted. However, effectiveness was the strongest and most significant element. It is important to highlight that, in this case, the military ethos alone was not sufficient to define self-legitimacy, with the influence of society's perception also being important.

Based on the above considerations, it can be said that the topic of procedural justice is fundamental to understanding police action in Brazil and its repercussions on everyday life. However, this type of study does not have the necessary frequency in the country, especially in the Amazon territory. This is a relevant topic due to the changing dynamics of violence in the North of the country, now characterized by environmental problems, the growing presence of organized crime, and a visible increase in urban violence.

Field Research With Civil Police Officers in Amazonas

The data presented at this point refers to the section of the questionnaire on the relationship between police and the community. The questions in the section addressed the following themes: (1) community policing, (2) cooperation between police and the community, and (3) procedural justice (ability to listen to the community, treatment of citizens, and trust in citizens). To analyze the data, an index of police officers' perceptions regarding their relationship with the community was created. The index summarizes in a single variable the information provided by a larger set of variables organized under the same theme. Furthermore, as it is a numerical variable, the index allows a series of statistical operations aimed at understanding the phenomenon studied. Therefore, the index addresses police officers' perception of the importance of the community. This is a measure of the perception of importance attributed by police officers to relationships established with the community.

In turn, the index is made up of six questions from the research instrument (here, we kept the number of each question in the instrument). Each is a statement about a certain aspect of the relationship between police and the community. For all of them, the respondent should inform their degree of agreement, with six response alternatives (categories), from the highest to the lowest degree (completely agree, agree, somewhat agree, slightly disagree, disagree, completely disagree—categorical variables with a scale ordinal). The following questions make up the perception index about the importance of community relations:

13. It is naive to trust citizens.
14. Police officers should not "waste time" listening to citizens' complaints about their problems.
16. In certain areas of the city, it is more useful for a police officer to be aggressive than to be courteous.
17. People who break the law do not deserve to be treated with respect.
18. In the police profession, making judgments based on people's appearance is inevitable.
19. Explaining your decisions to the public is a waste of time.

Table 10.1 presents the percentage and frequency of categories in each of the variables. Regarding question 13 (naivety and trust in citizens), there is a balance between the answers. However, it is possible to observe resistance around trust when it comes to the population, as 33.6% somewhat agree, 19.8% agree, and 2.7 completely agree with the statement. In other words, around 56.15 of the respondents registered, in some way, naivety in the act of trusting. This is relevant, given that trust is one of the pillars of procedural justice.

Question 14 also addresses the topic of trust by relating "waste of time" and "listening to citizens' complaints." In this case, there is a predominance of disagreement in relation to the statement with 39.3% completely disagreeing and 45.8% disagreeing. In this sense, listening to complaints is part of the police officer's daily work. Question 16 asks about a topic directly related to equal treatment by the police (the utility of aggressiveness varying depending on the region of the city). The majority disagreed with this perspective with respectively 30.9% disagreeing and 19.8% strongly disagreeing.

For question 17 (People who break the law do not deserve to be treated with respect), 46.7% disagree and 25.3% completely disagree. The vast majority reject the statement with a bias in favor of procedural justice. Regarding question 18 (In the police profession, making judgments based on people's appearance is inevitable), 36% disagree and 16.9%

TABLE 10.1 Percentage (and frequency) by category of variables that made up the perception index about the importance of the community

Categories/questions	Strongly agree	Somewhat agree	Slightly agree	Slightly disagree	Somewhat disagree	Strongly disagree
13	2.7 (7)	19.8 (52)	33.6 (88)	17.9 (47)	24.4 (64)	1.5 (4)
14	1.1 (3)	1.1 (3)	5.3 (14)	7.3 (19)	45.8 (120)	39.3 (103)
16	3.4 (9)	13 (34)	21 (55)	11.8 (31)	30.9 (81)	19.8 (52)
17	2.3 (6)	4.6 (12)	9.6 (25)	11.5 (30)	46.7 (122)	25.3 (66)
18	0.4 (1)	13 (34)	23 (60)	10.7 (28)	36 (94)	16.9 (44)
19	—	3.8 (10)	10.7 (28)	16.4 (43)	45.8 (120)	23.3 (61)

Source: Data gathered Civil Police of Amazonas 2014

completely disagree. Finally, question 19 (Explaining your decisions to the public is a waste of time) has 45.8% disagree and 23.3% disagree. In general, most issues present a favorable picture of procedural justice. The exception is question 13 focusing on the relationship between trust and naivety. On this specific topic, skepticism regarding cooperation is evident.

To better understand the answers, it is important to record the relationship between the variables. Thus, the greater the degree of agreement with each statement, the less the police officer understands community relations as important for policing. The greater the disagreement, in turn, the greater the importance attributed to community relations. This logic presided over the transformation of categorical variables into numerical variables, with the attribution of numbers to each of the response alternatives. To build an index capable of revealing the importance of the community, the highest values were assigned to disagreement and the lowest values to agreement, as follows: completely agree = 1, agree = 2, slightly agree = 3, slightly disagree = 4, disagree = 5, strongly disagree = 6.

In order to guarantee the validity and reliability of the measure, correlations between the variables were tested (Pearson correlation). The result of Cronbach's alpha test was 0.708 for the 6 variables.

Therefore, a summative scale was developed. For each respondent, the values of the alternatives marked in each question were added. This generated a scale ranging from 6 to 36. For purposes of better understanding, this scale was reconfigured to range from 1 to 10, with 1 representing the lowest level of importance attributed by police officers to community relations and 10 representing the highest level, high in importance. Thus, the higher the value of the index, the greater the importance attributed to the community.

The perception index regarding the importance attributed by police officers to community relations, for the researched sample, presented an average of 7.12 (on a scale of 1 to 10), with a standard deviation of 1.39. This demonstrates, about the survey respondents, the importance of relationships with the community. This is a central aspect of procedural justice, as seen previously. Graph 10.1 presents the histogram with the distribution of respondents along the scale constructed for the index.

Perception Index Regarding the Use of Police Force

The use of police force is another dimension associated with procedural justice. In the research instrument, there were six questions on the topic, dealing with aspects related to permission, rules, and investigation of the use of force by the police. To produce a more

Categories /questions	Strongly agree	Somewhat agree	Slightly agree	Slightly disagree	Somewhat disagree	Strongly disagree
13	2.7(7)	19.8(52)	33.6(88)	17.9(47)	24.4(64)	1.5(4)
14	1.1(3)	1.1(3)	5.3(14)	7.3(19)	45.8(120)	39.3(103)
16	3.4(9)	13(34)	21(55)	11.8(31)	30.9(81)	19.8(52)
17	2.3(6)	4.6(12)	9.6(25)	11.5(30)	46.7(122)	25.3(66)
18	0.4(1)	13(34)	23(60)	10.7(28)	36(94)	16.9(44)
19	-	3.8(10)	10.7(28)	16.4(43)	45.8(120)	23.3(61)

GRAPH 10.1 Histogram with the distribution of respondents (frequency) along the scale of the perception index on the importance of the community

complex measure of this dimension, the same procedure previously adopted for the importance attributed to the community was adopted concerning the use of force. The index reveals police officers' perception of the use of force. In this way, the index allowed us to analyze how police officers perceived the use of force in their daily lives.

The index was composed of four questions present in the questionnaire:

24. In some cases the use of more force than permitted should be tolerated.
25. The rules for police use of force are very restrictive.
26. The police are not allowed to use force as is necessary in many cases.
29. The investigation of improper use of force within the Amazonas Civil Police is very rigorous.

For all statements, the respondent should mark their degree of agreement, having at their disposal the same six alternatives presented for the questions that made up the community's importance perception index (from completely agree to strongly disagree). For the four questions, agreement represents the police officer's adherence to the use of force, while disagreement represents the opposite.

Table 10.2 presents the percentage of responses by category for each of the four questions. It is observed, in all cases, the percentages of responses for the degrees of agreement were higher than the percentages of responses for the degrees of disagreement, indicating, in general, a propensity to support the use of force: 13.7% and 31.7% said they completely agreed and agreed, respectively, with statement 24 (In some cases, the use of more force than permitted should be tolerated); for questions 25 (The rules for the use of force by the police are very restrictive), 26 (The police are not allowed to use force as is necessary in many cases), and 27 (The investigation of improper use of force within the scope of Civil Police of Amazonas is very strict), the percentages of these two categories were, respectively, 14.5% and 38.9%, 15.3% and 36%, and 19.1% and 34.7%.

The categorical variables were transformed into numerical variables (totally agree = 1, agree = 2, slightly agree = 3, slightly disagree = 4, disagree = 5, totally disagree = 6), in order to allow the construction of a summative scale, thus time, with a range from 4 to 24 (Pearson Correlation results are attached; the Cronbach's alpha value for the 4 variables was 0.71). The scale was reconfigured to range from 1 to 10, with 1 representing less resistance to the use of force (greater adherence to the use of force) and 10 representing greater resistance (less adherence). Thus, the higher the value on the scale, the greater the resistance

TABLE 10.2 Percentage (and frequency) by category of variables that made up the perception index on the use of force

Categories/ question	Strongly agree	Somewhat agree	Slightly agree	Slightly disagree	Somewhat disagree	Strongly disagree
24	13.7 (36)	31.7 (83)	17.9 (47)	7.6 (20)	21.4 (56)	7.6 (20)
25	14.5 (38)	38.9 (102)	19.1 (50)	9.9 (26)	15.3 (40)	2.3 (6)
26	15.3 (40)	36 (94)	12.6 (33)	7.3 (19)	22.6 (59)	6.1 (16)
29	19.1 (50)	34.7 (91)	18.7 (49)	9.5 (25)	15.6 (41)	2.3 (6)

Source: Amazonas Civil Police Survey 2014

Categories/ questions	Strongly agree	Somewhat agree	Slightly agree	Slightly disagree	Somewhat disagree	Strongly disagree
24	13.7(36)	31.7(83)	17.9(47)	7.6(20)	21.4(56)	7.6(20)
25	14.5(38)	38.9(102)	19.1(50)	9.9(26)	15.3(40)	2.3(6)
26	15.3(40)	36(94)	12.6(33)	7.3(19)	22.6(59)	6.1(16)
29	19.1(50)	34.7(91)	18.7(49)	9.5(25)	15.6(41)	2.3(6)

GRAPH 10.2 Histogram with the distribution of respondents (frequency) along the scale of the perception index on the use of force

and the lower the adherence to the use of force. Graph 10.2 shows the distribution of respondents along the scale of the perception index regarding the use of force. By reading it, it is possible to notice a greater concentration of respondents at the bottom of the scale, which had a mean of 4.48 (scale ranging from 1 to 10) and a standard deviation of 1.96. With this, it is possible to affirm that police officers support greater discretion in the use of force and fewer restrictions on its application.

Discussion

The importance attributed to relations with the community and support or resistance to the use of force are two constitutive dimensions of the same phenomenon, procedural justice. Therefore, there is a relationship between them. The hypothesis presented here is the following: resistance to the use of force is correlated with the importance of the community, and the greater the resistance to the use of force, the greater the importance attributed to relations with the community.

To test this hypothesis using two numerical variables (the two indices created), a linear regression model was tested. Its dependent variable is the index of perception about the importance of the community, and the independent variable (predictor) is the index of resistance to the use of force. According to the null hypothesis (Ho), there is no correlation between the dependent and predictive variables. For the alternative hypothesis (H1), there is a correlation between the dependent and predictive variables.

The model results confirm that there is sufficient evidence to reject the null hypothesis (H0). In other words, there is a statistically significant relationship between the predictor variable and the dependent variable. The Pearson correlation between the two indices was 0.44. Analysis of variance (ANOVA) indicates a p-value (significance) less than 0.001, confirming the rejection of the null hypothesis. The coefficient of determination (R^2) was 0.19 (Fávero and Belfiore 2021), meaning that 19% of the variation in the perception index regarding the use of cameras is explained by the variation in the resistance index to the use of force. In summary, the simple linear regression model showed that the variation in the index of resistance to the use of force explains the variation in the index of perception about the importance of the community [$F(1, 257) = 61.984$; $p < 0.001$; $R^2 = 0.19$]. The variation in the perception index about the importance of the community corresponds to 5.73 + 0.061 * variation of one unit in the index of resistance to the use of force.

The results of the regression model used to show that support for the use of force by police officers partially explains their perception of the importance of the community, based on the relationship proposed by the hypothesis: the greater the resistance to the use of force, the greater the importance attributed to the community. The percentage of variation in our dependent variable explained by the independent variable is 19%, showing that other variables affect this variation and opening space for new research on the topic. In any case, considering the countless factors that can affect the perception of the importance that police officers attribute to the community, it is significant that 19% of the variation can be attributed to the use of force.

References

Bradford, B. 2016. Policing and social identity: Procedural justice, inclusion and cooperation between police and the public. *Policing and Society: An International Journal of Research and Policy*, 24(1), 22–43.

Caldeira, T. P. R. 2002. The paradox of police violence in democratic Brazil. *Ethnography*, 3(3), 235–263.

Cubas, V. de O.; Castelo Branco, F.; Oliveira, A. R. de; Cruz, F. N. 2021. Predictors of self-legitimacy among military police officers in São Paulo. *Policing: An International Journal*, 44(6), 1140–1153.

Dantas, H. 2009. The academic training of police chiefs. In: Sadek, M. T. (Ed.). *Police Delegates*. Rio de Janeiro: Edelstein Center for Social Research, 22–50.

Eberhardt, J. L. 2016. *Strategies for Change: Research Initiatives and Recommendations for Improving Police-Community Relations in Oakland, California*. Stanford University, SPARQ: Social Psychological Answers to Real-World Questions.

Esparza, D.; Urgues Jr, A. 2020. The impact of centralization and professionalization of law enforcement on public opinion of the Mexican police. *Journal of Politics in Latin America*, 12(1), 104–120.

Fávero, L. P.; Belfiore, P. 2021. *Manual de análise de dados*. Rio de Janeiro: LTC.

Flom, H. 2019. Controlling bureaucracies in weak institutional contexts: The politics of police autonomy. *Governance*, 33(3), 1–18.

Frühling, H. 2009. Latin American police research: Where do we go from here? *Police Practice and Research*, 10(5), 465–481.

Goldsmith, A. 2005. Police reform and the problem of trust. *Theoretical Criminology*, 9(4), 443–470.

Haas, N.; Van Craen, M.; Skogan, W.; Freitas, D. 2015. Explaining officer compliance: The importance of procedural justice and trust within a police organization. *Criminology & Criminal Justice*, 15(4), 442–463.

Haller, M. B.; Kolind, T.; Hunt, G.; Søgaard, T. F. 2020. Experiencing police violence and insults: Narratives from ethnic minority men in Denmark. *Nordic Journal of Criminology*, 21(2), 170–185.

Hills, A. 2012. Lost in translation: Why the Nigeria Police fail to implement democratic reforms. *International Affairs*, 88(4), 739–755.

Hinton, M.; Newburn, T. 2009. *Policing in Developing Democracies*. Abingdon: Routledge.

Hough, M.; Ruuskanen, E.; Jokinen, A. 2011. Trust in justice and the procedural justice perspective: Editors' introduction. *European Journal of Criminology*, 8(4), 249–253.

Jonathan-Zamir, T.; Hasisi, B.; Margalith, Y. 2016. Is it what or how? The roles of high-policing tactics and procedural justice in predicting perceptions of hostile treatment: The case of security checks at Ben-Gurion Israel Airport. *Law and Society Magazine*, 50(3), 608–636.

Kang, I. 2022. Beyond street-level procedural justice: Social construction, policy shift, and ethnic disparities in confidence in government institutions. *Governance*, 35(3), 737–755. https://doi.org/10.1111/gove.12593

Leben, S. 2019. Exploring the overlap between principles of procedural justice and emotional regulation in the courtroom. *Oñati Socio-Legal Series*, 9(5), 852–864.

Lino, P. R. 2004. Police education and training in a global society: A Brazilian panorama. *Police Practice and Research*, 5(2), 125–136.

Murphy, C.; Tyler, T. 2017. Experimenting with procedural justice policing. *Journal of Experimental Criminology*, 13, 287–292.

Rolim, M.; Hermann, D. 2018. Confiança nas Polícias: percepção dos moradores e desafios para a gestão. *Sociologias*, 20(48), 188–211.

Sapori, L. F. 2018. The dual and civil-military models of policing in Brazil. In: Riccio, V. V.; Skogan, G. T. (Eds.). *Police and Society in Brazil*. London and New York: Routledge, 29–42.

Skogan, W. 2006. Asymmetry in the impact of police encounters. *Policing & Society*, 16(2), 99–126.

Skogan, W. 2015. Police survey. In: Maltz, M.; Rice, S. (Eds.). *Envisioning Criminology: Researchers on Research as a Process of Discovery*. New York: Springer, 109–118.

Sun, I. Y.; Wu, Y.; Van Craen, M.; HSU, K. K.-L. 2018. Internal procedural justice, moral alignment, and external procedural justice in democratic policing. *Police Quarterly*, 21(3), 387–412.

Sunshine, J.; Tyler, T. R. 2003. The role of procedural justice and legitimacy in shaping public support for policing. *Law and Society Magazine*, 37(3), 555–589.

Tankebe, J. 2008. Police effectiveness and police trustworthiness in Ghana: An empirical assessment. *Criminology & Criminal Justice*, 8(2), 185–202.

Terril, W.; Paoline III, E. A.; Gau, J. M. 2016. Three pillars of police legitimacy: Procedural justice, use of force and occupational culture. In: *The Politics of Policing: Between Force and Legitimacy, Sociology of Crime, Law and Deviance, 21*. Leeds: Emerald Group Publishing Limited, 59–16.

Trinkner, R.; Tyler, T. R.; Goff, P. A. 2016. Justice from within: The relationships between a procedurally fair organizational climate and police organizational effectiveness, endorsement of democratic policing, and officer well-being. *Psychology, Public Policy and Law*, 22(2), 158–172.

Tyler, T. R. 1997. Citizen discontent with legal procedures: A social science perspective on civil procedure reform. *American Journal of Comparative Law*, 45(4), 871–904.

Tyler, T. R. 2004. Increasing police legitimacy. *Annals of the American Academy of Political and Social Sciences*, 593, 593–608.

Tyler, T. R. 2011. Trust and legitimacy: Policing in the US and Europe. *European Journal of Criminology*, 8(4), 254–266.

Tyler, T. R. 2017. Procedural justice and policing: Rush to judgment? *Annual Journal of Law and Social Sciences*, 13, 29–53.

Van Craen, M.; Skogan, W. G. 2017. Achieving fairness in policing: The link between internal and external procedural justice. *Police Quarterly*, 20(1), 3–23. https://doi.org/10.1177/1098611116657818

Worden, R. E.; Mclean, S. J. 2017. Police legitimacy research: The state of the art. *Policing: An International Journal*, 40(3), 480–513.

Zanetic, A. 2017. Ação institucional, confiança na polícia e legitimidade em São Paulo. *Revista Brasileira de Ciências Sociais*, 32(95), 329508.

11
PRESSURE ON THE BRAZILIAN AMAZON BORDER AND STATE DISCRETION IN GRANTING ASYLUM TO VENEZUELANS

Janaína de Mendonça Fernandes

Introduction

The chapter analyzes the capacity of the Brazilian state to manage administrative processes in light of Brazil's migration legislation and the flow increase of Venezuelans in the northern borders of the country, the Amazonian border. It is worth noting right at the beginning that such law, despite recent advances, is still restrictive, and it would not account for two important flows of migrants to Brazil, the flow of Venezuelans and the flow of Haitians. It is necessary to observe such flow through the observation of two normative resolutions of the Brazilian State described subsequently.

Hence, we will observe part of the administration of immigration in Brazil through the processes that involve the entry of foreigners, describing the function of each agency involved in the legalization of an asylum seeker in Brazil, we will describe the bureaucratic procedures for granting or denying of asylum in Brazil. With this, we intend to clarify the function of each agency involved, helping to advance research on this theme, and pointing out possible bottlenecks in the administrative process of granting asylum. Still, the text discusses the capacity of the institutions of the criminal justice system in dealing with this problem.

Lastly, the analysis will focus on the role of the Brazilian Federal Police in this process.

In 2017, the law No. 13,445/2017 was enacted. The law named Migration Law observes the rights and duties of the migrant and of those who are visitors in Brazil; in addition, it regulates the entry and the stay and describes questions regarding the permanence of the foreigner in the country. The law also establishes principles and outlines guidelines for public policies regarding immigration in the country. The law gives migrants rights and presents itself as an opportunity to improve the policy and migration administrative processes in Brazil. In theory Law No. 13,445/2017 could improve and facilitate the processes of legalization and permanence of immigrants in Brazil, which could impact on their insertion in the labor market, if applicable, and promote access to public services to which such an immigrant would have rights, such as health, education and social assistance.

It should be noted that Brazil was one of the first countries in South America to be a signatory to the 1951 Convention, which served as the basis in 1997 for Law No. 9,474 of July 22, 1997; the Statute of Refugees, which provides other providences, such as the creation of CONARE (Comitê Nacional para os Refugiados, in literal translation: National Committee for Refugees); and a tripartite deliberative collegiate council, responsible for granting asylum in the country.

In relation to the large flow of Venezuelans, mainly from 2017 on, through the normative resolution No. 126/2017, the citizens of this country who wished to live in Brazil should have a temporary residence visa. This stems from the Venezuelan economic and government crisis, which resulted in the current humanitarian problem. Despite the aforementioned normative resolution, Venezuelans who wish to escape the crisis and live in Brazil can apply for asylum when crossing the border.

According to the Ministry of Justice, the process of requesting and granting asylum in Brazil takes an average of three years. However, this time may be longer or shorter depending on the applicant's entry conditions, on their nationality, among other factors. That is, the process of requesting and granting asylum is long and time consuming.

In addition, the increase in granting asylum to Venezuelan citizens may be a strategy or option for Brazilian immigration policy, given that the State has discretion to grant refugee status in Brazil. That is, the State can prioritize the granting of asylum to a given nationality to the detriment of others, even with the existence of normative resolution No. 126/2017.

The present chapter aims to analyze the pressure of the flow of Venezuelans on the Amazon border (Roraima) and its impact on the action of state institutions responsible for granting asylum, with particular interest in the actions of the Brazilian Federal Police. Still, the work analyzes the discretion in responding the asylum requests at the border in view of the bureaucratic difficulties observed in the current administrative process.

Method

This chapter made use of quantitative and qualitative methodologies, covering asylum seekers in Brazil with a process in progress at the National Committee for Refugees (CONARE) from the year 2011 on. Data were collected on the CONARE website, where the solicitations of recognition of refugee status in the *Refúgio em Números e Publicações* (Asylum in Numbers and Publications) section are found in a consolidated way (https://www.justica.gov.br/seus-direitos/refugio/refugio-em-numeros). These data are public, tabulated, and previously organized through reports accessible to anyone interested in the subject. Due to its presentation, there is a limitation on possible statistical crossings, that may limit some research conclusions. In addition, the research also used a qualitative methodology, through a bibliographical survey, through which a traditional narrative review was carried out.

The traditional narrative review does not use an exhaustive search on the subject in the literature and does not exhaust the sources of information, nor does it use the systematic survey technique. The methodology allows to search for texts on themes related to the object of study and is subject to the subjectivity of the authors, giving greater freedom in the use and consolidation of the theoretical framework. This procedure is applicable to academic works and facilitates the articulation of concepts to support the research carried out (Vosgerau and Romanowski, 2014).

By means of the legislation and consultation with the websites of ministries and official Brazilian and international agencies involved in the application process of asylum in Brazil, it was possible to map how an asylum seeker is given entry and legalized in Brazil. This mapping made it possible to describe the administrative process of granting asylum, as well as to observe its main problems and point out possible improvements in light of the new law in force. The analysis of documents (laws, normative resolutions, executive decrees, and other regulations) made it possible to observe the performance of each of the agencies. In this way, it was possible to understand the role of each of the agencies until the granting of refugee status to the applicant.

This mapping allowed to observe critically the administrative process of asylum request, highlighting possible bottlenecks through the design of diagrams and the observation of the number of existing and judged requests. In addition, we were able to observe the change in the profile of the applicant over time, with a considerable increase in the number of Venezuelans applying for asylum in Brazil. Particularly, there was an increase in requests in the state of Roraima, which today corresponds to 60% of the requests made in 2020. It is worth mentioning that 75.5% of the requests considered by CONARE in 2020 were registered in the states of the Federation that make up the northern region of the country, especially in the city of Pacaraima in the state of Roraima (Silva et al., 2021). According to Oliveira (2020),

> Low economic development is one of the main characteristics of the Roraima city of Pacaraima, which makes a dry border with Venezuela, along with the cross-border transit of citizens from both countries and the formation of binational families. Pacaraima is considered the "gateway" of Venezuelans in Brazil, being a small town located in Roraima and which has approximately 12 thousand residents (Brazilian Institute of Geography and Statistics, 2018). Pacaraima had all of its routine changed because of the border with Venezuela, through which at least 40,000 Venezuelans entered and remained in the country, according to Federal Police data (Agência Câmara de Notícias, 2018), at least 40,000 Venezuelans since 2013.
>
> *(Oliveira, 2020, p. 223)*

The poverty situation of the majority of Venezuelans who immigrate to Brazil is evident, which brings another point of attention to the Brazilian authorities, responsible for the reception of these asylum seekers. This pressure from immigrants is even greater due to the economic and social weaknesses observed in the state of Roraima. Such problem also reverberates in the fragility of the institutions of the criminal justice system in the region to deal with such a crisis, and, in particular, in the Federal Police.

Legislation and Administrative Processes

Together with the Asylum Law (federal law No. 9,474/1997), the new Migration Law (federal law No. 13,445/2017) operated important changes in the objectives, administrative processes, and rules that apply to foreigners who are in Brazil. Other instruments, such as the possibility of granting humanitarian visas, also supported such changes and facilitated the entry of different immigrants at natural and humanitarian risk in their countries of origin.

The humanitarian visa is a type of permanent visa to reside in Brazil. This visa type was created by the National Immigration Council and put into practice through the Normative Resolution (NR) 97/2012. Through NR 17/2013, the National Immigration Council pointed out the possibility of granting humanitarian visas to Syrians and corresponding countries.

It is important to point out that to apply for refugee status in Brazil, the applicant must, by law, do so within or at a border in the country. A humanitarian visa must be requested outside of Brazil, at the Brazilian consular authority present in the territory of the applicant's country. In addition, the humanitarian visa that is provided for in the Migration Law, Law 13,445/2017, still requires final regulation and detailing by the competent agencies.

Regarding Venezuelans, in 2017 a temporary residence visa was granted in Brazil through NR 126/2017, due to the economic and political crisis in the country.

In the application of the law 13,445/2017, three ministries are involved in the administration of immigration processes in Brazil, namely:

- Secretariat of Labor linked to the Ministry of Economy (former Ministry of Labor, MOL),
- Ministry of Foreign Affairs (MFA), and
- Ministry of Justice (MJ).

The Ministry of Labor, currently the Secretariat of Labor linked to the Ministry of Economy, has as a role within the migration policy to observe the migration from a labor perspective. In addition, this agency is responsible for registering workers in the formal labor market in Brazil, including foreigners working legally. The Ministry of Justice, as it also deals with humanitarian issues within the migration policy, observes the issue of granting asylum and visas of a humanitarian nature in Brazil. The Ministry of Foreign Affairs connects foreigners outside Brazil with the Ministry of Justice, in the case of the need for permanent visas, and with the Ministry of Labor, in the case of requests for work visas, through the diplomatic representations of Brazil abroad.

Other important agencies that also participate in the administration of immigration processes are:

- National Immigration Council (NIC), linked to the Labor Secretariat linked to the Ministry of Economy (former Ministry of Labor, MOL)
- General Immigration Coordination (GIC), which is an administrative sector of the Secretariat of Labor linked to the Ministry of Economy (former Ministry of Labor, MOL)
- Federal Police (FP), an autonomous agency linked to the Ministry of Justice
- National Committee for Refugees (NCR), linked to the Ministry of Justice

The National Immigration Council (CNIg) formulates the general guidelines of the country's immigration policy and has representation from other agencies, from civil society, and from the Federal Police (FP). The General Immigration Coordination (CGIg) decides on work permit requests for foreigners at national borders and provides technical and administrative support to the National Immigration Council (CNIg).

It is important to highlight the role of two organizations that are not part of the Brazilian State in Brazil's immigration policy, which are the Alto Comissariado das Nações Unidas para Refugiados (in literal translation: United Nations High Commissioner for Refugees) and Cáritas Brasil.

The Federal Police (FP) controls and guarantees the security of the country's borders, in addition to being responsible for registering foreigners entering Brazil. Regarding immigration, the FP observes national and public security by prosecuting, judging, and deciding on issues related to nationality, naturalization, expulsion, extradition, and deportation of foreigners.

It is up to the FP to receive the asylum application. This request follows an internal procedure and is submitted to judgment at the National Council for Refugees—CONARE, a collegiate agency linked to the Ministry of Justice. From then on, a protocol of the refugee request is issued by the Federal Police, such a document is valid while the applicant awaits the final judgment of CONARE. In theory, during this waiting period, the asylum seeker would be guaranteed access to health public policies, care for foreigners, and assistance in Brazil, in accordance with international human rights agreements to which Brazil is a signatory. Furthermore, according to the MJ website regarding asylum seekers and the FP:

> Applicants are people who have applied for asylum and started their processes, but still do not have a decision from Conare on their requests. After registering with Sisconare and completing the asylum application form, applicants must go to the Federal Police (FP) to register, collect biometric data and issue the Asylum Protocol, the identification document in Brazil. This document confers rights to applicants, in addition to a temporary residence permit.

In some FP units in Brazil, in this moment, the issuance of the Provisional National Migratory Registration Document (PNMRD) is also requested, which must be collected on site a few days later.

So, asylum seekers have two types of free identification document in Brazil:

1. Asylum Protocol—which has two models (Sisconare and SEI);
2. Provisional Document of National Migration Registry (PDNMR). (Ministry of Justice).

From the documents researched, it can be considered that there is an attempt by the State to outline a model of service to asylum seekers, based on the demands of the international community and with respect to the international human rights agreements to which Brazil is a signatory. However, there is currently the problem of the increase in the number of requests for asylum from border citizens in the states where it is possible to cross land borders, especially with Venezuela. These border states are precisely those with a deficit of structure on the part of the FP to deal with the demands of the refugees.

Having described the general functions of each agency, next we have prepared a matrix that describes in order the activities that each one involved in the asylum-granting process performs.

It should be noted that Cáritas, the entity responsible for managing the Refugee Reception Centers in Brazil, can support the applicant in the asylum application, directing this foreigner to document the request. When this occurs, the FP can forward the questionnaire

TABLE 11.1 Matrix of each part involved in the process and activities

Responsible	Activity
Foreigners at the border or in national territory	Document asylum request (declaration term) in the FP.
Federal Police	Submit asylum claim forms to the Ministry of Justice.
MJ (DEMIG)	Consolidate the request and send it to CONARE.
CONARE	Issue a provisional protocol (while the process is in progress) and forward such protocol to the FP. Request that the FP or another agency carry out the interview with the applicant to complement the process.
Federal Police	Communicate such protocol to the applicant so that, in possession of it, they can obtain CPF (Cadastro de Pessoas Físicas, in literal translation: Registration of Natural Persons) and work card. Schedule the interview with the applicant and consolidate a questionnaire on the asylum application to move forward with the process, when supported by CONARE.
FP or other agencies at the request of CONARE or at the request of the FP themselves	Conduct the interview with a lawyer and translator in the language of the asylum seeker, consolidate a questionnaire about the asylum request, and send an opinion to CONARE through the MJ (DEMIG).
MJ (DEMIG)	Communicate to CONARE the results regarding the interview and the questionnaire on the asylum claim.
CONARE	Prepare opinions for analysis by CONARE's own plenary and, from there, grant or reject the regularization of the refugee status in Brazil, communicating their decision to the Ministry of Justice.
MJ (DEMIG)	Inform the acceptance or refusal of the refugee request to the FP.
Federal Police	Providing of identity card for foreigners, regularization of refugees' status or requesting them to leave the country's borders.
Foreigners in national territory	Ensure that condition of stay is regularized or refused.

Source: Elaborated by the author based on researched legislation and information from the websites of the listed agencies.

about the refugee request to Caritas, and they can be asked to conduct an interview with a lawyer and translator in the applicant's language. At the end, Cáritas is responsible for forwarding the document for analysis by the Ministry of Justice (DEMIG). This role is important because, before being admitted to a center managed by Caritas, ACNUR checks whether the applicant can be considered a refugee.

From the knowledge of how it happens and who is responsible for each part of the asylum application in the country on, it is possible to observe that the judgment of the application for refugee status by CONARE depends on the action of several agencies of the Brazilian State. For this reason, joint work and sharing of information about the asylum claim should take place quickly and continuously. However, this is not what is observed in practice, because when considering the number of requests in relation to the number of cases judged by CONARE, there are a large number of requests without judgment. Table 11.2 shows the problem.

Thus, between 2011 and 2020, 265,729 asylum requests were made in Brazil and only 116,192 were judged by CONARE. Such numbers indicate that the asylum process is not judged with due speed. The Ministry of Justice themselves, on their website, point out the following question regarding the deadlines for requesting and granting asylum in Brazil:

> There is no specific deadline for carrying out each of these procedures. The analysis varies according to the nationality of the applicants, with the registration update of these applicants (making it possible to contact them when necessary), with the specific history of each applicant, with the complexity of the case, as well as with the information available on the country of origin. On average, requests are analyzed in 3 years, a period of time that can vary to more or less, depending on the variables listed.
>
> *(Ministry of Justice)*

From the understanding of the process of requesting asylum in Brazil and the analysis of the pertinent legislation, the analysis of the dynamics of the decisions will be carried out. As noted earlier, the problem of Venezuelans entering the northern border of Brazil will be discussed. In this particular aspect, regarding the Federal Police, we can note that there is a service protocol for asylum seekers, based on the regulations and the international agreements to which the country is a signatory.

The great question is the number of requests for asylum in border states, especially those with land borders in the north of the country. In these states, the Federal Police has serious limitations in terms of human and material resources and the support given by other agencies involved in the refugee process, which causes bottlenecks that directly impact the

TABLE 11.2 Number of asylum claims in relation to the number of asylum claims judged by CONARE per year

Year	Number of asylum requests per year	Number of asylum requests judged by CONARE per year
2011	1,465	107
2012	1,345	208
2013	6,810	643
2014	11,069	2,473
2015	15,906	1,742
2016	8,719	1,956
2017	32,009	1,304
2018	79,831	13,014
2019	82,552	33,453
2020	28,899	63,790
Total	268,605	118,690

Source: Consolidated by the author based on Silva et al. (2021)

efficiency of the Agency responsible for the activity, in addition to the assistance and protection of the refugee in Brazil. Without the refugee status request protocol that is issued by the Federal Police, the applicant remains in an irregular situation in the country and does not have access to the public policies to which he is entitled. In the next section, the flow of refugees and their impact on the territory will be analyzed.

The Flow of Asylum Seekers From Venezuela and Its Effects on the Borders of the Brazilian Amazon

Currently, the border service of asylum requests in the FP does not address the specific issues of land borders. This occurs mainly in the Amazon region, resulting in deficiencies in support actions for asylum seekers. Also, without the asylum request protocol issued by the Federal Police, access to public policies conferred by law is not possible. This discussion gained strength after the intensification of Venezuelan asylum requests by the State of Roraima. The migratory flow of Venezuelans to Brazil increased from 2015 on and intensified especially between 2017 and 2018 (Silva et al., 2021).

The increase in asylum grants is related to a political decision by the Brazilian government, which benefits them in relation to citizens of other countries. It should be noted that there is one of the normative resolution No. 126/2017, which would cover these citizens in terms of legalizing their housing in the country, however, there is a clear option for the design of the asylum, namely:

> . . . Considering the migratory flow to units of the Federation, especially in the North region, of foreign nationals from border countries who are not yet part of the said Residence Agreement, who are in an irregular migratory situation in Brazil and to whom do not apply the institute of asylum to remain in the country, resolves:
>
> Art.1 Temporary residence may be granted, for a period of up to 2 years, to foreigners who have entered Brazilian territory by land and are nationals of a bordering country, for which the Residence Agreement for Nationals of States Parties to the MERCOSUL and associated countries. . . .
>
> Art. 2 The foreigner who intends to benefit from this Normative Resolution and has requested asylum in Brazil must submit to the Federal Police units a declaration of preference for regularization of stay, indicating this Normative Resolution as the basis for his request.
>
> Single paragraph. The declaration of preference will be sent to the National Committee for Refugees (CONARE) for the administrative measures to be taken care of.

Such preference for granting asylum to Venezuelan citizens, despite No. 126/2017, can be demonstrated in Table 11.2, where we can observe the number of recognized refugees, according to country of nationality or habitual residence, Brazil, between 2011 and 2020, remembering that the flow of these citizens intensifies from the year 2017 on, the year of publication of the resolution. Among the reasons given by Venezuelan citizens for obtaining asylum, the one that stands out is "serious and widespread violation of human rights." However, despite this observation of the increase in the number of requests and the motivations that drive them at the borders and at the main entry points of this migratory flow according to Santiago (2019):

> [T]he human and material resources available at the Federal Police are limited (subject to annual budget limitations and a determined number of civil servants in the effective framework), so that, in a short time, there will be no conditions to expand capacity or reinforce the structure of the Frontier Unit through a mere reallocation of resources.

Although it does not have a simple and ready solution to the problem that arises, it is certain that, if it only adopts the ordinary standard of service performed in other immigration police units in the country, the Federal Police will not provide a satisfactory service. It is necessary to create a service process that can be applied in emergency situations like this one, which, given the constant world crises, tends to be repeated more frequently, with Brazil being a sure destination (Santiago, 2019, p. 18).

This fact can be observed at the main point of entry for Venezuelans: the city of Pacaraima in the state of Roraima. By means of these, requests are concentrated in the North region of the country, in particular the states of Roraima, Amazonas, and Acre, which have a great relevance in the number of asylum requests in Brazil. In 2020, 75.5% of asylum requests were registered in the states of the northern region of the country and 60% of asylum requests judged by CONARE originated in the state of Roraima (Silva et al., 2021).

Silva et al. (2021) also observe some results obtained by the Pesquisa de Informações Básicas Municipais—Munic 2018 (IBGE, 2017), in literal translation: Municipal Basic Information Survey—Munic 2018 (IBGE, 2017), in relation to the main cities of residence of asylum seekers in Brazil. When observing these two data, the authors point out that in the North region of the country there are shelters to support asylum seekers in the cities of Manaus (state of Amazonia), Boa Vista (state of Roraima), and Pacaraima (state of Roraima), federal units that receive especially Venezuelan citizens (Silva et al., 2021).

The Reference and Assistance Centers, which provide assistance to immigrants and legal support to asylum seekers or already recognized refugees, exist in Brazil only in five of the main cities of residence of asylum seekers, Boa Vista and Pacaraima in Roraima and the capital of São Paulo, Curitiba, and Foz do Iguaçu in Paraná (Silva et al., 2021).

Still in the state of Roraima, due to the large number of asylum seekers from Venezuela, *Operação Acolhida* (Welcome Operation) was created, a public policy instituted by the Brazilian State, with the objective of promoting the internalization and insertion of refugees in Brazil in the labor market. The *Operação Acolhida* installed 12 shelters in the city of Boa Vista in Roraima, in which it is possible for asylum seekers to have access to different forms of support from the Brazilian State, from food and shelter to support in their document regularization. In the vicinity of the Boa Vista Bus Station, a reception and support post was created to assist asylum seekers. This reception and support post also offers information services and basic infrastructure for temporary reception of immigrants (Casa Civil, 2022).

An interiorization and screening post was also installed in Boa Vista to support asylum seekers in regularizing their situation in the country and, through the Centro de Coordenação de Interiorização (CCI), in literal translation: Interiorization Coordination Center (ICC) carry out the interiorization of this applicant. It is important to highlight that the main strategy of the federal government to reduce the pressure on the northern borders of Brazil is the Interiorization Process of the Operação Acolhida; this strategy was designed as a response to the increase in the migratory flow due to the crisis in Venezuela (Casa Civil, 2022).

Finally, it should be noted that this chapter does not aim to critically analyze the Operação Acolhida, as this would require greater depth on issues related to the management and objectives of the operation, as well as the role of the State in the operationalization of the aforementioned program established by the Brazilian government. The focus of this chapter was to highlight the pressure of Venezuelan refugees on the northern border of Brazil and draw a parallel between this discretion in response to the pressure on the border, observing this fact in relation to the long administrative process of granting asylum.

Conclusion

It can be seen throughout the text that there has been a change in the profile of asylum seekers in Brazil, with considerable growth in the flow of Venezuelans. It is also possible to affirm the importance of the North region for the entry of this flow of asylum seekers in Brazil, being necessary to improve the management of immigration to speed up the judgment of asylum requests in Brazil, as well as to strengthen and expand the support equipment that these applicants receive.

Thus, after analyzing the numbers of asylum requests in Brazil and those assessed annually, it is possible to observe the presence of bottlenecks in the management of administrative processes related to refugees. These bottlenecks can be the reason why a process takes on average, in MJ's own words, three years. During this time, the asylum seeker, who is in a vulnerable situation, is prevented from consolidating their rights, established by the Immigration Law and the Asylum Law of Brazil. In this way, there is great pressure on the Federal Police to process these requests, since its protocol is a sine qua non condition for the refugee to gain access to the necessary documentation to live and work in Brazil, as well as to the public policies in force in the country. Thus, the Federal Police in Roraima increased its work demand throughout the humanitarian crisis that took place in Venezuela. There are hundreds of migrants who are waiting for assistance in search of migratory regularization. However, the human and material resources that the Federal Police have in the border region, especially in the state of Roraima, are limited with little possibility of expansion in the near future.

Such a situation may come to impact, in administrative terms, all asylum seekers in the country, regardless of nationality, because the increase in the flow of Venezuelans at the borders of Brazil can put pressure on CONARE's demand, deepening the existing bottlenecks. For these reasons, the adoption of the common standard of care already established in other immigration police units in the country will not speed up the processing of asylum requests. Therefore, there is a need to establish emergency exception standards to ensure the human rights of asylum seekers who enter the country through the Amazon region.

References

Casa Civil. 2022. Retrieved from https://www.gov.br/casacivil/pt-br/acolhida/sobre-a-operacao-acolhida-2. Accessed 03/29/24.

Comitê Nacional para os Refugiados (A). *Resolução Normativa CONARE no 102, de 12/01/2012. Dispõe sobre a concessão do visto permanente previsto no art. 16 da Lei nº 6.815, de 19 de agosto de 1980, a nacionais do Haiti* [Brasília, DF: s. n.]. Retrieved from https://www.legisweb.com.br/legislacao/?id=116083. Accessed 03/29/24.

IBGE—Instituto Brasileiro de Geografia e Estatística, Resultado da Amostra do Censo, Rio de Janeiro. (2017). Retrieved from http://www.ibge.gov.br/home/estatistica/populacao/censo2010/default_resultados_amostra.sHtm. Accessed 19/08/2024.

Oliveira, W. A. de. (2020). A Imigração dos Venezuelanos para o Brasil e a Atuação da Polícia Federal na Fronteira: uma análise sobre as solicitações de refúgio e residência temporária. *Revista Brasileira de Ciências Policiais*, 11(3), 231–263. https://doi.org/10.31412/rbcp.v11i3.657.

Santiago, R. G. D. (2019). *Proposta para melhoria do processo de atendimento de solicitantes de refúgio em estados fronteiriços, através da aplicação da soft systems methodology*, mimeo. https://unbral.nuvem.ufrgs.br/bd/items/show/2213. Available at 12th October 2024.

Silva, G. J.; Cavalcanti, L.; Oliveira, T.; Macedo, M. (2021). *Refúgio em Números*, 6th edition. Observatório das Migrações Internacionais; Ministério da Justiça e Segurança Pública (OBmigra)/Comitê Nacional para os Refugiados, Brasília, DF.

Vosgerau, D. S. R.; Romanowski, J. P. (2014). Estudos de revisão: implicações conceituais e metodológicas. *Revista Diálogo Educacional*, 14(41), 165–189.

PART III
Law and the Environmental Protection in the Amazon

12
INTELLECTUAL PROPERTY RIGHTS LEGISLATION AS A SOURCE OF INEQUALITY

A Case Study Based on Natural Genetic Resources From the Amazon Region

Marcos Vinícío Chein Feres

Introduction

This chapter[1] aims to analyze intellectual property rights legislation as a source of inequality, widening the gap between developed and developing countries, by facilitating the process of appropriation of natural genetic resources from developing countries, as well as by legalizing monopolization of these natural genetic resources by developed countries.

A preliminary literature review showed how *de-colonial thinking*, as formulated by Mignolo (2008), and colonial domination perpetrated by developed countries over the Southern countries, explained by Quijano (2000), are relevant concepts to be utilized so as to understand the nature of intellectual property rights and the idea of technological advancement. Central to grasping the idea of international regulations on intellectual property rights is Susan Sell's study on the TRIPS Agreement. Her study reveals how developed countries tend to organize international commerce in accordance with the logic of intellectual property rights (Sell, 2003). Intellectual property rights are logically conceived based on the idea of a legal monopoly, which reinforces the desire of transnational corporations to control a specific relevant market so as to increase their economic power. Emphasizing this perspective on transnational market power, Maskus (2012, p. 446) elucidates that "because IPRs [intellectual property rights] offer their owners the legal ability to exclude others from using their ideas or copying their expressive elements, they can establish breathtaking market power."

Moreover, Shiva's (1991, p. 2745) idea that the "corporate perspective views as value only that which serves the market" reveals the intrinsic value of intellectual property rights for corporate business to gain and extend its market power. In this context, Shiva (1991) also explains that third-world countries' agricultural practices or the use of their natural genetic resources are not taken as part of the technological advancement but rather as "primitive cultivars" or "mere traditional knowledge" quite distinct from science and technology. The ownership of biotechnological assets is totally divergent from the idea that all forms of life represent a common heritage as conceived by indigenous peoples in developing countries (Shiva, 1991).

Shiva (1991) also denounces how northern capitalist societies determine the process and the legal mechanisms of privatizing certain natural genetic resources via intellectual property rights. In this context, the WIPO plays a relevant international role in enforcing different types of policies and norms so as to expand property rights to the detriment of the socioeconomic interests of developing countries (Boyle, 2004).

Considering this preliminary literature review, the research question addressed in this chapter is what elements in international patent law and its institutional apparatus reveal traits of inequality between developed and developing countries. In order to understand this question, the chapter considers the case of natural genetic resources from Brazil. The normative bases of analysis are the 1994 Trade-Related Intellectual Property Rights Agreement (TRIPS), the 1992 Convention of Biological Diversity (CBD), the Nagoya Protocol, and the Patent Cooperation Treaty (PCT). The idea is not to determine if the legal instruments have been efficiently applied, rather the aim is to verify if these norms, and the World Intellectual Property Rights Organization's (WIPO's) institutional apparatus, are, in fact, deepening the inequality between developing and developed countries.

In summary, the aim of the chapter is to compare empirical facts concerning the use of Brazil's natural genetic resources with their legal treatment under international patent rights as recorded in the *patentscope*[2] database. The theory proposed is that, stemming from the case of the use of genetic resources from Brazilian biodiversity and the functioning of the *patentscope*, the institutional apparatus formed by international regulation bolsters the inequality in the distribution of intellectual property rights between developed and developing countries.

In order to corroborate the theory on the inequality in the distribution of intellectual property rights, empirical qualitative research was conducted, making use of the rules of inference developed by Epstein and King (2002) as well as the case study method proposed by Yin (2017).

The raw data extracted from the *patentscope*, combined with the specific knowledge related to the genetic resources from Brazilian biodiversity, were organized, systematized, and codified so as to substantiate the theory which may express either the efficacy or the inefficacy of the legal instruments aforementioned, as well as the effects of the legislation on developed and developing countries.

Methodology and Data Collection

In 2014, during a field trip in Manaus, an opportunity to go on a tour in the Ducke Amazon Forest Reserve presented itself to the author after a lecture at the Museum of Amazonia, a scientific research society. Jaime Diakara, a member of the *Desana*, an ethnic indigenous group from the Amazon region, was attending the lecture. Diakara invited the author and his assistant on a tour in the Ducke Forest Reserve. While there, Diakara pointed out a number of plants typical of the Amazon Forest and their utilization by the diverse indigenous tribes in the region. During the tour, every plant was photographed and catalogued in a field report. So far, the author and his team of assistants have researched two of these plants and their medical and cosmetic benefits, presented by Diakara, to verify if the genetic resource was registered as part of any patent applications on the database known as *patentscope*, specifically, *carapanaúba* and *curare* complex.

This is a pilot research project, which may produce results concerning other plants and animals typical of Brazilian biodiversity, not specifically focused on here. Nevertheless, it is necessary to analyze how the institutional apparatus was structured by international regulations; what the real intent of the authors, involved in the formulation of these regulations, was, and whether it is easy to find useful information about the patent system, not only for inventors but also for laypeople.

First of all, what is the patentscope? The patentscope is a database, organized and maintained by WIPO, in accordance with the PCT's legal requirements. It becomes apparent that the *patentscope* is a very relevant tool of analysis, as it is the international database available for all inventors and applicants from different parts of the world who intend to apply for a patent regarding a certain invention. It contains substantial information on patent applications, such as the description, designated country, and identification of the applicant and inventor. This information is crucial to verify the origins of the components of the final product, as well as the source of the patent application.

Having clarified the concept and the function of the patentscope, it is relevant to justify the choice to search the *patentscope* for patents granted for specific inventions containing natural genetic resources from Brazilian biodiversity. First, the *patentscope* is one of the most appropriate databases for full-text searching, as well as for exporting patent data (Jürgens & Herrero-Solana, 2015). Second, WIPO, the official international regulator of intellectual property, maintains the *patentscope*. Third, the *patentscope* is organized and structured in accordance with the PCT. Therefore, searching the *patentscope* may reveal relevant features of the contrast between developed and developing countries, as a consequence of the rules established, not only by TRIPS and CBD but also under the auspices of PCT. The PCT was conceived so as to facilitate the analysis of patents in various countries simultaneously, as well as to avoid the cost of translating the patent into different languages (Shear and Kelley, 2003). In sum, the PCT constitutes an instrument for accelerating the process of patent protection for those who are well equipped to submit international patent applications. For these reasons, the choice of the *patentscope* as the database for this research is especially appropriate, considering the nature of the study itself.

Having justified the choice of the *patentscope*, it is relevant to explain which natural genetic resources were selected and searched on the database and why. Due to the large number of patent applications, regarding all sorts of products and genetic resources, it was important to narrow the search in order to look for specific genetic resources commonly occurring in the indigenous areas in Brazilian territory. Therefore, the case study of the two aforementioned specific plants might shed light on the fact that patent applications filed by Western actors do not reveal the real source of the indigenous primeval use of those genetic resources.

Methodologically, stemming from the fact that the researcher can do more with documents than content analysis as stated by Charmaz (2014, p. 46), the strategy in this research is to understand the basic questions and apply them to the case study method utilized here as the main methodological technique:

Where do the data come from? Who participated in shaping them? What did the authors intend? Have participants provided sufficient information for us to make a plausible interpretation? And do we have sufficient knowledge of the relevant worlds to read their words with any understanding?

(Charmaz, 2014, p. 52)

In order to produce a logical model from empirical data, behind the utilization of the *patentscope*, under the auspices of the PCT, it was necessary to organize the data collected, bearing in mind the aforementioned questions. The analysis of the patents granted, concerning the two case studies of this chapter (*carapanaúba* and *curare* complex), will follow the analytical procedure conceived in accordance with the case study method formally designed by Yin (2017).

Where Do the Data Come From?

Following Robert Yin's (2017, p. 19) advice, a description of the procedure of data collection from the *patentscope* is required, for "your procedure and documentation need to distinguish your research case study from the other kinds of *non*-research case studies." The search for specific data on the *patentscope* was carried out in February 2019. On accessing the *patentscope* site (https://patentscope.wipo.int/), the tool, which initially appears, is "simple search." However, in order to fulfill the task of looking for natural genetic resources from Brazilian biodiversity as elements integrated in the patented invention, the advanced search presented itself as a more efficient tool, taking into consideration that it is possible to search for more features of the granted patent and the national phase of different offices all over the world.

It is important to acknowledge that the granting of a patent is a very complex administrative act, which requires a previous analysis by the international bureau and, then, each country designated in the patent file will proceed to the merits of the granting or the refusal of the patent proposed. More importantly, the applicant will always file the documents, expecting, not only an answer from the international bureau but also the approval and recognition of the patent in all the countries designated in the claim.

Once in the advanced search, the following option "*criteria: ALL Office(s): all Language: All Stemming: true*" was selected. The purpose was to execute a more thorough search, whose scope consists of scrutinizing the database, taking into account the entire content of the patent granted, the different national offices, and all languages of patent applications. The idea in the search mechanism is to combine the scientific name of the plant or the most relevant substance in the compound with the popular expressions used by locals and/or indigenous peoples. Thus, the keywords utilized in the search procedure were, in each case study, "*carapanaúba or Aspidosperma sp*" and "*curare or d-tubocurarine.*" The conjunction "or" is used so as to execute a search, which results in inventions containing in their descriptions either one of the expressions independently or both of them simultaneously.

Having defined the keywords and executed the advanced search, a new page popped up with the results, summing up all the patent applications that contained the keywords. The results were 230 patent applications listed for "carapanaúba or aspidosperma" and 247 patent applications for "curare or d-tubocurarine." The elements of identification that the patentscope provides, once the advanced search has been carried out, are the title of the patent, the country, the publishing date, the international patent classification, the application number, the applicant, and the inventor.

So as to be more practical, the method for showing the results was in descending order of publishing date with 200 applications per page. Finally, all the patent applications listed are hyperlinked to another page where detailed information about each application is available. Having collected the results of both cases, it was necessary to check, for each patent application, whether the patent was granted or not. In both cases, after the analysis of all the hyperlinked patent applications, the final results were that, out of 230 applications concerning "*carapanaúba*," only 61 were granted a patent, whereas out of 247 applications referring to "curare," only 91 were granted a patent.

However, at that specific stage of data collection, while reading the patents granted, it became apparent that there was a repetition of the same patent applications as part of the search process. It was crucial to solve this problem, looking more closely into the *patentscope* site. Patents with the same title were compared to confirm if they were part of the same "family" (jargon used by WIPO) so as to define patent applications submitted to different countries (designated countries), thus, retrieved from the database and, then, inserted, after each national phase, with the specific approval of two or more countries. In this case, it was possible to detect the original patent application as the source of all these different patent grants in accordance with specific national legislations and procedures. So as to find and confirm this information, certain features were cross-referenced, such as the inventor, the country, the applicant, and the description of the patent.

Findings

All the tables showing the patents granted were elaborated by the author, taking into account if they owned an international application number. Moreover, Tables 12.1 and 12.2 were organized, considering the designated country and the grant date. In order to find the designated country that granted and issued the patent, once the hyperlinked number is accessed, there is a tab where all the information about the national phase of the patent application is available, showing each country, which has already granted the specific patent. Basically, this information, before being referenced in Tables 12.1 and 12.2, was checked to confirm which designated country had effectively issued the patent.

Before completing the tables, it was essential to exclude, not only all the patent applications ("patent families") linked to an original patent application, as already explained, but also all the patent applications that were not directly connected with the natural genetic resource searched, that is, "*carapanaúba*" and "*curare*." These patent applications only utilized the natural genetic resource as an example, rather than a specific compound in the formula presented. Therefore, they were discarded.

Another relevant limitation of this research is the possibility that other essential elements contained in the natural genetic resources, studied in this chapter, may have been the object of appropriation in diverse patent applications. However, for the purposes of this specific research, it was necessary to limit the focus of the investigation.

Once verified the patent applications above, some of the applicants, in no specific order, were:

- *Foamix Pharmaceuticals, Ltd.*
- *Biogenic Innovations, LLC.*
- *Anteis SA.*
- *Neocutis SA.*
- *Wilfred-Ramix, Inc.*
- *Air Products & Chemicals, Inc.*
- *Trustees of Boston University*
- *The Scripps Research Institute*
- *California Institute of Technology*

TABLE 12.1 Carapanaúba or Aspidosperma sp.

Name	Designated country	Grant date
1. (EN) Composition of delivery system for personal care products	JP	02.03.2018
2. Compositions with modulating agents	US	11.08.2015
3. Use of methylsulfonylmethane (MSM) to modulate microbial activity	US	08.11.2016
4. Antioxidant compositions and methods of using the same	US	25.07.2017
	RU	24.05.2018
5. Peptides for skin rejuvenation and methods of using the same	US	28.06.2016
	MX	12.11.2018
	AU	05.04.2018
	SI	20.11.2017
6. (EN) Quaternary hetero atom compound	JP	22.12.2016
7. Composition for treating aids and associated conditions	US	08.07.2014
8. Foamable vehicle and pharmaceutical compositions thereof	US	02.05.2017
9. (EN) Polymer compositions for personal care products	JP	10.06.2015
10. Small molecule inhibitors of hepatitis C virus	US	03.11.2015
11. Quaternary heteroatom-containing compounds	US	02.09.2014
	EP	30.04.2014
12. Application of tannins to reduce odor emissions from animal waste	US	20.03.2012
13. Compositions and methods for the treatment of skin diseases and disorders using antimicrobial peptide sequestering compounds	US	25.04.2017
14. Oil and liquid silicone foamable carriers and formulations	US	02.12.2014
15. Polymeric compositions for personal care products	US	12.01.2016
	EP	13.09.2017
16. Cosmetic use of at least one ligand of the neuropeptide Y (NPY) receptor comprising agonist and antagonist of NPY, in a composition and as an agent for the maintenance and/or restoration of homeostasis of the e.g. epidermis	FR	31.03.2017
17. Synergistic pest-control compositions	US	27.05.2014
18. Composition with modulating agents	US	30.06.2015
19. Nutritional supplement for the prevention of cardiovascular disease, Alzheimer's disease, diabetes, and regulation and reduction of blood sugar and insulin resistance	US	13.09.2011
20. Hydrophilic, non-aqueous pharmaceutical carriers and compositions and uses	US	16.07.2013
21. Compositions and methods for increasing adipose metabolism, lipolysis, or lipolytic metabolism via thermogenesis	US	07.06.2011
22. Using plant extracts, or active ingredients purified from them, as lipolytic, slimming, and anti-cellulitis agents, in cosmetic, nutraceutical, or pharmaceutical compositions	FR	02.10.2009
23. A new process of the synthesis of 3',4'-anhydrovinblastine, vinblastine and vincristine	CA	26.06.2001
24. 7-bromo-beta-carboline compound and method for producing same	US	16.01.1990

Source: Elaborated by the author[3]

TABLE 12.2 Curare Complex and d-tubocurarine

Name	Designated country	Grant date
1 *—(FR2181806)	FR	22.08.1975
2 *—(FR2187297)	FR	03.12.1976
3 (US3998843) Quaternary ammonium compounds	US	21.12.1976
4 (US4029800) Neuromuscular blocking agents and antagonists	US	14.06.1977
5 (US4550113) 9-Amino-2,3,5,6,7,8-hexahydro-1H-cyclopenta(b)quinoline monohydrate hydrochloride as stimulant of neuro-muscular transmission of smooth muscles	US	29.10.1985
6 (US4734275) Anti-curare agents	US	29.03.1988
7 (WO1989001779) Molecular decoyants and methods of use thereof	FI	15.10.1997
	EP	31.05.1995
8 (CA2067754) Preparation for the application of agents in mini-droplets	CA	04.06.2002
9 (US5177082) Huperzines and analogs	US	05.01.1993
10 (US20050159398) Processes for the preparation of rocuronium bromide and intermediates thereof	US	25.08.2009
11 (WO2011009626) Compounds that inhibit muscle contraction	US	03.02.2015
	MX	29.10.2014
	EP	22.10.2014
12 (US20110104061) Treatment of renal hypertension or carotid sinus syndrome with adventitial pharmaceutical sympathetic denervation or neuromodulation	US	18.06.2013
13 (US20110250682) Formation of neuromuscular junctions in a co-culture comprising rat muscle cells overlayered with differentiated human spinal cord stem cells in a serum-free medium	US	24.04.2018
14 (WO2011133985) Formation of neuromuscular junctions in a defined system	USEP	16.09.2014
		26.12.2018
15 (US20120121675) Peptide-based compounds and compositions that inhibit muscle contraction	US	03.02.2015
16 (FR2970781) Procede de fabrication d'un support d'analyse et utilisation pour la detection de toxines	EP	22.04.2015
	US	11.09.2018
17 (wo2012136385) 6,7-dihydro-[1,3,4]thiadiazolo-[3,2-a][1,3]diazepin derivative and pharmaceutical composition containing the same as neuromuscular blocker or skeletal muscle relaxant, and method for the preparation	US	30.09.2014
18 (WO2013025963) Conversion of somatic cells into functional spinal motor neurons, and methods and uses thereof	US	26.09.2017
19 (US20130115694) Synthetic mammalian neuromuscular junction and method of making	US	16.09.2014
20 (US20140349884) Synthetic mammalian neuromuscular junction and method of screening for a candidate drug thereon	US	23.02.2016

* = no title available.
Source: Elaborated by the author[4]

- *The United States Of America, as represented by the Secretary of Agriculture*
- *L'Oreal*
- *Tyratech, Inc.*
- *HHC Formulations, Ltd.*
- *Greenpharma*;
- Kawaken Fine Chemicals Co., Ltd.

Having extracted the relevant data, some of the applicants, in no specific order, were:

- *Hoffmann La Roche*
- *Reckitt & Colmann Prod Ltd.*
- *Reckitt & Colman Products Limited.*
- *Bristol-Myers Company*
- *Nauchno-Issledovatelsky Institut Po Biologicheskikm Ispytaniyam Khimicheskikh Soedineny*
- *Research Corporation*
- *Gershoni, Jonathan, M.*
- *Ilcevc, Gregor; Yu Chao Mei; Tang Xi Can; Liu Jia Sen; Han Yan Yi*
- *Chemagis Ltd.*
- *Seward Kirk Patrick*
- *Mercator Medsystems, Inc.*
- *James Hickman, University of Central Florida Research Foundation, Inc.*
- *University of Central Florida Research Foundation, Inc.*
- *Lipotec, S.A.*
- *Centre Nationale de Recherches Scientifiques*
- *King Saud University*
- *President and Fellows of Harvard College*
- *Children's Medical Center Corporation.*

Codifying and Confirming the Theory Proposed

Taking into account Yin's (2017, p. 37–38) criteria for interpreting the case study's findings, it is crucial to think of this case study as "an opportunity to shed empirical light on some theoretical concepts or principles." So as to verify the initial theory of developed countries attempting to appropriate the natural genetic resources from developing states, it is logical to investigate who the inventors and the applicants are and where they originally come from, for these data should reveal, as indicial as this evidence may be, the nature and the core of this process of appropriation.

First, the applicants are the direct authors of the information available on the database, concerning the application of a patent. In this case, they are the ones responsible for shaping data in accordance with their ideas of prior art, conventional science, and the appropriation of natural genetic resources (Shiva, 1991). As far as intellectual property rights are concerned, the idea of prior art (also known as the state of the art) is essential to corroborate as well as determine the novelty and the inventive step of a product in a patent application (Spence, 2007).

Second, those who "own" the knowledge of prior art or have privileged access to knowledge have an advantage over others who might not have easy access to this knowledge. In fact, the inventors from developing countries, where biodiversity generates a wide possibility of new inventions, might be limited by local and financial contingencies, which do not affect inventors working from developed countries. This social and economic context is exacerbated by the powerful transnational corporations, which promoted and encouraged the approval of TRIPS (Sell, 2003). Moreover, corporate power is heavily concentrated in developed countries, reinforcing the thesis of private rights affecting public problems as well as strong intellectual property legislation limiting the development of poor countries (Maskus, 2012).

Mignolo (2008) asserts that the "*de-colonial*" way of thinking rests upon a necessary openness to new approaches in science and politics and the disentanglement of an array of possibilities concealed by the idea of modern rationality. Stemming from this assertion, it is important to consider whether the distribution of intellectual property rights is suffering from the effects of the colonialism derived from traditional forms of economic power and modern scientific rationality (Quijano, 2000). Thus, in order to empirically prove the existence of the remnants of colonial power in the realm of intellectual property rights, the next step was to confirm the nationality of the applicants, after organizing the aforementioned tables, pinpointing those applicants. In addition, it was necessary to verify the territorial domains of either the private corporation or the public institution involved.

A third table was elaborated to explicitly demonstrate the codes extracted from inventors and applicants, as it was fundamental to certify which country was effectively involved as the original territorial source of the patent application. In elaborating the codes below, the *patentscope* was found to be practically useless. After having extracted the data and organized Tables 12.1 and 12.2, a search was carried out utilizing Google tools. This might be seen as a limitation of this research, for it was impossible to avoid coming across homonymous or similarities among companies' names, which may not be detected utilizing Google miner. Nonetheless, the act of examining the original language of the patent application, the inventors registered in the database, and the patent applicants leads to a result, which demonstrates a more natural degree of uncertainty. As widely known in qualitative research, uncertainty is always part of the outcome (Epstein and King, 2002).

First of all, the corporations, the universities, or the governmental agencies shown as applicants were inserted in the Google search mechanism so as to verify their original location, their headquarters. Second, if one or more persons were exhibited as applicants, the same search procedure on Google was executed. In this specific case, it was necessary to validate whether the benefits of the research or the patent would be effectively transferred to the person's country of origin. It can be concluded that, in some cases, the independent inventors may be carrying out the research in a different country from their homeland.

In one instance, the *patentscope* did not provide the translation for one of the names of the applicant (patent # 1, Table 12.1); nonetheless, if that Japanese name is searched on Google miner, it appears to be the translation of "California Institute of Technology." At face value, Japan might be thought to be the original country of the patent application. However, after a simple search on the Internet, using the Google translator to confirm the search carried out, probably, the original invention was created by a Japanese citizen at the California Institute of Technology (*CalTech*) and the application was filed in Japanese as it was applied for in Japan, even though it cites *CalTech* as the applicant. All this uncertainty naturally emerges from either the sort of availability of cyberspace information or the veracity of Internet data (Yin, 2017). At this stage of the research, it has been impossible to check the veracity of the information.

Another challenging case in which the origins of the application have been difficult to ascertain, was patent #9 (Table 12.2), for the inventors and the applicants were the same. Researching the individuals in the application, it was possible to verify the relationship between one of them and a Chinese pharmaceutical company, that is, Tang Xi Can, one of the inventors who is a member of the Scientific Advisory Board at Jiangsu Simcere Pharmaceutical Company, Ltd.

Finally, Table 12.3 is organized as a means of codifying the likely origins of the applicants and, thus, demonstrating the true effects of 1994 TRIPS for developing countries, as already explicated by Shiva (1997) and Chang (2001). Both of the authors emphasize that TRIPS was imposed on developing countries by developed countries, reinventing some instruments of domination and the impediment of advancement, typical of colonial power, over developing countries.

Once codified for the countries and the continents whose applicants are disclosed on the *patentscope*, it is clear that 11 patent applications are originally from Asia, 13 applications from Europe, and 20 applications from North America. In fact, all of the countries that used Brazilian natural genetic resources are located in the northern hemisphere.

TABLE 12.3 The likely origins of the patent applications

Carapanaúba	Coding	*Curare*	Coding
1) United States	North America	1) Switzerland	Europe
2) Israel	Middle Eastern	2) United Kingdom	Europe
3) Canada	North America	3) United Kingdom	Europe
4) Switzerland	Europe	4) United States	North America
5) Switzerland	Europe	5) Russia	Europe
6) United States	North America	6) United States	North America
7) United States	North America	7) Israel	Middle Eastern
8) Israel	Middle Eastern	8) Slovenia	Europe
9) United States	North America	9) China	Asia
10) United States	North America	10) Israel	Middle Eastern
11) United States	North America	11) Spain	Europe
12) United States	North America	12) United States	North America
13) Switzerland	Europe	13) United States	North America
14) Israel	Middle Eastern	14) United States	North America
15) United States	North America	15) Spain	Europe
16) France	Europe	16) France	Europe
17) United States	North America	17) Saudi Arabia	Middle Eastern
18) Israel	Middle Eastern	18) United States	North America
19) United States	North America	19) United States	North America
20) Israel	Middle Eastern	20) United States	North America
21) United States	North America		
22) France	Europe		
23) Canada	North America		
24) Japan	Asia		

Source: Elaborated by the author

For instance, Artal (2012), in his article, explains the use of curare, typical of Central and South America, by the tribes in the highlands of the Orinoco and the Amazon rivers in the Amazon Region. The territorial source of curare is confirmed by Lee (2005) when describing the history of the origins of the poison (curare) developed by the indigenous tribes in the Amazon Region. Silva's (2015) dissertation, for example, confirms the existence of "Carapanaúba" or "*Aspidosperma sp.*" in the Amazon Region, revealing how the knowledge of making use of this genetic resource for medicinal therapy is passed on orally to the next generation of locals who use the medicinal properties of the tree and commercialize the natural products from "Carapanaúba" at the local market. Trindade et al. (2017) elucidate that "*Aspidosperma excelsum*" is a native plant from the Amazon region, verifying the geographical location of the plant. Therefore, Shiva's (1997) warning that developing countries' biodiversity is being appropriated by developed countries seems rational and reasonable. In addition, Sell's (2003) critique on TRIPS is also confirmed by the empirical data extracted from the *patentscope* for data reveal the developed countries as the main applicants of the patented products related to a natural genetic resource typical of a tropical country, specifically, Brazil. In fact, it is possible to argue that developing countries do not manage the international instruments made available by WIPO as efficiently as the developed countries (Boyle, 2004), for the applicants from developed countries seem to be more prevalent in the WIPO system, when applying for a patent application whose main element is a natural genetic resource extracted from a developing country, Brazil.

According to Susan Sell (2011, p. 22), "given the expansion of intellectual property rights and unequal distribution of economic and political power across the globe, developing countries face new challenges in navigating the system to their benefit." Sell (2011) writes this essay so as to comment on what has been achieved in the 15 years since the promulgation of TRIPS. Sell's (2011) statement is, in fact, corroborated by the data extracted from the *patentscope*. Obviously, developing countries, such as Brazil, do not have access to a system of *pseudo*-universal rights whose distribution is unequal among WIPO's State Members.

The increasing expansion of the intellectual property rights system is organized and elaborated so as to meet specific business and corporate interests (Boyle, 2004), which can be illustrated by the following applicants (extracted from both cases), for example, *Foamix Pharmaceuticals,* Ltd; *Hoffmann La Roche*; *L'Oreal*; *Bristol-Myers Company*; *Biogenic Innovations, LLC*; and *Greenpharma*. According to Yin (2017, p. 169), it is possible to import the strategies devised by Glaser and Strauss (2017, p. 46) on grounded theory to the case study, as he elucidates: "the procedures assign various kinds of codes to the data, each code representing a concept or abstraction of potential interest. You can apply such procedures to all case studies." This is why it is not unreasonable to link the substantive theory of inequality of distribution of intellectual property rights between developed and developing countries to Boyle's concepts and Sell's aforementioned hypotheses.

Sell (2011, p. 21) also expresses the idea that "vertical forum shifting may lead actors to deploy law in ways that reinforce, deepen, and exacerbate inequities—particularly between the OECD and the global south in the area of intellectual property." Sell (2011) criticizes how developing countries are being led by developed countries to adhere to bilateral agreements whose intent is more than TRIPS-plus. It is, in fact, US-plus (Sell, 2011). This conclusion is easily reached from the data provided earlier, because 19 out of 20 patent grants from North America originated in the United States. This means that the United States has the ownership of final products whose original compound is a natural genetic resource from Brazilian biodiversity.

According to Quijano (2000), colonialism expresses itself, not only by the dominance of economic power but also by the control of knowledge. Colonial power can be evidenced by the fact that a natural genetic resource, utilized by local peoples in countries in the Southern hemisphere, is appropriated and industrialized by countries in the Northern hemisphere so as to sell, either medicines or cosmetics, to the same countries from where the genetic resource had originally been extracted.

Moreover, it is obvious from their resistance to reformation or to flexibilization of the intellectual property rights regulations how reluctant developed countries have been to acknowledge the inequities caused by the international patent system. It is relevant to explain that, if the state of the art, as an essential concept embedded in the legal requirement of novelty, were taken seriously, the original use of natural genetic resources from developing countries should be considered as the prior art in the process of granting the patent application, thus, preventing the issuing of the patent. In those cases, the patent application file would not clearly reveal the limits of the state of the art that the application intends to overcome (Barbosa, 2011). This demonstrates how scientific knowledge is wielded as a means of domination and colonial power (Quijano, 2000), as indigenous knowledge is disregarded in the definition of *prior art*.

Reiterating Charmaz's (2014, p. 52) strategic questions: "Who participated in shaping them [the data]? [;] What did the authors intend?" it is quite obvious that developed countries, enforcing their colonial power, shape the intellectual property rights system by restricting the access of developing countries to information, knowledge, and technology, as well as appropriating the natural genetic resources originally located in developing countries. There is little doubt that theoretically there is no space for the development of de-colonial thinking (Mignolo, 2008) in the case of the intellectual property rights system. The idea of flexible rules stemming from the TRIPS Agreement is not evoked as a means of favoring the development of science and technology in developing countries. On the contrary, the main goal is to expand intellectual property rights so as to hamper new forms of creativity, technology, and knowledge in favor of new mechanisms of enforcement and policies concerned with the expansion of intellectual property rights (Boyle, 2004), as they are known nowadays.

As clarified by Glaser and Strauss (2017, p. 5), "grounded theory is derived from data and then illustrated by characteristic examples of data." Taking this last part of the strategy conceived by grounded theory applied to the case study method, the inequality of distribution of intellectual property rights between developed and developing countries, as pointed out in the aforementioned proposed theory, can be, not only extracted from the data provided earlier but also illustrated by features of the data, such as the functioning of the *patentscope* (predominance of patents granted to developed countries; the complexity of a structure, named "family of patents," as a means of classification of the same patent application being analyzed and granted by each Designated Country—it is a thicket); and the dominant presence of the United States as both Designated country (which has an expedited process of issuing patents) and original applicant. Furthermore, it is important to bear in mind that the formal theory, which is de-colonial thinking, developed by Mignolo (2008), was crucial in clarifying the theory of the inequality of distribution of intellectual property rights between developed and developing countries once the data collected in the *patentscope* were systematized and codified.

Conclusion

The purpose of this chapter is to analyze the cases of *Carapanaúba* and *Curare*, as pilot case studies by collecting data from the *patentscope*, the database of WIPO. The main target of the ongoing research is to provide empirical evidence for a theory on the inequality of distribution of intellectual property rights in the realm of the use of natural genetic resources and associated traditional knowledge. There is still much to be collected so as to make the theoretical construction more robust. Nevertheless, this first exploration confirms a series of criticisms put forward by different scholars and serves to demonstrate the validity of this proposed theory based on the appropriation, by developed countries, of natural genetic resources from developing countries.

One of the main limitations of this first research question is, in fact, the specificity of these two cases, though it is possible to confirm other case studies concerning the use of natural genetic resources by private companies and public institutions geographically located in developed countries. Nonetheless, this preliminary study should, at the very least, be interpreted as an important beginning of an ongoing process for the formulation of substantial evidence based on the appropriation of natural genetic resources from developing countries by developed countries.

Finally, this chapter provides specific data related to the use of natural genetic resources, typical of the Amazon Region in Brazil, as well as, natural genetic resources used by local tribes in the Amazon Region. Additionally, one of the keywords of each case study, used in the search tools of the *patentscope*, is also part of a local denomination of the plant, which indicates the provenance of the natural resource. It is also relevant to confirm that the use of the data miner from WIPO generates a "thicket" derived from complex search mechanisms and reinsertion of similar or equal data as a different hyperlink. To sum up, all the data extracted from the *patentscope*, once codified and categorized as done earlier, suggest the existence of empirical evidence indicative of the veracity of the theories proposed by previous scholars on the unequal distribution of intellectual property rights between developed and developing countries.

Notes

1 I acknowledge and thank FAPEMIG (Fundação de Amparo à Pesquisa do Estado de Minas Gerais), CNPq (Conselho Nacional de Desenvolvimento Científico e Tecnológico), and MCTI (Ministério da Ciência, Tecnologia e Inovação) for their financial support in making this paper possible.
2 This concept will be fully explained further on in the chapter.
3 I am indebted and grateful to my assistant Lívia Tambasco for her valued assistance with the collection of the data from the patentscope.
4 I am indebted and grateful to my assistant Amanda Carrara for her valued assistance with the collection of the data from the patentscope.

References

Artal, F. J. C. (2012). Curares y timbós, venenos del Amazonas. *Revista de Neurologia, 55*, 689–698.
Barbosa, D. B. (2011, July). Do requisito de suficiência descritiva das patentes. *Revista Da ABPI, 113*, 3–21. Retrieved from http://denisbarbosa.addr.com/arquivos/200/propriedade/requisito_suficiencia_patentes.pdf
Boyle, J. (2004). A Manifesto on WIPO and the Future of Intellectual Property. *Duke Law and Technology Review, 9*, 2–12. Retrieved from https://global.law.duke.edu/journals/dltr/articles/PDF/2004DLTR0009.pdf&oi=ggp

Chang, H.-J. (2001). Intellectual Property Rights and Economic Development: Historical Lessons and Emerging Issues. *Journal of Human Development*, 2(2), 287–309. https://doi.org/10.1080/14649880120067293

Charmaz, K. (2014). *Constructing Grounded Theory (Introducing Qualitative Methods Series)* (2nd ed.). London: SAGE.

Epstein, L., & King, G. (2002). The Rules of Inference. *The University of Chicago Law Review*, 69, 1–133.

Glaser, B. G., & Strauss, A. L. (2017). *Discovery of Grounded Theory: Strategies for Qualitative Research*. New York: Routledge, Taylor and Francis Group. Retrieved from http://a.co/7rQhsS8

Jürgens, B., & Herrero-Solana, V. (2015). Espacenet, Patentscope and Depatisnet: A Comparison Approach. *World Patent Information*, 42(June), 4–12. https://doi.org/10.1016/j.wpi.2015.05.004

Lee, M. (2005). Curare: The South American Arrow Poison. *Journal of Royal College of Physicians of Edinburgh*, 35, 83–92.

Maskus, K. E. (2012). *Private Rights and Public Problems: The Global Economics of Intellectual Property in the 21st Century (Kindle Locations 21–22). Kindle Edition.* (Peterson Institute for International Economics, Ed.), Book (1st ed.). Washington, DC: Peterson Institute for International Economics.

Mignolo, W. D. (2008). La opción de-colonial: desprendimiento y apertura. Un manifiesto y un caso. *Tabula Rasa*, 8, 243–281.

Quijano, A. (2000). Colonialidad del Poder y Clasificación Social. *Journal of World Systems Research*, VI(2), 342–386. https://doi.org/10.1017/CBO9781107415324.004

Sell, S. K. (2003). *Private Power, Public Law: The Globalization of Intellectual Property Rights* (1st ed.). Cambridge: Cambridge University Press.

Sell, S. K. (2011). TRIPS: Fifteen Years Later. *Journal of Intellectual Property Law*, 18(2), 1–29.

Shear, R. H., & Kelley, T. E. (2003). A Researcher's Guide to Patents. *Plant Physiology*, 132(3), 1127–1130. https://doi.org/10.1104/pp.103.022301

Shiva, V. (1991). Biotechnology Development and Conservation of Biodiversity. *Economic and Political Weekly*, 26(48), 2740–2746.

Shiva, V. (1997). Biodiversity Totalitarianism: IPRs as Seed Monopolies. *Economic and Political Weekly*, 32(41), 2582–2585.

Silva, F. de J. P. (2015). *Percepção e saberes do sistema produtivo de carapanaúba (Aspidosperma oblongum) no município de Manaus, Amazonas*. Universidade Federal do Amazonas. Manaus: Pró-Reitoria de Pesquisa e Pós-graduação.

Spence, M. (2007). *Intellectual Property*. Oxford: Oxford University Press.

Trindade, R. C. S., Kikuchi, T. Y. S., Silva, R. J. F., Vale, V. V., Oliveira, A. B., Dolabela, M. F., & Coelho-Ferreira, M. R. (2017). Estudo farmacobotânico das folhas de Aspidosperma excelsum Benth (Apocynaceae). *Revista Fitos*, 10(3). https://doi.org/10.5935/2446-4775.20160019

Yin, R. K. (2017). *Case Study Research and Applications: Design and Methods* (6th ed.), New York: Sage.

13

THE ENVIRONMENTAL PROTECTION IN FRENCH GUIANA

Normative Scheme and Stakes

Frédéric Bondil, Carole Hassoun, Mathilde Kamal-Girard, and Jean-Philippe Vauthier

French Guiana is a territory set in Amazonia, bordering both Brazil and Suriname. Its surface area is almost 84 000 km², covered at 96% with rainforest. The geographical location makes it a reservoir of an exuberant biodiversity:

> 5,400 species of higher plants (including ferns and flowering plants) have been inventoried, including 750 large trees and 300 orchids; there are also 186 mammals, 100 species of bats, 740 birds, 187 reptiles, 110 amphibians, 480 freshwater and brackish water fish and 350,000 to perhaps more than a million species of insects.[1]

In addition to this exceptional flora and fauna, the region also boasts significant underground resources, such as gold deposits, which are the best illustrations of the area's overall richness. Due to these specificities, French Guiana breeds serious and specific environmental crime issues. First and foremost is the illegal gold panning, which public authorities perceive as a real scourge and try to tackle consequently,[2] notably by setting up special operations[3] and enacting derogatory legal provisions.[4] No one can deny the environmental damage. One just has to think about the destruction of the Amazon rainforest and its components, or the significant pollution of soils and rivers, not to mention the dangerous consequences for human health. The risks brought by illegal gold panning justify the adoption of essential measures and provisions, in order to fight against this plague and preserve the Amazon biome. However, we can find and name other nuisances, such as protected species traffic, illegal fishing—with a singular aspect involving trafficking in fish bladders[5]—and *legal* gold panning and mining, which can also be a source of environmental damage. Protecting Guiana's biodiversity therefore seems both necessary and imperative. But how can French legislation, adopted over 7,000 kilometers away, meet the specific needs of a South American territory? If Montaigne wondered "*what truth these mountains bound, which is a lie to the world beyond?*" how can we conceive of a truth being the same in two worlds, separated not by bare mountains, but by an ocean?

If we refer to the French institutional organization, article 72-3 of the Constitution of October 4, 1958, states that: "*The Republic shall recognise the overseas populations within the French people in a common ideal of liberty, equality and fraternity,*"[6] distinguishing

DOI: 10.4324/9781003330653-17

four different types of local authorities. French Guiana is one of the overseas departments and regions ruled by article 73 of the French Constitution.[7] The latter are under the principle of *"legal assimilation,"* which means that *"statutes and regulations shall be automatically applicable,"* but also that *"they may be adapted in the light of the specific characteristics and constraints of such communities."* At first sight, French Guiana seems to be a territory where national law is likely to apply entirely, with some adjustments due to the local context, even though it seems a long way from mainland France. In this respect, it is possible to note a few particularities. The territory of French Guiana has seen the creation of an original land tenure system, called the *Zones de Droits d'Usage Collectifs* (ZDUC). This kind of environmental commons was set up in 1987[8] for *"communities of inhabitants who draw their means of living from the forest"*[9] and allows some exemptions for hunting, fishing, or the removal of soil and plants.[10] Besides, in 2007, the *Parc Amazonien de Guyane* (PAG),[11] the National Park of French Guiana, France's largest national park with a surface area of around 34,000 km², was created to carry out traditional environmental missions, as well as a more specific mission related to the presence of indigenous populations, creating a *"remarkable derogation system"*[12] for the exploitation of natural resources.[13] Presented as the *"common heritage of human beings,"*[14] the environment requires major protection through the implementation of effective and concrete tools at the national level but also and especially on the territory of French Guiana.

Even though they cast some light on the issue, these first answers are by no means sufficient. We shall examine them more deeply and thoroughly from the particular standpoint of the application of national law as an instrument for protecting the French Amazon. First, we will be looking at the general tools of environmental protection (I) and we will consider the specific means of the protection of the Guianese environment (II).

The General Tools of Environmental Protection

In order to understand the general means of protecting the Amazon in French Guiana, we first need to look at the normative framework (A), and then consider the role of the judicial judge, particularly with regard to ecological damage (B).

The Normative Framework

France is a unitary state, as ruled by the first article of the Constitution setting that the Republic is *"indivisible."* For a long time, the unity of the State was both political and administrative. In France, national sovereignty vests in the People,[15] who adopt legal rules, and these rules apply to the whole territory.[16] The Constitution, adopted on October 4, 1958, is the supreme one. From 1958, an ongoing evolution has changed the administrative unity into a decentralized organization,[17] whereas the political unity has been preserved.

French Guiana, which is the only part of the domestic territory that has boundaries into the Amazonian area, has a specific status inside the Frend decentralized state. Article L. 7111-1 of the General Local Authorities Code rules that French Guiana is:

> A territorial community ruled by the Article 73 of the Constitution which exercises the powers of overseas departments and overseas regions and all powers determined by statutes in order to take into account its specific characteristics and constraints.

French Guiana, designated as a *collectivité territoriale unique*[18]—a "single territorial community"—is allowed to have its own self-government, including a local assembly and a President, who is presently Gabriel Serville. Assisting the assembly are the Economic, Social, Environmental, Cultural and Educative Council of French Guiana, on the one hand, and the Grand Council of Amerindian and Bushinenge people, on the other hand. This local assembly takes decisions in all matters arising under powers.

Considering this normative framework, we can keep in mind that: (1) Constitution has normative effect on the whole territory; (2) national statutes usually apply on the whole territory, except from notwithstanding express clauses; and (3) self-governments can enact local administrative acts in order to deal with specific matters.

The Constitution

The French Constitution is a rather short formal Constitution. It sets out few fundamental rights, as it lays down no Title or Chapter dedicated to Human Rights; on the contrary to the Brazilian Constitution or most Constitutions enacted after World War II.[19] In France, constitutional fundamental rights are enshrined, but they are proclaimed in other documents than the Constitution itself. In 1971, the Constitutional Council, which rules on the conformity of Acts of Parliament and legal clauses,[20] has given constitutional value to all texts quoted by the Preamble of the Constitution[21]: the Declaration of 1789, the Preamble to the Constitution of 1946, and more recently the Charter for the Environment of 2004.[22] This textual and jurisprudential sedimentation is known as the *bloc de constitutionnalité*—the "constitutionality block."

The great principles of criminal law and environmental law are principally protected through these three declarations, which rule nothing specific to the Amazon. For instance, there is no similar clause to article 225 §4 of the Brazilian Constitution setting that the Amazonian rainforest is the heritage of the Nation.[23] The Charter for the Environment simply rules that *"the environment is the common heritage of all human beings."*[24]

There are few applications of these constitutional principles to French Guiana, and applications to the French part of the Amazon are even rarer. The only one is the February 18, 2022, decision ruled by the Constitutional Council.[25] In this ruling, the French constitutional judge had to deal with the constitutionality of statutory provisions allowing some mining concessions belonging to the *Montagne d'Or* (Golden Mountain) company *ipso jure*. The Constitutional Council has declared that various provisions of the mining code infringed the right to live in a balanced environment, the right to due respect for health, the duty to foresee and avoid the occurrence of any harm one may cause to the environment, and the duty to prevent such damage. Doing so, the Constitutional Council has ruled in favor of the full efficiency to environmental rights, making them prevail over other rights, and particularly over first-generation rights such as freedom of trade, freedom of contract, and property rights. The Constitutional Council has consequently given full legal effect to the constitutional principle that *"the safeguarding of the environment is a goal to be pursued in the same way as the other fundamental interests of the Nation."*[26] Having said that, it is not certain that the decision will lead to any tangible improvement in mining conditions in French Guiana, although it places great emphasis on the normative aspects of environmental protection. Even though the ruling does not ban mining concessions in general, it has brought legal gold panning to a halt in the facts. At the same time, illegal gold mining keeps on spreading across the Guiana Plateau, bringing with it pollution and crime.

Statutes and Regulation

French infra-constitutional norms scarcely deal with the Amazon itself. A skim through French (legifrance) and Brazilian (Normas.leg.br) legislation browsers makes it appear quite quickly. The word "*Amazonie/Amazônia*" and its related words stand out 62 times for the whole general rules (statutes, regulation, decrees) in France and more than 250 times in a similar normative corpus in Brazil, only taking into account the federal level. Amazon as such is a hardly present legal item in France. Indeed, all occurrences found are linked with the Amazonian Park.[27] Furthermore, "*general provisions for the national parks and those specific to overseas departments apply to the Amazonian Park in Guiana,*"[28] except from legal derogations, so that legal assimilation prevails, giving little way to Amazon-related rules at first glance.

However, in reality, the protection of the Amazonian area comes from other ways: criminal and environmental laws, which can have a particular application inside the geographical zone if they are appropriate. Many of these rules are laid down in codes such as the Mining Code, the Criminal Code, or the Environmental Code. For instance, article L. 110-1 of the Environmental Code defines as common heritage of the nation:

> Spaces, resources and natural environments on land and at sea, the sounds and smells that characterise them, sites, daytime and night-time landscapes, air quality, water quality, living beings and biodiversity.

In France, the whole environment is considered as national heritage and, consequently, so is the Amazon. In other words, the Amazon does not have a specific place inside the environment. Nonetheless, in the middle of the French part of the Amazon, such a special area does exist: the Amazonian Park. The delimitation of that zone allows to add another level of protection inside its boundaries, notably for native populations.[29]

As to the great principles of criminal law, they are contained in the Criminal Code. One major rule is related to the division of competencies between legislation and regulation: the law defines crimes and offenses, while regulation defines contraventions. Each of these norms determines the penalties applicable to those who committed the infringements.[30] Illegal gold mining and panning is defined as an offense punishable by five years' imprisonment and a €100,000 fine,[31] with the possibility of increased penalties.[32]

Policing the Amazon implies a necessary conciliation between these different norms, which can, in turn, complement each other, reinforce each other, and eventually give way to each other, in particular, because the specific laws will prevail over the more general rules.

The Role of the Judicial Judge in Environmental Damage: Compensation for Ecological Harm

While the main principles of French environmental law derive essentially from the Constitution and from legal and regulatory provisions, it is impossible to think about this law field without mentioning the central role of the judge and the importance of case law. Whether administrative, judicial, constitutional, European, or international, courts face a real challenge and have become the main protagonists in ecological awakening. They play an active part in the ongoing construction of environmental law and guarantee the efficiency of environmental rules. At the national level, the administrative courts appear to be the natural judges on nature and biodiversity protection litigation, given the harm done to the general interest, which is the specific concern of the administrative judge. In relation to administrative police, the Act n° 2008-757 of August 1, 2008, on environmental liability and various provisions for adapting to Community law in the field of the environment transposed a European directive on the prevention and repairing environmental damage.[33] Nevertheless, because of its transverse nature, and under pressure from civil society and environmental associations in particular, the environmental cause is also of great interest to the judicial courts. The protection of the environment, and ultimately of human beings falls under the judicial jurisdiction in the logic of liability and regulation of human activities. In order to preserve a healthy natural environment for human beings, and in accordance with article 1 of the French Charter for the Environment, the courts have the power to take action and, above all, to impose penalties on companies that engage themselves in harmful polluting activities[34] and fail, for example, to comply with their duty of environmental vigilance.[35] The Constitutional Council has emphasized that, under articles 1 and 2 of the Charter of the Environment, *"everyone has an obligation to be vigilant with regard to any damage to the environment that may result from one's activity."*[36] Moreover, courts can be confronted with specific situations, such as the ones we find in French Guiana, whose territory is covered by over 90% Amazon rainforest and suffers from illegal gold panning, with disastrous consequences on the ecosystem and human beings. Dealing with frequently imprecise texts, courts have been called upon to adapt the existing law and to show leadership and creativity in building the law of environmental civil liability, aiming at punishing attacks to the environment. Two main manifestations of the judicial judge's role are worth highlighting here: his role as co-author of the legal rules (1) and the importance of his punitive role (2).

The Judicial Judge as Co-Author of Environmental Civil Liability Law

The universality and flexibility of civil liability law have enabled judges to demonstrate their inventiveness in guaranteeing environmental protection,[37] without distorting the law. The judicial courts have thus been able to resort to the case law theory of abnormal neighborhood disturbances in order to put an end to an abnormal disturbance to the environment.[38] More significantly, they have enshrined pure ecological harm and defined it in the famous *Erika*[39] ruling as an *"autonomous objective prejudice"* to nature. However, it is taken for granted that compensable harm is nothing other than the injury to a legally protected individual interest, for civil liability law gravitates around the subject—and not the object—of law. Ecological harm, as it has been introduced by the *Cour de cassation*, the French judicial Court, deals exclusively with harm to nature. It is then intrinsically impersonal. This decision thus disregards a primary condition of reparation under usual judicial law, according to which the injury must be personal to the victim. The creative power of the courts has made the conditions of civil liability change. Nevertheless, the main purpose of liability law remains the need to establish a broken balance once again, by compensating an abnormally injured interest.

The legislator, directly inspired by case-law and doctrinal proposals,[40] recognized, by Act n°2016-1087 of August 8, 2016, for the reconquest of biodiversity, nature, and landscapes,[41] the existence of ecological harm, which was then codified within articles 1246 et seq. of the Civil Code. Article 1246 states that *"[a]ny person responsible for ecological harm is obliged to make reparation for it."* The law further defines this damage as *"a non-negligible harm to the elements or functions of ecosystems or to the collective benefits derived by man from the environment.*"[42] Presented this way, ecological harm covers a wide range of realities. Above all, compensation for ecological harm reveals a paradigm shift: it is no longer humans who suffer but nature and its biodiversity. One must therefore dissociate the objective harm suffered by the ecosystem from the subjective harm suffered by humans as a result of the attack on the environment.[43] This is not without disrupting the traditional *summa divisio* of persons and things, and the anthropocentric vision of man's relationship with nature. Considering the environment as a victim, and admitting that it is in some way a "creditor" of a debt of reparation, suggests a personification of nature. Compensation for ecological harm would therefore seem to be part of this growing desire to recognize nature's rights. The interactions between ecosystems and humans are highlighted in many countries and are constantly evolving. A river or a forest, for example, has been recognized as the holder of rights.[44] These interactions are also highlighted in French Guiana, in order to protect not only the territory's tangible and intangible heritage but also human health: it is thus proposed to recognize a new legal status for the Maroni River, the natural border with Suriname, to protect it from the dangers of illegal gold panning.[45] If proposals have been made to change the way nature is represented,[46] leading to clear changes,[47] French private law nevertheless remains faithfully attached to the *res/persona* distinction. It is generally accepted that the compensation for ecological harm calls for the recognition of a thing-victim whose protection must be ensured by courts,[48] without questioning the relationship between the human and the non-human.

According to the law, the judge shall then repair the attacks caused to the environment. However, the legal definition of ecological harm is restrictive: not all harmful actions to ecosystems are compensable, and only non-negligible attacks are.[49] It is nevertheless still necessary to agree on the notion of "compensable harm," which has not been defined by the legislator. Distinguishing harm and damage should bring useful enlightening. If the damage represents the environmental impairment suffered, the reparable harm would concern the abnormal consequences of this impairment for nature and biodiversity.[50] Consequently, environmental harm would not be compensated *ipso facto*. Only the serious consequences of such attacks, which would then be "*non-negligible*," would be subject to compensation. One must emphasize the importance of the discretion of the court, considering the abnormality of the damage caused to nature and biodiversity. Indeed, the judge will ultimately be the only one to characterize the ecological harm, assessing abnormality on a case-by-case basis. This is nothing new in the law of civil liability: the theory of abnormal neighborhood disturbances is based on a similar process, as it is up to the judge to assess the abnormality of the disturbance.

The Punitive Power of the Judicial Judge

In order to guarantee the effectiveness of environmental justice, the Biodiversity Act of August 8, 2016, gives courts decisive powers regarding the terms of reparation: on the one hand, the legislator imposes on the courts reparation in kind for ecological harm[51] as a priority and, on the other, recognizes preventive actions due to the singularity of litigation with a view to acting upstream of environmental damage. Independently of compensation for the harm, judges can then take reasonable measures to prevent the damage[52] before the injury to the protected interest has occurred. Judges can also put a stop to the unlawful act in order to avoid any future damage. These preventive powers granted to the judge are essential in environmental matters, as is reparation in kind, which is particularly well-suited to the specific nature of the harm in question. Other singularities are evident, notably the remarkable flexibility of the procedural rules. The law recognizes that the action for reparation of ecological harm is

> open to any person with standing and an interest in acting, such as the State, the French Biodiversity Office, local authorities and their groupings whose territory is concerned, as well as public establishments and associations approved or created for at least five years on the date the proceedings are brought, whose object is the protection of nature and the defence of the environment.

While the action appears to be designated on article 1248 of the aforementioned Civil Code at first reading, it is important to note that the indicated list is not exhaustive. Consequently, the action for reparation is open to any person with an interest in the matter, from which it follows that the latter has standing to sue. Incidentally, one can note that the approach is coherent when it comes to the "*common heritage of human beings.*"[53]

Nonetheless, these specific provisions raise limits to the courts' role, and especially to the effectiveness of their decisions. First of all, while the law recognizes reparation in kind as a priority, thereby impeding the judge's classic sovereign power in choosing reparation, the legislator did not take care to specify the possible measures of reparation in kind.[54] This lack brings difficulties for litigants, as it is up to the claimant to ask the judge for a precise and adequate remedy to the environmental damage.[55] Environmental law is however technical, complex, and sometimes fraught with scientific uncertainty. One should nevertheless underline that the judge will always be able to award damages "*in the event of de jure or de facto impossibility or inadequacy of remedial measures.*"[56] Once again, though, the judge's role is limited: damages must be "*allocated to the repair of the environment.*" In spite of its coherence, the rule goes against the principle of the free allocation of damages recognized by the judicial judge.[57] To make environmental justice truly effective, it will also be necessary to take into account the specific characteristics of the territory in question. The attacks on the Amazonian ecosystems caused by human actions raise essential environmental issues and could lead the courts to adapt their rulings to the territory's particular specificities and customs, in order to preserve not only its ecological heritage but also the health of the human societies living in close proximity to it. The Amazonian Park of French Guiana is a vivid example: in order to preserve an extremely rich biodiversity and the cultural heritage of the local and indigenous populations living within it, the Park's Charter, approved on October 28, 2013,[58] provides for derogatory provisions.[59]

The environmental law efficiency therefore remains relative, which justifies a quite rare level of litigation in civil matters. One can cast doubt on the cross-disciplinary nature of environmental law. While interdisciplinary is inevitably a strength, it is also one of the main weaknesses of environmental law, as it results in the dispersal of applicable standards. A number of proposals have been put forward, such as improving dialogue between the various players involved in the environment[60] or creating a new jurisdiction exclusively responsible for the protection of nature and biodiversity.[61] The need for environmental law to be clear and accessible is paramount, not only to ensure the protection of ecosystems and their functions but also to protect the rights of those subject to the law and to ensure environmental justice.

The Specific Tools of French Amazon's Environmental Protection

Within this complex body of legislation, which is not always conducive to effective environmental protection, there are nevertheless a number of specific means available to take into account the particularities of the Guianese context. These include the classic tools of criminal law, especially environmental criminal law (A), as well as the original provisions of the Amazonian Park of French Guiana (B).

The Particularity of Environmental Criminal Law in French Guiana

If there is one essential regulatory tool, it is criminal law, that is to say, *"the branch of law that defines society's exercise of the power to punish."*[62] Presented as such, criminal law appears to be the ideal means of ensuring environmental protection in general, and in the French Amazon in particular. However, the specific context of French Guiana still raises the question of its application. The principle of legal assimilation is fully applicable in criminal matters. The principle is enshrined in article 113-2 of the French Criminal Code, which states that *"French criminal law is applicable to offences committed on the territory of the Republic."* Any offense committed in French Guiana, and thus within the territory of the French Republic, is consequently subject to national criminal law, although this does not prevent certain foreign elements from being taken into account, including environmental offenses.[63] Having said that, it remains necessary to appraise how the environmental criminal law, whereas adopted at the national level, can meet the specific situation and specific delinquency[64] of this French territory located in South America. From this point of view, it should be noted that the protection of the French Amazon by repressive environmental law suffers from the inherent complexity of the discipline (1), as well as it should also be underlined that some adjustments have been made, notably in the fight against illegal gold panning (2).

The Inherent Complexity of Criminal Environmental Law

As various authors who have studied the issue point it out, criminal law is a complex body of law that *"is characterized by a wide dispersion of texts, a multiplicity of special incriminations and the unsuitability of some penalties ordered by the criminal courts."*[65] There are a large number of incriminating texts, scattered throughout various codes (Environmental Code, Rural Code, Town Planning Code, Public Health Code, Forest Code, Mining Code, etc., with the Penal Code occupying only a marginal position), and most of them are drafted in a way that makes it difficult to identify the constituent elements of the offence. Most of the time, they are *"'domino incriminations', with the Parliament describing the constituent elements of the offences in an imprecise manner, leaving it up to the executive to define their contours."*[66] Other authors also call attention to the fact that

> there is a constellation of heterogeneous incriminations related to fines or offences, which are specific to each environment (water, soil pollution, protection of animal species . . .), and are often little used in the absence of being clearly identified and prioritized.[67]

Also, the repression of environmental offenses appears to be somewhat complex, given the duality of penalties, which can be both criminal and administrative, but also because of a certain *"illogicality,"*[68] an *"inadequacy of the proposed penalties [which] is coupled with an inconsistency in the hierarchy of penalties.*"[69] Besides, the investigation and detection of environmental offenses are still subject to some specificities. In addition to officers and agents of the judicial police, as defined by the Code of Criminal Procedure, environmental inspectors are also competent under the conditions set out in article L. 172-1 of the Environmental Code, including certain civil servants and public agents belonging to government departments responsible for implementing the provisions of the Environmental Code, as well as those belonging to the French Biodiversity Office or to national parks. In many respects, environmental criminal law is dependent on special administrative policies. They were 25 before an Ordinance of January 11, 2012,[70] which further adds to the difficulty of repression.

As a result of this complexity, environmental criminal litigation accounts for only a small proportion of the activity of French criminal courts. In 2019, a joint evaluation mission by the Ministries of Justice and Ecological Transition made the scathing observation that "*environmental litigation has been neglected, rendering it invisible.*"[71] Between 2015 and 2019, this type of litigation accounted for less than 1% of all criminal cases, half the figure at the end of the 1990s,[72] when it was close to 2%.[73] In this context, one must notice that environmental law remains ineffective, although the observation is more optimistic as to criminal law as it is "*a sector that is significantly gaining ground.*"[74] Among the improvements, we should note the creation of "*regional centres specialized in environmental offences,*" notably in Cayenne,[75] by the Act of December 24, 2020.[76] These centers enable the handling of "*cases that are or appear to be complex, due in particular to their technical nature, the extent of the damage or the geographical area to which they extend*"[77] by dedicated magistrates and judiciary assistants. The same law also introduces a *convention judiciaire d'intérêt public (CJIP)*—a public interest judicial agreement—in environmental matters, which constitutes an alternative to prosecution applicable to legal entities and also allows for compensation for ecological harm.[78] In addition, there are provisions specific to French Guyana.

Adapting Criminal Environmental Law to the Context of French Guiana: The Case of the Fight Against Illegal Gold Panning

Notwithstanding both inherent difficulties in this field and the principle of the territoriality of criminal law, environmental law has managed to adapt itself to some extent to the Guianese specificities of environmental crime, especially in the fight against illegal gold panning. Several successive laws, most recently the "climate and resilience" Act of August 22, 2021,[79] have introduced a number of mechanisms designed to improve the effectiveness of the fight against uncontrolled gold mining in Guiana's soils and rivers, which is the cause of a great deal of environmental damage (deforestation, mercury pollution of water, destruction of ecosystems etc.).

In terms of substantive criminal law provisions, the Mining Code provides for offenses of direct relevance to the fight against illegal gold panning in French Guiana. Article L. 512-1, I bis of this code provides for a penalty of five years' imprisonment and a fine of 100,000 euros for the operation of a mine without authorization, or failure to comply with certain rules laid down for French Guiana concerning the possession and transport of mercury, all or part of a crusher or pump body (equipment used for gold mining), and the register to be kept by gold mine explorers and operators under article L. 621-15 of the Mining Code. Penalties for exploiting a mine without authorization are increased by article L. 512-2 and raised to five years' imprisonment and a fine of 375,000 euros when certain environmental offenses are involved; seven years' imprisonment and a fine of 1 million euros when all or part of the offense is committed within the boundaries of a national park, regional nature park, nature reserve, protected marine area or biological reserve; and ten years' imprisonment and a fine of 4.5 million euros when the offense is committed by an organized gang. In addition, the offense set out in article L. 621-8-3 of the French Mining Code also specifically concerns French Guiana, as it incriminates the loading, unloading, or transshipment of a boat, floating craft or floating equipment on French Guiana's inland waters, as part of an illegal gold panning activity. The penalty is three years' imprisonment and a fine of 100,000 euros. One should also note that article L. 512-3-1, created by the Act of August 22, 2021, makes foreigners guilty of one of the offenses defined in I bis of article L. 512-1 and article L. 512-2 liable to the additional penalty of deportation from French territory.

With regard to the rules of criminal procedure, article L. 621-8-4 of the Mining Code, created by the August 22, 2021, Act, empowers environmental inspectors, agents of the *Office National des Forêts (ONF)*—Forests National Office—and the *Office Français de la Biodiversité (OFB)*—Biodiversity French Office—to record violations of the Mining Code throughout French Guiana.[80] One should also mention the possibility of postponing the start of police custody,[81] as provided for by article L. 621-8 of the French Mining Code, when the transfer of persons arrested within the legal time limit for police custody raises insurmountable difficulties. Placers, where illegal gold mining takes place, are often located in the Amazon rainforest, several hours away from police and gendarmerie stations. This can create difficulties when it comes to calculating the length of police custody, which in principle starts from the moment the person is taken into police custody.[82] In addition, the starting point for customs detention[83] can also be postponed under this provision for offenses defined in article 414-1 of the Customs Code.[84] However, one should stress that, in all cases, the postponement may not exceed 20 hours until arrival at the premises where the measure is to take place and remains subject to the prior authorization of the public prosecutor or the investigating court.

Another derogatory mechanism worth highlighting is the possibility of destroying, immediately and on site, equipment seized as part of operations to combat illegal gold panning. The provisions of article L. 628-2-1 of the Mining Code are certainly justified by the practical impossibility of transporting equipment seized in the Amazonian Forest, such as a crusher, but it must be acknowledged that these measures call into question the respect for the rights of those prosecuted, since destruction takes place without any conviction being handed down by a judge.[85]

Finally, we should mention that the Climate and Resilience Act of August 22, 2021, created article L. 621-8-5 of the Mining Code, which provides for the introduction of identity checks, for the purposes of investigating and prosecuting offenses in connection with illegal gold panning,

> on the written requisition of the public prosecutor, on the territory of French Guiana and for the period of time that this magistrate determines and which may not exceed twenty-four hours, renewable on express and reasoned decision in accordance with the same procedure.[86]

This new provision enables a broader application of the ordinary types of controls provided for in article 78-2, paragraph 7, of the Code of Criminal Procedure, to which article L. 621-8-5, I, of the Mining Code refers, but above all, it enables the inspection of vehicles and boats, as well as the search of luggage, and the inspection of ships or any floating craft in territorial waters.[87]

Environmental criminal law is thus a special tool for protecting the French Amazon, but the Amazonian Park of French Guiana is another distinctive tool that needs to be developed.

A Remarkable Protected Area Under French Law: The Amazonian Park of French Guiana

The Earth Summit held in Rio de Janeiro, Brazil, launched the idea of creating a National Park in French Guiana. The project led by the French government transcribed the international blueprint for action on the environment, climate, and biodiversity. Doing so, France guaranteed the preservation of the Amazonian rainforest as a part of the Earth's "*green heart.*"[88] The environmental initiative had to deal with strong reluctance and sometimes sheer hostility. However, these expressions of opposition were somehow divided, into a power struggle confronting French Guiana's communities one against each other and each of them against the French State.[89] According to our opinion, it was a more general or more transverse resistance to an institution of environmental preservation that laid beyond this balance of power.

This kind of dissension happens frequently when Governments create protected areas. Some States in Africa or South-East Asia that met these problems have chosen to take action either by expulsing all inhabitants from the preserved areas or by prohibiting all human activities, including life-sustaining activities,[90] from them. These extreme solutions can be avoided, at least in France, due to "second generation" National Parks. The April 14, 2006, Act on National Park, modifying the July 22, 1960 Act, has contributed to promoting sustainable development, all the more since the 1992 Earth Summit, and has given a wider space to human interventions inside National Parks.[91] After more than ten years of tough discussions, the 2006 reform was essential to achieve the creation of the Amazonian Park of French Guiana by the February 27, 2007, Decree.[92] The legislative reform settles a new pattern consistent with local wishes. It also introduces special provisions in the Environmental Code for the Amazonian Park.[93] It realizes both a legal adaptation and a political compromise whose follow-ups are the Decree creating the Park, the Park's first Charter,[94] and the Conventions related to the implementation of Charter.[95]

The main characteristic of the Amazonian Park of French Guiana is that it does not only aim at conserving natural environments. It intends to protect human activities as well as the Amazonian biome. The Amazonian Park's support to the peoples inhabiting its borders is two-fold. First of all, the setting up and management of the Amazonian Park must not challenge past societal practices, which is what we will expose in the first part of these developments (1). The Amazonian Park also presents itself as a backing to the immobility suffered by the Amazonian human societies, which is what we will consider in the second part (2).

A Pacifying Park

The territorial organization of National Parks after the 2006 Reform was enough to limit the threat of lifestyle troublemaking rules. The legislation plans to juxtapose two areas in each park: a *zone de Cœur*—a "core zone"—a *zone d'adhésion* or *zone d'adhésion libre*—a "membership zone." The membership zone is determined by a principle of freedom (a). The core zone is ruled by an exemption system, which is more remarkable (b).

The Membership Zone and the Lack of Constraints

In this area, being part of the Amazonian Park is a choice. The 2007 Decree determines the towns or villages that are parts of the membership zone but fixes it only temporarily. Indeed, each town or village must bear it out by approving the Amazonian Park's Charter. Papaïchton, Saül, Maripasoula, and Camopi have made this choice.[96] Besides, nothing forbids these villages and towns to go back on their membership, either by rejecting the second Charter or any later one or by withdrawing from a more than 15-year Charter that has not been reviewed.[97]

There are no specific obligations to a territory's membership. The whole human activities, private or public, lucrative or not, are under usual regulation. Inside the membership zone or outside the National Park, the legislation is the same. As to hunting, farming, trading, or industrial logging, the National Parks' Charters only define orientations for the membership zone.[98] These orientations, including enforcement actions of the Charter, are mere recommendations. However, when towns[99] commit to abide by the Charter in Conventions related to its implementation,[100] or when the Charter transcribes legislative or regulatory provisions, notably dealing with environmental police or gold mining regulation,[101] the recommendations turn into mandatory rules.

The new constraints coming from instituting a National Park were far less likely to be avoided concerning the core zone.

The Core Zone and the Neutralization of the Constraints

In this central area, environmental protection establishes strong constraints to human activities,[102] even after the April 14, 2006, Act. The National Parks' Charters do not promulgate bare recommendations but objectives and measures with binding effect. As to the Amazonian Park, public authorities did not abolish the general regime from the core zone.[103] However, they have tried to soften or eliminate this ordinary regime for the benefit of the inhabitants of the Amazonian Park.

The way public authorities marked out the core zone was a strong contribution to this rules-softening, for they included only territories without permanent residents inside the core zone. But one should not conclude too quickly that the core zone is free of human beings, when it comes to the preservation of practices considered as legitimate. The combined provisions of April 14, 2006, Act, the Decree creating the Amazonian Park, and its first Charter define altogether a specific framework for the Amerindian and Bushinenge communities set in the National Park. These native and local communities do not have to comply with general prohibitions of hunting, fishing, harvesting unmanaged plants, and collecting minerals inside the Amazonian Park.[104] The exemption is valid for any personal or family consumption, if no marketing follows. Besides, plants and minerals can be used in manufacturing handicrafts, even if they are aimed to be sold to people outside the Park's traditional and non-resident communities.[105]

Saying that, we should not presume that the regulation inside the Amazonian Park only softens when it comes to *"the communities of inhabitants who generally make a living from the woods,*" as the expression from the Environmental Code goes.[106] Although the limits are stricter,[107] the National Park's other residents benefit from derogatory provisions to preserve their ways of life. The Decree creating the Amazonian Park allows them to hunt, fish, harvest unmanaged plants, and collect minerals if these activities are occasional.[108] They can use gathered plants, leaves, or stones to make household goods, except from handicraft production.[109]

The Amazonian Park is not only an institution that disturbs its inhabitants as little as possible. The Park supports them more directly or more positively.

A Park Encouraging Progress

The Amazonian Park must contribute to whatever its inhabitants wish to see evolving. The Statute specifically assigns this role to the National Park when it has to deal with the living conditions' general improvements. The Park has given itself this mission in order to help legal transformations.

A Park Supporting the Society's Progress

When it comes to the Amazonian Park of French Guiana, the Environmental Code does not limit its purpose to protecting and promoting the Guianese biodiversity. The Park must also "*serve the development of the communities of inhabitants who generally make a living from the woods, taking into account their traditional way of life*" and "*participate to a whole realizations and improvements in their social, economic and cultural aspects.*"[110] The Environmental Code links the Park's missions related to the peoples to the Charter's sustainable development project.[111]

The Charter prevents support to economic activities considered as non-sustainable. Particularly, it excludes any help to the gold mining sector.[112] On the other hand, the Charter insists on the development of nature-based tourism,[113] the sustainability of forest resources exploitation, as well as the promotion of local know-how.[114] Encouraging these activities is obviously out of the National Park's core business. The Charter underlines that the Park is not designed to replace the usual actors of business assistance. The Park must simply remain a helpful partner to get financial aid, technical support, or training actions. The Charter lets open the possibility for the Park to take the initiative in a "*vigourous economic development phase.*"[115] In fact, other institutions have few means to intervene, which gives a large extent to this enhanced facilitation. However, the Amazonian Park local life committee has stuck to what we can call a relay or spokesperson role to make the Local Government of Guiana act on road opening and digital isolation.[116]

The membership zone is clearly the main target of the development support, because development is a crucial stake for the towns and villages belonging to the Amazonian Park. The Charter does not completely omit the core zone, where the Decree creating the Park allows commercial activities "*associated to tourism,*"[117] making an exception to the general rule prohibiting them. The Park has shown ambition to contribute to develop light ecotourism structures, having little impact on the natural environment, whereas the area is principally dedicated to protecting biodiversity.[118]

The Amazonian Park's boldness is all the more impressive when it comes to encouraging legislative or regulatory changes.

A Park in Support of Law Progress

Apart from protected areas-related rules, provisions applicable to the Amazonian Park as well as to the rest of French Guiana or the whole French territory do exist. At first sight, the Park has no concern for them. However, it has already tried to make them its own.

The Park can intervene to make the implementation of these provisions more effective and efficient, for the sake of the inhabitants at least as much as for the sake of the ecosystems. The most significant example is related to gold mining regulation. The Charter goes further with the sole prohibition of gold mining in the core zone. It insists on the Amazonian Park and its agents' involvement against illegal gold mining, although the Park's action is presented by the Environmental Authority's observations[119] as subsidiary, the overseeing and cracking down on illegal gold mining belonging first to the Central Government.[120]

Another example is linked with the respect and protection of Amerindian and Bushinenge communities' culture and practices, by adapting national and European regulations. No need to determine if this kind of action is more difficult to carry out than the previous one. In a cooperative approach,[121] it realizes a variation of the regulations on hunting prohibition and protected species consumption.[122] These adaptations could make legal the ritual eating of spider-monkey, also called kwata, during funeral ceremonies. For sure, one can express reservations about the merits of this initiative and its chances of success. However, it confirms the singularity of the Amazonian Park of French Guiana among the environmental protection areas.

The regulation of the Amazon involves a necessary reconciliation between all these different standards and rules, which can, in turn, complement each other, reinforce each other, and eventually give way to each other, notably because the specific law will prevail over more general rules. In particular, these standards will be effective, thanks to the major intervention of the judge, presented as a key player in the preservation of ecosystems and their functions: he is the one who guarantees the effectiveness of standards through their application. In addition to these general aspects, repressive environmental law has a particular resonance in French Guiana, which contributes to better protection for this French portion of the Amazon. But originality does not stop at criminal law, and the unique provisions of the Amazonian Park of French Guiana clearly demonstrate not only the major interest in preserving the environment and its exceptional biodiversity but also the inescapable protection of the practices and activities of the communities present on the territory.

Notes

1 Lochon S., Linares S., "Conservation de la nature: les espèces protégées de la Guyane", *Revue forestière française*, AgroParisTech, 2003, 55, p. 323, hal-03449423.
2 Many public reports deal with the issue. See lately: Adam L., Serville G., Rapport . . . sur la lutte contre l'orpaillage illégal en Guyane, Assemblée Nationale, Rapport n° 4404, 31 juillet 2021. See also: Bas P., Darnaud M., Fichet J. L., Joissains S., Mohamed Soilihi T., *Rapport . . . pour une grande loi Guyane: 52 propositions*, Sénat, Rapport n° 337, 19 février 2020, specially p. 33 à 43.
3 The main of these special operations is the "Harpie" operation, which has been carried out jointly since 2008 by French Guiana's gendarmerie and armed forces, under the authority of the prefect and public prosecutor, and which *"aims to asphyxiate illegal gold mining zones and destabilize the underground economy on a long-term basis"* (*"vise à asphyxier les zones d'orpaillage clandestin et à déstabiliser durablement l'économie souterraine"*) de Rohan J., Dupont B., Berthou J., Antoinette J.-É., *Rapport d'information . . . à la suite d'une mission effectuée du 15 au 19 décembre 2010 en Guyane*, Sénat, Rapport n° 271, 1er février 2011, p. 27. About illegal gold panning

and other aspects of the delinquency in French Guiana, see Falxa J., "La Guyane, personne ne vous croira", *AJ penal*, 2019, p. 70.
4 See *infra*.
5 The swim bladder is the fish's organ for regulating its buoyancy. The swim bladder of the red acupa, a fish living in Guyanese waters, is highly prized on the Asian market, leading to an overfishing that threatens the survival of the species.
6 Montaigne, *Essais*, II, 12.
7 With Guadeloupe, Martinique, Reunion and Mayotte. See French Constitution, art. 73.
8 Decree n°87-267 of April 14, 1987 "amending the State domain Code and relating to State concessions and other acts entered into by the State in French Guiana with a view to the operation or transfer of its State-owned buildings", *JORF* of April 16, 1987, p. 4316.
9 Periphrasis avoiding the use of the terms "Native," "Amerindian," or "Maroon."
10 On the *ZDUC*, see notably Davy D., Filoche G. (coord.), *Zones de Droits d'Usage Collectifs, concessions et cessions en Guyane française: Bilan et perspectives 25 ans après*, Rapport IRD, avril 2014: https://horizon.documentation.ird.fr/exl-doc/pleins_textes/divers15-04/010064386.pdf.
11 Decree n°2007-206 of February 27, 2007 "creating the national park named "Amazonian Park of French Guiana", *JORF*, February 28, p. 3757.
12 Bondil F., "Le Parc amazonien de Guyane et l'exploitation des ressources naturelles. Réflexions juridiques à la lumière de la première charte du parc", *Revue juridique de l'environnement*, 2020, n° 4, vol. 45, p. 615; see also Aoustin T., "Le Parc amazonien de Guyane: un colosse aux pieds d'argile", *Revue juridique de l'environnement*, 2020, n° 4, vol. 45, p. 673.
13 About the Amazonian Park of French Guiana, see *infra*.
14 Charter for the Environment, Preamble (Constitutional Act n° 2005-205, March 1st, 2005, "on the Charter for the Environment", *JORF* n° 0051, March 2, 2005, p. 3697).
15 See French Constitution, art. 3.
16 Gicquel J., Gicquel J.-E., Droit constitutionnel et institutions politiques, *LGDJ*, 36ᵉ éd., coll. "Précis DOMAT", 2022, p. 87: "*Héritage du rousseauisme, la loi étant considérée comme l'expression d'une souveraineté unique et indivisible, elle acquiert les caractéristiques de cette dernière. La présence d'une loi nationale unique est la marque d'un État unitaire*"/"Inherited from Rousseau's theories, the law is considered to be the expression of a single and indivisible sovereignty, and thus acquires the characteristics of the latter. The presence of a single national law is the hallmark of a unitary State."
17 See French Constitution, art. 1st. Decentralised State "is characterised by the transfer of part of its regulatory powers to other administrative structures, which may be territorial authorities (territorial decentralisation) or public establishments (functional decentralisation). Decentralised local authorities administer themselves autonomously, but are subject to State supervision, in the form of either prior control or a posteriori control (legality control)" (Erhard T., Portelli H., *Droit constitutionnel*, Dalloz, 14ᵉ éd., coll. "HyperCours", 2021, p. 10: "*se caractérise par le transfert d'une partie de ses compétences réglementaires vers d'autres structures administratives, qui peuvent être des collectivités territoriales (décentralisation territoriale) ou des établissements publics (décentralisation fonctionnelle). Les collectivités territoriales décentralisées s'administrent de façon autonome, mais elles sont soumises à la tutelle de l'État, sous la forme soit du contrôle préalable, soit du contrôle a posteriori (contrôle de légalité).*" For a critical appraisal of the classifications of State forms, and particularly of the decentralised form, see Vandelli L., "Formes d'État: État régional, État décentralisé" in Troper M., Chagnollaud D. (dir.), *Traité international de droit constitutionnel*, Dalloz, 1ʳᵉ éd., coll. "Traités Dalloz", 2012, T. 2 Distribution des pouvoirs, pp. 53–76.
18 See General Local Authorities Code, art. L. 7111-1 and seq. and Electoral Code, art. 558-1 and seq.
19 See Favoreu L., et al., *Droit des libertés fondamentales*, Dalloz, 4ᵉ éd., coll. "Précis", p. 127: "*Dans toutes les Constitutions modernes, non seulement les catalogues de droits fondamentaux ne sont pas relégués dans des "préambules" sans valeur juridique, mais ils occupent une place centrale avec souvent une portée juridique renforcée, comme en République fédérale d'Allemagne où ils sont au cœur de la Loi fondamentale*"/"In all modern Constitutions, not only are the catalogues of fundamental rights not relegated to 'preambles' with no legal value, but they occupy a central place, often with enhanced legal scope, as in the Federal Republic of Germany, where they are at the heart of the Basic Law." See also: Hennette Vauchez S., Roman D., *Droits de l'homme et libertés fondamentales*, Dalloz, 5ᵉ éd., coll. "HyperCours", p. 197.

20 See French Constitution, art. 61 and 61-1.
21 Constitutional Council, decision n° 71-44 DC of 16 July 1971, Law completing the provisions of articles 5 and 7 of the Law of 1 July 1901 on association agreements. See Rousseau D., "La place du juge constitutionnel [Dossier: les évolutions de la Ve République]", *Les Cahiers français*, janvier–février 2001, n° 300, pp. 39–47; Robert J., "Propos sur le sauvetage d'une liberté", *Revue du droit public et de la science politique en France et à l'étranger*, 1971, pp. 11721–1204; note *JCP-G*, 1971, n° s.n.; Beardsley J. E., "The Constitutional Council and Constitutional Liberties in France", *The American Journal of Comparative Law*, Summer 1971, vol. 20, n° 3, pp. 431–452; Rivero J., note *AJDA*, 1971, pp. 537–542; Pizzorusso A., note, *Il foro italiano*, 1971; Hamon L., "Contrôle de constitutionnalité et protection des droits individuels", *Recueil Dalloz*, 1974, pp. 83–90; Haimbaugh G. D., "Was It France's Marbury v. Madison", *Ohio State Law Journal*, 1974, vol. 35, p. 910; Luchaire F., note, *Annuaire international de justice constitutionnelle*, 1991, n° VII-1991, p. 77; Philip L., Favoreu L., "Liberté d'association", *Les grandes décisions du Conseil constitutionnel*, Dalloz, 2009, pp. 180–199; Boudou G., "Autopsie de la décision du Conseil constitutionnel du 16 juillet 1971 sur la liberté d'association", *Revue française de droit constitutionnel*, 1er janvier 2014, n° 97, pp. 5–120; Favoreu L., Philip L., "Liberté d'association. Conformité de la loi au préambule. Protection des libertés publiques", *Les grandes décisions du Conseil constitutionnel*, Sirey, 1975, pp. 267–287; Hamon L., "Contrôle de constitutionnalité et protection des droits individuels. A propos de trois décisions récentes du Conseil constitutionnel", *Recueil Dalloz*, 1974, Chron. XVII, pp. 83–90; Lecoq-Pujade B., "1971, une révolution de palais?", *Revue française de droit constitutionnel*, juin 2022, n° 130, pp. 283–308; Rousseau D., "La décision du 16 juillet 1971, une ouverture démocratique", *Revue française de droit constitutionnel*, juin 2022, n° 130, pp. 309–314; Roux C., "Introduction (sur)plombante au cinquantenaire de la décision Liberté d'association", *Revue française de droit constitutionnel*, juin 2022, n° 130, pp. 275–282; Mongoin D., "Brèves de lecture théorique de la décision de 1971", *Revue française de droit constitutionnel*, juin 2022, n° 130, pp. 315–336; Philip-Gay M., "La décision Liberté d'association est-elle l'équivalent français de l'arrêt Marbury v. Madison?", *Revue française de droit constitutionnel*, juin 2022, n° 130, pp. 337–359; Manouguian A., "La décision du 16 juillet 1971 aux prises avec la diatribe de René de Lacharrière: une opinion toujours 'dissidente'?", *Revue française de droit constitutionnel*, juin 2022, n° 130, pp. 361–375; Eck L., "Faut-il constitutionnaliser la décision du Conseil constitutionnel du 16 juillet 1971?", *Revue française de droit constitutionnel*, juin 2022, n° 130, pp. 377–391.
22 See earlier, Constitutional Law, n° 2005–205.
23 See Brazilian Constitution, art. 225 §4°.
24 Charter for the Environment, see earlier.
25 Constitutional Council, decision n°2021–971 QPC of 18 February 2022, France Nature Environnement [Extension *ipso jure* of certain mining concessions]. See Scanvic F., Chevalier C., "Mines: l'éternité et le couperet", *Bulletin de droit de l'environnement industriel*, mai 2022, n° 99, p. 6; Brett R., "Un coup d'arrêt à la ruée vers l'or guyanais?", *Revue juridique de l'environnement*, juin 2022, n° 2–2022, pp. 389–402; Memlouk M., "La prolongation des concessions minières à l'épreuve de la Charte de l'environnement", *Bulletin de droit de l'environnement industriel*, juillet 2022, n° 100, pp. 35–42; Savonitto F., "Une décision environnementale historique", *Le blog du CERCOP, questions constitutionnelles*, 4 juin 2022; Rrapi P., "Au Conseil constitutionnel, la montagne d'ord accouche d'une souris verte", *Revue française de droit constitutionnel*, décembre 2022, n° 132, pp. 939–945; Cartier E., "Un grand pas en avant pour la protection de l'environnement: décision n° 2021–971 QPC du 18 février 2022, France nature environnement [Prolongation de plein droit de certaines concessions minières], *in* Chronique de droits fondamentaux et libertés publiques (janvier-juin 2022)", *Titre VII [En ligne]*, octobre 2022, n° 9.
26 Charter for the Environment, Preamble.
27 See Environmental Code, art. L. 331-1 to L. 331-15-7; Forest Code, art. D. 172-3.
28 Environmental Code, art. L.331-15-1.
29 Environmental Code, art. L. 331-15-3.
30 Penal Code, art. 111-2.
31 Mining Code, art. L. 512-1, I-bis.
32 Mining Code, art. L. 512-2 and seq. About these infringements, see *infra*.
33 *JORF* n°0179 of August 2, 2008, p. 12361; Directive 2004/35/CE, Parliament and Council, April 21, 2004.

34 See not. Cass., crim., March 22, 2016, n°13-87.650; *D.*, 2016, 1236, note Epstein A.-S., 1597, chron. Laurent B., Ascensi L., Pichon E. et Guého G.; *AJ pénal*, 2016, 320, note Perrier J.-B.; *RSC*, 2016, 287, obs Robert. J.-H.; *RTD civ.*, 2016, 634, obs. Jourdain P.; *JCP*, 2016, 647, note Bacache M., 648, note Parance B., 1117, n°3, obs. Bloch C.; *AJDA*, 2016, 638; Court of Appeal, Cayenne, February 24, 2022, n°21/00085.

35 See Truilhé E., Hautereau-Boutonnet M., *Le procès environnemental. Du procès sur l'environnement au procès pour l'environnement*, Rapport de recherche, Mission de recherche Droit et Justice, 2019, pp. 132–145; Hautereau-Boutonnet M., *La responsabilité civile environnementale*, Dalloz, 1re édition, coll. "Dalloz corpus", 2020, spéc. n°87 et s.; *Le Code civil, un code pour l'environnement*, Dalloz, coll. "Les sens du droit", 2021, 191 p.

36 Constitutional Council, April 8, 2011, n°2011–116 QPC; *RDI*, 2011.369, étude Trébulle F.-G.; *D.*, 2011.1258, note Rebeyrol V.; *D.*, 2298, obs. Mallet-Bricout B. et Reboul-Maupin N.; *AJDA*, 2011.1158, note Foucher K.

37 The protection has constitutional value, Constitutional Council, January 31, 2020, n° 2019–823 QPC.

38 About the dismantling of relay antennas, see Court of Appeal, Montpellier, September 15, 2011, n°10/04612; Court of Appeal, Versailles, February 4, 2009, *SA Bouygues Telecom c/Eric X*, n°08/08775.

39 The judgment is named after the Maltese oil tanker involved in the case, which sank off the coast of Finistère while carrying 30,000 tonnes of heavy fuel oil, causing a major oil spill and polluting around 400 kilometers of French coastline. Cass., crim., September 25, 2012, *Erika*, n°10–82.938; *D.*, 2012.2711, note Delebecque Ph.; *D.*, 2557, obs. Trébulle F.-G.; point de vue Neyret L.; 2920, obs. Roujou de Boubée G.; *Environnement et développement durable*, 2013/3, p. 19, note Bacache M.; *AJDA*, 2013.667, étude Huglo C.; *JCP*, 2012, 1243, note le Couviour K.; *JCP*, 2013, 484, n°5, obs. Bloch C.; *AJ pénal*, 2012, 574, note Montas A. et Roussel G.; *RTD civ.*, 2013.119, obs. Jourdain P.; *Gaz. Pal.*, 24–25 oct. 2012, note Parance B.

40 See not. Jegouzo Y. (dir.), *Pour la réparation du préjudice écologique*, Rapport remis au Garde des Sceaux, 17 septembre 2013.

41 *JORF*, n° 0184, August 9, 2016.

42 Civil Code, art. 1247.

43 See Environmental Code, art. L. 142-3-1 on the environmental class action. See also the distinction made between pure ecological harm and moral prejudice of the environmental associations, Cass. Crim., June 29, 2021, n°20-82.245; *D.*, 2021.1564, obs. Perrier J.-B.

44 See, for instance, New Zealand, which recognized the Whanganui River as a legal person (Te Awa Tupua Act, March 20, 2017), and the Colombian Supreme Court, which gave the Colombian Amazon legal personality (Colombian Supreme Court of Justice, 5 April 2018, no. STC4360–2018).

45 See, not. Karpe Ph. et Tiouka A., "La politique de lutte contre l'orpaillage sur le fleuve Maroni en Guyane française", 17 mars 2022, hal-03611201.

46 A relationship of co-viability is encouraged in order to preserve *"living together"*, see, in this respect, Barrière O., et al., *Coviabilité des systèmes sociaux et écologiques. Reconnecter l'Homme à la biosphère dans une ère de changement global*, éd. Matériologiques, coll. "Essais", 2019; See also, Camproux-Duffrène M.-P., "L'admission dans le Code civil de la réparabilité du préjudice écologique; lésion d'un intérêt commun", in *Mélanges en l'honneur de Jean-Michel et Patrice Storck, Liber amicorum*, Dalloz, 2021, pp. 31–43, who assesses that *"it is time to move on frome a right to dominate nature to a right to relationships ans links between humans and non-humans"* (spec. p. 32; *"qu'il est temps de passer d'un droit de domination de la nature à un droit de relations, de liens entre humains et non-humains"*) by recognizing a *"natural common"* (*"commun naturel"*); Neyret L., Atteintes au vivant et responsabilité civile, préf. Thibierge C., Paris, LGDJ, 2006; Hermitte M.-A., "La nature, sujet de droit?", in Annales, Histoire, Sciences Sociales, 2011, pp. 173–212.

47 On June 29, 2023, the Provincial Assembly of the Loyalty Islands in New Caledonia recognized marine turtles and sharks as subjects of law. See also Act no. 2015-177 of 16 February 2015 on the modernization and simplification of the law and procedures in the fields of justice and home affairs, which established a new protective status for animals, now considered to be "sentient living beings" (Civil Code, art. 515-14).

48 See not., Hautereau-Boutonnet M., "L'évolution des formes de préjudice: le cas du préjudice écologique", *Les cahiers Portalis*, 2022/1, n°9, pp. 19–26, spec. p. 25.

49 The limitation was ruled conform with the Constitution: Constitutional Council, February 5, 2021, n°2020–881 QPC.
50 This distinction is explicitly set out in the civil liability bill published on March 13, 2017, which includes the environmental cause into its provisions in a sub-section entitled *"special rules for compensation for loss resulting from environmental damage."* See not., Hassoun C., *L'anormalité dans le droit de la responsabilité civile, contribution à la recherche d'une unité en responsabilité civile extracontractuelle*, sous la direction de J. Julien, thèse, Toulouse, 2018, spéc. n°212.
51 Civil Code, art. 1249.
52 Civil Code, art. 1252.
53 See *supra*.
54 Contrary to administrative police provisions, see Environmental Code, art. L. 162-6 and seq., resulting from Act n°2008-757 of August 1st, 2008, see earlier.
55 The plaintiffs can rely on the existing nomenclature for environmental damage, which distinguishes between damage caused to humans and damage caused to the environment, see Neyret L. et Martin G.-J. (dir.), *Nomenclature des préjudices environnementaux*, LGDJ, Paris, 2012.
56 See Civil Code, art. 1248 al. 2; about the Marseille Calanque National Park case, see Criminal Court, Marseille, March 6, 2020, n°1505; Court of Appeal, Aix-en-Provence, June 29, 2021, n°20/01931.
57 See, for instance, Cass. Civ., 2nd, July 7, 2011, n°10–20.373; crim., June 2, 2015, n°14–83.967.
58 Decree n°2013-968 "approving the charter of the Amazonian Park of French Guiana", *JORF*, October 30, 2013, p. 17664.
59 See *infra*.
60 Notably between judicial and administrative courts, the latter ordering the State to pay compensation for the ecological harm regarding the provisions of the Civil Code: see Administrative Court, Paris, February, 3, 2021, nos 1904967, 1904968, 1904972, 1904976/4–1, as to the environmental harm caused by failure to meet greenhouse gas emission reduction targets; Administrative Court, Paris, June, 29, 2023, n°2200534/4–1, which recognizes the existence of an ecological harm resulting from the *"widespread, diffuse, chronic and long-lasting"* (*"généralisée, diffuse, chronique et durable"*) contamination of waters and soils by the use of plant protection products. See also, *L'environnement: les citoyens, le droit, les juges—Regards croisés du Conseil d'État et de la Cour de cassation*, Documentation française, coll. "Droits et débats", 28 octobre 2022, 145 p.
61 See not. Agoguet D., "Une révolution citoyenne pour la justice et l'écologique: vers un juge de la protection environnementale", *Revue juridique de l'environnement*, 2020/3, pp. 425–429.
62 Pin X., *Droit pénal général*, Dalloz, coll. "Précis", 14ᵉ éd., 2023, p. 2, n° 2.
63 See not. Lagoutte J., "L'application dans l'espace de la loi pénale environnementale", *Gaz. Pal.*, 16 mai 2023, n°16, p. 61.
64 See *introduction*.
65 Prieur M., Bétaille J., Chendet A.-M., Delzangles H., Makowiak J., Steichen P., *Droit de l'environnement*, Dalloz, coll. "Précis", 8ᵉ éd., 2019, p. 1247, n° 1501; see also Jaworski V., "L'état du droit pénal de l'environnement: entre forces et faiblesses", *Les Cahiers de droit*, 2009, vol. 50, n° 3–4, p. 889; Gogorza A., "Le droit pénal de l'environnement", *Dr. pénal*, 2013, dossier 4.
66 Jaworski V., "L'état du droit pénal de l'environnement: entre forces et faiblesses", see earlier.
67 Agoguet D., Atzenhoffer D., Delbos V., Corsini C., "Les incriminations environnementales", *Revue Justice Actualités* n° 25, *La justice pénale environnementale*, juin 2021, p. 84.
68 Gogorza A., "Le droit pénal de l'environnement," see earlier.
69 Jaworski V., "L'état du droit pénal de l'environnement: entre forces et faiblesses", see earlier. The author notes: "How can we justify the fact that harming the conservation of endangered animal or plant species is punishable by a maximum of six months' imprisonment and a fine of €9,000, when the simple theft of any object is punishable by three years' imprisonment and a fine of €45,000? Why is it that anyone picking an edelweiss is liable to six months' imprisonment and a fine of €9,000, whereas the deliberate disturbance of a nesting peregrine falcon is at best a fifth-class offence punishable by a fine of €1,500?" ("*Comment justifier que le fait de porter atteinte à la conservation d'espèces animales ou végétales menacées d'extinction soit puni au maximum de six mois d'emprisonnement et de 9 000 euros d'amende, alors que le vol simple d'un objet quelconque est sanctionné d'un emprisonnement de trois ans et d'une peine*

d'amende de 45 000 euros? Comment expliquer que celui qui cueille un edelweiss encourt six mois d'emprisonnement et 9 000 euros d'amende, alors que la perturbation intentionnelle d'un faucon pèlerin en train de couver ne constituera au mieux qu'une contravention de cinquième classe punie de 1 500 euros d'amende?").

70 Ordinance n°2012-34 of January 11, 2012 "Order simplifying, reforming and harmonising the administrative and judicial police provisions of the Environment Code", *JORF* January 12, 2012, text n°6; V. Agoguet D., Atzenhoffer D., Delbos V., Corsini C., "Les incriminations environnementales", see earlier.
71 Cinotti B., Landel J.-F., Agoguet D., Atzenhoffer D., Delbos V., *Une justice pour l'environnement. Mission d'évaluation des relations entre justice et environnement,* Ministère de la transition écologique et solidaire, Ministère de la justice, Rapport final, octobre 2019, p. 17.
72 Bouhoute M., Diakhaté M., "Le traitement du contentieux de l'environnement par la justice pénale entre 2015 et 2019", *Infostat Justice,* avril 2021, n° 182: http://www.justice.gouv.fr/art_pix/stat_Infostat_182.pdf
73 Agoguet D., Atzenhoffer D., Delbos V., Corsini C., "Les incriminations environnementales", see earlier.
74 Bénézech F., "Approche globale de la délinquance environnementale: le rôle des procureurs de la République", *Revue Justice Actualités* n° 25, *La justice pénale environnementale,* juin 2021, p. 22.
75 Act n°2020-1672 of December 24, 2020 "on the European Public Prosecutor's Office, environmental justice and specialised criminal justice", *JORF,* December 26, 2020, text n°4.
76 Decree n°2021-286 of March 16, 2021 "designating the regional centres specialising in environmental offences pursuant to articles 706-2-3 of the Criminal Procedure Code and L. 211-20 of the Judicial Organisation Code and adapting the Criminal Procedure Code to the creation of assistants specialising in environmental matters", *JORF,* March 17, 2021, text n°15.
77 Criminal Procedure Code, art. 706-2-3.
78 Criminal Procedure Code, art. 41-1-3. See also Bénézech F., "Approche globale de la délinquance environnementale: le rôle des procureurs de la République", see earlier.
79 Act n°2021-1104 of August 22, 2021, "combating climate change and building resilience to its effects", *JORF* n° 0196 of August 24, 2021, text n° 1, see not. Gindre E., Falxa J., Lavric S., Vauthier J.-P., "Droit des Outre-mer. Chronique de droit pénal, procédure pénale, droit pénitentiaire, politique criminelle", RSC 2022, p. 905.
80 Prior to the Act of August 22, 2021, only environmental officers could benefit from such authorization, issued by the Cayenne public prosecutor, which was only valid within the territorial limits of the Amazonian Park of French Guiana.
81 Under the terms of article 62-2 of the Code of Criminal Procedure, police custody is "*a measure of constraint decided by a judicial police officer, under the supervision of the judicial authority, whereby a person against whom there are one or more plausible grounds for suspecting that he has committed or attempted to commit a crime or an offence punishable by imprisonment is held at the disposal of investigators.*"
82 Initially, article L. 621-8 allowed this deferral for the offence provided for in article L. 615-1 of the French Mining Code, which makes it a criminal offence to mine without authorization, provided that mining was accompanied by attacks to the environment referred to in article L. 512-2, I and II, of the same code. Since the law of 22 August 2021, the deferral can apply to any mining operation without authorization, regardless of any attacks to the environment, and also to the offence under article L. 621-8-3 of the Mining Code.
83 A measure different from police custody, but which also consists of a temporary deprivation of liberty, decided by a customs officer in the event of a customs offence punishable by imprisonment and when this measure is justified by the requirements of the customs investigation. See Customs Code, art. 323 and seq.
84 This provision incriminates: "*1° The fact of exporting native gold from French Guiana either without an itemised declaration or under cover of an itemised declaration not applicable to the goods presented, or by concealing the goods from inspection by the customs service; 2° Holding or transporting native gold within the customs radius of French Guiana without presenting either a transport document, or a document issued by a person legally established in the customs territory, or a document certifying that the native gold is intended for legal export.*"
85 Lingibé P., "Le droit pénal en outre-mer: entre principes d'égalité et de réalité", *AJ pénal,* 2019, p. 68.

86 Mining Code, art. L. 621-8-5, I.
87 Mining Code, art. L. 621-8-5, II to IV.
88 To catch the importance of the international background, see Le Prestre P., *Protection de l'environnement et relations internationales: les défis de l'écopolitique mondiale*, Paris, A. Colin, 2005, 477 p.
89 See not.: Aubertin C., et Filoche G., "La création du parc amazonien de Guyane: redistribution des pouvoirs, incarnations du 'local' et morcellement du territoire", in Aubertin C. et Rodary E. (Eds.), *Aires protégées espaces durables?*, Marseille, IRD Editions, 2008, 163–185.
90 For situations of high tension in East Africa from the early days of British colonization, see Boutrais J., "Pastoralismes et aires protégées d'Afrique de l'Ouest en regard de l'Afrique de l'Est", in Aubertin C. et Rodary E., op. cit., Marseille, IRD Editions, 2008, 215–246.
91 About this striking change, see also, with a somehow provocative title: Cans C., "Les parcs nationaux sont morts: vive les parcs nationaux de développement local", *AJDA*, 2006, 1431–1436. Compare with Alban N. et Hubert G., "Le modèle des parcs nationaux français à l'épreuve du territoire", Vertigo, Vol. 13, n° 2, sept. 2013, on the denial of any real guiding idea in the French reform of 2006.
92 Decree n°2007-266, *JO*, February 29, 2007, p. 3757. *Addendum* welcoming this text: Untermaier J., "Le parc amazonien de Guyane, huitième parc national français (décret n° 2007-266 du 27 février 2007)", *Revue juridique de l'Environnement*, 2008, 2, 135–155.
93 Environmental Code, art. L. 331-15-1 to L. 331-15-7.
94 Approved by Decree n° 2013-968 of October 28, 2013 (*JO* October 30, 2013, p. 17664). The opportunity for revision of the Charter must in principle be submitted to the park's board of directors no later than 12 years after its approval (Environmental Code, art. L. 331-3, II, al. 1).
95 Concluded with all the member municipalities since the end of 2016, and accompanied by framework agreements between the PAG and other public or private institutions, ranging from the communities of municipalities of West and East Guyana (CCOG and CCEG) to the EDF company and the French Guiana Academy.
96 The communes of Papaïchton joined rapidly in December 2013 and Saül in February 2014, while cancellations of municipal elections delayed the accession of the commune of Maripa-Soula until June 2014 and that of the commune of Camopi until May 2015.
97 Environmental Code, art. L. 221-3, II.
98 Forming the part III of the first Charter of the PAG.
99 Or other partners (see *supra*).
100 Even then real obligations for the public do not seem to be based directly on the agreement, but only on municipal by-laws, the legality of which the administrative judge may have to assess.
101 See spec. for the Charter of the PAG, Orientation I-3 Participer à l'objectif d'éradication de l'orpaillage illégal (Helping to eradicate illegal gold mining).
102 With the legal definition of the core area(s) of national parks as *"terrestrial and maritime areas to be protected"*(Environmental Code, art. L. 331-1, al. 2).
103 With the definition of the Objectives for the core zone and their implementation measures in part IV of the 2013 Charter.
104 Environmental Code, art. L. 331-15-3 and R. 331-21 and Decree of February 27, 2007, art. 19 to 22.
105 Decree of February 27, 2007, art. 22, 3°, which does not make it possible to define very clearly the prerogatives of the communities of inhabitants over the resources of the core zone as a simple right of use within the meaning of French civil law, quite distinct from the right of enjoyment or exploitation (for a reminder of this distinction: Reboul-Maupin, N., *Droit des biens*, Dalloz, 8ᵉ éd., coll. "HyperCours", 2020, n° 245 seq.). Compare with the inclusion of an insert on the *zones de droits d'usages collectifs* (ZDUC), in the Part I of the Charter of the PAG, La charte, un projet pour les territoires concernés par le Parc amazonien de Guyane ("The charter, a project for the territories concerned by the Amazonian Park of French Guiana").
106 Art. L. 331-15-3.
107 Compare with Aubertin C., et Filoche G., "La création du parc amazonien de Guyane: redistribution des pouvoirs, incarnations du "local" et morcellement du territoire", see earlier, on highlighting the legal provision of a simple possibility and not an obligation to give preference to traditional communities.
108 Decree of February 27, 2007, art. 25, 1° à 3°.

109 Decree of February 27, 2007, art. 25, 3°.
110 Environmental Code, art. L. 331-15-5.
111 Environmental Code, art. L. 331-15-5, in fine.
112 At the same time, gold miners are referred to the specific unit responsible for supporting the legal mining profession (Charter of the PAG, Stake (III)).
113 Charter of the PAG, Measure III-2-5-1.
114 Charter of the PAG, Orientation III-2.
115 Charter of the PAG, Orientation III-2.
116 PAG, CVL, Actions en cours, Désenclavement (PAG website, 2023).
117 Decree of February 28, 2007, art. 11.
118 Charter of the PAG, Objective III-2. Recall the invitation from the French National Parks Portal to organize the tourism strategy according to the realities of each park's territory. At the very least, we agree that, in relatively sparsely populated French Guiana, which is far from international air links, tourism is not the main threat to safeguarding the heart of the Amazon Park. Compare with *Courrier International*, 14 juin 2021, "Les parcs nationaux américains pris d'assaut par les touristes" on the growing concerns about mass tourism in the major parks of the western United States.
119 Autorité environnementale, Conseil général de l'environnement et du développement durable, 2012. Avis délibéré sur l'évaluation environnementale du projet de charte du Parc amazonien de Guyane, n°Ae: 2012–61, 14 nov., 2 Le projet de charte: présentation et prise en compte de l'environnement par le projet, www.cgedd.developpement-durable.gouv.fr.
120 See spec., Sub-orientation I-3–3 and Sub-objective I-2–3.
121 See Barrière O. et Faure J.-F., "L'enjeu d'un droit négocié pour le Parc amazonien de Guyane", *Natures Sciences Sociétés*, 2012/2, vol. 20, 167–180.
122 Charter of the PAG, Part 2, Principe général (C), Adapter les politiques publiques et les réglementations aux réalités du territoire ("General Principle (C), Adapting public policies and regulations to local realities").

14
LOGOSPIRACY IN THE LEGAL AMAZON

Raimundo Pontes Filho

Introduction

The Amazon has been a territorial, socio-environmental, cultural, and symbolic space characterized not only by rich socio-biodiversity and a vast tropical rainforest but also by several socio-legal complexities that potentially contribute to the production of the context of violence and public insecurity, in particular the *logospirate* processes.

The need to highlight *Logospiracy* in the Legal Amazon or *logospirate* processes in the region began with perplexity at the insufficiency of the notion of biopiracy to account for countless processes that took place over time and, in some cases, still persist in the Amazon.

Such *logospirate* dynamics occurred throughout the process of social formation in the Amazon and continue to manifest themselves, especially in the form of violations of the rules that protect or should protect the quality of the environment, environmental resources, traditional knowledge associated with the use of biodiversity, labor rights, compensation rights of indigenous peoples, traditional populations, national society, and the State itself.

Such occurrences are found in research, studies, academic investigations, and official records, including those from remote times. They are present in reports and narratives treated by regional historiography. The essential dialogue with anthropological and sociological works on the region is also used. Finally, the return to understanding jurisprudence, doctrine, and national laws regarding these *logospirate* processes is equally necessary.

Under this interdisciplinary orientation, therefore, we seek to study, understand, discuss, and unveil the phenomenon of *Logospiracy*, taking the Brazilian Legal Amazon as its context. *Logopiracy* takes different forms and tones but inevitably leaves its trail of destruction, extermination, and cultural and physical annihilation.

The Logos and the *Logospirate*

In the search for the formative principle of the universe, nature, beings, values, and knowledge, as occurs among different peoples and cultures, Greek mythology, philosophy, and science strived to understand reality as a whole. The first Greek philosophers, the pre-Socratics, each postulated a reality, an essence or an original and founding principle of

DOI: 10.4324/9781003330653-18

all beings, of all things, and all *physis*. This original foundation of everything that exists, called arché (arqué), presides over and organizes the entire universe, each of these philosophers represented in element(s) of nature, to be revealed and disseminated by the Logos (rational thought, ordered speech, clarifying word).

It was water for Thales of Miletus (approx. 625 to 558 BC). For Anaximander (approx. 625 to 547 BC), the Apeiron (the unlimited) would be the founding principle of all things. For Anaximenes (approximately 585 to 528 BC), air would be the arché, the forming particle of all physis, nature, or universe(s). For Pythagoras of Samos (approx. 580 to 497 BC), this structuring principle of all reality would be the number or the numerical principle, as all things would represent numbers.

For Heraclitus of Ephesus (approx. 540 to 470 BC), this essence that formed life, reality, intelligence, knowledge, and values would be the Logos itself. It would be much more than just revealing the arché of all physics. Logos would impart movement, diversity, and antagonism to reality, as represented in the fire. For Parmenides of Eleia (approx. 530 to 460 BC), the principle and foundation of all reality, the arché, is permanence, static, that lasts forever, the eternal expressed in the absolute, unique, immutable "being," one, immobile and infinite: being is; non-being is nothing.

For Empedocles of Agrigento (approx. 490 to 435 BC), the essence of the universe and the primordial principle of all things is not in a single element of nature but comes from the combinations between four elements: water, air, fire, and earth. For Democritus of Abdera (approx. 460 to 370 BC), the essence of physics, which forms all things, are invisible and indivisible particles, which he called atoms. The atom corresponds to "being" and the void or vacuum (absence of atoms) to "non-being." Being "is" according to the arrangements between atoms. The existence of a vacuum allows movement to occur. Atoms would move in a vacuum.

The original Greek thinkers did not understand the same thing as this essence or principle that forms and organizes reality. However, they understood that all things would create one, that plurality would result in unity, diversity in the one, and the ordering of the chaos in the cosmos.

The Heraclitus Logos assumes a broader dimension and scope, positioning itself as the forming essence and organizing principle of all reality, of physis—nature or the universe; however, distinguishing itself from the others, it would be able to take into account the unity in dynamics of diversity and antagonism, of transience and permanence of reality. The Logos of the Ephesian singular is not only the path to search for the primordial essence, arché but the very essence or principle that generates, structures, and orders all things in the universe (Pontes Filho, 2017, p. 55)

When this Logos is reduced, fragmented, or corrupted, it converts itself into a logospirate, and its manifestation occurs with the harmful dynamics and harmfully impactful processes that constitute Logospiracy. The Heraclitic Logos does not deny or camouflage the chaos present in reality but reveals it and even denounces it in the search to overcome it, trying to make the cosmos prevail from this eternal struggle of the real, forming the one, the totality, the cosmic physis.

In opposition to the Logos, the logospirate seeks to disguise, camouflage, and even deny chaos. Often, in the form of multiple promises, including progress and prosperity, with a view to imposing themselves in a unique, exclusive, and totalitarian way, the logospirate tries to belittle diversity and disapprove the right to freedom to be different, to diverge, and to antagonize. With excessive greed and greed for control and homogenization, the logospirate tends to make chaos prevail in the form of injustice, violence, illicitness, criminality, naturalized and systemic corruption, symbolic garbage in the media and social networks, tons of solid waste that reveals degrading models of production and consumption, of egocratic, political, economic, religious and extremist perversions, clearly manifesting itself in Logospiracy.

Considering that it does not demean, reduce, disintegrate, or fragment knowledge, values, and traditions of different peoples and cultures, the Heraclitic Logos operates as an analytical tool, an instrument of observation and critical reflection, a valid epistemological lens to survey, analyze, "diagnose," and confront the logospirate, preventing it from continuing to devour sociocultural diversity, the environment, and the fundamental rights of different societies, populations, and communities, such as those in the Brazilian Amazon.

Logospiracy

Addressing the problem of Logospiracy in the Legal Amazon is a very challenging task, given the dynamic nature of the topic, and it is open to research, criticism, and academic contributions. The concept of Logospiracy is more appropriate for understanding intervention processes in the Amazonian context than that of Biopiracy. The notion of Logospiracy is significantly broader and encompasses the idea of Biopiracy, which is limited and insufficient to deal with processes that, in addition to the irregular appropriation of resources and knowledge, involve the undue exploitation of human labor, whether through slave labor or the reduction to a condition analogous to slavery, either through the precariousness of labor relations. Thus, Logospiracy is something with a broader scope and extension than Biopiracy.

There is no legal definition for the notion of biopiracy, and it is up to us to resort to doctrinal understanding to shed light on this notion. So let's start with what Vandana Shiva explained about this biopirate process:

> Five hundred years after Columbus, a secular version of the same colonization project is underway through patents and intellectual property rights (IPD). The Papal Bull was replaced by the General Agreement on Tariffs and Trade, GATT. The principle of effective occupation by Christian princes was replaced by effective occupation by transnational companies supported by contemporary rulers. The vacancy of land was replaced by the vacancy of life forms and species, modified by new biotechnologies. The duty to incorporate savages into Christianity has been replaced by the duty to incorporate local and national economies into the global market and to incorporate non-Western systems of knowledge into the reductionism of the commodified science and technology of the Western world. The creation of property through the piracy of other people's wealth remains the same as it was 500 years ago." (Emphasis added)
>
> *(Shiva, 2001, p. 24)*

In the same vein, in an article in the magazine *Hiléia* in which he postulates criminal protection against biopiracy in the Amazon, Fernando Dantas and others clarify that biopiracy "can be considered unauthorized appropriation of the genetic heritage of a region, including species of fauna, flora and traditional knowledge associated with biodiversity" (Dantas, 2008, p. 207). It is, therefore, evident that the notion of biopiracy is limited to the undue or illegitimate appropriation of resources, goods, and traditional knowledge, disregarding a fundamental aspect of Logospiracy—the issue of the exploitation of human labor.

In the investigative path to understanding Logospiracy, the first clue is the conception of Logos, present since archaic Greek philosophy and throughout the history of philosophical and scientific thought, which reveals the extent of this category as the primary tool for analysis of the phenomenon of Logospiracy.

This logo, which marks, structures, and organizes societies, sometimes representing their way of being and living in a group, can be plundered, deformed, extinguished, and pirated by other logos. In a broad sense, this is what we intend here to call Logospiracy. From this perspective, it is important to carefully reflect on the construction of this analytical instrument, Logospiracy, to purify the purely ideological contents that it may have, reaffirming the scientific validity of understanding a phenomenon with universal characteristics and harmful impacts, including considering the events that occurred in the Legal Amazon.

Thus, the meeting and confrontation between the "Logos" of groups and civilizations, one pirate/predator and another plundered/prey, has been part of the historical process of the most diverse societies at all times, including those of Amazon. It is a process that invents and reinvents the logic of confrontation between the structuring principles and values of peoples, groups, and societies over time in different geographic and symbolic or immaterial spaces, whose effects are impactful in the most distinct fields of social life.

In this sense, Logospiracy covers a long journey through time, manifesting itself in the most different spaces, contexts, and times. So, it is no exaggeration to say that it has almost always been present in geography and human or sociocultural history.

Logospiracy has been present throughout history, since the slavery-based economies from the old empires to the religious obscurantism of the Middle Ages to the advent of modern rationality. It is on cultural, political, and economic models, including instrumentalizing science and technologies. It constitutes a structuring characteristic and a driving axis of postmodernity or liquid modernity, as is the globalization of the technical-scientific-informational environment. The society of information, production, and consumerism deforms, degrades, and decomposes in different aspects, including indicators of solid waste and expressions of symbolic waste (Pontes Filho, 2017).

Logospiracy consists of the process that disintegrates cultures, disrupts people, their traditions, and the symbolic universe, plunders nature and knowledge, and annihilates populations, collectivities, and communities, including native and traditional ones, constituting an impactful dynamic of deprivation, harm, and violations of fundamental rights, constituting a crime against biodiversity, sociocultural diversity and social labor relations, seriously violating human dignity, however, not yet adequately foreseen or typified. Despite this, several illegalities result from logospirate practice, such as the undue, unauthorized, or illegal appropriation of natural goods and substances, traditional knowledge and knowledge, human work, and the harmful disintegration of values that structure the belief system and the culture of socially diverse peoples.

Nowadays, this confrontation between pirated Logos versus plundered Logos takes place under the dynamics of the globalization of the market economy governed by perverse financial speculation and the fundamentalist neoliberal conception of the economy, which imposes the inhumane reduction of the State's social responsibility. They were done terribly during the Covid-19 pandemic, in 2020, causing immeasurable damage in terms of human losses.

Logospiracy coexists in line with what Milton Santos called perverse globalization, centered on the contemporary double tyranny of money and information (Santos 2008, p. 37), which promotes materialist, sensorial consumerism, reifying everything for disposal, including the body itself.

Logospiracy irregularly appropriates not only resources, environmental goods, and traditional knowledge but also values, beliefs, or world views and work subject to precarious relationships or similar to slavery, to which groups and populations are subjected, mainly those native and traditional ones, including in the Brazilian Legal Amazon.

This alignment between capitalism and Logospiracy could not be more in tune. As Octavio Ianni explains, capitalism "is a simultaneously social, economic, political and cultural process of vast proportions, complex and contradictory, more or less inexorable, overwhelming" (1999, p. 171).

One of the effects of this contemporary logospirate process would be the loss of the centrality of the spirit, of the human logos built from classical and humanist culture, culminating in what master Milton Santos called the disturbance of spirits resulting from the predominant globalization in progress.

From the last decades of the 20th century, it was a matter of building, in international legal instruments, a system of legal protection over intellectual property, including copyright, which opened space to consider the civil and criminal liability of those who focus on the practice of Logospiracy, that is, those who act as logospirates, violating the rules of the system of legal protection of this knowledge, forms of expression and life that constitute the logos of societies. Logospiracy can be understood in modern times as a violation of the rules of this legal protection system, giving rise to reparations and compensations based on international law.

Thus, it is explained that the practice of Logospiracy goes beyond the idea of biopiracy and violates a set of rights, offending labor, individual, and collective rights associated with the compensation rights of States, national societies, native peoples, and traditional populations. For this reason, the Brazilian Legal Amazon is not just a case but the ideal scenario, par excellence, for the practice of Logospiracy.

The Brazilian Legal Amazon

The Legal Amazon is a political concept describing the states and regions in Brazil's North, Center-West, and Northeastern regions. The limits were established in 1953, and they correspond to the following Brazilian states: Acre, Amapá, Amazonas, Mato Grosso, Pará, Rondônia, Roraima, Tocantis, and part of the state of Maranhão. The region comprises an area of around 5.0 million square kilometers (59% of Brazilian Territory). It hosts 56% of Brazil's indigenous population.[1] It brings together the largest environmental collection on the planet: water resources, minerals, fish, wood, fauna, flora, broadleaf forest, diverse peoples, and traditional knowledge, among other environmental assets.

In reality, it constitutes an expressive subcontinent, reaching nine countries: Brazil, Bolivia, Colombia, Ecuador, Guyana, French Guiana, Suriname, Peru, and Venezuela, in an area of more than 7 million square kilometers. According to the National Institute of Research in the Amazon (INPA), the figures for the Amazon are impressive:

- an area of 7,584,421 km^2; an immensity of lands, waters, and forests that brings together fauna, flora, minerals, and various native cultures, representing 7% of the planet's

surface or the 20th part of the Earth's surface, 2/5 (two-fifths) or 4/10 (four tenths) of South America, and 3/5 (three-fifths) of Brazilian territory
- 1/3 (one-third) of the world's broadleaf forest reserves
- brings together more than 50% of the world's biodiversity
- 15 trillion m³ is what rains annually in the Amazon basin
- 48% of rainwater is used and evapotranspired by the Amazon ecosystem, with the other 52% drained by rivers, considering that scientific studies have shown that in tropical forest ecosystems, 25% of the water evaporates, 50% is transpired, and 25% drained by rivers
- net oxygen production, on average, of 96 tons per year, which represents 0.000008% of the output of the Earth's atmosphere, highlighting the small participation of the Amazon in the global production of this gas, absorbing, however, specific amounts of carbon gas (CO_2), functioning as a kind of ecological filter
- is home to around 17 million inhabitants, fewer than three-thousandths of the world's population, with a density of around 3.4 inhabitants/km²
- Subsoil abundantly rich, in both quantity and quality, in mineral matter (cassiterite, manganese, iron, gold, oil-gas, titanium, bauxite, gypsum, niobium, copper, diamond, uranium, etc.)
- Has 17% or around 1/5 (one-fifth) of the planet's water resources considered suitable for human consumption. The Foz do Rio Amazonas has, depending on the time of year, a volume of water that corresponds to between 100 m³ and 300 m³ per second, which, considering the average of 200 m³ per second, represents that the daily consumption of a city of 2,000 inhabitants would be supplied by one second of the river.

The Amazon, by bringing together this diversity of natural resources and ecosystems, in addition to vast social diversity, specifically forms a subcontinent that consists, from this perspective, as Márcio Souza says, of a "multinational and pluricultural territory formed by billions of years of geological and which houses thousands of plant specimens, animals and many people" (Souza, 2001, p. 15).

These characteristics contributed to arousing, at different times, varied external pressures on the region, being reissued today through international projects to globalize it, such as projects such as "Great Lakes of the Hudson Institute" and "Carretera Marginal de la Jungle."

During Brazil's military dictatorship, the strategy was the occupation of the Brazilian Amazon led by significant projects in the region: road network (Transamazônica, Perimetral Norte, Cuiabá-Santarém, Porto Velho-Manaus, Belém-Brasília, etc.), urban network, Sudam, Suframa, Proterra, Polamazônia, PGC—Grande Carajás Program and others.

Given the growing external interest in the Amazon and the progressive scarcity of environmental resources on the planet, the Amazon Cooperation Treaty emerged at the end of the 1970s of the 20th century, aiming to promote the rapprochement and development of the territories of the Amazon countries:

Motivated by this growing international greed, the Amazon countries came together in 1978 to sign the Amazon Pact, a political attempt to unify interests and objectives in exploring the region.

(Oliveira, 1979, p. 11)

The Amazon Cooperation Treaty (TCA), a multilateral legal instrument of Public International Law signed between the Amazon countries (Brazil, Bolivia, Colombia, Ecuador, Guyana, Peru, Suriname, and Venezuela), effectively reflects this concern, even when it reaffirms the principle of national sovereignty in its Amazonian territories, by establishing that:

> **Article IV:** The Contracting Parties proclaim that the exclusive use and exploitation of natural resources in their respective territories is a right inherent to the sovereignty of the State, and its exercise will have no restrictions other than those resulting from International Law. (Our emphasis).
>
> *(Amazon Cooperation Treaty (ACT), 1978)*

This shows that Amazonian countries perceive the critical position of the Amazon in the face of internal and external economic and geopolitical scenarios, given the region's rare environmental characteristics. This makes it relevant to approach the impacts of Logospiracy on Legal Amazon in a context of perverse globalization. Given this, one must question the effects of Logospiracy on the Brazilian legal Amazon.

Impacts of the Logospiracy in Brazilian Legal Amazon

Once the notion of Logospirataria and the geographic and historical space in which it occurs in this analysis—the Legal Amazon—have been clarified, it is time to discuss its harmful impacts on the Amazon.

Returning to the idea of Logospiratism, in its epistemological significance, to understand the harmful impacts on socio-environmental reality due to the occurrence of Logospiracy processes in the Legal Amazon allows questions and postulations, the consequences of which certainly include legal aspects and judicial measures.

Attesting to the occurrence of Logospiracy in the Legal Amazon is recognizing that genetic heritage resources and traditional knowledge associated with the use of biodiversity produced in the region are being irregularly appropriated alongside the undue exploitation of human labor through precarious work relationships or even the worst-case scenario (reduction to the analogous condition of slavery), violating the legal rules that protect the rights of indigenous peoples, societies, traditional populations, and the State itself.

As a result, the inaugural postulation is that the impacts caused by the practice of Logospiracy in the Brazilian Legal Amazon primarily affect national sovereignty, understanding it as a political-structural institute that characterizes the State and gives it powers to represent national society, indigenous peoples, and traditional populations of the region on the domestic and international scene. Logospiracy violates the rights of the fundamental political-legal entity that has the duty, in the sphere of the international community, to represent the interests of members of the Brazilian State, including indigenous peoples, traditional populations, and national society.

The Convention on Biological Diversity (CBD), ratified by more than 160 signatories, is a multilateral instrument of public international law and has influenced the current legislation of several countries on access to genetic heritage, access/protection of associated traditional knowledge, and fair distribution and equitable benefits arising from the economic use of genetic resources, safeguarding the sovereignty of each national State over the genetic heritage of its territory. The CBD also forms the basis of Brazilian legislation on the subject.

Professor Sebastião Marcelice Gomes opportunely clarifies, in the article "Genetic Heritage: legal implications relating to the right of access," that:

> The CBD establishes "that States have sovereign rights over their biological resources" and promotes an advance about the previous paradigm of humanity's shared heritage. However, it is necessary to analyze the legal implications of this paradigm shift regarding biological resources and define the exact dimension of state sovereignty.
>
> *(Gomes and Chaves, 2015, p. 175)*

The author aforementioned proposes a model of joint and responsible sovereignty by the provisions of the Convention on Biological Diversity:

> This study does not share the view that a State has its sovereign power weakened by being linked to international organizations; however, in the case of national States' ownership of their biological resources, the CBD carves out joint sovereignty, as it should not prevent Contracting Parties from accessing these resources.
>
> *(Gomes and Chaves, 2015, p. 177)*

As long as public law and also legal transactions of a private nature do not institute policies and legal devices that inhibit the looting and undue appropriation of traditional resources and knowledge (TCs) or encourage the development of research to make better use of Amazonian biotechnologies, they will be helplessly watching the neocolonial Logospiracy of plants, wild animals, active ingredients, CTs originating from the Amazon forest without significant consequences, in particular through the application and granting of patent registrations, as can be seen in Table 14.1.

TABLE 14.1 Patents on products from Amazonian plants required in several developed countries

Product	Number of patents	Countries
Castanha-do-Pará	72	USA
Andiroba	2	France, Japan, EU, USA
Ayahuasca	1	USA (1999–2001)
Copaíba	3	France, USA, WIPO
Cunaniol	2	EU, USA
Cupuaçu	6	Japan, England, EU
Curare	9	England, USA
Espinheira Santa	2	Japan, EU
Jaborandi	20	England, USA, Canada, Ireland, WIPO, Italy, Bulgaria, Russia, South Korea
Amapá-doce	3	Japan
Piquiá	1	Japan
Jambu	4	USA, England, Japan, EU
Sangue de dragão	7	USA, WIPO
Tipir	3	Japan
Unha de gato	6	USA, Poland
Vacina de sapo	10	WIPO, USA, EU, Japan

Source: World Intellectual Property Organization (WIPO)

Some of these patent registrations were questioned and invalidated. Still, the vast majority, without resistance, usually followed the registration procedure with the regulatory entity and obtained the rights for commercial exploitation without bearing responsibilities for compensation to the people and communities that developed the respective traditional knowledge associated with genetic heritage for the sharing of benefits aimed at the conservation and sustainable use of biological diversity itself, and for compensation from the State that represents the providers above of traditional knowledge in the international legal sphere.

In view of these questions, it is clear that the research and study of Logospiracy can unfold at more specific levels of investigation and subside discussions about different undertakings—institutional, private, or official—regarding the impacts on the Brazilian Amazon.

Conclusions

The impactful tentacles of Logospiracy spread throughout the planet, also reaching the Brazilian Amazon, especially after the encounter between the region's native peoples and people of European origin.

Several logospirate consequences resulted from this historical (dis)encounter for the Amazonian aboriginal populations: indigenous slavery, imposition of colonial models and the respective detribalization and deculturation (e.g., the Lusitanization imposed in the Pombaline period), wars and massacres imposed by the colonizers, looting of natural resources (tropical products and articles called backlands drugs) and traditional knowledge associated with biodiversity developed by Amazonian populations and communities, diseases that decimated indigenous groups and populations, among other harmful impacts.

> One fact, however, is indisputable: in seventy years of Portuguese colonization, indigenous peoples were exterminated from the Amazon delta, the island of Marajó, and the lower Amazon, forcing the Portuguese to look for Indians in the Western Amazon and go up towards the Solimões and tributaries such as the Negro and Japurá rivers.
> *(Freire, 1994, p. 34)*

Currently, Logospiracy continues to manifest itself in the Brazilian Legal Amazon in the most different forms of processes that are harmful to the environment and the rights of sociodiversity in the region. The most frequent ones assume the following social configurations:

a) in the irregular exploitation of human labor or reduction to a condition analogous to slavery;
b) the misappropriation of natural resources and biodiversity;
c) the looting or plundering of associated traditional knowledge created and developed by different groups and native communities;
d) impacts caused by mining activities or mineral extraction;
e) in the forgetting, loss, and eradication of practices, customs, and symbolic traditions of the Amazon (folklore, legends, festivals);
f) the radicality of expressions of violence and criminal events in the region;
g) in the production of a significant amount of solid waste, lack of appropriate destination and treatment for it, a situation that also reflects the effects of symbolic waste, including those that try to diminish or belittle regional traditions and cultures;

h) corruption and lack of assistance on the part of the State, nationally and regionally, to deal with and confront situations of health, social, economic, and public security crises, mainly due to the gradual dismantling of essential public services, which has had a detrimental impact on the population in the Amazon, especially in 2020, considering the effects of the new coronavirus pandemic.

These are certainly the main forms of manifestation of Logospiracy today in the Brazilian Legal Amazon, which allows us to see the need for even more comprehensive and in-depth research on the problem.

Note

1 Available on https://www.ipea.gov.br/desafios/index.php?option=com_content&id=2154:catid=28#:~:text=A%20Amaz%C3%B4nia%20Legal%20%C3%A9%20uma,5%2C0%20milh%C3%B5es%20de%20km%C2%B2 at 04/02/24

References

Amazon Cooperation Treaty (ACT). 1978. Available at https://otca.org/en/wp-content/uploads/2021/01/Amazon-Cooperation-Treaty.pdf.
Dantas, F. 2008. A necessidade de tutela penal contra a biopirataria na Amazônia. *Hiléia: Revista de Direito Ambiental da Amazônia*. Ano 6–7, n°. 11–12.
Freire, J. R. B. 1994. *A Amazônia Colonial (1616–1798)*. 5ª ed. Manaus: editora Metro Cúbico.
Gomes, S. M., Chaves, M. do P. S. R. 2015. Patrimônio genético: implicações jurídicas relativos ao direito de acesso. In: Filho, Guajarino et al. (eds.). *Biotecnologia e (Bio)Negócio no Amazonas*. Manaus: Edua.
Ianni, O. 1999. *Teorias da Globalização*. 5ª. ed. Rio de Janeiro: ed. Civilização Brasileira.
Oliveira, A. E. 1979. Ocupação Humana. In: Salati, Enéias (org.). *Amazônia: desenvolvimento, integração, ecologia*. São Paulo: Brasiliense/CNPq.
Pontes Filho, R. P. 2017. *Logospirataria na Amazônia*. Lisboa, Portugal: Chiado Editora.
Santos, M. 2008. *Por uma outra globalização: do pensamento único à consciência universal*. 17ª ed. Rio de Janeiro: Record.
Shiva, V. 2001. *Biopirataria: a pilhagem da natureza e do conhecimento*. Petrópolis, RJ: Vozes.
Souza, M. 2001. *Breve história da Amazônia*. 2ª. ed. Rio de Janeiro: Agir.

15

THE BRAZILIAN AMAZON BETWEEN GEOPOLITICS AND LAW

Guilherme Sandoval Góes[1] and Antonio dos Santos[2]

Thematic Introduction

Among the main themes of constitutional theory that needs to be better examined in Brazilian academia is the multidisciplinary epistemic approach involving legal and strategic studies related to the challenges and perspectives of the sustainable development of our Amazon.

In fact, the Brazilian Amazon is a doubly privileged geographical region, to the extent that, at the same time, it is full of natural resources, such as its incomparable biodiversity (rich in different plant and animal species), its important mineral reserves, abundant fresh water, and vast expanses of tropical forest. In addition, the Amazon plays a crucial role as a strategic vector for containing the greenhouse effect, acting as a carbon sink of global proportions, an essential factor for climate regulation on a global scale.

In addition to the issues of its natural resources and its role in protecting the environment and regulating the climate, a third element can also be added, which is the intrinsic relationship between indigenous peoples and nature, a theme so well addressed by Arthur Cézar Ferreira Reis, in his pioneering work "História do Amazonas" (1931).

His reflections on the regional identity and economic potential of the Amazon are fundamental for the understanding of the current theory of the Strategic Rule of Law, inspired by Geolaw, envisioned here as the branch of science that studies the epistemic encounter between geopolitics and law.[3]

It is in this context that emerges the relevance of an in-depth analysis of the challenges faced by the region in terms of environmental preservation and sustainable development. It should be noted, therefore, that it is necessary to unveil the Amazon region from the perspective of geopolitics, in order to understand how the relationship between territory and power was and is present in the occupational process of the Amazonian territory. In fact, since the first contact between indigenous peoples and European colonizers, the Amazon has always been seen as a strategic area, in terms of both natural resources and geographical position.

Throughout history, several countries and groups have sought to control and exploit this region, which has led to territorial conflicts and geopolitical disputes that continue to this day, such as the Essequibo issue, involving Venezuela and Guyana.

DOI: 10.4324/9781003330653-19

In short, as already highlighted, the Amazon continues to be a space of international interest, not only for its biodiversity and economic potential but also for its importance in regulating the global climate and maintaining environmental balance.

Contrary to what it may seem, neither economic exploitation nor environmental preservation deserves to receive the sacred mantle of the sole codifier of the Amazon. That is why this article encompasses the debate on the place of the Amazon, both in the field of geopolitical theory and in the field of legal theory. In addition: the place of the Amazon in Brazil's Grand Strategy and the place of the Amazon in the 1988 Brazilian Constitution

In general terms, this means that, in order to carry out its function of distributing justice and guaranteeing fundamental rights for the Amazonian population, the 1988 Brazilian Constitution cannot be left out of the geopolitics of the Amazon, in the same way as the geopolitics of the Amazon, in its task of promoting the development and reduction of poverty in this region, cannot remain alien to the constitutional text, and must faithfully follow the norms of the Democratic Rule of Law and the international legal order of civilized nations.

Without the evolution of multidisciplinary studies of geolaw, it will be difficult for Brazil to transform its full development potential into an effective national power, always remaining a developing country, of late modernity.

In this sense, Cristina Soreanu Pecequilo accurately highlights:

> The more efficient the conversion of potential power into actual power, the greater the possibility of a state acting in the international system. One more example: Brazil is considered one of the largest producers of raw materials and holder of biodiversity in the world, but the processing of many of these raw materials is not carried out here, but abroad. Brazil, therefore, has potential power that it cannot convert into real power, allowing others to add value and achieve dominance from its resources, leaving many of the resources unexploited.
>
> *(Pecequilo, 2005, pp. 57–58)*

With this, it is easier to understand the concept of strategic cores or actors, conceived here as an expansion of the traditional concept of triple helix (companies, universities/research institutions, and government), which acting in full synergy, should promote national development, eliminate poverty and marginalization, in addition to reducing social and regional inequalities, within a free fair and solidary society, as outlined in items I to IV, of article 3, of the Brazilian Constitution.[4]

In general terms, it should be noted that the term "Strategic Rule of Law" should be interpreted as an attitude of the Democratic Rule of Law, which coordinates the actions of different strategic centers, including its own performance, whether as a regulator, financier, or executive body. Without this coordinating action by the State, there will be no national development and, in its wake, there will be no guarantee of social rights, including the dignity of the human person of the most vulnerable Brazilians, notably the indigenous communities and riverside populations of the Amazon.

With regard to the Amazon's Grand Strategy, for example, Meira Mattos (2011) already highlighted the importance of geography, territory, and its characteristics in the exploration and application of political power by the State. In this sense, it showed that elements such as the size, geodetic position, neighborhood, maritime access, and topographical nature of a territory could favor or hinder the formulation of a development strategy. As an example, Meira Mattos cites the difference between the Mississippi Valley and the Amazon Valley, pointing out that the exploration and establishment of a developed society in the Mississippi Valley required less human effort compared to the Amazon Valley.

This is due to the characteristics of each region, such as population density, availability of natural resources, navigability of rivers, among other factors, hence the relevance of formulating a great strategy for the region, obeying the constitutional principles and the international norms regulating the protection of the environment.

This vision is fundamental to understand the concept of the Strategic Rule of Law, which brings into contact the geopolitical, legal, and social dynamics in different regions of the country. Under the influence of the Rule of Law, the country must seek the development of the Amazon without departing from the pillars of democracy and the constitutional feeling of justice and without neglecting the international rules arising from the protection of the environment.[5]

In this context, it is believed that the great challenge of constitutional theory in the 21st century will be to analyze, with due academic density, the theoretical foundations of the Strategic Rule of Law, whose innovation is the construction of a new constitutional framework that balances free enterprise and the opening of world trade with the dignity of the human person, national development and social justice.

Therefore, it is urgent to introduce this new field of legal science into the Brazilian legal culture, with an epistemological focus aimed not only at the constitutional issues of national life but also at the strategic consequences of judicial decisions.

Anyway, this is the thematic spectrum of this article.

Amazon and Geopolitical Relevance

The Amazon represents a considerable geopolitical challenge. This region extends over nine countries on the South American continent, corresponding to 6.9 million km², which represents the largest biome in the world. Its magnitude is representative and of great complexity. This Brazilian biome is equivalent to 4,196,943 km², also called the Legal Amazon, and is in the center of South America.

Its territory is home to more than 30% of the Earth's biodiversity. It is the largest tropical forest in the world (equivalent to 15 European countries), with 3.52 million km² of native vegetation; In terms of vegetation, it is the largest ecosystem in the world, with tropical forests and grasslands, where there are about 2,500 species of trees and 30,000 species of plants, out of the hundred thousand that exist in South America (IBGE, 2011).

The Amazon is the largest hydrographic basin on the planet, which holds about 20% of the fresh water on the earth's surface, thus representing the most important transport and articulation system in the region, with 23,000 km² of navigable rivers and 2/3 of the Brazilian hydroelectric potential. Its main mineral riches are gold, tin, niobium, petroleum, natural gas, potash, limestone, manganese, iron, aluminum, diamond, chromium, and lignite.

This Amazonian potential is highlighted in several works, as can be seen in the quote transcribed next:

> Located in the north-central part of South America, covering the territories of Brazil, Bolivia, Peru, Ecuador, Colombia, Venezuela, Guyana, Suriname and French Guiana

(French overseas territory), the Amazon region occupies around 7,800,000km², which corresponds to 40% of the total area of South America. Boasting in its domains about 30% of the tropical forests and $1/_3$ of the genetic stock of the Earth, the Amazon biome stands out as the world's largest reserve of biodiversity.

(Queiroz, 2011, p. 280)

A source of mineral wealth and unknown or unquantified biodiversity, which attracts the interest of other countries, as already mentioned: "There is the presence of numerous foreign non-governmental organizations that, under the pretext of protecting the region or its inhabitants, try to research and map these sources, posing a risk to national sovereignty" (Dos Santos and Ribas, 2020).

The strategic relevance and international dimension of the Amazon can be measured by the attention that the world has been giving to the region for its important role in climate change and the abundance of natural resources increasingly demanded by the economy around the world. Such attention has alerted the Amazonian countries to the care that the region deserves under the threat of contesting their own sovereignty over these territories (Antiquera, 2006, p. 19).

As the extensive natural resource potential that exists in the Amazon and the crucial role the region plays in global climate change are better known, global attention on the region's fate is increasing.

Becker clarifies this issue:

The northern border corresponds to the strip of the Legal Amazon that borders seven countries in South America, constituting the most extensive border segment in Brazil, representing about 70% of the total Brazilian land border area. This dimension is one of the aspects that accounts for its strategic importance, which is also dictated by the position of the Amazon itself in relation to the rest of the country and abroad.

(Becker, 2009, p. 57)

The emphasis on the international dimension of the Amazon is consolidated in a phrase by Ignacy Sachs, a precursor of sustainable development:

We are all Amazonians, since the future of our species on planet Earth will depend to a large extent on the fate that will be given to the Amazon rainforest, a great dispenser of climates and regulator of the water regime, in addition to having a very rich biodiversity.

(Sachs, 2008, p. 1)

The Amazon has demanded special attention from the Brazilian Ministry of Foreign Affairs since the 1970s. At the initiative of the Brazilian state, the implementation of the Amazon Cooperation Treaty (ACT) was proposed, which had the political objective of bringing together the Amazonian countries in order to neutralize the submission of the region to international regimes that would reduce the sovereignty of the Amazonian countries.

In the 1990s, with the focus on increasing efficiency in the design and implementation of multilateral initiatives based on sustainable development, the Amazon Cooperation Treaty Organization (ACTO) was created. The implementation of ACTO resulted from the approval of an amendment to the ACT, which configured this new institution.

In this way, the Pan-Amazonian countries were structured to provide answers to state and non-state actors regarding the capacity to effectively manage the region and protect their sovereignty within a world system undergoing profound and rapid geopolitical reconfiguration.

Nowadays, sovereignty is a contested concept. Although we do not share this view, we argue that responses to the Amazon challenge should be efficient and conditioned by current paradigms and supported by public policies in tune with national environmental preservation.

Power relations in a changing world affect the regional geopolitical context, requiring a minimum dose of realism from the Brazilian State in the management of the national interest.

Considering the complexity of the regional biome and its intersectional character, the Amazon is always an interdisciplinary discussion, not just an environmental one. Thus, an interagency project is required for the implementation of public policies of any nature in that region.

Due to its physical dimensions, the natural wealth, and varied ecosystems existing in its territory, and also the result of its leading role as a food exporter, Brazil will always be the focus of the international scenario. In recent decades, the environment has been used as a non-tariff barrier against *commodity-producing* developing countries, as a way of subjugating developing countries and maintaining the *status quo* of the previously existing order.

Economic development is a necessary condition for the advancement of society. It must be considered in its search that environmental preservation is also important, which must coexist with the other without canceling the parts, so that they are balanced in meeting the sustainability of the projects.

The Amazon has always been the object of diplomatic and military attention of the Brazilian state. The need for cooperation among the Amazonian countries was seen as an essential aspect to develop the region and neutralize the risks of interference. A quote from Moniz Bandeira highlights the theme:

> The development of the Amazon depended, however, on cooperation with neighboring countries, since seven of Brazil's ten international borders were located almost entirely in that region, totaling 12,114 km, which represented about 80% of the total of its land border. Thus, with the purpose of increasing cross-border development, the Ministry of Foreign Affairs, during the government of General Ernesto Geisel (1974–1979), undertook the negotiations, under the responsibility of Ambassador Rubens Ricupero, for the celebration, on July 3, 1978, of the Amazon Cooperation Treaty.
>
> *(Bandeira, 2010, p. 81)*

Therefore, there is an urgent need to formulate an Amazon's Grand Strategy, which is capable of providing for the development of the region and protecting biodiversity and the rights of indigenous peoples and riverine populations.

This is the great challenge of the country's academic thought, which is to merge the studies of Geopolitics and Law (Geolaw), with the arduous mission of unveiling the intricate geopolitical game of the hegemonic countries, which project to the world the Kantian-Wilsonian rhetoric of axiological protection values for the environment and human rights, but which, in real life, practice the Machiavellian-Hobbesian aspect of international relations.

Geolaw, the Strategic Rule of Law, and the Development Centers of the Amazon

This thematic segmentation begins, highlighting that the elaboration of the "Amazon's Grand Strategy" has the potential to be the main initiative to guarantee the fundamental rights of indigenous and riverine populations.

The formulation of such a strategy can be crucial for the protection of these communities that have a deep connection to the land and depend on it for the preservation of their cultural, linguistic, and biological diversity. Guaranteeing their rights is, therefore, not only a matter of social justice but also a strategic necessity for Brazil, including the positive exponential gain that our international projection can acquire within the Global Governance System.

Additionally, the strategy has the potential to play a significant role in the environmental preservation of the Amazon, which is one of the richest and most diverse ecosystems in the world, and its protection is vital for global climate regulation and the health of our planet. Its great challenge is to build a strategic archetype capable of finding the balance between the need for environmental conservation and the economic and social development of the Amazon region.

Thus, in order to harmonize these constitutional values that put national development and environmental protection in tension, the Amazon's Grand Strategy must seek the principle of practical agreement, which presupposes mutual concessions between these two constitutional provisions of the same normative dignity.

Therefore, when applying the constitutional norms that embody the Strategic Rule of Law, judges and courts must take into account the principle of practical concordance, the interpretation of which points to the reconciliation between national geopolitical interests and respect for the rights of indigenous communities, on the one hand, and global interests related to environmental protection and the preservation of biodiversity, on the other.[6]

In other words, neither does environmental protection have a hierarchy over national development nor does national development have supremacy over the former. It is up to the Brazilian State to promote these two constitutional values in a balanced manner, based on mutual concessions, as already highlighted. Thus, the formulation of Amazon's Grand Strategy will require the participation of all sectors of Brazilian society, including federal, state, and municipal governments, companies, universities and research institutes, and civil society organizations, but it will also require political will and strategic cooperation from the Global Governance System to safeguard ecosystem services essential to humanity.

In addition, following in the footsteps of General Carlos de Meira Mattos (1980) thought, the construction of a pan-Amazonian community is highlighted, whose geopolitical vision recognizes the importance of the Amazon for Brazil and proposes regional cooperation as a way to promote development and integration in South America, that is, it proposes the economic and social development of the region in a coordinated manner. It should be noted that the strategy advocated by Meira Mattos, developed in the book *A Pan-Amazonian Geopolitics*, published in 1980, aims to integrate the Amazon region as a whole, taking into account its common ecological challenges.

In this regard, it is worth mentioning the creation, in 1978, of the Amazon Cooperation Treaty signed by several countries in the region, including Brazil, Bolivia, Colombia, Ecuador, Guyana, Peru, Suriname, and Venezuela. Here it is worth a very important geopolitical observation, namely, the fact that French Guiana is not part of the treaty as a signatory country, insofar as it is an overseas territory of France.

Now, it is necessary to ask, what are the reasons why France is not part of this first Amazon cooperation initiative? Is it a resistance from France itself or an opposition from the other Amazonian countries?

In our opinion, strategically speaking, it would be essential for France to integrate into the Amazon Pact as a whole. Placing the European country that most contests Brazil's performance in the environmental preservation of the Amazon would be a big step toward the effective protection of this region. It leaves it to the reflection of Brazilian jurists, legislators, journalists, military, and diplomats to analyze the negative and positive points of France's integration into a cohesive geopolitical bloc of the Pan-Amazon.

However, regardless of France or any other country or multilateral organization of Amazonian integration, it is urgent for Brazil to formulate an autochthonous model, considering the geopolitical breadth of the region and guaranteeing its environmental preservation, in accordance with the legitimate aspirations of the international society of democratic nations.

It is time to reject meticulously crafted Kantian-Wilsonian rhetorical speeches from countries and multilateral organizations that only serve to aggravate the cycle of poverty of indigenous communities and riverine populations in the Amazon. As Ives Gandra rightly ponders, in the words below, the sovereignty of the Amazon is Brazilian and we should not give it up:

> In 1991, Roberto Campos and I participated in a seminar of the Konrad Adenauer Foundation, in Bonn, Germany, in which we debated with two professors of the institution, among other economic topics, those presented by them, the internationalization of the Amazon. They argued that the Amazon, as a universal heritage, should be under the supervision of nations, not Brazil. Evidently, Roberto, more diplomatic, and I, more forceful, countered the proposals of the German masters. I even joked that you, who have destroyed their own forests for centuries, now want us, instead of reforesting Europe, in order to maintain its comfort, to guarantee it, through Brazil, sacrificing a considerable portion of our territory and handing it over to the leaders of the developed countries? Yes, we should preserve the Amazon Rainforest, but, as a sovereign nation, selling, in an eventual preservation market—today, carbon—the cost of maintenance in values consistent with being borne by developed countries, because the forest to be preserved corresponds to the size of a considerable portion of Europe.
>
> *(Martins, 2023, p. 217)*

Indeed, the Amazon is not only a matter of the Brazilian State and not a national issue for the Amazonian countries but also a matter of global interest due to its essential ecosystem services for humanity,[7] which include, among others, the regulation of the global climate, by absorbing large amounts of carbon dioxide from the atmosphere; the protection of the greatest biological diversity on the planet, with millions of species of plants, animals, fungi and microorganisms, which enables the development of new medicines, foods and materials; and the supply of water from the recharge of aquifers, the maintenance of rivers, and the regulation of rainfall patterns in the region and around the world.

From the perspective of geolaw, it is clear that judicial decisions related to the Amazon can have repercussions that go beyond national borders and can affect geopolitical relations between countries and multilateral organizations of the Global Governance System, for example, World Trade Organization (WTO), International Monetary Fund (IMF), Organization for Economic Co-operation and Development (OECD), and various UN Commissions and Conventions, among them, The 2030 Agenda and the UN Intergovernmental Panel on Climate Change (IPCC).

It will certainly not be a strategic initiative of the WTO, or the IMF, or the OECD, or the UN System, or France, or the United States, or China, or any other country or international organization that will formulate a great strategic model for the economic and social development of the Amazon, with geopolitical latitude to transform Brazil into an energy and environmental superpower in the context of democratic nations.

This responsibility lies with the Brazilian State, which should receive support and investment from the international community, notably from multinational companies that should be encouraged to make direct investments in the Amazon region, exploiting its enormous potential in terms of natural resources and biodiversity through the formation of joint ventures and public-private partnerships with Brazilian companies.

It is not advisable to embark on the traditional dynamics of providing subsidies and facilities to national or foreign companies without the necessary counterpart that strengthens the Amazonian triple helix, that is, coordinated actions between government, companies, and academia that enhance industrialization and the production of high value-added products, with international competitiveness and mandatory integration into global value and innovation chains.

In essence, here is the founding basis of the Amazon's Grand Strategy: to drive the creation of new strategic nuclei and strengthen existing ones through a regulatory framework that encourages the emergence of competitive companies in the global market, focusing on the comparative advantages inherent to the characteristics of the Amazon.

These companies can be state-owned or private, national or multinational, and should be supported by substantial investments, both public and private, with or without temporary subsidies, in order to advance the synergy of the Amazonian triple helix.

As a matter of fact, the Brazilian state must, among many other things, strategically establish regulatory frameworks for the Amazon, in order to create high-tech industries linked to its unique biodiversity (Brazilian and/or multinational biotechnology, pharmaceutical, and cosmetic companies); develop river transport as a means of regional integration and reduction of logistical costs for the production of riparian communities; exploit the potential for energy generation from renewable sources, such as hydroelectric, solar, wind, and biomass energy; encourage the formation of large tourism companies based on the natural beauty and biological diversity of the Amazon, with the potential to attract millions of tourists annually; and incentivize companies focused specifically on reforestation and conservation of the Amazon rainforest for sale in the global carbon credit market.

In short, with the right strategy for the Amazon region, Brazil has the opportunity to become an energy, tourism, environmental, and biotechnological powerhouse on the global stage. Thus, the future vision of the Amazon is, at the same time, complex and multidimensional.

On the one hand, it requires the creation and strengthening of high value-added companies, which, operating from the Amazonian territory, can compete internationally in the links of innovation, supply, and value chains, thereby generating, at the same time, the preservation of biodiversity and the reduction of poverty and regional and social inequalities, in accordance with article 3 and its paragraphs of the 1988 Constitution.

On the other hand, large investments in universities and research and technology centers in the Amazon region are equally important, as they contribute to leadership in brands and patents of Amazonian products, promoting the local economy based on the traditional knowledge of indigenous peoples and the rich and unique biodiversity of the region. In other words, without violating the rights and culture of indigenous peoples and local communities, the Amazon's Grand Strategy must promote their well-being, guaranteeing them the minimum legal content of human dignity, namely, guaranteeing them social rights to health, education, culture, housing, leisure, and equal opportunities.[8]

There is no dichotomy between the economic development of the Amazon and aggression against the cultural rights of indigenous peoples. Brazilian society needs to overcome this rhetoric of supposed Kantian-cosmopolitan nature, which in reality is nothing more than a Machiavellian-Hobbesian rhetoric that accuses the Brazilian State of trying to neutralize the cultural values of indigenous communities in the Amazon. Stephen Baines goes so far as to assert that:

> With the construction of the BR-174 highway between 1970 and 1977, which connected Boa Vista and the entire territory of Roraima to the rest of Brazil, there was a very rapid growth of the non-indigenous population and an accelerated economic development in the region. From 1985 onwards, the border region became the target of the Calha Norte Project, which intensified, in an unprecedented way, the cultural integration policies that had been imposed over the centuries. The establishment of the Calha Norte Project (PCN in [P]ortuguese), as argued by Oliveira (1990), aims to implement infrastructure in the northern border of Brazil, under the justification of protecting it, reinforcing national sovereignty, preventing drug trafficking, and the entry of guerrillas from neighboring countries. However, the undeclared reasons for the PCN would be the implementation of infrastructure to open up the region to economic development, especially through large mining projects in the Guianese Massif, rich in deposits of cassiterite, diamonds, gold, and other minerals.
>
> *(Baines, 2004, p. 73)*

What good is it to celebrate the normative strength of the Constitution in a vigorous Democratic State of Law, committed to the historical rights of indigenous communities, when we see the indignity and poverty in which these brave Brazilian brothers live, without health care, without basic sanitation, without virtually any support from anyone. It is necessary, therefore, to develop a strategy for the Amazon region that reconciles the process of regional development with environmental preservation and the cultural diversity of indigenous peoples. However, this strategy must be conceived autonomously, without being influenced by foreign strategic nuclei.

In fact, the influence of external strategic actors can undermine this objective, using even lawfare, which, in the name of the Democratic State of Law, neutralizes the strategic actions of the Brazilian state regarding economic development and the human dignity of indigenous peoples.

These forces often manage to deregulate and deconstitutionalize legal norms of late modernity underdeveloped countries, thus facilitating the exercise of their economic power in the region within this context of fourth-generation legal warfare.

At this point, Ignacio Ramonet brings to light the vision that:

Democratic voting has very little influence on the internal functioning of these three major actors (associations of states, global companies, and large groups of media or finance, and non-governmental organizations—NGOs). This great mutation of the world, which empties the meaning of democracy, has settled in without being noticed and without the political leaders themselves being aware of it.

(Ramonet, 2003, p. 12)

The strategic actions of lawfare can lead to a loss of vitality in democracy on the periphery of the world system (countries of late modernity, as is unfortunately still the case in Brazil), as it is affected by forces promoting legal deregulation in favor of large multinational companies and their economic interests.

In the same vein, the lesson of Charles J. Dunlop:

Law fare is a concept that is ever more frequently discussed in government, academic, and media circles. Regrettably, that discussion is not as informed as it might be. The purpose of this commentary is to clarify what law fare means by discussing how it originated, how it is being used by opposing sides in modern conflicts, and what some of the challenges are as we look ahead. Although I have tinkered with the definition over the years, I now define "law fare" as the strategy of using—or misusing—law as a substitute for traditional military means to achieve an operational objective. As such, I view law in this context much the same as a weapon. It is a means that can be used for good or bad purposes.

(Dunlap, 2008, p. 146)

Reinterpreting Carl von Clausewitz, now with shades of postmodern stateness, one can say that "law is the continuation of geopolitics by other means," it is worth explaining: legal warfare is the new warfare of postmodernity, fourth-generation warfare, in which legal-constitutional maneuvers will be used as substitutes for maneuvers of armed forces, aiming to achieve certain fundamental State objectives, whatever their nature (foreign policy, economic, national/military security, psychosocial, or scientific-technological) (Góes, 2020a, p. 23).

Unfortunately, the Brazilian literature in this epistemological field is still incipient, that is, it is a practically unexplored topic in Brazil. We do not have any major academic work on this subject, as in Italy, for example. There, there are several scholars, among them the jurist Natalino Irti, with the work "*Norma e Luoghi. Problemi di Geo-Diritto.*" whose dominant scientific line studies the relations between the deregulating forces of the economy and technology and the law on the periphery of the world system (Irti, 2005).

In this way, Philip Bobbitt (2003), in the United States and the United Kingdom, has developed a dense literature on the relationship between national strategy, constitutional law, and international law, highlighting the idea of the state market.[9]

This lack of geolaw vision in Brazil makes it difficult, for example, to understand that a certain state, without using its armed forces, can destroy the main centers of gravity of a possible geopolitical adversary, using only the legal sphere. In essence, lawfare is the war of strategic nuclei of adversary countries seeking to control global value and innovation chains, notably those of high added value and intense technology. In short, this is the main form of warfare unfolding between the United States and China.[10]

Only with this more sophisticated thinking will Brazil have the capacity to articulate the strategic nuclei of the Amazon, transforming all the potential power of the region into real power and, with this, projecting the country as an environmental and energy superpower in the concert of nations. It is urgent, therefore, to reconcile the principles of geoverdism (a term coined by Thomas L. Friedman),[11] with the premises of economic development in the Amazon region based on its biodiversity and its different ecological subsystems.

While geolaw analyzes how the geopolitical aspects of world power influence the formulation of regulatory frameworks for strategic sectors of the economies of peripheral countries, the Strategic State of Law emphasizes the need to insert local actors (companies-universities-government) into global value, production, and innovation chains.

In this sense, the concepts of geolaw and the Strategic State of Law form the scientific basis of the statesman in his task of promoting national development, in the same way that they constitute the scientific basis of the judge in his task of deciding on a fundamental geopolitical question of the Brazilian State.

Conclusion

The binomial of national development and environmental security should be the guiding axis of the Amazon's Grand Strategy, considering environmental preservation and sustainability as relevant aspects. National development will continue to be pursued as a means to reduce regional imbalances, in line with the construction of a homogeneous and socially just national state. This national effort should be guided by the principles of sustainability and environmental preservation.

Brazil needs to articulate a robust foreign policy in cooperation with its Amazonian neighbors, while remaining vigilant in the context of a world order under reconstruction. The multilateral condition of the Amazon points to regional cooperation as a relevant instrument to prevent potential interference or interventions from extraregional actors.

Brazil must refine its public policies to reconcile internal development needs and economic exploration with international commitments to environmental preservation, as assumed by the Brazilian state.

Consequently, this work analyzes the perspectives of formulating a Amazon's Grand Strategy that aligns with the concepts of geolaw and Strategic State of Law. This study highlights the importance of a multidisciplinary approach between geopolitical theory and constitutional law theory, considering the influence of external strategic cores on the legal order of late-modern countries, as unfortunately remains the case with Brazil.

In the first instance, an intersection was investigated between the concepts of geolaw and the Strategic State of Law, which provides an epistemic view to understand the relationships between geopolitical and legal variables. Geolaw deals with the connections between law and geopolitics, considering the power dynamics among national states. On the other hand, the Strategic State of Law refers to the use of legal strategies to achieve national objectives, which, in the case of Brazil, align with the fundamental goals outlined in articles I to IV of our Constitution.

Rigorously, these provisions in article 3 of the Constitution establish guidelines for Brazil's Grand National Strategy, which should aim not only for national development but also for eradicating poverty and marginalization, as well as reducing social and regional inequalities within a free, just, and solidary society. Thus, the concepts of geolaw and the Strategic State of Law can assist in formulating this Grand Strategy, including the dimension related to the Brazilian Amazon.

As observed throughout this work, these concepts promote a more sophisticated scientific approach that recognizes the importance of the matrix of interconnected impacts involved in formulating development strategies and interpreting legal norms—both constitutional and international. Therefore, this multidisciplinary approach contributes to advancing constitutional theory by providing analytical and strategic tools to address the complex challenges faced by the state in promoting the social well-being and fundamental rights of Brazilian citizens, including those living in the Amazon region.

Therefore, let us not forget the impacts of judicial decisions on the country's geopolitical future, particularly concerning the future of the Amazon.[12] From the perspective of geolaw and the Strategic State of Law, constitutional interpretation becomes increasingly complex. Beyond the semantic and syntactic aspects of the constitutional text, it is essential to consider the global geopolitical landscape and its implications for conflicting strategic cores, especially multinational companies vying for market dominance.

That's why this academic work sought, from the outset, to further develop the idea of a hermeneutics of development for the Amazon, with an exegetical model capable of harmonizing regional development, environmental preservation, and the cultural diversity of indigenous populations.

Through the systematization undertaken, it was possible to demonstrate that statesmen and legislators must rethink a new state paradigm, considering new forms of international relations and fresh approaches to interpreting the Constitution. The envisioned solution must prioritize strengthening and expanding the strategic cores (companies-universities-government) operating in the Amazon region.

Therefore, Brazil urgently needs to move away from a geopolitically submissive stance toward global centers of power and reclaim lost time. In doing so, it is crucial to recognize that the Constitution and the Grand Strategy of the country must walk hand in hand.

With these considerations, this academic work concludes, emphasizing that in the era of geolaw, the Amazon's Grand Strategy must align with both economic development and environmental preservation in the region, while safeguarding the constitutional rights of indigenous communities and riverside populations.

The Amazon's Grand Strategy faces the challenge of fostering innovation, productivity, and international competitiveness for companies and universities operating in the region. This alignment should contribute to a broader vision of a green, diversified, and highly complex economy. It involves improving the business environment and increasing the country's qualified international participation, thereby promoting employment, income distribution, and the reduction of social and regional inequalities.

Notes

1 Coordinator of the Postgraduate Program in International Security and Defense (PPGSID) at the Brazilian War College; Emeritus Professor at the School of Command and General Staff of the Army; Postdoctoral researcher in Geopolitics, Culture, and Law at the Brazilian Air Force University; Doctor of Law from the State University of Rio de Janeiro; Leader of the Geopolitics Research Group of Brazil at the Superior War School of Brazil; Constitutional Law Professor at

the School of Magistracy in Rio de Janeiro and at Cândido Mendes University; Member of the Examination Board of the Getúlio Vargas Foundation for the Brazilian Bar Association (OAB) Exam; Invited speaker at the William J. Perry Center for Hemispheric Defense Studies, WJPC, USA (2019–2023); Diplomate of the United States Naval War College, Class 48, Newport, Rhode Island (1996). Email: guilherme.sandoval@terra.com.br.

2 Master's degree holder and Specialist in International Security and Defense from the Brazilian War College—ESG. Analyst in Geopolitics, Security, and Defense at the Strategic Studies Center of ESG, Rio de Janeiro (Brazil). Researcher at the Laboratory of Simulations and Scenarios of the Naval War College. Email: czosantos@yahoo.com.br.

3 Consequently, everything seems to indicate that geolaw heralds a new scientific era in which statesmen, strategists, judges, democratic legislators, constitutionalists, internationalists, and legal practitioners in general must rethink the connections between legal norms and state strategic action. Within this framework of multidisciplinary complexity, geolaw emerges as the ultimate scientific frontier—whether in geopolitics or law. It encompasses both geopolitical control of law (constitutionalization of geopolitics) and legal control of geopolitics (judicialization of geopolitics) (Góes, 2020b, p. 108).

4 By strategic cores, we mean all those actors, entities, companies, or segments—whether private or state-owned—that are economic, commercial, technological, academic, scientific, financial, regulatory, or industrial. These actors should be capable of effectively participating in international competition within the global chains of production, knowledge, and value, with or without investment from the Brazilian state.

5 Essentially, a Strategic State of Law is synonymous with a Democratic State of Law that coordinates its strategic actions for the common good. Therefore, it is the responsibility of the country's Grand Strategy to establish synergies between its state-owned or private companies and universities and government agencies. The aim is to promote the achievement of the four fundamental objectives of the Brazilian state outlined in the 1988 Constitution.

6 It is crucial to emphasize once again the scientific relevance of the concepts of geolaw and the Strategic State of Law. These concepts underscore the idea that judicial decisions must be informed by a comprehensive understanding of the geopolitical power dynamics among nations. This understanding ensures that judges and courts are equipped to apply the principle of practical concordance in cases of normative conflict involving the protection of human rights for indigenous peoples, environmental preservation, and the promotion of economic and social development in the Amazon region.

7 Such essential ecosystem services for humanity should, among other things, aim to (a) establish partnerships between universities and research institutes focused on Amazon biodiversity and new technologies for sustainable use of natural resources; (b) encourage industry and the development of green technologies, such as renewable energy and biotechnology; (c) implement zoning and territorial planning policies in the Amazon, protecting conservation areas and promoting sustainable agricultural and forestry practices; (d) enhance monitoring and environmental enforcement systems in the Amazon to combat deforestation, organized crime infiltration, illegal mining, and other environmentally harmful activities in the region; (e) invest in low-impact environmental river transportation projects in the Amazon, utilizing existing river navigation companies; and (f) scientifically develop traditional knowledge held by indigenous communities, using it to create new strategic cores linked to biodiversity, particularly in the field of pharmaceuticals, with a portion of the profits benefiting these communities' well-being.

8 In this context, José Luiz Borges Horta argues that establishing the milestones of strategic constitutionalism encourages a broad reconsideration of the material and formal aspects of the constitutional state, particularly in three relatively unexplored fields: political, economic, and cultural (Horta, 2012, p. 789).

9 In Bobbitt's words: Perhaps this conviction stems from my unusual personal history. Sometimes I feel not only that I was destined to write this book but also that I might be one of the few who would wish to do so. After all, over the past 25 years, I led a dual life. As a professor, I divided my time between Texas and England. In the United States, I teach constitutional law at the University of Texas; in the United Kingdom, I lectured on nuclear strategy, first at Oxford and later at King's College in London (Bobbitt, 2003, p. 3).

10 It is truly melancholic to note that in Brazil, this scientific lineage is still in its infancy, lacking greater doctrinal and jurisprudential development. However, it must be acknowledged that the

so-called permanent legal warfare (Lawfare) between the United States and China, whether due to global neoliberal leadership or the technological competition for control of the McLuhanian global village, is a reality. What we aim to demonstrate here is not traditional warfare but rather commercial warfare that transforms into legal battles. This clearly underscores that the Constitution indeed has a strategic dimension that cannot be neglected.

11 This is a philosophy that I would like to call "geo-verdism." We, the geo-greens, seek to unite environmentalists who want to reduce the use of fossil fuels causing climate change, evangelicals who want to protect God's green planet and all of His creation, and geostrategists who aim to decrease our dependence on crude oil because it fuels some of the world's worst regimes (Friedman, 2007, p. 469).

12 Let me explain further: once a specific strategic issue of the Brazilian state becomes a matter for the judiciary, an ill-considered decision by the Supreme Federal Court, made without taking into account the complex geopolitical dynamics with other sovereign states, can have disastrous consequences for the lives of thousands of Brazilians. For instance, it could lead to the destruction of a major Brazilian company, resulting in widespread unemployment.

References

Antiquera, D.C., 2006. *A Amazônia e a Política Externa Brasileira: Análise do Tratado de Cooperação Amazônica (TCA) e sua transformação em Organização Internacional (1978-2002)*. Dissertação (Mestrado em Relações Internacionais) - Instituto de Filosofia e Ciências Humanas, Campinas, Universidade de Campinas.

Baines, S. G., 2004. A fronteira Brasil-Guiana e os povos indígenas. Revista de Estudos e Pesquisas, FUNAI, 1(1), 65-98.

Bandeira, L. A. M., 2010. Geopolítica e Política Exterior: Estados Unidos, Brasil e América do Sul. Brasília, FUNAG.

Becker, B. K., 2009. *Amazônia: geopolítica na virada do III Milênio*. Rio de Janeiro: Garamond.

Bobbitt, P., 2003. A guerra e a paz na história moderna. O impacto dos grandes conflitos e da política na formação das nações. Rio de Janeiro: Campus.

Dunlap, C. J. 2008. Lawfare Today: A Perspective. In: Yale Journal of International Affairs, Winter, p. 146-154.

Friedman, T., 2007. O mundo é plano: uma breve história do século XXI. Rio de janeiro: Objetiva.

Góes, G. S., 2020a. A judicialização da geopolítica como última fronteira epistemológica do neoconstitucionalismo. In: Adaylson Wagner Sousa de Vasconcelos, ed., Instituições da democracia, da Cidadania e do Estado de Direito. Ponta Grossa: Atena.

Góes, G. S., 2020b. Geopolítica e Constituição à luz do Estado Democrático de Direito. Revista Austral: Revista Brasileira de Estratégia e Relações Internacionais 9(18), 107–31.

Horta, J. L. B. 2012. Urgência e emergência do constitucionalismo estratégico. Revista Brasileira de Estudos Constitucionais, 23, 783-806.

IBGE - INSTITUTO BRASILEIRO DE GEOGRAFIA E ESTATÍSTICA. 2011. Geoestatísticas de recursos naturais da Amazônia Legal. IBGE: Rio de Janeiro.

Irti, N., 2005. Norma e Luoghi. Problemi di Geo-Diritto. Roma-Bari: Laterza.

Martins, I. G. da S. M., 2023. Os reais interesses sobre a Amazônia. Revista do Ministério Público do Estado do Rio de Janeiro 90, 217-218.

Mattos, C. M.,2011. Geopolítica, v. III. Rio de Janeiro: Editora FGV.

Mattos, C.M., 1980. *Uma Geopolítica Pan-Amazônica*. Rio de Janeiro: Biblioteca do Exército Editora.

Pecequilo, C. S. 2005. Introdução às relações internacionais. Temas, atores e visões. Petrópolis: Editora Vozes.

Queiroz, F. A., 2011. *Hidropolítica e segurança: as Bacias Platina e Amazônica em perspectiva comparada*. PHD. Thesis (Doutorado em Relações Internacionais)-Universidade de Brasília.

Ramonet, I., 1998. A Geopolítica do Caos. Petrópolis: Vozes.

Reis, A. C. F., 1931. História do Amazonas. Manaus: Officinas Typographicas de Augusto Reis.

Sachs, I., 2008. Amazônia: laboratório de biocivilizações do futuro. Available at http://dowbor.org/2008/10/amazonia-laboratorio-de-biocivilizacoes-do-futuro-outubro-2008- 2.html/. Access on 10th April 2021.

Santos, A., Ribas, L. M., 2020. Amazônia, Interesse Nacional e Soberania Brasileira: planejamento, desenvolvimento sustentável e defesa. Revista Argumentum, 21(2), p. 627-662.

INDEX

Note: Page numbers in *italic* indicate a figure and page numbers in **bold** indicate a table on the corresponding page.

Alonso, A.M. 32
Amazonas 2, 14, 17–18, 63–64; Association of Police Commissars 21; Environmental Agency 21, 22; Environmental Protection Agency 25; Federal Police Commissar 21–22; illegal lodgers in 22, 24–25, 27; Northern Family (FDN) 67; State University 21; *see also* Civil Police; rule of law
Amazon Cooperation Treaty (ACT) 109; amendment to aims of 115; Article IV on exclusive use and exploitation of natural resources 208; defensive-protectionist period of 115; emergence at the end of 1970s of 20th century 207; objectives criticized by member countries 114; political objective of 215; polycentric governance analysis through regulatory framework 110
Amazon Cooperation Treaty Organization (ACTO) 5–6, 109–120, 119n10, 215; Andean-Amazonian region 110–112, *111*; capabilities for dealing transnational threats 113–116; formation of 115; Resolution RES/XIII MRE-OTCA/04 119n10; Strategic Agenda 117; UNASUR compared with 112–113
Amazon Fund 18, 28n3
Amazon Protection System (SIPAM) 69
Amazon Surveillance System (SIVAM) 69
Andean-Amazonia 109–112, *111*
Andean Community of Nations (CAN) 76, 78
annual intercensal growth rates *91*
Antaihua, J. 37

Apuí 3, 14, 18–19, 21–23; deforestation rates in **20**
Arawak Army 41
arché (arqué) 203
Artal, F.J.C. 177

Baptiste, B. 56
Becker, B. 62, 215
Belém Declaration 115, 118, 119n9
Bertolin, P.T.M. 126
Binational Border Attention Centers 78
Binational Border Commission (COMBIFRON) 77
biopiracy 3, 6, 17, 103, 117, 202–206
Bobbitt, P. 221, 224n9, 225
Bolivia 1, 36, 63–64, 66, 102, 103, 113, 206, 214, 217
Bonelli, M.D.G. 126, 130, 134, 135
Börzel, T.A. 16
Botero, R. 51
BR-174 highway 220
BR-429 (highway) 107n5
Brazil 1, 107, 145, 222; autochthonous model 218; biodiversity of 168–169, 178; decrease of homicide rates in 2; defense and intelligence of 68–71; deforestation in 18, **19**; documents for asylum seekers 157; drug trafficking in 63–64; effect of asylum seekers on borders 160–162; environmental problem in 18; Federal Constitution 4, 8, 13, 22, 62, 68–71, 126, 130, 142, 183, 213; Federal Police (FP) 153, 156–157, 160; General Immigration Coordination (CGIg)

156; government efforts to control border points and land crossings 55; Grand Strategy 213, 216–217, 219–220, 222–223, 224n5; issue of ghettoization in 132, 138; issues of fires and illegal logging in 13, 103–104, 106; judiciary 225n12; migration legislation and administrative processes 155–160; Ministry of Foreign Affairs 156; Ministry of Justice 127, 156; Ministry of Labor 156; National Immigration Council (CNIg) 156; no access to *pseudo*-universal rights 177; organized crime and violence 66–67; percentage of women in police organizations *131*; police agencies and forces in **128**, 130–132; Reference and Assistance Centers 161; security concern in 63–64, 68–71; support and investment from the international community 219; *see also* Rondônia; Legal Amazon; Legal Amazonia
Brazilian Forum on Public Security (FBSP) 6, 67, 71, 103, 127
Brown, J. 136
Buzan, B. 109, 111–112

Calha Norte Project 220
Campos, R. 218
Cano, L. 33
carapanaúba complex 168, 170–171, **172**, **176**, 177, 179
Carrington, K. 125–126, 130, 132, 136, 138
causal chain 110, *110*, 116, 118, 118n3
Center for Studies on Crime and Public Security (CRISP) 6, 127
Center for Studies on Organizations and People (NEOP) 6, 127
Centro de Coordenação de Interiorização (CCI) 161
Chang, H.-J. 176
Charmaz, K. 169, 178
Charron, N. 16
Civil Police (Amazonas) 126–127, **128**, 142–151; composition of 143–144; dimensions of procedural justice 144–146; field research carrried out with officers 146–150, **149–150**; overview 142–143; web survey conducted for 143–144; *see also* Amazonas
coca 98; collectors 95; legalization of 37; policies for eradication of 56; production/cultivation 32–38, 42, 47, 50, 52, 54, 56–58, 79, 95; trafficking 32, 37–38, 42
cocaine 37–38, 64, 66–67, 78; commercialized for medicinal purposes 35; flow routes from the Andean-Amazonian region *111*; imported by Colombian drug traffickers from Bolivia 36; increase in exports after the Colombian Civil War 2; increase in international demand for 36

Colombia 1, 18, 46–60, 64, 84, 94; Armed Forces 84; conflict on Ecuadorian territory 79; corruption and collusion, as obstacle to law enforcement in 48–49; crimes in 47–58; criminal organizations in 5deforestation in 50–53, **53**; drug trafficking in 97; Environmental Crimes Law of 2009 57; exploitation of nature reserves in 52–55; failure of law enforcement agencies in 48; against global drug threat 80; guerrilla groups in Ecuador 81; illegal minery and mining activities in 55–56; illegal trafficking of species in 49–50, 57–58; impact of peace agreement with the FARC guerrillas 47, 54; increase of armed conflict in 95; lack of social fabric and community control in 49; Law 2250 of 2022 57; Law of Environmental Crimes 57; Ministry of Defense 58; Ministry of Environment and Sustainable Development 57–58; Plan Colombia 78–79; presence of political and criminal entities in 47–48; regulations for combatting crime and devastation 56–58; security risks from terrorist and drug trafficking organizations 74; threat of criminal gangs to indigenous reservations in 52–55
Comando Vermelho (CV) (criminal organization) 67
Commission of Enquiry on the Coca Leaf 35
Complexo Anísio Jobim 2
CONARE (Comitê Nacional para os Refugiados, National Committee for Refugees) 154–155, 157–162, **158–159**
Connell, R. 138–139
Convention on Biological Diversity (CBD) 168–169, 208–209
Convention on International Trade in Endangered Species of Wild Fauna and Flora (CITES) 57, 117, 119n13
Correa, R. 80
corruption: coca legalization and 15, 37; deforestation 105; due to illicit economies and organized crime 42; in illegal logging 38; involving public officials 17, 55, 65, 107; as obstacle to law enforcement in Colombia 48–49
crimes 5, 22; in Colombia 47–58; against women 132; *see also* environmental crimes
criminal entities, in Colombia 47–48
criminal environmental law 188–191
criminal gangs, in Colombia 46–49, 53, 55, 59
criminal justice institutions 3–5, 17, 20, 22, 23, 26
criminal law 183–184, 188, 189, 194
criminal organizations 2, 4–5, 17, 23, 56, 62–71; biopiracy 6; described 65–66; issue of border security 63–64; legal/institutional

framework 68–71; organized crime and violence 66–68; use of forces to control territories 17
Cubas, V. de O. 146
curare complex 168, 170–171, **173**, **176**, 177, 179

de-colonial thinking 167, 175, 178
De Echave, J. 39, 42
deforestation 18, 59, 105, 128, 224n7; carried out by companies 49; in Colombia 2, 49–54, **53**, 57–58; corruption 105; cultivation of coca causing 37–38; dealt by law enforcement institutions and judicial authorities 14; defined 17; due diligence in case of 23; evolution of **19**; monitoring through satellite 27, 28n2; preventing cultivation of coca to prevent 58; rates in Apuí and Lábrea **20**; in Rondônia 103; strategies to combat 56
Democratic Rule of Law 213
devastation, strategies to combat 56–58
Diakara, J. 168
disputes 67; Ecuador 75–77; FARC guerrillas involved in territorial 51; geopolitical 212; illicit crop cultivation and illegal mining 53; political leaders in Peru involved in 82
Donohue Jr, R. H. 130, 132, 134
drug trafficking 17, 31, 67, 74, 77–80, 97; in Andean-Amazonian region 111; in Brazil 64, 66; coca production and 34–38, 42; in Colombia 76–77, 88, 95; international 69, 103; in Lago Agrio, Ecuador 97; linked to terrorist groups 41; by organized criminal groups 63, 66
Dunlop, C. J. 221

Easton, D. 81
Eberhardt, J. L. 144
Echeverry, N. 54
ecological harm 55, 184–187, 189, 198n60
Ecuador 4–5, 34, 48, 74–85, 93–99, 100n1; Armed Forces 41, 75, 77, 81–82, 84; Comprehensive Border Development Plan 79; connection of political system with Amazon 81–83; Defense White Paper 79; development models in 88–92; drug trafficking in Lago Agrio 97; institutional influences and weaknesses of 81; institutions and regimes in 83–84; issues of wealth, disputes, and borders 75–77; organized crime, violence, and migration in 77–81; *see also* Lago Agrio
environmental civil liability law 185–186
environmental crimes 14, 23, 28, 48, 106, 189; causing global illicit financing 119n4; illegal mining in 56; limited resources for investigation of 26; in Rondônia 103

Environmental Crimes Law of 2009 (Colombia) 57
environmental protection, in French Guiana 181–201; biodiversity in 181; core zone and the neutralization of the constraints 192–194; environmental criminal law in 188–194; normative framework 182–184; role of judicial judge in environmental damage 184–187
Escobar, A. 100n3
Executive Unit for Northern Development (UDENOR) 78

failed states 15, 16, 22, 112, 119n5
Família do Norte (Northern Family) 2
Federal Attorney Office (Porto Velho) 23
Federal Police (Porto Velho) 22–23, 68, **128**, 153–154; asylum claims **158**, 159–161; dealing with environmental law 104; National Immigration Council (CNIg) 156; role in removing invading loggers 105; role of 157; technical and anthropological training of 106
Fénix (intelligence and military operation) 79–80
Filippi, E. 119n8
fires 3, 21, 52, 56, 115; deforestation and 14, 27, 51; illegal logging and 13, 18–19, 21, 25, 27–28, 50; monitoring of 27
First Northern Command (PCN) (criminal organization) 67
fragile states/statehood 15, 16, 22, 28, 110, 112; issues of land regulation in 23; in Rondônia 103–104
France 9n1, 191, 218, 219; Constitutional Council 183; integration into the Amazon Pact 218; issues of national sovereignty 182; Mining Code 190, 199n82; statutes and regulation 184
French Guiana 63; authoritarian governments in 1; biodiversity and geography of 181; the Constitution 183, 195n17; environment statutes and regulation 184; General Local Authorities Code 182–183; legal gold panning and mining 181, 183, 185–186, 189–191; National Parks 182, 191–192; Parc Amazonien de Guyane (PAG) 182; as single territorial community 183; Zones de Droits d'Usage Collectifs (ZDUC) 182; *see also* environmental protection, in French Guiana
Friedman, T. L. 222
frontier, Amazonia as 21, 24–25, 32–33, 42, 50–51, 56, 63–64, 96–98

Gavião People 105–106, 107n4
GDP growth 16, 76, 129
General Agreement on Tariffs and Trade (GATT) 204

geolaw 8, 212–225, 224n3, 224n6; environmental preservation and sustainable development 212; relevance of 214–216; Strategic Rule of Law and the Development Centers 217–222
geopolitics 212–223
geo-verdism 225n11
Getulio Vargas Foundation (FGV) 127
Ginsburg, T. 15
Glaser, B. G. 177–178
glass ceiling 136, 138–139
Global Governance System 217, 219
Gomes, M. 209
Gootenberg, P. 35
Grand Strategy (Brazil) 213, 216–217, 219–220, 222–223, 224n5
grilagem (land grabbing) 5, 51, 53, 104, 107n1
grileiros 22–23
grounded theory 177–178
guerrillas 1, 2–4, 48, 82, 98, 220; criminal activities and 46; FARC 47, 51, 54, 75; narco-guerrillas 77; Shining Path and MRTA 41; threats to indigenous populations and settlers 78

Haass, R. 110
habilitación (compulsory indebtedness) 38
"Harpie" operation 194n3
Helman, G. 119n5
Hermann, D. 146
Herndon, W.L. (Commander) 31
"high-policing practices" 144
Horta, J. L. B. 224n8
Huanacuni, F. 113
human trafficking 17, 31–37, 40–41, 42, 48
hydroelectric power plants, Rondônia 103–106

IIRSA *see* Regional Infrastructure Integration Initiative
illegal fishing 57, 119n4, 181–182, 192, 195n5
illegal gold panning 181, 185–186, 189–191
illegal logging 21, 31–32, 38, 42, 119n4; in Colombia 46; fires and 13, 17–19, 21, 27–28; indigenous population as victim of 5; monitoring of 27; in Rondônia 103–104, 106
illegal mining 39–40, 46–47, 49, 51, 53, 55–57, 76, 80, 118, 224n7; criminal gangs involved in 49, 55
illegal wildlife trafficking, Colombia 49–50, 58
illicit economic activities 42–43
Impact on Ecuador of Aerial Spraying Conducted in Putumayo as Part of the Plan Colombia (report) 78
indigenous organizations 32–34, 41–42, 83
indigenous peoples/population 31, 33–34, 37, 38, 54–55, 78, 83, **93**, 132, 212, 220; being victims of necropolitics and violence in Rondônia 102–103, 106; damage by hydroelectric dams to indigenous lands 107; effect of military intervention on life of 59; effect of modernization on 94; indigenous women working in police agencies 6, 132, 140; Morona Santiago 92; protection of human rights for 224n6; protection of natural resources and 104; recognition of the rights of 53; represented as savage and violent 32; use of coca by 35; violence against, in Rondônia 103
indigenous reservations, in Colombia 47, 52–53
indigenous women 6, 132, 140
institutional influences, Ecuador 81
institutional resources 26–27
intellectual property rights legislation 167–179; data collection 168–171; inventors and applicants in 174–178; research findings 171, **172–173**; research methodology 168–170
intelligence, Brazil 62–71, 77, 79–80, 106
International Monetary Fund (IMF) 80, 219
International Police Cooperation Center (CCPI) 117
Interpol (International Criminal Police Organization) 38

judicial judge: as co-author of environmental civil liability law 185–186; punitive power of 186–187; role in environmental damage 184–187
Judiciary Police *see* Civil Police (Amazonas)

Kang, I. 145
Kilonzo, N. 119n13

labor relations, in Rondônia 104
Lábrea, Amazonas 14–15, 18–19, 21–23; deforestation rates in 20; Transamazônica 22
Lago Agrio, Ecuador 88–101; about 92–94; borders and multidimensional interconnection of 97–99; commercial exchange on the border of 97; development models in 88–92; geopolitics 99–100; human geographic space 94–96; importance of oil in economy of 96; security and integration with national states 99–100; *see also* Ecuador
land grabbing 5, 51, 53, 59, 104
land regulation 23
Lara, R. 89
Lasso, G. 80, 84n1
laws/regulation 23, 144–145, 188–191; Act n° 2008-757 185; Asylum Law (Brazil) 155, 162; in Colombia 56–58; Constitutional Amendment 105, 140, 140n5; Democratic Rule of Law 213; environmental civil liability 185–186; Forest and Wildlife law 42; geolaw 8, 212–215, 224n3, 224n6; Immigration Law

162; Law 2250 of 2022 (Colombia) 57; Law of Environmental Crimes (Colombia) 57; Migration Law (Brazil) 153, 155; Strategic Rule of Law 213–214, 217–222, 224n5; *see also* environmental crimes; rule of law (RoL)
Le Billon, P. 98
Legal Amazon 63; area *129*; deforestation in 18; geography of 66; Logospiracy/Logospirate in 206–210; motivations for women joining the police 135; percentage distribution of women police officers *133*; PRODES rates 1998–2021 **19**, 28n2
Legal Amazonia 6, 127, 132–138; aim of 140n6; municipalities and population in *129*; transport fatalities in 130
legal assimilation 182, 184, 188
Lemay-Hébert, N. 16
limited statehood 16
Logospiracy/Logospirate 202–211; biopiracy 204; described 204–206; in Legal Amazon 206–210; Logos and 202–204
Logospiratism 208
Long, G. 113
Lottholz, P. 16
Loveman, B. 81
Luhmann, N. 81
Lutz, B.M.J. 125

Madeira Complex 104, 107n3
Manaus 2, 3, 18, 19, 168, 207
Marks, T. 112
McCaffrey, B. 77
Meira Mattos, C. de 213–214, 217; *A Pan-Amazonian Geopolitics* 217
Melendez, A. 37
Mignolo, W.D. 167, 175, 178
migration 67, 90, 97, 126, 128, 161; Brazilian policy 154–160; in Ecuador 77–81, 88; Migration Law (Brazil) 153, 155; in Venezuela 80
modern (modernity)/modernization 93–94, 100n3, 205, 213, 220–221
Moreno, L. 80
Mott, M.L. 126
Musumeci, L. 134

Nagoya Protocol 168
National Indigenous Organization of Colombia (ONIC) 54
National Integration Program (PIN) 128
National Parks: French Guiana 184, 191–192, 201n118; role in encouraging progress 193; role in supporting the society's progress 193; in support of law progress 194
National Security Council (COSENA) 82
nature reserves, exploitation in Colombia 52–53
necropolitics, Rondônia 102–103

Netherlands 9n1, 46
Noboa, G. 78
Nolte, D. 113, 119n7
normative framework 8, 114, 182–184
Northern Family (FDN) (criminal organization) 2, 65, 67
Nyström, J.W. 31

Obando, É. 51
oil price 76
Oliveira, W. A. de. 155
Operação Acolhida (Welcome Operation) 161–162
Operation Artemisa (Colombia) 58–59
Organization for Economic Co-operation and Development (OECD) 219
Organization of Indigenous Peoples of the Amazon (OPIAC) 54
organized crime 17, 23, 31, 37, 65, 83, 110; in Brazil 66–67, 69; in Ecuador 77–81; defined 65; illicit economies and 42; poverty and 112
Ostrom, E. 118n2
ovayeri (Asháninka warriors) 41

A Pan-Amazonian Geopolitics (Meira Mattos) 217
Parisada, N. 37
Pascual, L. 37
Patarroyo, M.E. 58
Patent Cooperation Treaty (PCT) 168–169
patents 169–171, 178, **209**, 220
patentscope 168–171, 175–179
peace agreement: with FARC 4, 47, 54; with Peru 74, 77
Pecequilo, C.S. 213
Penal Police Force 128, 140n5
perception index **147**, 148; on use of police force 148–150
Pereira, B. 49
Peru (Peruvian State) 1, 18, 33–34, 63; coca production and drug trafficking in 34–38; *Empresa Nacional de la Coca* (ENACO) 42; human trafficking and sexual exploitation in 40–41; illegal gold mining in 38–40; illegal logging in 13, 21, 38; illicit economic activities and violence 42–43; Ministry of the Environment 39; Peace Agreements 74, 77; Peruvian Ombuds Office 40; Tupac Amaru's guerrillas in 2, 36, 41
Pizango, G. 37
Plan Colombia 77–78, 95
police 22–23, 26, 139; cessation of custody of 190; challenges faced in controlling illegal logging or drug trafficking 42; challenges in reform of 138; collusion between criminals and 49; combined actions against cross-border illicit activities 117; controlling

illegal crossings 80; deployed in remote areas 48; failure to secure indigenous lands 105–106; federal 68, 136, 140n1; institutionalization of 127, **128**, **133**; legitimacy of 145–146; Penal Police Force 140n5; in procedural justice 148–149; used by Ecuador against the Colombian conflict 78; use of river for surveillance 55
police action 145; in indigenous lands of Rondônia 103–106; in Oakland 144; procedural justice in Brazil 146
policewoman 125–140; in Brazil and Amazonia 130–132; composition of 132–134, **133**; day-to-day activities of 136–138, *137*; deployment location of *139*; distribution of duties in Legal Amazonia *137*, 138; inclusion of 126, 130–138; motivations for being policewoman in Amazonia 134–135, **135**; research topics on 127–130, **128**; survey 127
polycephalic geopolitical model 111, 118
Porto Velho 19, 23
Portugal 9n1
poverty 17, 93, 98, 110–112, 155, 213, 218–220
Primeiro Comando da Capital (PCC) (criminal organization) 67
procedural justice 143–148, 150
Procópio, A. 115
PRODES project 18, **19–20**, 28n2
protected area 38, 54, 57–58, 190, 194
punitive power, of judicial judge 186–187

Quijano, A. 167, 178

rainforest *114*, 181, 183; conservation 2, 215–219; effects of destruction 52–53; illegal gold mining in 190; illegal gold panning in 185; map of *114*; protected by the Brazilian Federal Constitution of 1988 13; in urban areas 8
Ramonet, I. 221
Ratner, S. 119n5
Redondo, D.C. 34
Regional Infrastructure Integration Initiative (IIRSA) 77, 99; Manta-Manaus project 100; Waterway Putumayo project 100
Region of Ecuador (RAE) 88, 90; development model 89; ethnic self-identification in 92
registration of lands 17, 22, 24, 54, 210
Reyes, R. 80, 100n1
Roldós, J. 89
Rolim, M. 146
Rondônia 23–26, 102–107; deforestation in 105; environmental crimes in 103; fragile states/statehood in 103–104; hydroelectric power plants 103–106; illegal logging in 103–104, 106; illegal sale of land in 104; indigenous peoples as victims 102–106; labor relations in 104; National Indian Foundation (FUNAI) 104–106; police action in indigenous lands of 103–106; *see also* Brazil
rule of law (RoL) 14–20, 109, 111; Belém Declaration 115; importance of 16; research methodology 20–21; research result 21–27; state capacity to uphold the 21, **21**; *see also* Strategic Rule of Law

Sachs, I. 215
Sant'Anna, A.A. 17
Santos, M. 206
Schöneich, S. 119–120n14
Schultze-Kraft, M. 84
security 99–100; in Brazil 63–64, 68–71; in Ecuador 74–85; in Rondônia 102–103; threats due to organized crime 80
Sell, S. 167, 175–177
sexual exploitation 40–41, 59
Sharisho, C. 37
Shining Path *(Sendero Luminoso)* 36, 41
Shiva, V. 167–168, 176–177, 204
Silva, G. J. 161
Skogan, W. 6, 17, 143–145
Soares, B. 134
Soberón, R. 37
social fabric, Colombia 49
South American Defense Council (CDS) 100, 113
Souza, M. 207
sovereignity 80, 82, 83, 115–116, 182, 187, 208–209, 215, 218, 220
Spain 9n1
Special Amazon Education Commission (CEEDA) 114–115, 119n8
Special Commission for Health in the Amazon (CESAM) 114, 119n8
Special Commission for Indigenous Affairs in the Amazon (CEAIA) 114, 119n8
Special Commission for Science and Technology in the Amazon (CECTA) 114, 119n8
species trafficking, in Colombia 49–50, 56–58
state failure *see* failed states
state fragility *see* fragile states/statehood
Strategic Rule of Law 213–214, 217–222, 224n5
Strauss, A. L. 177–178
Suñé, N. 113
Superintendency of Development for the Amazon (SUDAM) 140n6, 207
Supreme Federal Court 225n12
Suriname 1, 63, 113, 181, 186, 206, 208, 214, 217
sustainable development 2, 8, 51–52, 57–58, 60, 116, 119n10, 140n6, 191, 212, 215

Tankebe, J. 145–146
Trade-Related Intellectual Property Rights Agreement (TRIPS) 167–169, 175–178
traditional knowledge 167, 179, 202, 204–206, 208, 210, 220
Trindade, R. C. S. 177
Trinkner, R. 145
Trujillo, P. 89, 95, 100n1
Tupac Amaru Revolutionary Movement-MRTA 2, 36
Tyler, T.R. 144–145

Ucko, D. 112
UN Intergovernmental Panel on Climate Change (IPCC) 219
Union of South American Nations (UNASUR) 100, 110, 119n7; Amazon Cooperation Treaty Organization (ACTO) and 112–113, 117
United Nations: Council on Narcotic Drugs 35; Minamata Convention in 2013 57; Single Convention on Narcotic Drugs 35
United Nations Environment Program (UNEP) 38
United Nations Office on Drugs and Crime (UNODC) 51–52, 56; on percentage of policewomen in the Americas countries 130, *131*
United States 76, 80, 219, 221–222; coca production and commercialization 42; legal warfare between China 225n10; National Security Strategy 77; policewomen in 130; pressure for eradication of coca leaves 35; on trust in police 145; War on Drugs 78
United States Agency for International Development (USAID) 78
urban violence 1, 3, 17, 59, 88, 103, 146
Uribe, Á. 79

Van Craen, M. 145
Varese, F. 67
Vega, Garcilaso de la 32, 34
Venezuela 1, 18, 51, 63, 80, 113, 153–162, 214, 217; effect of asylum seekers on borders Brazil 160–162; legislation and administrative processes 155–160
Versteeg, M. 15–16
Vinicius Macedo, M. 119n8
violence 2, 33; in Brazil 66–67; in Colombia 47–56; in Ecuador 77–81; in indigenous lands 37, 102, 103–106; in Peru 42–43
von Clausewitz, C. 221

Waever, O. 109, 111–112
women in policing *see* policewoman
Women's Emancipation League, objective of 125
World Intellectual Property Rights Organization (WIPO) 167–169, 177, 179
World Order 2.0 110, 116
World Trade Organization (WTO) 219

Yasuní-ITT Initiative 80
Yin, R. 170, 174
Young, C.E.F. 17

Zanetic, A. 146

Printed in the United States
by Baker & Taylor Publisher Services